P9-CFJ-328

TEACHING
CHILDREN
SCIENCE

YORK COLLEGE
PENNSYLVANIA
Servire est vivare

LIBRARY

TEACHING CHILDREN SCIENCE

Joseph Abruscato

University of Vermont

PRENTICE-HALL, INC. Englewood Cliffs, New Jersey 07632

Library of Congress Cataloging in Publication Data

ABRUSCATO, JOSEPH.
    Teaching children science.

    Includes bibliographies and index.
    1. Science—Study and teaching (Elementary)
I. Title
LB1585.A29   372.3′5′044   81-11951
ISBN   0-13-891754-X

*Editorial/production supervision and interior
design by Linda Schuman
Cover design by Diane Saxe
Manufacturing buyer: Edmund W. Leone*

© 1982 by Prentice-Hall, Inc., Englewood Cliffs, N. J. 07632

All rights reserved. No part of this book
may be reproduced in any form or
by any means without permission in writing
from the publisher.

Printed in the United States of America

10   9   8   7   6   5   4   3   2

ISBN 0-13-891754-X

PRENTICE-HALL INTERNATIONAL, INC., *London*
PRENTICE-HALL OF AUSTRALIA PTY. LIMITED, *Sydney*
PRENTICE-HALL OF CANADA, LTD., *Toronto*
PRENTICE-HALL OF INDIA PRIVATE LIMITED, *New Delhi*
PRENTICE-HALL OF JAPAN, INC., *Tokyo*
PRENTICE-HALL OF SOUTHEAST ASIA PTE. LTD., *Singapore*
WHITEHALL BOOKS LIMITED, *Wellington, New Zealand*

LB
1585
A29
.1982

This book is dedicated to
Anne Marie
Elizabeth
Charlotte
who give meaning to life.

Contents

chapter 6
How Can I Help Handicapped and Gifted Children Get the Most out of Science? 90

part 2
THE EARTH AND THE COSMOS: METHODS, CONTENT, DISCOVERY ACTIVITIES, AND DEMONSTRATIONS

chapter 7
How to Plan and Teach Earth/Space-Science Learning Units 109

chapter **9B**
**The Cosmos: Discovery Activities
and Demonstrations** 185

part **3**
**THE LIFE SCIENCES: METHODS,
CONTENT, DISCOVERY ACTIVITIES,
AND DEMONSTRATIONS**

chapter **10**
**How to Plan and Teach Life-Science
Learning Units** 203

chapter **11A**
Plants and Animals: Content 220

chapter **17**
The Ecology Crisis: Understanding and Preserving the Relationship between Ecosystems and the Environment— Discovery Activities and Demonstrations 393

chapter **18**
The Energy Crisis: Conserving the Energy We Have and Searching for Alternative Energy Sources—Discovery Activities and Demonstrations 410

APPENDIXES

Preface

Flexibility. Excellence in living and excellence in teaching demand flexibility—the ability to respond in a positive way to the different individuals and situations we meet. *Vive la différence!* We are different from one another and that is precisely what makes life beautiful and *extremely* interesting.

Responding with flexibility to the needs of children is a challenge that requires many resources. Perhaps the most important resource that you have or will have is *people*: colleagues with whom you can comfortably share ideas, challenges, and the joy that comes from working with children. I hope that you find many such individuals during your teaching career. It is also helpful to have other sources of inspiration, practical ideas, and activities that can be drawn upon as you develop learning experiences for children. A *book* can be such a resource. This book has been designed to be such a resource for you. I hope that through it I will have helped you enable hundreds and thousands of children to see, for perhaps the first time, the trees with the lights in them.

Joseph Abruscato
Burlington, Vermont

Acknowledgments

There are so many people who have assisted me in the development of this book. First of all there is my dear friend and colleague Jack Hassard, who encouraged me to begin this venture. He and I have worked together on many projects in the past and will continue to work together in the future.

Many elementary teachers helped develop the science activities, demonstrations, field trips, bulletin boards, learning centers, and other materials contained in this book. They include Lynn Cluff, Molly McCloskey, Christine Varney, and Douglas Varney. Their participation in various phases of this project has helped to ensure that the book is a *practical* volume that can be used by both preservice and inservice teachers.

I would like to thank Mary Louise Wasko, who, with this project, has transformed four book manuscripts from C− handwriting (as certified by my third-grade teacher) to typed copy. Susan Franko and Barbara Matthews have also kindly assisted me at every step of this journey. The unfailing cheerfulness and extreme competence of all these individuals is a source of great pleasure to me.

The "Teacher Talk" sections of the first six chapters consist of excerpts from interviews with many teachers. These interviews are reported in full in *Case Studies in Science Education, Volume I*, published by the National Science Foundation.

How This Book
Is Organized

PART 1 PLANNING FOR LEARNING (Chapters 1–6)

These chapters are designed to sharpen your thinking as you develop the long-term and short-term teaching plans that will put your children in contact with the wonders of their natural environment. Each chapter includes:

1. *A Look Ahead*: a list of the topics discussed in the chapter.
2. *Text*: a discussion of a number of specific topics.
3. A section called *"Going Further"*: learning activities that will help you pursue in more depth various issues and problems raised in the chapter.
4. *Teacher Talk*: excerpts from interviews with teachers who work daily with children that will stimulate your own thinking and your discussions with others.
5. *A Summary*: to help you review the main ideas in the chapter.
6. *Suggested Readings*: a list of books and articles that will help you extend your analysis of the main points discussed in the chapter.

PART 2 THE EARTH AND THE COSMOS
(Chapters 7, 8A, 8B, 9A, 9B)

Chapter 7 How to Plan and Teach Earth/Space-Science Learning Units

This chapter begins with a description of a teaching incident that will focus your attention on earth/space-science experiences in the elementary curriculum. Included in the chapter are *lists of earth/space-science concepts and processes* you may wish to include in teaching units, *practical ideas for relating earth/space-science topics to other parts of the elementary curriculum, sample learning centers, sample field trips, sample bulletin boards,* and many other ideas for working with earth/space-science topics in the elementary classroom.

Chapters 8A and 9A   Earth/Space-Science: Content

These chapters are designed to give you science content that can serve as a foundation for your teaching of earth/space-science units. It is content written for you, the teacher.

Chapters 8B and 9B   Earth/Space-Science: Discovery Activities and Demonstrations

These chapters provide you with discovery activities and demonstrations appropriate for elementary-school children engaged in earth/space-science units. The initial discovery activities and demonstrations are presented in great detail: they include *instructional objectives, lists of needed materials, motivational ideas, directions,* and *key discussion questions* (with some possible children's responses). Following detailed explanations of specific discovery activities and demonstrations are a selection of additional activity and demonstration ideas. *Activities and demonstrations that will be of special interest to younger children (grades K−3) are marked with an asterisk.*

PART 3   THE LIFE SCIENCES (Chapters 10, 11A, 11B, 12A, 12B)

Part 3 follows the same format as Part 2 but focuses on the *life sciences.*

PART 4   THE PHYSICAL SCIENCES (Chapters 13, 14A, 14B, 15A, 15B)

Part 4 follows the same format as Parts 2 and 3 but focuses on the *physical sciences.*

PART 5   THE SUPERSAVERS (Chapters 16, 17, 18)

There are three very serious problems that face *today's* children that have not received, in my opinion, sufficient attention in other elementary-science methods books: the depletion and pollution of our *natural resources,* the irreparable harm being done to the *ecology* of our planet, and the limitations of our supply of *energy.* I think elementary-school children need experiences that prepare them for the challenges occasioned by these problems. To help you achieve a science classroom where members are attentive to these three contemporary problems, I have prepared a chapter of discovery activities and demonstrations for each of them. They are:

Chapter 16   The Natural-Resources Crisis: Saving the Water, the Soil, and the Air We Breathe—Discovery Activities and Demonstrations

THE APPENDIXES

THE MOMENT OF LEARNING

Then one day I was walking along Tinker Creek thinking of nothing at all and I saw the tree with the lights in it. I saw the backyard cedar where the mourning doves roost charged and transfigured, each cell buzzing with flame. I stood on the grass with the lights in it, grass that was wholly fire, utterly focused and utterly dreamed. It was less like seeing than like being for the first time seen; knocked breathless by a powerful glance. . . . I had been my whole life a bell, and never knew it until at that moment I was lifted and struck.

Annie Dillard
Pilgrim at Tinker Creek

TEACHING
CHILDREN
SCIENCE

part 1

Planning for Learning

chapter 1

What Is Science?

Have you ever had the pleasure of watching a young child discover a rabbit? The child usually seems to enjoy the process much more than the rabbit does. The hugging, squeezing, and petting child feels the rabbit's warmth, its softness, and its gentleness. The rabbit, on the other hand, is probably a bit worried about the intentions of its new friend. The rabbit need not fear, for this human has loving and not stew on his mind.

The child will hold and play with the rabbit for a long time, for there are powerful motivating forces at work here: the child's feeling of oneness with nature and the child's curiosity about the surrounding world. The child, the rabbit, and you and I are all made of the same "stuff." We are all disposed to behave in ways that will help us make sense out of the world in which we find ourselves. We are curious because we cannot survive unless we learn. For just as the rabbit must learn of lettuce leaves and foxes, we must learn of the pleasures and harm that can come to us during our brief sojourn on this planet.

Now that we are adults, our curiosity and wonder about our surroundings may be less intense than it was when we were children. Although our childhood curiosity may sometimes have exasperated our parents, grandparents, and teachers, it was and continues to be an important factor in our lives. It is innate curiosity that is the source of the shortest and yet most powerful words known to humankind—why, what, when, and how.

Do you remember the curiosity of your childhood? Do you remember asking:

Why is the sky blue?

What is thunder?

When is yesterday going to come again?

How does the moon stay up in the sky?

Perhaps you still remember the one question that seemed to always temporarily immobilize even the most responsive of adults:

Why can't cats have puppies?

I believe that although we are no longer children, somewhere in each of us repose some glowing embers of innocent, childlike curiosity. I hope that this chapter will begin a journey that will rekindle your curiosity and also lay the foundation for the development of the practical skills that you will need to help children use their abilities to the fullest as they explore and make sense out of their world.

Figure 1—1. (*Source:* Sybil Shackman, Monkmeyer)

YOU, CHILDREN, AND SCIENCE:
SOME FEARS, SOME HOPES, SOME DREAMS

As I write this page I am thinking about you. Although I do not know you personally, I think I already know you pretty well. I know you through the personalities and competencies of hundreds and perhaps even thousands of preservice teachers and inservice teachers with whom I have worked over the years. I also know you through knowing myself and reflecting on my own fears, hopes, and dreams as I approached the first classroom in which I had children in my charge and science as the medium through which I would engage their minds.

I also know you through the expectations you have of yourself. I believe that you wish to become an excellent teacher. If you are presently teaching, you are undoubtedly motivated to become a better teacher tomorrow than you are today. You are probably confident of your ability to teach reading, the language arts, and the social studies. I think you are fairly confident in your ability to teach arithmetic. And finally, I think you are a little uneasy about the prospect of teaching children science.

I think you may *fear* that science will be:

1. Hard for children to understand. You may even have expended a great deal of energy trying to stay away from science courses in high school and college because of their presumed difficulty.
2. A subject that may encourage children to ask you questions for which you may not have the answers.
3. A rather "messy" subject that will require you to use strange, bubbling, colored liquids, electrical devices that can cause shocks, and chemicals that can go flash, pop, or bang.
4. A subject that requires the "cutting up" of creatures large and small. (Let it be known that the author is one of the world's most squeamish persons in this respect. As an undergraduate and graduate student, he developed elaborate schemes to avoid dissecting *anything*, and he now publicly thanks all those laboratory partners who upon observing his apparent bumbling elected to carry out the procedures themselves.)
5. A subject requiring activities that can result in loud talking, overexcitment, and unruly behavior among the children.

I think I know what some of your *hopes* are:

1. Your hope that through study and help from others you will be able to teach children science.
2. Your hope that the questions the children ask will not be too hard.
3. Your hope that when you teach science the children will remain under reasonable control.
4. Your hope that your curriculum coordinator, principal, and superintendent will be patient with you while you get your feet on the ground in the teaching of science.

I think I know some of your *dreams*:

1. Your dream that your classroom will be a happy, exciting, and productive place in which your children learn about themselves as they learn all the school subjects, including science.

5

2. Your dream that the children you teach will go forth to other grade levels well prepared for the challenges they will face.

3. Your dream that in some way you will make a difference in children's lives, that you will help them acquire the knowledge, skills, and attitudes that will encourage them to dream—and to do.

Every page in this book represents my effort to help you to overcome your fears, sharpen your hopes, and fulfill your dreams as a teacher. Let us now begin.

WHAT IS SCIENCE?

Science is somewhat like an elephant. If you wish to understand it, you must begin by recollecting the old fable about the three blind men and the elephant. Each observed a different portion of the elephant's anatomy, and in so doing developed an understanding of the nature of the elephant that was very different from the understanding gained by his friends. To the man who touched and felt the texture, width, and length of the elephant's leg, the elephant was like a giant tree supported by a massive trunk. To the man who felt the elephant's trunk, the elephant seemed to be a serpent. Of course, the man who carefully inspected the posterior region of the elephant reached a far different conclusion!

Science also has a variety of facets. Three of them will have central importance throughout this book. Science is the name we give to a group of *processes* through which we can systematically gather information about the natural world. Science is also the *knowledge* gathered through the use of such processes. Finally, science is characterized by those *values and attitudes* possessed by people who use scientific processes to gather knowledge.

Science as the Processes of Inquiry

A newborn infant babbles, gurgles, wriggles, and reaches out to touch the world. Each day of life commemorates that very first day. Each day you and I reach out to our surroundings and wonder. We are human and we are wonderers.

The clamor of your alarm clock this morning summoned you to face once again the essential questions of life and of living. We spend our hours in the sometimes mundane activities of a busy day, and yet there is a fundamental restlessness. It is the restlessness that comes from being a wonderer. Most of us want to know who we are, why we are here, and what our future will be, and we strive to make sense out of our present state. This fundamental drive to inquire is as much a part of human life as breathing and eating—we simply have a need to know.

Some people are afraid to be curious. They just do not want to know. They live out their lives dully, ever confident that "curiosity killed the cat." Curiosity didn't kill the cat—ignorance did. As a matter of fact, if it wasn't for curiosity there wouldn't have been a cat to begin with. It is only curious cats that produce kittens!

Those who are bored with life have somehow lost their curiosity. I hope that you haven't lost yours. I hope that your curiosity constantly motivates you to ask why, what, when, and how. You are going to be surrounded by children who have

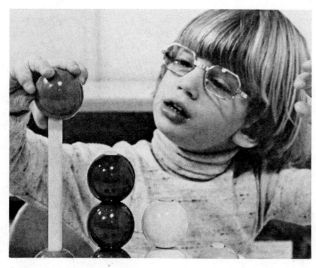

Figure 1—2. The child reaches out, touches, and wonders. (*Source:* Lew Merrim, Monkmeyer)

not lost their curiosity. Your challenge will be to mesh your curiosity with theirs as they develop an understanding of the natural world. The challenge is really not very difficult, since children bring so much energy and natural curiosity to the quest. All children seem to be scientists at heart.

OBSERVATION

Observation is the principal means by which we listen for nature's answers to our questions. Merely being present when nature responds to our curiosity is not enough. Real observation requires that you focus and direct your senses, for nature does not reveal its secrets to just any passerby. Annie Dillard writes eloquently of her experiences as she became an observer of her surroundings:

> A fish flashes, then dissolves in the water before my eyes like so much salt. Deer apparently ascend bodily into heaven; the brightest oriole fades into leaves. These disappearances stun me into stillness and concentration; they say of nature that it conceals with a grand nonchalance, and they say of vision that it is a deliberate gift, the revelation of a dancer who for my eyes only flings away her seven veils. For nature does reveal as well as conceal: now-you-don't-see-it, now-you-do.

She recalls the noise of migrating red-winged blackbirds who had apparently landed near Tinker Creek and her futile attempt to observe them.

> One day I went out to investigate the racket; I walked up to a tree, an Osage orange, and a hundred birds flew away. They simply materialized out of the tree. I saw a tree, then a wisk of color, then a tree again. I walked closer and another hundred blackbirds took flight. Not a branch, not a twig budged: the birds were apparently weightless as well as invisible. Or, it was as if the leaves of the Osage orange had been freed from a spell in the form of red-winged blackbirds; they flew from the tree, caught my

eye in the sky, and vanished. When I looked again at the tree the leaves had reassembled as if nothing had happened.

She persisted and decided to try for a better vantage point.

Finally I walked directly to the trunk of the tree and a final hundred, the real diehards, appeared, spread, and vanished. How could so many hide in the tree without my seeing them? The Osage orange, unruffled, looked just as it had looked from the house, when three hundred red-winged blackbirds cried from its crown. I looked downstream where they flew, and they were gone. Searching, I couldn't spot one. I wandered downstream to force them to play their hand, but they'd crossed the creek and scattered. One show to a customer.[1]

The children we teach need many opportunities to apply and test their powers of observation as they engage in science activities. Through observations they gather information and organize it so as to achieve a greater understanding of phenomena. Our effort needs to be one that helps children reach out and observe.

[1]Annie Dillard, *Pilgrim at Tinker Creek* (New York: Bantam Books, 1978), pp. 17–18. Copyright © 1974 by Annie Dillard. Reprinted by permission of Harper & Row, Publishers, Inc.

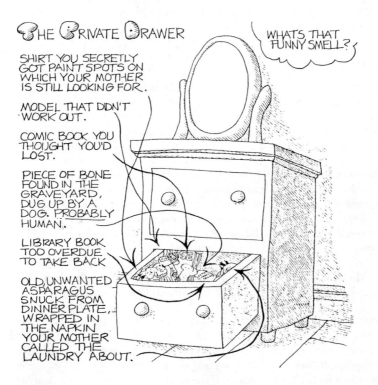

Figure 1–3. (*Source:* Reprinted by permission of Richard Marek Publishers, Inc. from NUTS by Gahan Wilson. Copyright © 1979 by Gahan Wilson.)

What did you collect as a young child? Did you have a secret bag full of magic stones? Did you have a scrapbook of leaves? Did you cut out pictures of television and movie stars and gather all the information you could find about each of your favorites? Did you tape the pictures to the back of your bedroom door or pin them to a bulletin board? Perhaps in some remote corner of an attic or basement you still have a bag of those very special seashells gathered on a quiet beach, a shoe box crammed with old bubble-gum cards, an old, yellowing autograph book filled with the signatures of your special friends, or perhaps a collection of well-worn Nancy Drew mysteries.

Most children are avid collectors. Collecting is very close to a process that is at the heart of science. A scientist is first and foremost a person who observes the natural world and attempts to bring it under some sort of structure. Children's collections reflect our natural tendency to observe and classify. As a matter of fact, observation and classification are processes that undergird not only science but also most other forms of human exploratory activity.

The collections that you made as a child or perhaps are still making as an adult really represent a combination of the processes of *measurement* and *classification*. They represent measurement since your decision to include or exclude a particular object or artifact (for example a seashell or a picture of a rock-music star) was probably based upon the extent to which it "measured up" to some set of standards. You had to decide if the seashell was too big or too small or if it retained too "fishy" a smell. Such decisions were based on comparisons you had to make between the object and certain criteria.

Figure 1–4. The child makes "sense" of the world by observing and classifying. (*Source:* Suzanne Szasz, Photo Researchers, Inc.)

Observation, classification, and measurement are basic processes used by science to explore the natural world. In combination these three processes enable science to utilize yet another process—that of *hypothesizing*. A hypothesis can be thought of simply as an educated guess. As children and now as adults we base much of our verbal behavior and indeed our actions on the hypotheses we make.

Have you ever observed the humorous situation of an infant turning to an adult male who is not his or her father and saying "Daddy"? Hypotheses are all based on previous experience. Consequently, the validity of a hypothesis we make depends on the amount and quality of our previous experience. The history of science is really a history of the continual refining and improving of hypotheses. The child misapplying "Daddy" has made an error that is not different in kind from the hypothesis that the world is flat.

These processes of science—observing, measuring, classifying, and hypothesizing—as well as others shown in Figure 1–5 all enable scientists to explore the environment and make educated guesses.

CONCEPTS

Energy can be changed in form.

Matter can be changed in form.

The total amount of matter and energy in the universe never changes but is just changed in form.

PRINCIPLES

Objects that are dropped increase in velocity as they approach the earth's surface.

Like poles of magnets will repel each other.

Unlike poles of magnets will attract each other.

For every action there is an equal and opposite reaction.

PROCESSES

Observing	Communicating
Classifying	Hypothesizing
Using Space/Time Relationships	Experimenting
Using Numbers	Controlling Variables
Measuring	Interpreting Data
	Defining Operationally

Figure 1–5. Sample Concepts, Principles, and Processes of Science

Science as Knowledge

Gently a soft breeze teases a tree leaf. The breeze grows into a gust of wind as the sky is ominously darkened by approaching storm clouds. A bright flash of lightning cleaves the sky and a burst of thunder rolls across the land. On a far horizon a funnel-shaped cloud touches the earth and begins a frantic hop-scotching dance that rips apart all that is in its path. A hundred kilometers away meteorologists huddle around a radar screen and use the processes of science to gather knowledge about the storm.

Processes of science yield a body of knowledge that we commonly refer to as the content of science. This body of knowledge includes the facts gathered, the generalizations or concepts that unify these facts, and a set of principles that can be used to make predictions. Facts, concepts, and principles are the content of science.

The principles of science are commonly referred to as laws. Like poles of magnets repelling each other, the movement of a satellite around the earth, and the suicidal journey of salmon on their way upstream to spawn—all represent the operation of natural laws. Science to a very large measure is the search for underlying laws that can be used to predict behavior.

It is reported that when Albert Einstein was asked why he used one soap for both washing and shaving he replied, "Two soaps? That is too complicated." Scientists do not seek to discover the most complicated laws that can be imagined. Rather, the scientist's goal is to discover the simplest laws that can explain a phenomenon.

If we emphasize just the facts of science, children will learn that science is an accumulation of factual knowledge. By emphasizing just the concepts of science, children will learn that science is a set of generalizations. If we emphasize solely the principles of science, children will learn that science is but a set of predictions. What we must do as we help children experience science is to develop activities that will encourage them to learn more than the facts, more than concepts, and even far more than the principles—for science also manifests an underlying system of values.

Science as a Set of Values

All human activities, whether the writing of beautiful poetry, the painting of a landscape, the singing of a song, or the doing of a scientific experiment, reflect the values held by those who actually carry out the activities. When we think of values from an artistic point of view we tend to think of values such as beauty and truth. What then are the values of science?

There are many values of science that can be emphasized as we help children experience the processes and learn the content of science in the classroom. Six that I have found to be of particular interest to teachers are:

Truth	Originality
Freedom	Order
Skepticism	Communication

There are other values that guide the activities of scientists, but these six seem to be the most relevant to the developmental needs of children.

Since science seeks to explain truth and make sense out of our natural world, it has as its most basic value the search for *truth*. The scientist seeks to discover not what should be but rather what *is*. The high value placed on truth applies not only to the discovery of facts, concepts, and principles, but also to the recording and reporting of such knowledge.

The search for truth is predicated on yet another important value—*freedom*. Real science occurs only when the investigator is able to operate in an environment that provides him or her with the freedom to follow paths wherever they may lead. As one philosopher of science noted, "Science cannot prosper where there is constraint upon daring thinking, where society dictates what experiments may be conducted, or where the statement of conclusion may lead to loss of livelihood, imprisonment, or even death."[2] History is full of examples of scientists who had to pay a very high price for publicly affirming the results of their work.

Do you believe everything you read? Are you a bit skeptical of things you hear about? Do you take things at face value? If you answered no to any or all of these questions, then you will readily understand why science values *skepticism*. The products of science are the results of questions put to the natural world. Astronomer Carl Sagan has reflected on the importance of this predisposition to raise questions: "Science is based on experiment, on a willingness to challenge old dogma, on an openness to see the universe as it really is. Accordingly, science sometimes requires courage—at least the courage to question the conventional wisdom."[3]

Children are full of surprises. Their answers to questions often reflect considerable *originality* of thought and expression. For example, a group of schoolchildren were asked, "What are some ways to save energy?" Some of their delightful responses are shown in Figure 1-6.

The content and processes of science are characterized by an underlying *order*. Scientists not only gather information, they organize it. Without an organizational scheme and underlying order, all the knowledge that has been gained by science would be of little value. The scientist values not just knowledge, but knowledge that is organized.

Children should understand that scientists not only explore the natural world but also *communicate* the results of their explorations to others. Without extensive communication, the progress of science would be limited. This, of course, is true of all forms of human activity. Progress can occur only when people have a knowledge and understanding of information and concepts developed by others.

These six values pervade not only science but all other areas of human understanding. As a teacher of science you need to help children understand that science is more than a set of facts and more than a group of processes. Science is also a human activity that has as its framework a set of values that are important in day-to-day life.

[2]Bentley Glass, *Science and Ethical Values* (Chapel Hill, N.C.: University of North Carolina Press, 1965), p. 90.
[3]Carl Sagan, *Broca's Brain* (New York: Random House, 1979), p. 13. © 1979. Used with permission.

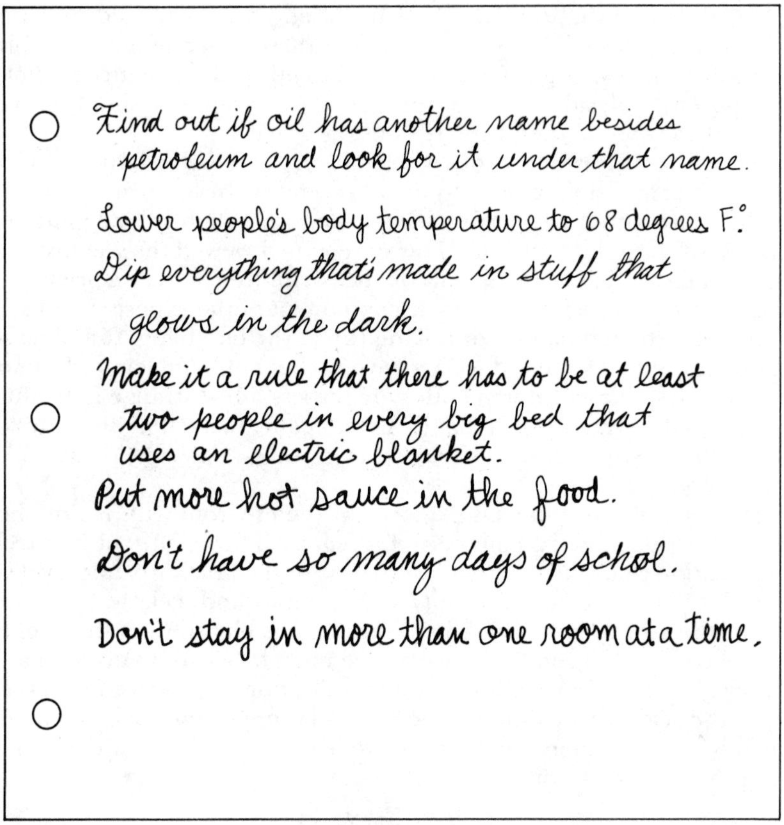

Find out if oil has another name besides petroleum and look for it under that name.

Lower people's body temperature to 68 degrees F.°

Dip everything that's made in stuff that glows in the dark.

Make it a rule that there has to be at least two people in every big bed that uses an electric blanket.

Put more hot sauce in the food.

Don't have so many days of school.

Don't stay in more than one room at a time.

Figure 1–6. Children's Answers to the Question—"What Are Some Ways to Save Energy?" (*Source: "Elementary Energy Savings," The Chronicle of Higher Education*, 18, no. 21 [July 30, 1970], 8.)

THE SCIENTIST: WHO IS SHE?

Did the title of this section jar you a bit? If it did, you are now aware of one of your own prejudices about scientists. The image of the scientist held by the citizenry is stereotyped with respect not only to the sex of scientists but to other characteristics as well. In a classic study of how high school students view scientists, Mead and Metraux reported the following common perceptions:

> The scientist is a brain. He spends his days indoors, sitting in a laboratory, pouring things from one test tube into another. . . . He can only eat, breathe, and sleep science. . . . He has no social life, no other intellectual interests, no hobbies, or relaxations. . . . He is always reading a book. He brings home work and also brings home creepy things.[4]

[4]M. Mead and R. Metraux, "Image of the Scientist Among High School Students," *Science*, 126, no. 3270 (August 30, 1957), pp. 384–390.

It is doubtful that this image of the scientist has changed much over the years. The attitudes of the students making these observations probably reflect the views of society at large. The sexism in the choice of pronoun does not seem to be a purposeful utilization of "He" for "He or She"; rather, it simply bears out the strength of the stereotype of the scientist as a male.

One of my favorite activities with children, and with adults as well, is to ask them to perform a simple task: to draw a scientist. In most cases the scientist is generally represented as a bespectacled male with a slightly mad glint in his eyes and a crop of straggly white hair. This stereotyped view of the scientist as a rather strange character limits our ability to help children perceive science and the individuals who guide it as a valuable component of the experience of schooling. Few can resist the temptation of poking fun at the bumbling, fumbling scientist. The point is not that science does not have its share of bumblers and fumblers but rather that all fields of human endeavor possess a few strange individuals. The real harm of the stereotype is that it encourages ridicule that dissuades children from thinking positively about science or science-related fields as an eventual career choice.

The scientist is simply an explorer of the environment. He or she is very similar to the poet and the painter in this regard. The scientist utilizes techniques for exploration that are different from those of the poet or painter, yet shares in their goals. The artist looks for unity and harmony and seeks ways to express the results of the search in a way that is comprehensible; so does the scientist.

As we help children learn science we must take care to do so in a way that emphasizes the discovery of content, the utilization of processes, and the importance of the scientist to society. The task is large but the tools are many. All it requires is a commitment on your part to learn as much about children and the teaching of science as you can.

GOING FURTHER

On Your Own

1. Consider your present feelings about teaching children science, and identify the factors that influence your attitude. If you have worked with children while they are experiencing science, what conclusions can you draw about their attitudes toward science?
2. If possible, interview an elementary teacher to find out how he or she would answer such questions as: What do children think science is? What materials for learning science are available in your school? Do you feel prepared to teach science? If the teacher has taught for a few years, ascertain whether his or her attitudes about the teaching of science have changed. Develop additional questions to use during the interview.
3. Do some library research to determine the role that science and technology have played in shaping our present-day society. Consider such questions as: Would society be better served if science were pursued only for the sake of technology that results from it? Does the scientist occupy a "prestige" position in modern society? What responsibility does the scientist have for communicating the results of his or her work in an understandable way to the public?

4. If you were to teach science to a group of rural children, what aspects of science would you stress? Consider the same question using a suburban and an urban school environment as a frame of reference. In each case highlight the arguments for and against the statement "The purpose of schooling is to liberate children from their parochialism."

With Others

5. Role-play a conversation between a parent who believes in each of the following statements and a teacher who does not.
   a. It is more important for children to learn to read and write than it is for them to learn science.
   b. Too much time is wasted in school when the children do science activities.
   c. Science causes children to think about things that they have no business thinking about.
6. Have each member of your group interview a different scientist or person in a science-related profession, asking each of the following questions as well as others that the group members develop. Then meet as a group to compare the responses you gathered.
   a. What motivated you to become a scientist (other science-related career)?
   b. To what extent did your experience in elementary school influence your eventual career decision?
   c. Do you feel that your work directly affects individuals and society in general?
   d. What advice would you give to a teacher who wanted to do a good job planning and doing science activities with children?

TEACHER TALK: SPRINGBOARDS FOR DISCUSSION

- "The only difference between boys and girls in science is snakes and worms and that doesn't last long."

- "I think teaching them rigour and method is a useful thing to do. The danger, though, is that you end up just pacifying them. The science that is going to affect their lives isn't the five stages of writing a lab report. It is nuclear power, pollution, recombinant DNA research. Those are the things I want them to know about, and I want them to be able to pursue things for themselves, not just because they are in a course or a textbook."

- "Science education which only a few years ago was largely optional and integrated in the lower grades has not become a major responsibility of the school. . . . Today, if the teacher is to meet her responsibility she must help the children, in ways appropriate to their maturity, to understand causal relationships and systematic approaches to the observation of phenomena. Moreover, even the young child must become more informed about the place of science and technology as major factors in modern life."

- "What is the nature of science? Is it new ways of looking at things we usually take for granted, or is it knowledge at new frontiers? Is it methodical, disciplined and perhaps sometimes boring; or is it imaginative, free-wheeling and perhaps sometimes incoherent?"

SUMMARY

Some people feel that science is a difficult subject to teach elementary-school children. Actually, just a moderate amount of effort can make the teaching of science enjoyable for both the teacher and the children. Science has a variety of facets. Three that are of particular significance are (1) its processes, (2) the knowledge gathered through the use of these processes, and (3) the values and attitudes that underlie the scientific enterprise. Children need to have an understanding of the various facets of science as well as the manner by which science is applied to society. The application of science to daily life is known as technology, and those who apply science to the solving of problems are scientists. Peoples' stereotypes of scientists can be a problem. Scientists are commonly depicted as wizened, aged men who spend their time madly mixing strange concoctions in test tubes. Such stereotypes serve to isolate the doing of science from the remainder of human activity, suggest that scientists are a strange group of people, and imply that only men do science.

SUGGESTED READINGS

ASIMOV, I., "Pure and Impure: The Interplay of Science and Technology," *Saturday Review*, 6(June 9, 1979), 22–24.

CHAMPAGNE, A. B., and L. E. KLOPFER,"Problem Solving as Outcome and Method in Science Teaching: Insights from 60 Years of Experience," *School Science and Mathematics*, 81, no. 1(January 1981), 3–8.

BRONOWSKI, J., *The Ascent of Man*. Boston: Little, Brown, 1973.

BROWN, R. A., and R. G. LUCKOCK, "Dreams, Daydreams, and Discoveries: Inspiration of Scientists," *Education Digest*, 44(February 1979), 32–34.

CAREY, W. D., "Science and Public Understanding," *Science*, 204(May 25, 1979), 797.

DILLARD, A., *Pilgrim at Tinker Creek*. New York: Bantam Books, 1978.

RICHMOND, B., "This Must Be Science, the Teacher's Manual Says So," *Science and Children*, 18, no. 5(February 1981), 12–13.

SAGAN, C., *Broca's Brain*. New York: Random House, 1979.

SHAW, J. M., and M. J. PUCKETT CLIATT, "Science Is What Scientists Do," *Science and Children*, 18, no. 6(March 1981), 16–17.

STAHL, R. J., "Working with Values and Moral Issues in Content-Centered Science Classrooms," *Science Education*, 63(April 1979), 183–194.

YAGER, R. E., "Nutrition: A Basic Strand of School Science," *School Science and Mathematics*, 81, no. 2(February 1981), 159–162.

chapter 2

Why Teach Science?

A LOOK AHEAD

Your science classroom will be a special place—a very busy and happy place where children learn about themselves and others as they become actively involved with the "things" and "stuff" of science. You will be their guide as they open their minds and perhaps their hearts to the possibility not only of learning but of learning how to learn.

All the children you teach will face the complexities of life in the twenty-first century. Robert Heinlein has prophesied the following responsibilities for tomorrow's adults:

A human being should be able to change a diaper,

plan an invasion, butcher a hog, conn a ship,
design a building, write a sonnet, balance accounts, build a wall, set a bone, comfort the dying, take orders, give orders, cooperate, act alone, solve equations, analyze a new problem, pitch manure, program a computer, cook a tasty meal, fight efficiently, die gallantly. Specialization is for insects.[1]

If Heinlein is correct, you and I have a responsibility to help children develop *all* their talents and abilities to their fullest. Clearly, science and its application to daily life should be a very important component of

[1]Robert A. Heinlein, *Time Enough For Love* (New York: Putnam, 1973) pp. 265–66. Reprinted by permission of G. P. Putnam's Sons. Copyright © 1973 by Robert A. Heinlein.

Figure 2–1. (*Source:* SAPA II, Module 42, p. 3. Science . . . A Process Approach II, American Association for the Advancement of Science. Used with permission.)

the curricula we develop and the learning experiences we provide.

One expression that you will hear again and again during your teaching career is "teaching the whole child." I have always been amused at hearing people use the expression, since I immediately conjure up visions of someone teaching only parts of the child. Can you imagine a teacher thinking, "Now, I am going to teach that child's elbow a thing or two!"

It is the whole child who comes to school and it is the whole child whom we must teach and reach. The fullest possible development of a child's mind, heart, and body would seem to be the basic purpose of education. We should seek to help children develop intellectually, emotionally, and physically in our schools and in our classrooms. Each of these major goals can be thought of as a domain of human learning. In recent years the terms *cognitive, affective,* and *psychomotor* have been widely used by educators to signify the intellectual, emotional, and physical aspects of children's development. An understanding of specific cognitive, affective, and psychomotor goals as well as more general goals, such as the development of creativity, critical thinking, and career awareness, will provide you with a framework for developing curriculum materials.

SPECIFIC GOALS OF SCIENCE EDUCATION

The Cognitive Domain

"An empty wagon makes the most rattle" was an expression used again and again by one of my teachers. It probably revealed her belief that the brain was a vehicle that operated best when it was filled. She certainly made a valiant and only partially successful attempt at filling my own mind. However, I *do* remember her expression, yet I do not remember the facts that she attempted to teach. I think that I remember her words because they bore sufficient meaning to have engaged my mind. Perhaps she knew all along that the facts would evaporate but that I would learn something else as a result of being taught by her—and she was right.

Much of our time in schools is spent on experiences that require us to think. The cognitive development of a child consists of his or her acquisition of knowledge and formation and use of concepts and principles. The cognitive domain clearly encompasses both the "content" portion of science and the "process" portion. The child can discover the content of science by applying the processes of inquiry during science activities, by reading, through class discussion, and through many other media.

Benjamin Bloom and others have suggested that there are six levels of cognitive learning:[2]

> Knowledge
> Comprehension
> Application
> Analysis
> Synthesis
> Evaluation

[2]Benjamin S. Bloom, ed., *Taxonomy of Educational Objectives* (New York: McKay, 1976), p. 18.

As you consider learning goals that may be appropriate for elementary science, this hierarchy may prove helpful. The list proceeds from the simple to the complex: knowledge requires the least amount of cognitive skill, evaluation the most.

Figure 2–2 is a list of the types of science activities, organized by cognitive level, that teachers use to encourage a child's cognitive growth.

LEARNING LEVEL	SAMPLE PROCESS SKILLS	SAMPLE ACTIVITY
6. Evaluation	Choosing	Choosing a well-balanced meal for hot lunch.
	Evaluating	Selecting the proper materials to use in building a home for a classroom pet.
5. Synthesis	Designing	Inventing a flashlight using a battery, wires, and a bulb.
	Presenting	Presenting in proper order a group of pictures that show the life cycle of a frog.
4. Analysis	Comparing and Contrasting	Comparing and contrasting a caterpillar and a butterfly.
	Organizing	Organizing an assortment of weather information to make a weather chart.
3. Application	Demonstrating	Demonstrating a lunar eclipse using a flashlight, a globe, and a rubber ball.
	Estimating	Estimating the amount of litter on a playground from the amount on one square meter.
2. Comprehension	Describing	Describing how the seasons change.
	Summarizing	Summarizing information read in a chapter by making a drawing.
1. Knowledge	Labeling	Labeling the parts of a flower.
	Defining	Defining the term "liquid state of matter."

Figure 2–2. Cognitive Learnings, Related Processes, and Sample Science Activities

The Affective Domain

Grunts and crunching sounds from one alder indicated that the small porcupine was still feeding, oblivious of the gathering darkness. Darkness was welcome to the deer mice that lived in the forest; the meadow's edge resounded with patterings and bumps as they emerged to look for seeds and berries.

A buoy lit up across the passage. The water was dim and gray now, a gulf broken only occasionally by the fluke of a spouting whale. The whales' ponderous breathing sounded close in the dimness, as though the great animals were rising just outside the cove.

The tide was in. It covered the sand beach completely, and its wavelets lapped at the driftwood logs. The sloping garden of wildflowers was a vague, greenish mass beneath the black of the trees. Some buzzing creature, sphinx moth or hummingbird, paused above a lacy cow-parsnip umbel for a moment.

The seam of the vapor trail was reversed—a pale streak against the dark sky. Directly above the cove, the first small star began to shine. It was past midnight.[3]

There is much beauty around us. It is a gift that we need to help the children in our classrooms become aware of and enjoy. The teaching of science gives us many opportunities to bring out the emotional response of children to their world. When you teach science the development of a child's feelings about the world should be an important goal.

The science experiences that you provide for children encourage the acquisition of values that will lead to a positive attitude toward science, schooling, the development of appropriate relationships with others, and the natural world. The beautiful poem in Figure 2–3 expresses the importance of the child's environment in the development of positive attitudes. As teachers we need to create classroom learning environments that foster each child's affective growth.

Without a conscious effort by the teacher to realize the goal of affective development of his or her students, a classroom discussion of the vastness of the universe is simply a discussion about empty space. The very same lesson, when taught by a teacher who tries to emphasize attitudinal development, evokes a child's feelings of wonder and joy about the vastness of space.

A lesson about a caterpillar becoming a butterfly is simply about a caterpillar and a butterfly unless the teacher attends to the affective development of children. But the same content can be taught in a way that encourages the child to stop, to think, and to develop feelings about the near miraculous transformation of a humble caterpillar into a gossamer-winged butterfly.

The Psychomotor Domain

Children need to develop the ability to operate their bodies in such a way that they can manipulate their environment. Such manipulation requires a coordination between what the mind wills and what the body is able to perform. Young children in our classrooms need to learn to develop both their gross and their fine motor

[3]David Rains Wallace, "This Tangled Brilliance," *Sierra*, 64, no. 2 (March/April 1979), 38. Used with permission.

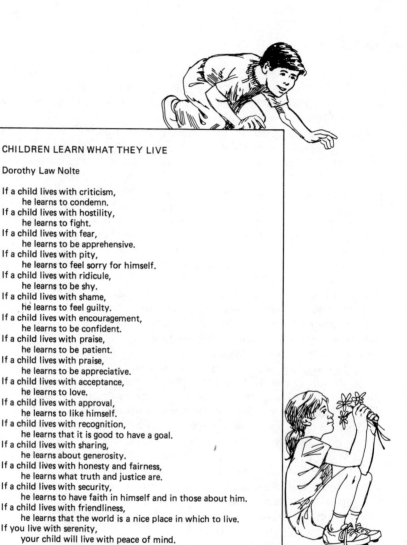

CHILDREN LEARN WHAT THEY LIVE

Dorothy Law Nolte

If a child lives with criticism,
    he learns to condemn.
If a child lives with hostility,
    he learns to fight.
If a child lives with fear,
    he learns to be apprehensive.
If a child lives with pity,
    he learns to feel sorry for himself.
If a child lives with ridicule,
    he learns to be shy.
If a child lives with shame,
    he learns to feel guilty.
If a child lives with encouragement,
    he learns to be confident.
If a child lives with praise,
    he learns to be patient.
If a child lives with praise,
    he learns to be appreciative.
If a child lives with acceptance,
    he learns to love.
If a child lives with approval,
    he learns to like himself.
If a child lives with recognition,
    he learns that it is good to have a goal.
If a child lives with sharing,
    he learns about generosity.
If a child lives with honesty and fairness,
    he learns what truth and justice are.
If a child lives with security,
    he learns to have faith in himself and in those about him.
If a child lives with friendliness,
    he learns that the world is a nice place in which to live.
If you live with serenity,
    your child will live with peace of mind.

With what is your child living?

Figure 2–3. (*Source:* Dorothy Law Nolte. Copyright Dorothy Law Nolte.)

abilities. Gross motor skills can be developed through such science activities as the assembly and use of a simple lever, the use of hoes and rakes to care for a school vegetable garden, or the shaping of sand on a sand table into a river delta. Children also need experiences that require fine motor skills. These skills can be developed through such activities as cutting with scissors, drawing lines with pencils and rulers, and sorting seeds on the basis of physical characteristics.

Some psychomotor experiences in the study of science require the taking apart of objects. Old alarm clocks, broken musical instruments, and even ripe fruits and vegetables can be used to develop a child's ability to disassemble things. These psychomotor activities are given a cognitive dimension when we ask children to predict what they will find, organize and classify the parts they uncover, and finally hypothesize about the function that each part performs. Similarly, children can be given the parts of a mechanism, such as a plastic skeletal model of an animal, and be asked to assemble them into a whole. Activities that require assembling and disassembling can all be used to integrate psychomotor and cognitive goals.

GENERAL GOALS OF SCIENCE EDUCATION

Creativity

> "Well, if that is the *full* moon, where did the *empty* moon go to?"

Would that question have taken you by surprise? It is a wonderful question asked by a child who is creatively thinking and learning. The development of a child's creative ability is an important goal of the elementary-school curriculum and of science education in particular. The child who is developing and displaying creativity is one who is applying his or her cognitive, affective, and psychomotor abilities in a way that yields new ideas, skills, products, or questions. During a science experience children manifest creativity by inventing concepts that have not yet been covered in class or in science readings; developing original skills, such as a new way to feed the fish in the classroom aquarium the proper amount of food automatically; inventing a product such as an "over-the-vacation classroom-plant-waterer"; and formulating in-class questions such as the one about the destination of the "empty" moon.

DENNIS the MENACE

"HE'S HYPHENATIN' TILL SPRING, JOEY... ALL YOU HAVTA DO IS DUST HIM ONCE IN AWHILE."

Figure 2–4. Note how Dennis creatively uses science vocabulary. (*Source:* Field Enterprises. © Field Enterprises, Inc. Used by permission of Hank Ketcham.)

Because of the high value placed on originality in the discipline of science, creativity is a natural goal of science education. The best way for us to foster creativity in children is to model creativity in the teaching techniques we use. Creative learning cannot occur in a classroom environment that does not reflect creative teaching.

In order to be a creative teacher you will probably have to take a few risks. At times you will have to depart from the tried and true. At times you will have to encourage children to ask questions that you might be tempted to discourage. At times you will have to depart from the curriculum and carefully thought out lesson plans. Perhaps most important, you will need to strive constantly to find ways to encourage and elicit the creative abilities of the children with whom you work, their parents, and the teachers and administrators who make up the total school environment. The task is a large one, but you have a great advantage: science as an area of study provides a rich environment for creativity.

Critical Thinking

"Science educators now generally agree that the purpose of education from kindergarten through high school is to prepare students for life, not for university entrance."[4] If we are to accomplish the worthy goal of directing our science instruction toward helping children and youth to face life's challenges and opportunities, we will need to help children utilize their full intellectual powers as they experience science.

If we use science activities that engage children in the processes of inquiry discussed in Chapter 1, they will have many opportunities to apply their critical-thinking skills. As a child learns science he or she has an opportunity to verify reasoned judgments. This testing of the validity of a conclusion is a natural part of doing science. To foster critical thinking in children, all you need to provide are opportunities for them to "think" about situations—that is, to reason out explanations and then create ways to test these answers. Neither step requires sophisticated materials or special learning environments.

Figure 2–5 is an extensive list of questions that can be used to elicit critical thinking in children. Note that the materials with which the children test their conclusions are simple and highly relevant to the *real* world of the child: soap bubbles, balloons, and of course paper airplanes. All these are readily available—particularly the paper airplanes!

Good Citizenship

Have you ever thought of raising rainbow trout in your basement? This imaginative solution to world hunger comes from a Mr. Karl Hess, a citizen who is unwilling to let the knowledge of science and technology rest solely in the hands of scientists and engineers. Hess found he could supply much of his neighborhood with protein by raising rainbow trout in plywood tanks in apartment basements

[4]Marjorie Gardner, "Ten Trends in Science Education," *The Science Teacher*, 46, no. 1 (January 1979), 31.

1. What kind of soap *solution* seems to make the best bubbles?
2. Are some *brands* of liquid soap better than others for making bubbles?
3. If the copper wire is shaped into a *square*, can "squarish" bubbles be produced with it?
4. Do *different* shapes and sizes of copper wire *loops* make different shapes and sizes of bubbles?
5. If the liquid soap solution is *heated* or *cooled* are the resulting bubbles any different?
6. How *long* can a soap bubble last?
7. How *big* can a soap bubble be?
8. Do "fat" balloons behave differently from "skinny" balloons when the air is released?
9. Do *large* balloons fly farther than *small* ones?
10. Can you figure out a way to make a balloon fly in a *straight* line?
11. If a paper clip is taped to one side of a balloon, will it "fly" the same as before?
12. Can you figure out how to make a *balloon rocket* using string (as a guide), a soda straw, and tape?
13. How *far* can you get your balloon rocket to go?
14. What happens if a *parachute* is attached to the open end of the balloon and the blown-up balloon is then released?
15. Can you make a *paper airplane* that really flies?
16. What type of *paper* seems to work best in making airplanes?
17. Is it possible to make a *"flying wing"* type of plane?
18. How does attaching a *paper clip* affect the flight of a plane?
19. If one *wing* is smaller than the other, what happens to the plane's flight?
20. Can you build a plane that makes a *circle* and returns?
21. Can you build a plane that makes a *loop*?
22. What kind of design seems to be the best *glider*?
23. Does the *weight* of the paper affect the flight of the plane?
24. How *small* can paper planes be made and still fly rather than just "dropping down"?
25. How *large* can paper planes be made before they fail to glide well?
26. Is it possible to make a *cardboard* airplane fly like one made of paper?
27. Will a *round* plane fly?
28. How does the size of the *wing* affect the plane's flight?
29. Can a *jet plane* be made using balloons?
30. What would happen if a paper plane *contest* was organized in your school?

Figure 2−5. Questions to Stimulate Thinking (*Source:* Ronald G. Good, *How Children Learn Science.* New York: Macmillan, 1977, pp. 283−284. Reprinted with permission of Macmillan Publishing Co., Inc. Copyright © 1977 by Ronald G. Good.)

(for about a dollar a pound in costs). He also raised bumper crops of tomatoes on empty rooftops, growing them in liquid nutrients rather than in soil. The "community technology" involved in the trout raising was the knowledge that a few cups of vacant-lot soil in the trout tanks produced bacteria that removed destructive ammonia from trout waste; that discarded washing machines provided fine water-recirculation systems; and that the calcite chips available in any garden store were perfect for filters.[5]

The citizen who has at least a basic knowledge of science has a distinct advantage over the person who is scientifically ignorant. The scientifically literate person will be able to make informed judgments about the relative merits of government-proposed courses of action that have a scientific or technologic dimension. Each person's life is heavily influenced by science and technology. Environmental pollution, space exploration, health care, and other science-related issues are constantly in the news, and they must have the attention of the "average" citizen if big government, big business, and local, state, and federal agencies are to act in responsible ways. The citizenry has a responsibility to keep itself informed of scientific and technologic developments and to offer suggestions for changes in policy and action that can help alleviate human problems. By the way, Mr. Hess's trout-raising system produces three tons of protein per year per basement!

Tomorrow's adults will need to be aware of the concepts and processes that undergird the earth/space, physical, and life sciences. It will be their influence and tax money that will promote the exploration of the universe, the determination of the structure of matter, and the improvement or destruction of the ecology of the planet. Our job as teachers is to help children prepare themselves for responsible citizenship in tomorrow's world.

Expanded Career Awareness and Diminished Sex-Role Stereotyping

What do you want to be when you grow up? was the question asked of kindergartners. On the boys' list: astronaut, truck driver, trainman, and policeman. The girls' list included ballerina, librarian, stewardess, movie actress, mommy, and princess. Next the children were asked, "What would you like to be if you were the other sex?" A little boy said, "Well, I guess if I were to grow up to be a girl, then I'd have to be nothing." And then one little girl answered, "Well, if I were a boy, I would grow wings and fly across the city. I could do anything. . . ."[6]

The wistfulness in the little girl's words brings me sadness. She is so young and yet so very worldly. Someone has already put *STOP* signs on roads to her future.

The excluding of females from life's possibilities is obviously a societal problem. We could all opt to simply "let George or Georgette take care of it" and

[5]William K. Stuckney, "Official Circles," *Omni*, 1, no. 11 (August 1979), 127. Copyright 1979 by Omni Publications International, Ltd. and used with the permission of the copyright owner.

[6]Letty Cottin Pogrebin, quoted in *Instructor*, 86, no. 8 (April 1977), 22. Copyright © 1977 by The Instructor Publications, Inc. Used by permission. The study reported by Pogrebin was conducted by the University of Pittsburgh.

divest ourselves of the responsibility for a solution, but we cannot do this. If we believe in equality of opportunity, then we have an obligation to correct sex-role stereotyping with every group of children we teach. Teachers can make a difference in the way a child perceives his or her potential. Over the years we have probably inadvertently reinforced the societal view that science has gender and in so doing denied countless children the opportunity to consider science and science-related fields as vocational possibilities. This reinforcement of sex-role stereotyping harms boys as much as girls: the girls learn that science is not for females, and the boys learn that girls don't like to do science.

"Nearly 100% of all nurses, but only 7% of all doctors, are female. Ninety-nine percent of all engineers are male."[7] These figures emphasize the obvious

[7]Walter Smith and Kala M. Stroud, *Science Career Exploration for Women* (Washington, D.C.: National Science Teachers Association, 1978), p. 2.

Figure 2–6. Remember, stereotyping harms boys as much as it harms girls. Your classroom should involve everyone in activities. (*Source:* SAPA II, Module 42, p. 4. Science . . . A Process Approach II, American Association for the Advancement of Science. Used with permission.)

differences between the career choices of males and those of females. The challenge to the elementary-school teacher is that of building career awareness in children, not necessarily helping children choose a career. If your children do not become aware of the appropriateness or importance of the careers of individuals with scientific training, they will be considerably handicapped as they approach the career choice that they will make in their adolescence. Career awareness is a special problem not only for the girls we teach but also for boys and girls who are members of racial and ethnic minorities. You will be able to do a great deal to expand children's perceptions of themselves and of what they can become. The science experiences that children have under your guidance can serve not only to teach them science but also to help them see the wonderful possibilities that lie in their future.

GOING FURTHER

On Your Own

1. Think about the role of science and technology in what you have done so far today—the foods you've eaten, the modes of transportation you may have utilized, the creams, lotions, and ointments you may have applied to yourself, the prescription or patent medicines you may have ingested, your reliance on electrical energy, and so forth.

2. Have you ever felt that you did not have enough scientific knowledge to understand fully a news broadcast dealing with a current event that involved science and technology? If so, what was the event? What parts of the report puzzled you? What cognitive, affective, or psychomotor learnings would have helped you achieve a better understanding of what happened? Did the report mention any ways in which the event might affect society?

3. Review Figure 2–2. Which of the cognitive levels and processes listed there were stressed in the science activities experienced as an elementary-school student? What advice might you consider giving your former teachers about the goals of the elementary science curriculum?

4. Think about a science activity that you recently observed in a classroom. If you have not observed one recently, think of one that you would like to present to a group of children. Analyze the observed or fictional activity, and try to determine the extent to which it would help children attain cognitive, affective, or psychomotor goals.

5. In recent years, have you observed any scientific or technologic developments that reflected a high degree of creative ability on the part of scientists or people in science-related fields? Which developments struck you as having the most potential significance for society? In what ways did the developments reflect the ability of people to look at things in new ways? What could you do as a teacher to foster creativity in your classroom?

With Others

6. Prepare a list of science- or technology-related issues that are currently facing the people in your community. Discuss the issues, and determine what each group member's position is on each. Now have each group member identify the extent to

which schooling, parents, and the media have influenced his or her opinion. How significant was the influence of schooling? What are the implications of this significance, or lack of it?

7. Have each member of the group construct a newsprint or blackboard chart that represents his or her recollection of a typical elementary-school day. Include each subject and the approximate amount of time devoted to it. Compare the schedules and note whether science is included. If so, discuss its relative emphasis.

8. Discuss the effects of the potential role models with which your parents, teachers, textbooks, and the media provided you. Can you recall your level of career awareness as an elementary-school child? What did you want to become? Why? If you are a woman, what factors tended to turn you away from a scientific career? If you are a man, reflect upon any stereotypes you had (have?) about women and science. Discuss the extent to which you have observed members of ethnic or racial minorities depicted by the media as having science-related careers.

TEACHER TALK: SPRINGBOARDS FOR DISCUSSION

- "[F]irst graders love science. It is exciting and different. By the time they get to junior high some are saying, "Oh no, not science!" When first and second graders get excited about science—magnets are fun you know—they squeal with delight. We somehow manage to take out that fun as we go along. I don't know how we do it."

- "You can't say that's exciting [floating corks in water]. I want experiments you can do which get them all off saying, 'Wow! How did that happen?' Something that really challenges and excites."

- "Actually I really enjoy science. But I haven't had the time, with all the other things to teach, to put time into developing a science activity. Actually the children enjoy it. We sent the children to the environmental lab and they came back bubbling."

SUMMARY

There are many reasons for teaching science. The facts, concepts, principles, and processes of science make a contribution to the child's cognitive development. The development and application of values such as truth, freedom, skepticism, originality, order, and communication can all be part of a child's science experiences. These values represent an important component of a child's affective development. Science activities can also provide children with many opportunities to develop and refine their gross and fine motor skills. The fostering of creativity, critical thinking, and an understanding of the relationship of science to society are also feasible goals of science teaching. Finally, the teacher can use science experiences to help children develop a positive attitude toward science and an awareness of careers in science and science-related fields.

SUGGESTED READINGS

American College Testing Program, *Women in Science and Technology.* Iowa City: ACT Publications, 1976. 16 pp.

Career Awareness. Elementary Science Packet 7. Washington, D.C.: National Science Teachers Association, n.d.

HARBECK, M. B., and P. MARCUCCIO, "Science in the Lives of Children," *Childhood Education*, 55 (November/December 1978), 94–96.

JENKENS, E., ed., *American Black Scientists and Inventors.* Washington, D.C.: National Science Teachers Association, 1975. 79 pp.

KLOPFER, L. E., "Editorial: Scientific and Technological Literacy for All: A National Policy," *Science Education*, 65, no. 1 (January 1981), 1–2.

KREINBERG, N., *I'm Madly in Love with Electricity, and Other Comments about Their Work by Women in Science and Engineering.* Berkeley, Calif.: Lawrence Hall of Science, 1977. 37 pp.

McCORMACK, A. J., "Creativity: A Funny Thing," *Science and Children*, 16 (March 1979), 48–50.

MORAVCSIK, M. J., "Creativity in Science Education," *Science Education*, 65, no. 2 (April 1981), 221–227.

SMITH, W., and K. STROUD, *Science Career Exploration for Women.* Washington, D.C.: National Science Teachers Association, 1978. 77 pp.

"So You Say You Want to Be a Scientist," *Science Quest*, 52 (April 1979), 32–33.

STANBURY, G. M., "Elementary Science Programs: A Principal's Perspective," *Science and Children*, 18, no. 4 (January 1981), 15.

STUCKNEY, W., "Official Circles," *Omni*, 1, no. 11 (August 1979), 22, 127.

WELCH, W. W., L. E. KLOPFER, G. S. AIKENHEAD, and J. T. ROBINSON, "The Role of Inquiry in Science Education: Analysis and Recommendations," *Science Education*, 65, no. 1 (January 1981), 33–50.

Western Electric, *Legacy for All: A Record of Achievements of Black American Scientists.* n.d. 27 pp.

chapter 3

How Do Children Learn Science?

"I Led the Pigeons to the Flag"

The most saluted man in America is Richard Stans. Legions of school children place their hands over their hearts to pledge allegiance to the flag, "and to the republic for Richard Stans."

With all due patriotic fervor, the same kids salute "one nation, under guard." Some begin with "I pledge a legion to the flag," others with "I led the pigeons to the flag." This is not a new phenomenon. When they come to "one nation, indivisible," this generation is as likely to say "one naked individual" as a previous generation was to murmur, "one nation in a dirigible," or "one nation and a vegetable."

"The Stars Bangled Banger" is a great source for these creative mishearings: "the Donzerly light," "oh, the ramrods we washed," "grapefruit through the night" that our flag was still there.

Figure 3–1.

Then there is the good Mrs. Shirley Murphy of the 23rd Psalm: "Shirley, good Mrs. Murphy, shall follow me all the days of my life." (Surely, goodness and mercy would not lead us into Penn Station.)[1]

Children are always learning something. Sometimes what they learn is not what we as teachers or parents intend. The teacher in a rural setting announcing a language-arts unit on Pulitzer Prizes may really be announcing a science unit on the reproduction of chickens as some children hear "pullet surprises." Human learning depends on many factors, and the examples above reveal but one of them—the learner's previous experience. In order to become an effective teacher you must first develop a good understanding of how children learn.

How did you learn science in elementary and high school? Was science a group of facts that you memorized? Did you learn science as you would learn a foreign language—paying close attention to the study of new vocabulary words? Was the emphasis on learning science through hands-on activities? Did your teachers emphasize the acquisition of the general concepts that underlie the sciences? Did you learn science by reading about it or by actually doing it?

If you view science or any other field as simply a mass of knowledge that has to be internalized, then you will probably bring that assumption to your own teaching. If, on the other hand, you view science as a body of knowledge and processes that is best understood by grasping the general concepts that permeate it, you will bring that assumption to your teaching. Your present view of learning has been shaped to a large measure by your teachers and their beliefs about human learning. Similarly, your beliefs will affect the children that *you* teach.

CHILDREN, LEARNING, AND SCIENCE

Wouldn't it be nice if someone could tell you how children learn? The implications of such a proposition are profound. Teaching would be a great deal easier if some genie could leave a message in each teacher's mailbox tomorrow morning that simply said:

Children learn by . . .

If you found such a message, you could simply use the explanation as the basis of your teaching all through the day. Think of all the happy children leaving school at the end of the day, feeling the pride that comes from having learned. Think of all the happy teachers who would leave school knowing that they really accomplished something. Think of all the happy parents who would finally hear appropriate responses from their children during mealtime interrogations initiated with the question "What did you learn in school today?" Think of all the school principals and school-board members who could sleep soundly knowing that children had *learned*.

Unfortunately, even at this point in the twentieth century we must approach our teaching with a lack of certitude about how children learn. All we have to rely upon are theories of learning. The spectrum of our contemporary knowledge about learning is bounded by two major sets of theoretical constructs, each by itself

[1]William Safire, "I Led the Pigeons to the Flag," *The New York Times Magazine*, May 27, 1979, p. 9. © 1979 by The New York Times Company. Reprinted by permission.

inadequate to describe how children learn. Consequently, we must approach our teaching with humility about the state of our knowledge of learning, yet we must muster self-confidence in our ability to synthesize and apply the most salient propositions that emerge from two very diverse explanations of the phenomenon we call learning:

1. The cognitive view, based on the work of David Ausubel, Robert Gagné, Jerome Bruner, and Jean Piaget
2. The behavioral view, based on the work of B. F. Skinner

THE COGNITIVE VIEW OF LEARNING

Figure 3–2. What is this a drawing of? (*Source:* Begelski, B. R. and Alampay, D. A. The role of frequency in developing perceptual sets. *Canadian Journal of Psychology,* 15[1961], 205–11. Page 206, Figure 1. Copyright [1961] Canadian Psychological Association, reprinted by permission.)

What is Figure 3–2 a drawing of? Ask others to look at the drawing and give their opinion. If you discuss the drawing with them you will find that it can spark a very lively argument. This drawing and others like it reveal the principal beliefs held by theorists who feel that human learning depends upon the mental processes of the learner. Cognitive-learning theorists believe that what we learn depends primarily upon *us.* In marked contrast, behaviorists believe that learning is controlled by our *external* environment.

David Ausubel

Ausubel believes that learning should be a deductive process. In other words, children should be presented with a general concept and should then proceed to specifics. From this point of view, the quality of learning depends on the teacher's ability to organize concepts, principles, and ideas so that the child has experiences that continually fit new learnings into the more general learnings that preceded them.

What would you have seen in the ambiguous drawing in Figure 3–2 if *prior* to your looking at it a person had asked you one of the following questions: (1) What kind of animal is this a picture of? (2) Do you know this scientist's name? If you were asked the first question, you would probably see a mouse or a rat in the picture. If you were asked the second question, you would probably see a man (as we have noted, scientists are unfortunately typically stereotyped as men). Cognitive-learning theory has as one of its tenets the idea that what we perceive and what we understand is based on a general tendency to organize information into a meaningful whole.

If this is indeed the case, then we as teachers can play an important role in children's learning by structuring experiences so that they take advantage of this natural tendency. One way of accomplishing this is the use of what Ausubel refers to as advance organizers.[2] The two questions about Figure 3–2 are examples of advance organizers. What each of them does is dispose the learner (in this case, the reader—which I hope is the same thing) to make sense out of an experience *before* the experience occurs. Here the advance organizers were questions; they can also be statements, lists of topics, pictures, or many other things.

SOME IMPLICATIONS OF AUSUBEL'S WORK

Clearly, Ausubel's work can give you a number of helpful ideas about planning science experiences for children. In particular, try to use advance organizers and a variety of other techniques that will connect what the children are presently learning to what they have previously learned. Figure 3–3 suggests various ways to put Ausubel's ideas to work in your classroom.

Jerome Bruner

Bruner believes that an important part of your role as a teacher is to provide children with activities that will help them see the underlying ideas, concepts, relationships, or patterns in science. According to Bruner, children should always learn inductively—that is, from the specific to the more general.

To help children organize their learning, Bruner suggests, you should develop "coding systems" that will enable them to place new information within the larger scheme of things. For example, when you are teaching children about plants and animals you could have them group new information about each under specific categories, such as "reproduction" and "use of oxygen."

The results of Bruner's research suggest that you should try to nurture intuitive thinking in children. That is, you should encourage them to make guesses based on incomplete evidence. They can then check on the accuracy of their guesses by carrying out science activities, and in this way maintain their interest in the subject matter at a high level.

When you face the larger issue of curriculum development for the science classroom, you may wish to refer to Bruner's more general ideas about the importance of teachers providing young children with the basic structural elements of science (in a simplified form) and then moving to more complex presentations of the structure in the upper grades. This progression from simple to complex can be accomplished through the use of activities that foster discovery learning. If you teach young children you will probably need to provide more assistance to children involved in discovery learning than to older children.[3]

[2] Anita Woolfolk and Lorraine McCune Nicolich, *Educational Psychology for Teachers* (Englewood Cliffs, N.J.: Prentice-Hall, 1980), pp. 217–218.

[3] Adapted from the ideas of Woolfolk and Nicolich, *Educational Psychology for Teachers*, pp. 211–214.

Practical
Applications:
Using Ausubel's Ideas
in the Science Classroom

1. Use advance organizers.
   EXAMPLES • List, pronounce, and discuss science vocabulary words prior to lessons that use new science lessons.
   • Role-play possible situations that may develop on a field trip prior to a field trip.
   • Prepare and display a bulletin board that displays the major components of a learning unit prior to beginning the unit with the children.
2. Use a number of examples.
   EXAMPLES • Ask the children to give examples from their own experience related to science phenomena observed in class.
   • Use pictures and diagrams to show various examples of such things as constellations, animals, clouds, plants, etc.
3. Focus on both similarities and differences.
   EXAMPLES • Discuss how plants and animals are the same and different.
   • Compare various types of rocks.
   • Explain what conventional and alternative energy sources do and do not have in common.
4. Present materials in an organized fashion
   EXAMPLES • Outline the content of particularly complicated lessons.
   • Organize the materials needed for science activity so that a sign indicates whether they are to be used at the beginning, middle, or end of an activity.
5. Discourage rote learning of material that could be learned more meaningfully.
   EXAMPLES • Have children give responses to questions in activities or textbooks in their own words.
   • Encourage children to explain the results of science activities to one another.

Figure 3–3.

SOME IMPLICATIONS OF BRUNER'S WORK

Each time you think about a science lesson you are going to present or a learning unit you intend to develop, you may wish to consider how Bruner's work can guide your planning. In particular you may wish to ask yourself whether your plan proceeds from the specific to the general, from the simple to the complex, and from the concrete to the abstract. You should also check your lesson plans to see if they encourage discovery learning through challenging questions or ideas that will get children to make "guesses," or hypotheses, before they engage in science activities. Figure 3–4 can help you evaluate your planning and teaching.

Practical Applications:

Using Bruner's Ideas
in the Science Classroom

1. Emphasize the basic structure of new material.
   EXAMPLES • Use demonstrations that reveal basic principles—the demonstration of the "laws" of magnetism by using similar and opposite poles of a set of bar magnets.
   • Encourage children to make outlines of the basic points that are made in textbooks or discovered through activities.
2. Present many examples of the concept you are teaching.
   EXAMPLES • When presenting an explanation of the phases of the moon, have the children observe the phases in a variety of ways—direct observations of the changing shape of the moon in the evenings, demonstrations of the change in reflected light in a sun, earth, or moon model using a flashlight and spheres, and looking at diagrams of the sun-moon-earth positions.
   • Using magazine pictures to show the stages in a space shuttle mission, have the class make models that show the stages in a space shuttle mission and list the stages of a space shuttle mission on the chalkboard.
3. Help children construct coding systems.
   EXAMPLES • Invent a game that requires children to classify rocks.
   • Have children maintain a scrapbook in which they keep collected leaf specimens that are grouped according to observed characteristics.
4. Apply new learnings to many different situations and kinds of problems.
   EXAMPLES • Learn how scientists estimate the size of populations by having children count the number in a sample and then make estimates of the numbers of grasshoppers in a lawn *and* in a meadow.
5. Pose a problem to children and let them find the answer.
   EXAMPLES • Ask questions that will lead naturally to activities such as "Why should we wear seat belts?" and "What are some ingredients that most junk foods have?"
   • Do a demonstration that raises a question in the children's minds, e.g., levitate a washer using magnets or mix two colored solutions to produce a third color.
6. Encourage children to make intuitive guesses.
   EXAMPLES • Ask the children to make a guess at the amount of water that goes down the drain each time a child gets a drink of water from a water fountain.
   • Give the children magazine photographs of the evening sky and have children guess the locations of some major constellations.

Figure 3—4.

Robert Gagné

Gagné suggests that there are at least eight types of learning. The accompanying list contains a brief description of each and an example from elementary-school science.[4]

Type of Learning	Description	Example
1. Signal Learning	Classical conditioning as studied by Pavlov.	(Obviously, we do not use classical conditioning in the science classroom.)
2. Stimulus–Response Learning	The learner displays a learned behavior in response to a stimulus.	The child moves away from a liquid that seems to be boiling too rapidly.
3. Chaining	The learner acquires a succession of stimulus–response connections.	The child performs a series of operations to create a product, such as making a plaster cast of an animal footprint.
4. Verbal Association	The learner uses a series of words, phrases, or sentences whose connections to other meanings are based on previous learning.	The child names the planets in our solar system in order according to their distance from the sun.
5. Multiple Discriminations	The learner acquires the capacity for making a number of identifying responses to various stimuli.	The child learns the names of commonly observed trees.
6. Concept Learning (Classifying)	The learner acquires the capacity to make a response to a group of stimuli that are characteristics of an entire class of objects or events.	The child uses a term such as *mammals* when observing a cow.
7. Principle (Rule-governed) Learning	The learner acquires the capacity to make a response that includes two or more concepts.	The child uses the term *deciduous* appropriately in describing a tree that loses its leaves in winter. This reflects a grasp of the concepts of deciduous, tree, and leaves.
8. Problem Solving	The learner uses two or more previously acquired principles to produce a new capability.	Using two principles (laws) of motion, the child explains why race-car drivers wear seat belts.

In recent years Gagné has focused a great deal on the specific outcomes of learning experiences. These "end products," according to Gagné, can be viewed as intellectual skills, verbal information, attitudes, motor skills, and cognitive strategies. If you evaluate the quality of learning in your classroom, these end products can help you focus upon the range of learning opportunities that you have provided.

[4]Based on Alfred DeVito et al., *Developing Children's Thinking through Science* (Englewood Cliffs, N.J.: Prentice-Hall, 1970), pp. 132–135. This list originally appeared in Gagné's *The Conditions of Learning* (New York: Holt, Rinehart & Winston, 1965), pp. 31–61.

Practical Applications:

Using Gagné's Ideas
in the Science Classroom

1. Stimulus-response learning

    EXAMPLE • Provide repetition of the stimulus-response connection with immediate reinforcement—praising solutions to problems or providing answer keys for children's use after doing worksheets or questions at the end of a textbook selection.

2. Chaining

    EXAMPLE • Perform the necessary links in the correct order, reinforce the final link, and provide for necessary prompting and repetition. For example, after demonstrating how a length of glass tubing is bent and inserted into a rubber stopper safely, have the student perform the same operations with verbal instructions from you.

3. Verbal association

    EXAMPLE • Reinstate verbal links in the proper order with intermediate "coding" links. Reinforce the correct response and provide for necessary prompting and repetition. "Ism," for example, might remind the individual of the three major groups of rocks: igneous, sedimentary, and metamorphic.

4. Multiple discriminations

    EXAMPLE • Present the stimuli in a manner that emphasizes distinctiveness, such as noting the peculiar effect produced when feldspar reflects light, or making reference to the "little pegs" at the base of each spruce needle, or identifying the peculiar wing structure of the swallowtail butterfly. Confirm correct responses and provide for repetition.

5. Concept learning (classifying)

    EXAMPLE • Present a variety of stimuli representing the concept class, each of which has a connection with a common response. Verify acquisition by presenting a novel stimulus member of the class. For instance, after separating a variety of leaves, stems, and flowers into monocot or dicot groups, introduce a number of unfamiliar flowering plants for classification into either division.

6. Principle learning ("rule-governed" learning)

    EXAMPLE • Inform the learner of the expected performance and invoke the recall of component concepts or principles by verbal instructions. Verify acquisition by asking the learner to demonstrate the principle. For example, after observing that heating makes air expand, heating makes oxygen expand, and heating makes carbon dioxide expand, the student might make the more abstract generalization that "heating makes gases expand."

7. Problem solving

    EXAMPLE • Inform the learner of the expected performance and invoke recall of previously learned concepts or principles by verbal guidance. Verify by asking the learner to demonstrate in a specific instance. To illustrate: the student might use information gained in observing a candle burn out in closed pint-sized jar to predict how long a similar candle would burn when placed in a closed quart-sized jar.

Figure 3-5.

SOME IMPLICATIONS OF GAGNÉ'S WORK

According to Gagné, the eight types of learning constitute a hierarchy extending from signal learning (the simplest to acquire) to problem solving (the most complex). If you were to follow Gagné's approach to learning in your work with children, you would arrange the learning environment so that children would have many opportunities to master the various types of learning. Your ultimate goal would be the children's attainment of skill in problem solving. The list of specific examples in Figure 3−5 may prove helpful to you.[5]

Jean Piaget

When you were a very young child did you believe any of the following things?

> The sun or the moon followed you when you were out taking a walk.
> Anything that moves is alive.
> Clouds were really strangely shaped creatures.
> Dreams come in through the window while you're asleep.
> Your dolls were real people.

A curiosity about the beliefs held by young people started Jean Piaget's lifelong search for an understanding of the manner by which children think and perceive. Piaget's interest in the way in which children viewed the world around them was sparked by his reading of the childhood recollections of a deaf-mute.

Much of Piaget's early work with children has contributed to our understanding of the way in which young children view the world. Implicit in this understanding is the belief that it is the child who brings meaning to the world, and not vice versa. This is quite consistent with the cognitive-learning theorist's view of learning as being an internal process.

An exploration of childhood egocentrism is only one component of Piaget's work. There is another component, one that may have a greater impact on you, the classroom teacher. Piaget proposed that each of us progresses through distinct stages of intellectual development. This is a controversial notion, since it is at odds with those who believe that the child can learn virtually anything at any time—as long as what is to be learned is presented properly.

THE STAGES OF COGNITIVE DEVELOPMENT AND THEIR CHARACTERISTICS

This section lists the characteristics that Piaget believed are displayed by children at various stages in their intellectual development.

Sensorimotor Knowledge (0 to 2 years)

1. An object "exists" only if the child can see, feel, hear, touch, or taste it. Anything outside his or her perceptual field does not exist.
2. Random physical searching sometimes uncovers hidden objects.
3. The child acquires knowledge solely by interacting with his or her immediate environment.

[5]DeVito et al., *Developing Children's Thinking through Science*, p. 134.

4. Knowledge gathered in this stage serves as the foundation for representational knowledge.
5. The child's "world view" is based solely on the knowledge directly available to him or her at a particular instant in time.
6. The child imitates the behaviors of adults and the movement of objects through arm, hand, and body movements.
7. During this stage the child progresses from reflex behavior to the ability to perceive that objects and people have permanence and can be the cause of events.

Preoperational (Representational) Knowledge (2 to 7 years)

1. Children in this stage tend to talk "at" one another. They engage in monologues with one another that tend to be unrelated. (Some of us seem to still display this characteristic from time to time!)
2. Organized language and the use of symbols begins.
3. The child is still oriented perceptually—that is, to the here and now. Logical thinking is relatively limited. The child operates on the basis of intuition rather than logic.
4. The child is still primarily egocentric: other points of view are not fully understood.
5. The child begins to think in terms of simple classes. For example, he or she learns that *animals* includes dogs, cats, cows, and so forth.
6. The child becomes goal-directed and displays trial-and-error behavior when striving for a goal.
7. The child has some difficulty understanding that objects have multiple properties. For example, he or she is not completely aware that a block simultaneously possesses color, weight, height, depth, hardness, and other qualities.
8. The concepts of time and space are difficult. The child's estimates of such durations as the time elapsed before, during, and after an event vary from clock time. Space

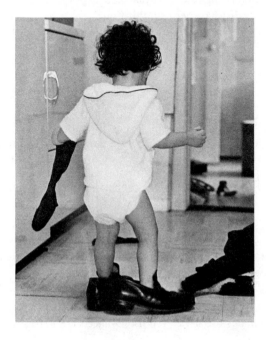

Figure 3–6. What stage of development might this child be in? (*Source:* Alice Kandell, Rapho/ Photo Researchers, Inc.)

consists solely of the area he or she is familiar with: that there are people or things in different cities or countries is difficult for the child to understand.

9. The child does not "conserve" such quantities as mass, weight, or number. For example, an equal volume of orange juice placed first in a short wide glass and then in a tall narrow glass is perceived as having changed in amount.

10. The child uses magical or animistic explanations for phenomena—for example, "Dreams come in the window when I sleep" and "The sun is moving across the sky during the day because it is trying to follow me."

Concrete Operations (7 to 11 years)

1. The child can carry out elementary logical thought processes, particularly those dealing with concrete objects.
2. The child can group objects into classes and can arrange elements of a class in order.
3. The child understands the conservation of length, area, weight, and volume.
4. The child understands the concept of reversibility.
5. The child has difficulty isolating variables and then relating them to one another.
6. The child's thought processes become less egocentric.
7. The child begins to develop an understanding of the concepts of space and time.

Formal Operations (12 years through adulthood)

1. The child is able to think very abstractly.
2. The child can consider many alternative solutions to a problem.
3. The child is able to isolate a variable in a problem and consider its role and those of related variables.
4. The child is able to make a sound hypothesis before experimenting.
5. The ability to abstract enables the child to think in terms of metaphors.
6. The child can abstract the underlying principles that seem to govern a phenomenon.
7. The child is able to think about his or her own thinking.
8. The capacity to solve very complex verbal problems evolves as a result of the child's ability to manipulate the meanings represented by symbols.

THE PIAGETIAN TASKS AND THE CHILD'S ABILITY TO CONSERVE

Researchers evaluate the stage of cognitive development possessed by a child primarily through the use of diagnostic activities that have become known as Piagetian Tasks. These tasks essentially require children to deal with situations that test whether they understand that the number or amount of something remains constant even if its appearance or arrangement is modified. This ability is known as *conservation*. The following list describes the various types of conservation that are evaluated:

Conservation of number: the number of elements in a group remains the same even if the elements are rearranged.

Conservation of substance: the amount of a substance remains the same even if its shape is altered.

Conservation of length: the length of an object (or line) does not change if it is displaced in space.

Conservation of area: the surface covered by members of a set of objects remains the same even if the objects are rearranged.

Practical Applications:

Using Piaget's Ideas
in the Science Classroom

1. *Infants* in the sensorimotor stage (0 to 2 years)
   EXAMPLES • Provide a stimulating environment that includes eye-catching displays, pleasant sounds, human voices, and plenty of tender loving care so that the infant becomes motivated to interact with the people and things in his or her perceptual field.
   • Provide stuffed animals and other safe pliable objects that the child can manipulate so as to acquire the psychomotor skills necessary for future cognitive development.
2. *Preschoolers and children in the primary grades*: The preoperational stage (2 to 7 years)
   EXAMPLES • Provide natural objects such as leaves, stones, twigs, etc. that the child can manipulate.
   • Toward the end of this stage provide opportunities for the child to begin grouping things into classes—that is, living/nonliving, animal/plant.
   • Toward the end of this stage provide experiences that give children an opportunity to transcend some of their egocentricism—that is, having them listen to other children's stories about what was observed on a trip to a zoo.
3. *Children in the elementary grades*: The stage of concrete operations (7 to 11 years)
   EXAMPLES • Early in this stage children should have many experiences to use their acquired abilities with respect to the observation, classification, and arrangement of objects according to some property. Any science activities that include the observation, collection, and sorting of objects should be able to be done with some ease.
   • As this stage continues you should be able to introduce successfully many physical science activities that include more abstract concepts such as space, time, and number, for example, making measurements of length, width, height, and weight of objects, counting the number of swings of a pendulum in a given time.
4. *The middle school child and beyond*: The stage of formal operations (12 years through adulthood)
   EXAMPLES • Children in this stage are able to deal with abstractions rather easily; consequently, emphasis can be placed on the general concepts and "laws" that govern observed phenomenon. Such projects and activities include the prediction of the characteristics of an object's motion based on Newton's Laws, the making of generalizations about the outcomes of a potential imbalance among the producers, consumers, and decomposers in a natural community, etc.
   • Children in this stage should be encouraged to make hypotheses about the outcomes of experiments in absence of actively doing them. A key part of the process of doing activities in your classroom might appropriately be "pre-lab" seniors in which the child writes down hypotheses about outcomes.

Figure 3–7.

43

Conservation of weight: the total weight of fragments of an object is equal to the weight of the original object.

Conservation of volume: the volume of a liquid remains the same regardless of the size and shape of the container in which it is placed.

A sampling of diagnostic activities that you may wish to use to study some of the conservation abilities of children is included in Appendix A of this book.

SOME IMPLICATIONS OF PIAGET'S WORK

If children do pass through distinct stages of cognitive development, then your challenge as a teacher is to be sure that the learning experiences you provide match the cognitive abilities of the children. The children must somehow have experiences that neither bore them nor frustrate them.

THE BEHAVIORAL VIEW OF LEARNING: B. F. SKINNER

The name B. F. Skinner should bring to mind a theory that attempts to explain the phenomenon of human learning in a rather simple and straightforward manner. The word *simple* is not used in a pejorative way here. Rather, it is intended to signify a view of learning that does not espouse a complex account of human thinking and behavior. Although many people in education summarily reject the so-called Skinnerian approach to learning, I believe that some elements of it can be applied in the classroom. The following discussion focuses only on those principles of behavioral psychology that seem to me to be most relevant for the elementary teacher of science.

SOME IMPLICATIONS OF SKINNER'S WORK

Behavioral psychology deals essentially with an individual's behaviors and the way his or her environment affects those behaviors. Some view it as placing undue emphasis on this power of the environment.

The essential element of behavioral psychology as conceptualized by Skinner is the effect of the environment on the individual's behaviors. According to Skinner, the individual "emits" behaviors and the environment "operates" on these behaviors by providing specific consequences for them. *Operant-learning* theory proposes that behavior is virtually controlled by the environment. The implications of this theory for teaching are enormous, for if we accept it we must then pay close attention to the learning environment we are providing.

If the behaviors emitted by a child in our classroom are ultimately determined by the classroom environment, we should be spending most of our planning and teaching time creating an environment that will result in the behaviors we call learning. In operant-learning theory those components of the environment that have the effect of increasing the frequency or strength of a behavior are known as *reinforcers*. In the classroom both *tangible* and *intangible* reinforcers are present. Tangible reinforcers include such things as getting good grades, winning a prize in a science fair, earning free time to work on special projects, earning the privilege of introducing a resource person who is going to speak to the class, and earning the privilege of being caretaker for classroom plants or animals. Figure 3–8 emphasizes the point that tactics such as extra schoolwork should not be used as punishment for misbehavior. The emphasis should always be on what the child does properly.

Intangible reinforcers are such things as praise from the teacher and approval from classmates—the general recognition by others of the worthiness of what a child does. Behaviorists tell us that the use of both tangible and intangible reinforcers can exert considerable influence on the behavior of children.

The fostering of a positive and productive learning environment is a process that can draw successfully on some of the basic principles of operant-learning theory. Whether or not you choose during your teaching career to incorporate behavioral principles such as those discussed above will be a personal and professional decision on your part. Regardless of your choice, you will need to evaluate continually whether the specific techniques that you use are providing a fruitful and pleasant learning environment for children without eroding their dignity and your own. Figure 3–9 lists some practical applications of behavioral psychology to the science classroom.

Figure 3–8. (*Source:* United Features Syndicate. © 1964 United Features Syndicate.)

Practical
Applications:
Using Behavioral Principles
in the Science Classroom

1. Reinforce positive behavior.
   EXAMPLES • Use praise when a child completes a task or project well, for example, write notes to children on completed science activity reports or homework assignments.
   • Tell children who do a particularly good job at "cleaning up" after a particularly messy science activity that you appreciate their effort.
   • During group discussion of the results of science activities, praise children who make contributions.
2. Reinforce effort.
   EXAMPLES • Thank children for trying to answer questions during class discussions.
   • Praise children whose behavior on trips improves with each field trip.
   • Praise children who try to make a detailed drawing of observed phenomenon even if the drawings are not complete.
   • Praise children for trying to work cooperatively on small group science activities.
3. After a behavior is established, reinforce the behavior at irregular intervals.
   EXAMPLES • Surprise the class with special visitors to class or field trips during particularly challenging units.
   • Take individual photographs (slides) of children at work on long-term (multiweek) science projects and present slide shows unannounced at various times during the project.

Figure 3–9.

GOING FURTHER

On Your Own

1. Imagine that you want a group of preschool or early-primary-grade children to have two learning experiences, one focusing on changes in the seasons and the other on animal babies. What results could you draw from Piaget's research that would apply to such learning experiences for children at this stage of cognitive development? What would be one way in which you could apply the results of Piaget's research to a lesson on each of these topics?
2. Reflect on your own experience of science when you were at the stage of concrete operations. Can you recall any ways in which your learning experiences conflicted with Piaget's theories?
3. Briefly discuss how the results of Ausubel's, Bruner's, and Gagné's work might be applied to science lessons on the following topics:
   a. space travel to Mars

   b. reproduction of flowers

   c. violent weather (hurricanes, tornadoes, etc.)

4. To what extent do you feel that the behaviorist view of the learning process can or should be applied to the science classroom? What practical considerations must be taken into account? What ethical questions must the teacher resolve?

5. Interview an elementary teacher of science to ascertain the extent to which he or she makes decisions from the point of view of behavioral- or cognitive-learning theory. Ask the teacher to give you examples of such decision making.

6. Interview an elementary-school curriculum coordinator or principal to determine the extent to which the basic learning theories discussed in this chapter are applied to curriculum development or teaching practices. Try to find examples.

On Your Own or with Others

7. Brainstorm a list of specific ways in which you could organize a science-learning environment so that it capitalizes on the points of view espoused by:

   a. Ausubel

   b. Bruner

   c. Gagné

   d. Piaget

   e. Skinner

8. Ask children at various grade levels what science topics strike their interest. What conclusions do you reach about the science interests of children and the appropriateness of particular science topics for children of various ages?

9. On the basis of your own work with children or observations of others working with children, what strikes you as the prime reason(s) for a child being interested in science or science-related topics? To what extent do you feel that a child's interest in science is related to his or her learning? If you are doing this activity as a member of a learning group, compare and contrast your observations with those of the others.

TEACHER TALK: SPRINGBOARDS FOR DISCUSSION

- "What is observation? Now close your eyes! Close eyes! Mattie, your eyes aren't closed. You're peeking. O.K. Everyone's eyes closed? Now tell me, what am I wearing today?"

- "When a child asks how a bird stands on a wire, a more reasonable answer can be found from holding a bird and observing, than from any amount of verbal explanation by a teacher. I try now to give a child an answer. The question means curiosity and that means opportunity for learning—not for getting what's in me into him."

- "The things that turn on third graders are things which they have seen or heard about but never really understood."

- "I'm not as concerned with what to teach, or how to teach it, or how to order the curriculum as I am with how do students really learn science. That is going to be different from how students learn math, motor skills, other things. How do we get students to higher cognitive levels of synthesis, application? What kind of training do I need at this? Experience has not revealed that to me or to my colleagues."

SUMMARY

Children are always learning something. In order to help children achieve cognitive, affective, and psychomotor learnings in science you will need to develop a viewpoint about the nature of learning itself. Psychologists have developed various theories of learning. If we placed these theories on a continuum, cognitive theories would be at one end and the behaviorist theories at the other. The former explains learning as an internal phenomenon based on the learner's changing perceptions of the world. The latter suggests that learning can best be explained as changes in the learner's overt behavior as a result of reinforcement. Your understanding of children and your efforts to plan and teach effectively will depend very much upon your own beliefs about learning.

SUGGESTED READINGS

AUSUBEL, D. P., and J. D. NOVACK, *Educational Psychology: A Cognitive View*. New York: Holt, Rinehart & Winston, 1978.

BRUNER, J., *On Knowing: Essays for the Left Hand*. Cambridge: Harvard University Press, 1979.

BYBEE, R., "Science Education Policies for an Ecological Society: Aims and Goals," *Science Education*, 63, no. 2(April 1979), 250.

COWAN, P. A., *Piaget with Feeling*. New York: Holt, Rinehart & Winston, 1978.

FULLER, E. W., MAY, D. H., and BUTTS, D. P., "Science Achievement of Third Graders Using Visual, Symbolic, and Manipulative Instructional Treatments," *Journal of Research in Science Teaching*, 16(March 1979), 129–136.

GAGNÉ, R., *The Conditions of Learning*. New York: Holt, Rinehart & Winston, 1965.

HART, L. A., "Don't Teach Them; Help Them Learn," *Learning*, 9, no. 8(March 1981), 38–40.

MORRIS, J., *Psychology and Teaching*. New York: Random House, 1978.

MUSSEN, P. H., J. J. CONGER, J. KAGAN, and J. GEIWITZ, *Psychological Development: A Life Span Approach*. New York: Harper & Row, Pub., 1979.

"Piaget and Education: A Symposium," *Journal of Education*, 165(Winter 1979), 5–101.

SCHMECK, R., "Improving Learning by Improving Thinking," *Educational Leadership*, 38, no. 5(February 1981), 384–385.

VICTOR, E., "Jean Piaget: 1896–1980," *Science and Children*, 18, no. 3(November/December 1980), 6.

WOOLFOLK, A. E., and L. McC. NICOLICH, *Educational Psychology for Teachers*. Englewood Cliffs, N.J.: Prentice-Hall, 1980.

How to Plan Learning Units, Daily Lessons, and Assessment Strategies

THE WATER RAT AND THE SEA HORSE

How will you plan your teaching so that children will learn? One way for you to develop your response to this fundamental question is to first consider the extremes of planning styles that may be used. Since this is a rather emotionally charged topic, I would like to take it up by having two very interesting animals present their approaches to the teaching and learning process. (The use of animal metaphors would seem to be an educationally appropriate technique for me to employ, since you are now aware that you have achieved the Piagetian stage of formal operations.) I should point out that any resemblance to any educator living or dead is neither implied nor intended. On the other hand . . .

Allow me now to introduce two experts in the field of educational planning: the water rat and the sea horse.

The Parable of the Water Rat

"Hullo, Mole!" said the Water Rat.

"Hullo, Rat!" said the Mole.

"Would you like to come over?" inquired the Rat presently.

"Oh, it's all very well to talk," said the Mole rather pettishly, he being new to a river and riverside life and its ways.

The Rat said nothing, but stooped and unfastened a rope and hauled on it; then lightly stepped into a little boat which the Mole had not observed. It was painted blue outside and white within, and was just the size for two animals; and the Mole's whole heart went out to it at once, even though he did not yet fully understand its uses.

The Rat sculled smartly across and made fast. Then he held up his fore-paw as the Mole stepped gingerly down. "Lean on that!" he said. "Now then, step lively!" and the Mole, to his surprise and rapture, found himself actually seated in the stern of a real boat.

"This has been a wonderful day!" said he, as the Rat shoved off and took to the sculls again. "Do you know, I've never been in a boat before in all my life."

"What?" cried the Rat, open-mouthed: "Never been in a—you never—well, I—what have you been doing, then?"

"Is it so nice as all that?" asked the Mole shyly, though he was quite prepared to believe it as he leant back in his seat and surveyed the cushions, the oars, the rowlocks, and all the fascinating fittings, and felt the boat sway lightly under him.

Figure 4–1. (*Source:* SAPA II, Module 15, p. 5. Science . . . A Process Approach II, American Association for the Advancement of Science. Used with permission.)

"Nice? It's the *only* thing," said the Water Rat solemnly, as he leant forward for his stroke. "Believe me, my young friend, there is *nothing*—absolutely nothing—half so much worth doing as simply messing about in boats. Simply messing," he went on dreamily: "messing—about—in—boats; messing—."

"Look ahead, Rat!" cried the Mole suddenly.

It was too late. The boat struck the bank full tilt. The dreamer, the joyous oarsman, lay on his back at the bottom of the boat, his heels in the air.

"—about in boats—or *with* boats," the Rat went on composedly, picking himself up with a pleasant laugh. "In or out of 'em, it doesn't matter. Nothing seems really to matter, that's the charm of it. Whether you get away, or whether you don't; whether you arrive at your destination or whether you reach somewhere else, or whether you never get anywhere at all, you're always busy, and you never do anything in particular; and when you've done it there's always something else to do, and you can do it if you like, but you'd much better not. Look here! If you've really nothing else on hand this morning, supposing we drop down the river together, and have a long day of it?"

The Mole waggled his toes from sheer happiness, spread his chest with a sigh of full contentment, and leaned back blissfully into the soft cushions. "What a day I'm having!" he said. "Let us start at once!"[1]

The Parable of the Sea Horse

Once upon a time a Sea Horse gathered up his seven pieces of eight and cantered out to find his fortune. Before he had traveled very far he met an Eel, who said,

"Pssst. Hey, bud. Where ya' going?"

"I'm going out to find my fortune," replied the Sea Horse, proudly.

"You're in luck," said the Eel. "For four pieces of eight you can have this speedy flipper, and then you'll be able to get there a lot faster."

"Gee, that's swell," said the Sea Horse, and paid the money and put on the flipper and slithered off at twice the speed. Soon he came upon a Sponge, who said,

"Pssst. Hey, bud. Where ya' going?"

"I'm going out to find my fortune," replied the Sea Horse.

"You're in luck," said the Sponge. "For a small fee I will let you have this jet-propelled scooter so that you will be able to travel a lot faster."

So the Sea Horse bought the scooter with his remaining money and went zooming through the sea five times as fast. Soon he came upon a shark, who said,

"Pssst. Hey, bud. Where ya' going?"

"I'm going out to find my fortune," replied the Sea Horse.

"You're in luck. If you'll take this short cut," said the Shark, pointing to his open mouth, "you'll save yourself a lot of time."

"Gee, thanks," said the Sea Horse, and zoomed off into the interior of the Shark, there to be devoured.

The moral of this fable is that if you're not sure where you're going, you're liable to end up someplace else—and not even know it.[2]

The surest way to stifle your professional growth is to decide that you will always be a water rat or always be a sea horse. The teaching of children, in my opinion, requires that you develop a wide variety of approaches and specific techniques. On the one hand, you must learn to provide experiences that are sufficiently discovery-based to capture the imagination and power of a child's intellect as he or she unlocks the mysteries of a given phenomenon. Yet you will also need to be able to plan some learning experiences in a more systematic, goal-directed manner.

[1]Kenneth Grahame, *The Wind in the Willows* (New York: Dell, 1969), pp. 4—6. Used with permission.

[2]From *Preparing Instructional Objectives*, Second Edition, by Robert F. Mager. Copyright © 1975 by Pitman Learning, Inc., Belmont, California. Reprinted by permission.

THE SCOPE OF THE SCIENCE CURRICULUM

Imagine observing a tiny gnat walking across a pebble as lightning flashes in the sky. How would each component of this scene fit into the area of knowledge we call science? The tiny gnat is understood through biology, the science of living things. The origin and characteristics of the pebble are understood through the earth/space sciences. The energy of the lightning flash and the atoms and molecules that make up the gnat and the pebble are understood through the physical sciences. Each component of the scene represents one part of the *scope*, or breadth of content, of what we call science. To summarize, science is generally thought to include the earth/space sciences, the biological sciences, and the physical sciences.

The earth/space sciences represent our knowledge of the origins of the universe and of our earth in particular. The earth/space sciences include astronomy, geology, meteorology, and other areas of study. Among the earth/space-science topics commonly taught in elementary school are

1. The stars, sun, and planets
2. The soil, rocks, and mountains
3. The weather.

The biological sciences include botany, zoology, and ecology. These disciplines are usually represented in the science curriculum as

1. The study of plants
2. The study of animals
3. The study of the relationship between plants and animals
4. The study of the relationship between living things and the environment.

The physical sciences include physics and chemistry. Physics is concerned with the relationship between matter and energy. Chemistry is concerned with the manner through which various types of matter combine and change. In the elementary school the following topics would be considered part of the physical-sciences component of the science curriculum:

1. The study of forces
2. The study of energy
3. The study of the chemical changes that matter undergoes.

THE SEQUENCE OF THE SCIENCE CURRICULUM

A knowledge of the scope of science will help you decide what topics can be reasonably included within the body of science experiences that you will present to children. However, one important question remains to be answered about these topics: in what order should they be presented? For example, should children learn about the earth they live on before they learn about the structure and function of their bodies? Or, should the sequence be reversed? Should children learn about the ways in which they use electricity prior to learning about the

52

sources of electrical energy? Should children learn about eggs before they learn about chickens?

There is no definitive answer to the question of sequence. However, here are three guidelines that may help you as you consider the place of science in a child's school experience.

1. Since no learning can occur if the learner is unattentive to the experience, any decision you make among curricular choices should favor those topics that will generate the most learner involvement and interest.
2. As a general rule, organize learning experiences from the child outward. That is, select experiences that relate first to the child and then to the science content. In teaching electricity, for example, have children consider how they use electricity before they study its source.
3. In general, when deciding whether to expose children to a concept that can be considered concretely or abstractly, select the concrete approach first. For example, when teaching the cause of the phases of the moon demonstrate the phenomenon in a concrete way (the traditional demonstration uses a globe and a stationary flashlight shining on an orange that a child moves in orbit around the globe) prior to a general and more abstract discussion.

UNIT PLANNING

Teaching units can be interdisciplinary. For example, a second-grade science unit on energy conservation could become a science and social-studies unit on community workers and the energy they use.

You may want to reflect on the learning units you experienced as a child. Can you remember any of the science units you studied? If so, what kinds of activities did you carry out during the unit? Did your teachers seem to have a general plan for the units?

What Is a Unit Plan?

Coliseum Scoreboard

Lions   7
Christians   0

Whenever I see a cartoon or hear a joke that has this punch line, I usually think of substitute teachers. What is a score that might have represented a day with a substitute when you were a child? How did the day's contest usually begin? If you were a particularly mischievous child, you probably enjoyed observing the look of fear in the substitutes' eyes, the unsureness of their speech, and the aura of anxiety that seemed to precede them as they took their first steps from the doorway to the teacher's desk. A whole day of fun and games at the coliseum was sure to follow.

You may be thinking, "Well, what does all this have to do with unit planning?" It has everything to do with unit planning! The substitute teacher usually did not stand a chance because he or she had no idea of what to do, how to do it, where the class had been, and where it was going. Similarly, children whose full-time teacher lacks a sense of the "big picture" have in effect a new substitute teacher every day of the school year. Each day the children have a learning experience that is not part of any larger context is a school day that relates neither to the past nor to the future. Our children deserve far better treatment. They need appropriate learning experiences in science and in all subjects, activities that will reflect their teacher's concern with goals and that will involve them cognitively, affectively, and physically. To accomplish this, dedicated and professional teachers *plan*.

Unit plans take a variety of forms. The list of possible components in Figure 4–2 may prove useful to you when you develop your own unit plans.

Can Unit Plans Be Used in Schools That Have Science Textbooks?

Did you have your own science textbook in elementary school? Many schools use textbooks or curriculum guides as organizing elements for the curriculum. With some creative planning on your part, such materials can be an important starting point for the development of meaningful science experiences for children. After

COMPONENT	PURPOSE
Rationale	Helps you think through the reasons for doing a unit on a particular topic
*Instructional objectives	Help you focus on the intended outcomes of the unit
Listing of science concepts and processes that will be emphasized	Helps you focus on both the major ideas and methods of science that should be stressed
Content outline (for the teacher)	Helps you review the content that will provide the foundation for the learning experience
*Daily lesson plans	Help you think through learning activities in the context of the daily time allotment for science
Materials list	Helps you make certain that you have all the materials needed for science activities that occur in daily lessons
Audiovisual materials and supplementary materials list	Help you make certain that you have such things as film, filmstrips, cassette tape, and the necessary equipment for media that will be used
*Assessment strategies	Help you consider informal and formal ways to assess the extent to which children achieved cognitive, psychomotor, and affective growth during the unit

*Considered in greater detail later in this chapter.

Figure 4–2.

diagnosing student needs and interests you can utilize a portion of a textbook or a curriculum as a basis for a unit plan. Such materials can serve as key sources of information, activities, and teaching suggestions.

Too many teachers with access to these materials use them as an excuse not to plan. This is quite unfortunate, since modern science textbooks and curriculum guides provide many useful resources for the teacher. Consider, for example, the following unit-planning information found in recent editions of three major elementary-school science series.

Gateway to Science (McGraw-Hill)	Holt Elementary Science (Holt, Rinehart & Winston)	Understanding Your Environment (Silver Burdett)
Overview of the Program	Unit Concepts	Unit and Lesson Concepts
Scope and Sequence	Unit Preparation (identifying with lessons will need science materials)	Philosophy and Objectives
Objectives	Science Learning Center	Lesson Materials
Science Background	Unit Opener (unit opening idea)	Lesson Capsule (lesson plan)
Science Words	Lesson Background	Extension
Teaching Schedule	Objectives	Science Background
Materials List for Optional Activities	Material Needed/Group	Science Equipment
Enrichment Bibliography	Material Needed/Lesson	Resource Material
Chapter Tests and Enrichment Activities	Basic Teaching Plan Optional Ideas	Bulletin Board Ideas

Teacher's editions and school curriculum guides can make the planning process easier for you. However, they should be used only as helpful tools and not as substitutes for planning.

How Do I Write Learning Objectives?

"I want my children to feel *really* mellow about science."

For some teachers at some time in some setting, this may be an appropriate learning outcome. However, it is so vague that to think of science activities having the intended result would be rather difficult. Indeed, it would be difficult to invent a curriculum that would result in "mellow" feelings, let alone "really mellow" feelings!

This is not to say that every lesson in every setting requires specific objectives. However, when you *do* wish to have children learn specific content, processes, or affects, unambiguous and clearly written objectives can prove very useful. Wherever possible, the children you teach should be involved in developing and discussing objectives. By involving them in the process of determining objectives, you will probably increase the appropriateness of the objectives and the likelihood of their attainment.

Let's look now at the skills you will need in order to write focused objectives. Such objectives are typically written for each lesson or major learning activity in a unit plan. There are three types of learning objectives that you may wish to include in a unit plan: cognitive, psychomotor, and affective. Cognitive objectives deal with mental processes such as the grasping of concepts, the acquisition of knowledge, and the mastery of a science process. Psychomotor objectives concern manipulative skills. Affective objectives deal with the development of student attitudes and values.

The central characteristic of a learning objective is the specification of the behavior that the child is likely to exhibit as a result of the learning process. When

Figure 4–3. Do you think that this boy may be doing a science activity that is cognitive, affective, *and* psychomotor in character? Why? (*Source:* SAPA II, Module 6, p. 10. Science . . . A Process Approach II, American Association for the Advancement of Science. Used with permission.)

you write a learning objective be sure to specify the action you wish the child to perform. Attempt to answer the question, What will the child be able to do? Here are some key performance words that you will find useful as you write instructional objectives:

1. Write	8. Explain orally
2. Bake	9. Construct (make)
3. Measure	10. Select
4. Sing	11. Define
5. Paint	12. Label (a diagram)
6. List	13. Name
7. Solve	

Here are some examples of objectives you might include in various unit plans.

Unit Topic	Sample Objective
1. Force and Motion	Measure how high a tennis ball will bounce when dropped from different heights.
2. Electrical Circuits	Draw a simple series circuit.
3. The Nervous System	Name the five senses.
4. Protecting Our Environment	Write a poem about preventing water pollution.
5. Good Nutrition	Bake a batch of cookies that do not require sugar.
6. Ecology	Draw a picture that shows one way in which animals and plants depend on each other.
7. The Changing Earth	Construct a model of a volcano.
8. Energy Conservation	Make a poster that shows five ways to save electrical energy in school.
9. Violent Weather	Define the term *hurricane*.
10. Using Electrical Energy	List five safety rules for using electrical appliances.

The science activities presented in this book include learning objectives that specify the expected student behavior. These objectives will probably be specific enough for most schools. However, some school systems require the teacher to establish objectives that are even more specific.

LESSON PLANNING

How Do I Write a Lesson Plan?

Do you know what "winging it" is? It is the process of walking into the classroom completely unprepared and inventing a lesson on the spot. Perhaps with many years of experience you will have the knowledge and teaching ability to occasionally wing it. Even so, I recommend that you plan all lessons you teach. It may not be necessary to write lesson plans that include all the components discussed. You should, however, have some type of plan every time you work with children. Please, don't wing it!

There are wide variety of approaches to lesson planning. You will ultimately devise a format that fits your teaching style. I have always felt that the *process* of making a lesson plan is probably more important than the plan itself. The lesson-planning process forces you to think through a variety of factors that will increase the likelihood of your lesson being successful.

Let us now consider two different lesson-plan formats that may be useful to you as you develop your own approach to lesson planning:

Format	Topic	Grade	Figure
1.	Finding Out Whether an Object Sinks or Floats	First	4−4
2.	A Nutritious Lunch	Fourth	4−5

Sample Lesson-Plan Format 1

LESSON-PLAN COMPONENTS

1. Objectives
2. Materials
3. Preparation
4. Development
5. Appraisal
6. Extension
7. Transparency Original
8. Activity Sheets (3)

COMMENTS

This lesson plan has considerable detail yet seems to be easy to work with. The teacher will be using a rather wide variety of media to teach the lesson. In particular, note the use of a song, a transparency, and a variety of hands-on science activities. The lesson places heavy emphasis on involving the children in science processes. This process orientation is evidenced by the hands-on activities, the objectives, and the nature of the appraisal. Notice that the teacher will have what is essentially a process-observation checklist in the appraisal section.

Here are some points you may wish to pay special attention to as you study this lesson-plan format:

1. The materials section distinguishes between materials that the teacher will need and materials that the student will need. This will help keep the teacher organized as he or she prepares to teach the lesson.
2. The preparation section enumerates the procedures that the teacher must carry out before the lesson. For example, starting the growth of seedlings is something that is often necessary in teaching science.

FINDING OUT WHETHER AN OBJECT FLOATS OR SINKS

OBJECTIVES

Demonstrate excitement of discovery, respect for diverse opinions, questioning attitude, insistence on evidence, and respect for materials.

Construct predictions about the behavior of certain objects in water. (predicting, communicating, inferring)

Demonstrate a method of checking predictions. (manipulating, observing)

Distinguish between objects that sink and objects that float. (communicating, classifying)

MATERIALS

For the teacher		For each child
knife	cork	scissors
pine cone	fork	paste
shell	plastic vial with lid	crayons
leaf	overhead projector	Activity Sheet 1
marble	transparency film	Activity Sheet 2
coin	large water container, transparent	Activity Sheet 3
pencil	chart paper	
buttons	soap	
clothespin		
felt tip pen		

PREPARATION

1. Obtain an overhead projector.

2. Make a transparency from the pattern on Page 46.

3. Duplicate copies of the Activity Sheets from the originals on Pages 47-49.

4. Partially fill an aquarium, gallon jar, or some other clear container with water.

5. Post the chart paper where it will be easy to record the children's predictions. Divide the paper into two columns, Float and Sink.

Figure 4—4. Lesson-Plan Format 1 (*Source:* Excerpted from the Curriculum Guide *Grouping Things* Level I, "Finding Out Whether an Object Sinks or Floats" [Towson, Md.: Baltimore County Board of Education], pp. 41—49. Used with permission.)

DEVELOPMENT

    1. Begin the activity by saying:

            Have you ever played with
            toys when you take a bath?

    Allow time for a few responses. Tell the children to listen as you
    either sing or recite the words of the little song about a child who
    also likes to play in the bathtub.

My Submarine[1]

_____

[1] Material from GROWING WITH MUSIC BOOK 1, Related Arts Edition by
Harry R. Wilson, Walter Ehret; Alice M. Knuth, Edward J. Hermann, and
Albert A. Renna. 1971 Prentice-Hall, Inc., Englewood Cliffs, N.J.
Reprinted by permission.

Figure 4–4. *(cont.)*

Encourage the children to talk about the song. Ask:

What was the child playing with?

What was he pretending it was?

What happened to the bar of soap?

Possible
Responses

It floated.

It stayed on top of the water.

It sank.

It went to the bottom of the water.

Continue the discussion by asking:

If an object stays on top of water, what
word do we use to tell what it does?
(floats)

If an object goes to the bottom of water,
what word do we use to tell what it does?
(sinks)

2. Project the transparency and allow time for the children to look
at the picture. Select volunteers to name the objects that are
pictured. Ask:

What are the children doing with the knife?

What do you think they will do with the
other objects?

Let's all be scientists and predict what would
happen to each of the objects in the picture if
we put them in water. Will they sink or will
they float?

Allow a few minutes for the children to observe the transparency
and to make their predictions.

3. Distribute the three Activity Sheets. Tell the children to look care-
fully at the pictures on Activity Sheet 1 and name the pictured objects.
Tell them to cut out one object at a time and place it on the sheet
Sink if they think the object will sink in water, or place it on the sheet
Float if they think it will float.

This is an exercise in predicting. The
predictions will be tested later so the
pictures should not be pasted on at this
time.

Figure 4–4. (cont.)

Allow time for the children to cut the pictures and place them on the sheets. Circulate around the room, listening to the children's comments while they work. Be prepared for differences of opinions and questions. Try to stay out of this discussion but do encourage the children to give reasons for their opinions.

4. After all the children have arranged their pictures to represent their predictions, say:

> Now that you have decided what you think each object will do, let's test them and see what really happens.

Have one volunteer at a time come up to demonstrate what happens when the real object is placed in water. As each object is tested, record the result on the chart paper in the proper column.

Compare the actual results with the children's predictions by asking:

> What did you think _____ would do?

> What made you think so?

5. After all the objects have been tested, tell the children to paste the pictures on the appropriate sheet. Remind them that the chart is the record of what actually happened when the real objects were put in the water.

APPRAISAL

Check the attainment of the objectives as you observe the children working with the actual objects and with the pictures. These behaviors indicate success:

> Tells about experiences at home with objects that sink and float.

> Offers to bring in objects from home to test.

> Resists the temptation to splash water.

> Smiles at his correct predictions.

> Offers reasons for his predictions.

> Mentions that his sister can float more easily than he can.

Figure 4–4. (cont.)

FOR EXTENSION

1. Make a mural. Encourage the children to bring in objects or pictures of objects that will sink or float.

+---+
| These objects will float. |
| |
| ~~~~~~ |
| blue water |
| |
| These objects will sink. |
+---+

Have the children tape along the surface of the water those objects and pictures of objects that will float, and at the bottom of the mural those things that will sink. Keep a bowl of water available so that the children can check the objects.

2. Set up a learning station with a box of objects, some that sink and some that float. Provide a bowl of water in which the children may test the objects to see if they will sink or float.

Transparency Pattern

Prepare a transparency showing two children trying to float various objects in a bowl of water. Include such things as clothespins, corks, forks, butter knives, coins, and so on.

Figure 4—4. (cont.)

Figure 4–4. (cont.)

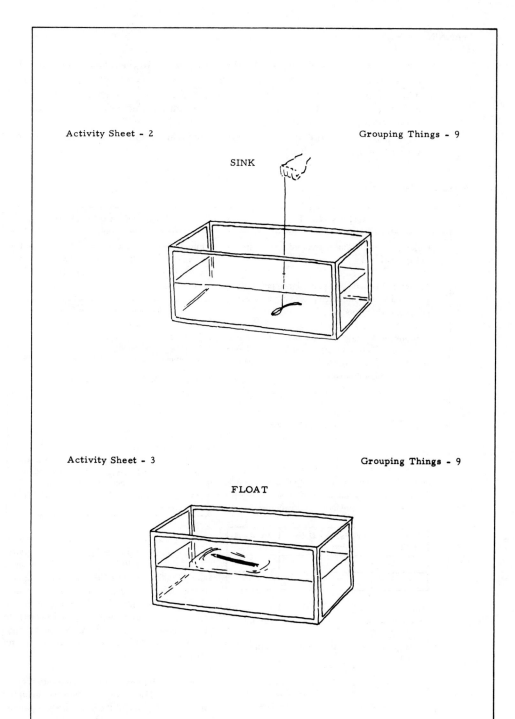

Activity Sheet - 2   Grouping Things - 9

SINK

Activity Sheet - 3   Grouping Things - 9

FLOAT

Figure 4–4. *(cont.)*

3. The song will help the children develop an awareness of the relationships among what they learn. In this case music and science are being integrated.
4. The children will be expected to maintain a record of what they do during the activities. There is a wall chart to be filled in as well as the activity sheets that will require some cutting and pasting.
5. The "learning station" suggested in the extension section is yet another medium that can be used with this lesson.

Sample Lesson-Plan Format 2

Activity No. 1	Comments to Teachers
Objective: To plan, prepare, and serve a lunch in the classroom.	**Time Required:** Planning: 15 to 30 minutes; purchasing or collecting food: two days; preparing food and serving meal: two to three hours.

Materials Needed: Hot plate, large pot, paring knife, can opener, stirring spoon, measuring cup, measuring spoons, calorie counter.

Procedure: A suggestion for a lunch is given below. Teachers and other adults should feel free to plan with the entire class or with an appointed planning committee.

> **Menu**
> Vegetable Soup
> Peanut Butter or Cheese Sandwich
> Orange or Apple
> Cookie
> Milk

Place the menu on chart paper or the chalkboard. List the Four Basic Food Groups with space for each of the foods in the menu.

Meat or meat substitute	Vegetables and fruits	Dairy products	Bread and cereals

Name a committee to list the calories and/or vitamins in the meal using a calorie counter.

Other committees which might be appointed include:

Food Collecting	Table Setting
Food Preparation	Cafeteria Liaison
Table Decoration	Parent Support
	Clean-up

> **Vegetable Soup (Serves 8-10°)**
> No. 2½ can tomatoes, chopped but undrained
> 1 tbsp. melted butter or margarine
> 1 small chopped onion
> 1 lb. ground beef (this can be eliminated if budget is small)
> 1 medium size can of mixed vegetables
> 3 cups water
> 2 beef boullion cubes
> 2 tsp. salt
> ½ tsp. sugar
> ¼ tsp. basil
> ½ tsp. pepper
> Saute onion in butter; add beef and brown well. Stir in remaining ingredients. Bring to a boil, stirring frequently. Simmer 25 minutes.
> ° Multiply proportions according to the size of the total group.

Making peanut butter for the sandwiches would be an interesting project to add to this activity. To do this, add a little salt and a tablespoon of any oil that does not solidify at room temperature to a cup of roasted, shelled peanuts. Drop the whole thing into a blender. Press the button and relax. It may take some time to complete the transformation from nuts into peanut butter. Give the machine a chance and do a little stirring.

There are a variety of ways to facilitate preparing a meal. For example, a cafeteria manager may provide some of the basic foods, a parent-support committee could solicit donations, or

Figure 4–5. Lesson-Plan Format 2 (*Source: F.O.O.D for Thought*, U.S.O.E., Department of Health, Education and Welfare. Published by Project FOOD, Durham City Schools, Durham, North Carolina.)

Activity No. 1 *(continued)*	Comments to Teachers
The table decoration committee should decide on specific plans and collect the necessary materials before the date of the lunch.	each child could be assigned to provide a specific food.
The table setting committee should approach the cafeteria staff and request the use of plates and utensils from the general supply. It could write a letter to the cafeteria manager, giving the number of plates, bowls, etc., needed and the date of the lunch; or the teacher can make special arrangements with the manager. Disposable utensils and plates are another alternative.	The food could be purchased during a field trip to the grocery store. If the teacher wishes, the activity could be combined with information about health ratings of restaurants, employee cleanliness, etc.
Allow enough time to prepare the soup and sandwiches. Some teachers have suggested making two pots of soup on hot plates to reduce the time it takes to cook in one large pot.	
Ask each child to wash his hands before he prepares food. The food might be prepared as an early morning activity and eaten at the appropriate lunch time period.	

Figure 4—5. *(cont.)*

LESSON-PLAN COMPONENTS

1. Concept Statements
2. Objective
3. Materials Needed
4. Procedure
5. Time Required

COMMENTS

This lesson is a good example of giving children an opportunity to apply their science learnings. The children will do more than read and talk about good nutrition: they will plan, serve, and of course eat a nutritious lunch. As you plan lessons you will need to keep inventing ways to make them come alive. This lesson does that.

The lesson requires a high degree of cooperative effort. Seven possible student committees are enumerated. If you intend to foster cooperative action in a learning experience, a list of the needed committees, work groups, and so on should appear on your lesson plan.

This lesson plan assumes a fair degree of previous teaching experience. It does not include components that will probably be included in the actual teaching of the lesson, such as questions and evaluation activities. The teacher using this plan would probably build these components into the lesson as it evolved.

Here are some additional points you may wish to consider as you study this format:

1. The time required for the lesson has been considered beforehand. This is very important, since lessons that require much time will affect the amount of attention that can be given other portions of the curriculum. If you teach in a departmentalized elementary school, the teaching of such lessons will require the indulgence of the teachers of other subjects.
2. Such activities as the class planning of menus and the acquisition of foodstuffs (and possibly cooking appliances), require a great deal of cooperation among the children. In addition, the cooperation of the school cafeteria managers must be obtained. The teacher attempting this type of lesson needs to have a plan; "winging it" would probably be disastrous.
3. The combined wisdom and experience of a group of teachers working in concert produced a plan that seems extremely workable. It is an example of the benefits to be had when a team of teachers cooperatively plans experiences for children.

ASSESSMENT

"What dja git?"
"She gave me a C!"

Is this part of a familiar classroom conversation that you have overheard? Perhaps you have made such comments yourself. By developing and using a wide variety of assessment techniques you can help children learn to think in terms beyond "What dja git?" Tests are but one way of assessing learning; there are many others you may wish to use as you teach.

Anecdotal Records

Date _____

John Hall, age 7
Grade 1
Last week the children in my class watched baby chicks being hatched in the incubator.
This morning, John came into the room bursting with excitement. "My mother's gone to the hospital to get our baby out!" he said. "How nice," I replied. "Will she be home soon?" "I don't know," he answered. "I don't know how long it will take the baby to get out."[3]

This note, written by a first-grade teacher to herself, tells a great deal about young John and his understanding of his world. By taking the time to write down notes about classroom occurrences the teacher has found a way to assess what John is learning. Notes to yourself can help you assess how well both the children *and* you are doing.

During science activities you will find yourself interacting with the children—

[3]Reported by June E. Lewis and Irene C. Potter, *The Teaching of Science in the Elementary School* (Englewood Cliffs, N.J.: Prentice-Hall, 1970), p. 49.

helping them arrange materials and equipment, listening to what they are saying, and watching what is going on. This interaction can be an excellent opportunity for you to gather information about the progress of the class as a whole or of particular students. To accomplish this you will need some way to record your observations before they escape from your consciousness. Here are some hints:

1. Whenever you place an observation on paper be sure to write down the date. You may even want to include the time.
2. Make the writing of notes a habit. Prior to the lesson remind yourself that you are going to be writing down observations.
3. Consider focusing your observations on cognitive, affective, and psychomotor progress that you observe. Your notebook could take the form of a daily chart that has a column for each. Such a chart will help you keep track of your observations.
4. Be sure to tell the children that you will be writing notes to yourself about how things are going. You may even suggest that they do the same. If so, at the end of each week you can have a full-class discussion of your observations and their observations.
5. Review your anecdotal records in detail when you come to the end of a teaching unit. This will enable you to assess the effectiveness of the learning activities in which the children participated.

Student Logbooks

Children can maintain science logbooks in which they write their reactions to particular activities. Here are some suggestions for implementing their use:

1. Discuss with the class the use of a science logbook and your expectations of it. Indicate such things as where they should be kept and how often you will review them.
2. Have the children construct their own logbooks. Provide the necessary notebook paper, paper for covers, and staples.
3. Encourage the children to divide each page of their logbook into particular questions and address these questions each time they write in the book. The questions could include:
   a. What did I do?
   b. What did I learn?
   c. How do I feel about learning about _____ (topic)? _____
4. Encourage them to write in their logbooks every day and provide time for them to do so.
5. Schedule time at the end of each teaching unit for the children to discuss some of the things they have written.
6. Keep your own science logbook throughout the year. Be sure that the children are aware that you are also keeping track of what you are learning.
7. The science logbooks can be a very effective part of the materials that you make available for such festive occasions as Parents' Night or Back-to-School Night.

Tests

The use of written tests for children learning science can provide *some* evidence of their progress in acquiring knowledge or understanding concepts. Keep in mind that paper-and-pencil tests suffer from a number of limitations, the most obviou being a child's verbal fluency. Obviously, a child who is a good reader and is capable of writing effectively is going to achieve higher scores on written science tests than his or her peer who does not have such capabilities. Be aware that written tests in the elementary school may tell you more about a child's language-arts skills than about his or her science achievements!

Written tests are usually composed of objective and essay questions. Here are some suggestions on how to construct and use written tests.

1. Maintain a balance between questions that simply assess knowledge gained and questions that assess the application of knowledge.
2. Maintain a file of questions that you use as well as notes on how individual items could be improved. After giving a test ask the children which questions gave them the most difficulty and why they had problems with these items. You may find that various items are confusing to children even though they appeared clear to you when you wrote them.
3. Grade the completed test quickly. By providing children with prompt feedback you will be able to help them focus their study habits so that they are more adequately prepared for future tests.
4. As you prepare a test, cross-reference each item to the cognitive objectives of the teaching unit. This can ensure that you will be acquiring a measure of student progress over the full range of the unit's objectives. It will also be useful for you to maintain a chart showing the number of children answering each question correctly. This will help you assess the extent to which unit objectives were achieved.
5. Prepare the children for tests in the same way that you would prepare them for other experiences in your classroom. Provide them with directions concerning what to study and how to study. You may also wish to take some classroom time to discuss how to take a test.

Assessing Affective Development

"Boy, do I hate science!"

If one of your children made this not very subtle comment, you might be led to conclude that his or her affective development toward science has been less than adequate. Our only real basis for assessing students' affective growth is our observation of the affect-laden behaviors they exhibit. Their smiles, frowns, comments, in-class behavior, and out-of-class behaviors related to science will indicate the extent to which they are developing favorable attitudes toward science.

The child's affective development should be one of your primary concerns. The assessment of the extent to which children develop favorable attitudes toward science and the doing of it is, of course, rather hard to measure. Your own intuition based on your interactions with the children in your classroom will (with increased years of classroom teaching experience) lead you to some conclusions about the affective development of individuals as well as the full classroom. There do exist some tools that can complement your intuition with some tangible information ʾout affective development. Figure 4–6 consists of items that you may wish to upon to create an affective-development checklist. Your own observations of and conversations with teachers can provide other observable behaviors may wish to include in your checklist.

Likes and Prefers to:

read science books
read science magazines
read scientific articles
  in the newspaper
read about scientists
read about inventions
read science fiction
make collections
play science games
own science toys
own science equipment
see science TV programs
see science films
go to science fairs
go to museums
go to planetariums
go on science field trips

Does:

pursue science hobbies
experiment
plan experiments
plan original experiments
suggest plans for exploring
  inquiries
construct science equipment
construct science models
  and charts
try to invent
participate in science fairs
use correct vocabulary
try to predict what will
  happen on the basis of
  his previous learnings
observe the world around him
theorize
do independent research
avoid jumping to conclusions
seek proof
understand and use controls

talk about scientific
  things and events
report on scientific news
ask good science questions
detect difference between
  truth and fiction
persevere in methods of inquiry
  and research
apply his science learnings
  to new situations
see relationships

Believes in and Practices:

the scientific method
causal relationships
using more than one resource
repeating experiments to
  validate his results
questioning his results
checking his results
consulting authorities
debunking superstitions

Willing to and Does:

change his opinion if sufficient
  evidence warrants it
admit mistakes and try to
  correct them
admit he doesn't know
give credit to others when
  credit is due
accept the possibility of error
  in available resources
make allowance for human
  error
criticize and evaluate his
  own work
contribute ideas
accept responsibility
believe in scientific progress
believe in the future of science

Figure 4—6. Listing of Affecting Behaviors (*Source:* Lewis and Potter, *The Teaching of Science in the Elementary School*, © 1970, p. 49. Reprinted by permission of Prentice-Hall, Inc.)

On Your Own

1. The way in which you plan for teaching will probably depend a great deal upon your general outlook on the nature of teaching and how children learn. To bring these perceptions into focus, respond to each of the following statements:
   a. Careful planning is consistent with the manner in which I carry out life activities.
   b. Planning can restrict flexibility.
   c. I never had a teacher who planned.
   d. Children will learn regardless of how much teachers plan.

2. Use your knowledge and previous experiences to extend each of the following statements:
   a. For me, an example of an extremely boring science unit would be . . .
   b. For me, an example of a very interesting science unit would be . . .
   c. It would be fairly easy to integrate a unit on space travel with a unit on . . .
   d. Some ways to include children in the planning process are . . .

3. Review the lesson-plan formats discussed in this chapter. Then select a science topic appropriate for the grade level you are most interested in and develop a lesson plan for the topic. If possible, teach the lesson to a group of children or peers who role-play children.

4. Do you remember any science lessons in elementary school that "fell apart" due to lack of proper planning? What were the specifics of the situation? If you have no such recollection, consider factors that might cause a science lesson to go awry.

5. Select one grade of elementary school. If you were able to choose the science units to be taught the children at this level, which units would you select? In what order would you teach them? How much of the school year would you spend on each unit?

On Your Own or with Others

6. Brainstorm a science activity for each of the following science units:
   a. Indoor gardening
   b. Animals with pouches
   c. The changes in the seasons
   d. Earthquakes
   e. Friction.

   When you are done, try to place the activities in the most appropriate order in which they could be taught.

7. Interview an elementary-school teacher (or a group of teachers) to ascertain
   a. His or her general approach to planning—for example, whether he or she uses a school science curriculum or a textbook series, and how flexible he or she can be in using such materials
   b. How he or she plans teaching units
   c. How he or she plans daily lessons
      The assessment techniques he or she typically uses
      What activity he or she would suggest for someone who has yet to plan a science unit for children.

8. Role-play a job interview between a school principal and a teaching candidate for one or more of the following positions:
   a. Kindergarten teacher
   b. First-grade teacher in a self-contained classroom
   c. Third-grade teacher in a self-contained classroom
   d. Fourth-grade science teacher in a departmentalized school
   e. Fifth-grade teacher in a self-contained classroom
   f. Sixth-grade science teacher in a self-contained classroom.

   During the interview the "principal" should ascertain the candidate's opinions and possible skills for science teaching by asking about:
   a. The science content and experiences appropriate for children at that grade
   b. The planning style the prospective teacher would use.
   c. Assessment strategies the teacher would use.

   If you are not doing this activity as part of a learning group, list the comments that the prospective teacher might make during an interview for one of the above positons.

TEACHER TALK: SPRINGBOARDS FOR DISCUSSION

- "When things go badly, check to determine whether your plans were adequate; chances are they were not."

- "We have general to basic students [in science class]. I think the only way to reach them is to teach them something they can relate to—i.e., no abstractions. I have left the book almost entirely in order to teach things they can relate to and enjoy, and I find I get more response and motivation in this way."

- "Science has gone down over the past decade. We have changed the curriculum to try to adjust to this decline. . . . I lectured, did everything 'wrong' (according to contemporary pedagogy) and my students loved it. High interest, high achievement. Now I am doing everything I know to recapture that interest. Changing my teaching, group discussions, student activities, films, kits. But it's gone, all gone

SUMMARY

Good teaching requires good planning. The science curriculum for chil typically consists of a number of learning units. These are long-term plan science experiences that focus on a particular topic. Daily lesson plans ar component of a unit plan. Two sample lesson plans and a discussion of ea found in this chapter. As a science teacher, you will need to assess whethe children are learning and how well you are teaching. Anecdotal records, s logbooks, and other techniques can be used to assess the quality of learn instruction in your classroom.

SUGGESTED READINGS

BRONFENBRENNER, U., "Our Schools Need a Curriculum for Caring," *Instructor*, 88, no. 7(February 1979), 34–36.

CHANEY, B., and D. ZJAWIN, "Our Dinosaur Sits in the Front Row," *Instructor*, 90, no. 8(March 1981), 44–51.

HARBECK, M. B., "Accountability through Curriculum," *Science and Children*, 16, no. 2(October 1978), 19–21.

HUNTER, M., and D. RUSSEL, "How Can I Plan More Effective Lessons?" *Instructor*, 87, no. 2(September 1977), 74–75.

LEWIS, J. M., "Answers to Twenty Questions on Behavioral Objectives," *Educational Technology*, 21, no. 3(March 1981), 27–31.

MAIN, E. D., "Interrelating Science with Other School Subjects," *Science and Children*, 18, no. 5(February 1981), 26–27.

POPHAM, W. J., *Educational Evaluation*. Englewood Cliffs, N. J.: Prentice-Hall, 1975.

RUDMAN, M. K., "Evaluating Students: How to Do It Right," *Learning*, 7, no. 2(October 1978), 50–53.

SMITH, B. O., and D. E. ORLASKY, *Curriculum Development: Issues and Insights*. Chicago: Rand McNally, 1978.

WILLIAMS, H. et al., "Designing Science Lessons to Promote Cognitive Growth," *The Science Teacher*, 46, no. 1(January 1979), 26–29.

chapter 5

Discovery Learning

INQUIRY, CURRICULUM MODELS, AND CLASSROOM ORGANIZATION/MANAGEMENT

The teacher who walks in the shadow of the temple, among his followers, gives not of his wisdom, but rather of his faith and his lovingness. If he is indeed wise, he does not bid you enter the house of his wisdom, but rather leads you to the threshold of your own mind.[1]

Kahlil Gibran speaks poetically here of the teacher and the very important role that he or she plays in helping children learn. I believe he is saying to us that we can never help children learn if we tell them everything they need to know.

Children need opportunities to act on their natural curiosity, to use the processes of science to explore their world and learn. We refer to children's use of the processes of science to uncover knowledge and concepts as *discovery learning.* Helping a child make discoveries is not an easy task, but it is an enjoyable one. To see the smiles and hear the exclamations of joy of children who are learning through discovery is a special gift that only teachers receive. If you wish to receive this gift, you must be prepared to give a great deal.

You may believe that you can effect discovery learning simply by putting children in direct contact with science materials; nothing could be further from the truth. Your role in discovery learning is substantial. Among other things, you will have to use effective questions to motivate inquiry, use demonstrations to pique curiosity, be knowledgeable about discovery-based curriculum models that you can turn to for ideas and activities, and organize and manage a productive and exciting learning environment. This chapter will help you develop your skills in this very important area of good science teaching.

[1]Kahlil Gibran, *The Prophet* (New York: Knopf, 1967), p. 96. Reprinted by permission of Alfred A. Knopf, Inc. Copyright 1923 by Kahlil Gibran and renewed 1951 by Administrators C.T.A. of Kahlil Gibran Estate, and Mary G. Gibran.

Figure 5–1. (*Source:* David Strickler, Monkmeyer)

INQUIRY—TEACHING TECHNIQUES

One very important teaching skill that can foster inquiry is that of piquing children's curiosity and focusing their knowledge and abilities by asking them questions. Some people feel that asking questions is a straightforward process that does not require any real skill—after all, we all know how to ask questions. True, all teachers ask questions of children. However, the real issue is whether the questions that are asked help children learn. A considerable amount of research has gone into discovering the kinds of questions we ask of children and the manner in which we ask them. The results of a few of these analyses may surprise you.

Analyzing the Questions You Ask

When I visit a classroom I sometimes feel that I have stepped back in time to the Spanish Inquisition. I am always astounded at both the number of questions the teacher asks and the amount of time they take up. The extent to which questions dominate our teaching is surprising. In a review of both old and new research on the questioning behavior of teachers, Glen McClathery notes that

> Probably the first empirical research on questioning-and-answering behavior was a 1912 study by Stevens, who found that teachers did 64 percent of the talking in high school classrooms and that they asked questions at the astounding rate of two to four per minute, or about 395 questions per day. A school principal interviewed in the study asked, "When do they (students) think?"
>
> Hyman suggests that a third of all classroom discourse consists of questions. King, while analyzing a tape of a reading lesson she had given, was startled to find that she had asked so many questions (59 in 30 minutes). Bellack documented that the teacher dominates the structuring, soliciting, and reacting moves (86 percent, 85 percent, and 81 percent respectively). The student, on the other hand, reacts infrequently (19 percent), but dominates the responding move (88 percent).

We not only ask too many questions, McClathery found, we tend to ask one type of question much more often than others:

> Haynes analyzed questions asked in a sixth-grade history class and discovered that 77 percent called for factual answers. Guszak's studies similarly showed that about 80 percent of questions asked required recall of facts, as did a study by Schreiber. In a pilot study done in 1970, Galloway and Mickelson verified that 70 to 80 percent of the questions asked by elementary teachers were of the memory variety. And Gall estimates that about 60 percent of teachers' questions require recall; about 20 percent require students to think; and the rest are procedural.[2]

If you intend to use questions that truly foster inquiry among children, then you will need to develop a way to analyze your questioning behavior. One place to

[2]*Analyzing the Questioning Behavior of Science Teachers* by Glen McClathery in *What Research Says to the Science Teacher*, edited by Mary Budd Rowe, © 1978, National Science Teachers Association, p. 14. Used with permission.

begin is in a pamphlet by Patricia Blosser, who describes the types of questions that teachers ask:

> *Managerial Questions* are those used by the teacher to keep the classroom operating, to move activities (and pupils) toward the desired goals for the period or lesson or unit. Such questions as "Does everyone have the necessary equipment?" "Will you turn to page 15, please?" or "Who needs more time to finish the experiment?" are classified as belonging to this category.
>
> *Rhetorical Questions* are used by teachers to reinforce a point or for emphasis. "The green coloring matter in plants is called chlorophyll, right?" or "Yesterday we said there are three major groups of rocks: igneous, sedimentary, and metamorphic, okay?" fit into this category. Teachers asking rhetorical questions do not really anticipate receiving an oral student response, although they sometimes get one.
>
> *Closed Questions* are those for which there is a limited number of acceptable responses or "right answers." "What happened when you switched from low to higher power magnification" or "What are plant cell walls made of?" are questions which anticipate certain answers. It is expected that students have already had contact with the information requested from a teacher lecture, class activity, assigned reading, or some visual aid (film, filmstrip, chart, demonstration).
>
> *Open Questions* anticipate a wide range of acceptable responses rather than one or two "right answers." They draw on the student's past experiences but they also cause students to give opinions and their reasons for these opinions, to infer or to identify implications, to formulate hypotheses, or to make judgments based on their own values and standards. Examples of Open Questions might include, "If you were to design a science display for the school bulletin board, what would you include in the display and why?" "What do you suppose life on earth might be like with weaker gravity?" "What should be included in a project to improve the school environment?" or "If you suspected that you were the carrier of some genetic abnormality, would you have children?"[3]

Figure 5−2 summarizes these four types of questions and their functions. For a comprehensive discussion of ways to improve the questions you ask in science class, see the *Handbook of Effective Questioning Technique*, also written by Patricia Blosser.[4]

Using "Wait Time": The Pause That Refreshes Discovery

Have you ever heard of wait time? It is one way to increase the effectiveness of the open questions you use (as well as all other questions). Wait time simply means sufficient time for children to think about questions prior to responding. Our questioning behavior tends to follow a certain pattern: we ask a question, receive a response from a child, and then make an immediate reaction. Both Blosser and Mary Budd Rowe, in their analyses of ways to improve questioners' behaviors, stress the importance of pausing at appropriate times during the question-asking process. There are two types of wait time you need to keep in mind when you ask questions:

[3]Patricia Blosser, *How to Ask the Right Questions* (Washington, D.C.: National Science Teachers Association, 1975), pp. 2−3. Used with permission.

[4]Worthington, Ohio: Education Associates, 1973.

QUESTION TYPE	QUESTION FUNCTION
Managerial	To keep the classroom operations moving
Rhetorical	To emphasize a point or to reinforce an idea or statement
Closed	To check the retention of previously learned information or to focus thinking on a particular point or commonly held set of ideas
Open	To promote discussion or student interaction; to stimulate student thinking; to allow freedom to hypothesize, speculate, share ideas about possible activities, etc.

Figure 5—2. Major Types of Questions Teachers Ask (*Source*: Patricia Blosser, *How to Ask the Right Question*. Washington, D.C.: National Science Teachers Association, 1975. Used with permission.)

1. The pause that follows the question that you ask.
2. The pause that follows the child's response.

In studying 800 tape recordings of science lessons, Rowe made some astounding findings regarding the amount of wait time employed by teachers. She reported, for example, that on the average children are expected to commence their reply to a question within nine tenths of a second. If a child doesn't answer within this time (wait time 1), the question will be repeated, placed in another form by the teacher, or asked of another child. In other words, within a very short time of asking a question, teachers either ask another question or comment on the original question.[5]

An increase in wait time can make a significant impact upon the inquiry behavior of children in the classroom. Rowe suggests that increasing wait time to an average of over three seconds results in the following observable changes in the verbal behavior of children:

1. The length and number of students' responses increase.
2. "I don't know" and failures to answer decrease.
3. The incidence of speculative thinking increases.
4. More evidence—followed or preceded by inference—is expressed.
5. The number of questions asked by children increases.
6. Contributions from "slow" students increase.[6]

Wait time does indeed seem to be a pause that refreshes the learning process. Think about it each time you work with children.

[5]Mary Budd Rowe, *Teaching Science as Continuous Inquiry* (New York: McGraw-Hill, 1975), p. 274.
[6]*Ibid.*, p. 257.

Using Demonstrations as Springboards for Discovery

"Do it again!"

That exclamation should bring joy to your heart after you do a science demonstration for children. Those three words are a clear message to you that you have made contact with a child's mind.

In recent years I have observed a deemphasis on the use of demonstrations in elementary-science classrooms. It seems that a long overdue reemphasis on having children do activities has taken the teacher out of a very important role—that of showing children phenomena that they cannot efficiently, effectively, or *safely* discover for themselves. The science demonstration can be an important tool for promoting inquiry in children since it has enormous potential for focusing attention upon a phenomenon. The demonstration can raise many questions for children that can be addressed in greater detail by individual science activities.

Demonstrations, of course, can be misused in the classroom. They should never replace the child's involvement in science activities. Moreover, they should not be used solely to reproduce phenomena that children have already read about. Demonstrations can be very effective in intensifying children's curiosity about a unit to be studied, clarifying confusion resulting from the attainment of contrary results by children who have carried out identical science activities, and tying together various cognitive, affective, and psychomotor learnings at the end of a learning unit.

This book includes elementary-school demonstrations for the life, physical, and earth sciences. Other sources of science demonstrations may be found in the list of references at the end of this book. Bear in mind that by using larger equipment or materials you can transform into a demonstration virtually any science activity you feel your children should experience as a class.

There are a number of considerations in presenting an effective demonstration. Figure 5–3 is a demonstration checklist that you can use to assess the effectiveness of science demonstrations that you or others do.

USING TEXTBOOKS TO ENCOURAGE DISCOVERY LEARNING

There are many ways in which textbooks can help children experience the processes of science. Current textbooks are quite different from the texts of just a few years ago. The most significant difference is that virtually all the major science textbooks now available include hands-on science activities. If the science teaching materials available to you during the school year include a set of textbooks, you and the children will have access to numerous science activities appropriate for use at your grade level. Modern science texts contain a wealth of experimental learning possibilities that may be easily overlooked by teachers.

The activities in a textbook series, of course, reflect a particular scope and sequence of science content. If you have the freedom and the desire to create your own science curriculum, the textbook can still be quite useful. By omitting some of the structure present in the textbook's directions to the child, you can modify the activities so that they place more emphasis on discovery learning.

_____ 1. Did the teacher begin the demonstration promptly or did children have to wait an excessive amount of time while the teacher got prepared?

_____ 2. Was the demonstration essentially simple and straightforward or was it elaborate and complex?

_____ 3. Could *all* the children in the class observe the demonstration?

_____ 4. Did it seem as if the teacher had pretested the demonstration or was there evidence that this was the first time the demonstration had been tried—e.g., missing equipment, confusion in the sequence of steps?

_____ 5. Was the teacher able to create a bit of drama with the demonstration as a result of purposely puzzling situations or unexpected (to the children) outcomes?

_____ 6. Did the demonstration endanger the health or safety of the children?

_____ 7. Did the demonstration seem to "fit" the learning unit under study?

_____ 8. Was the demonstration appropriately introduced, carried out, and concluded?

_____ 9. Did children have an opportunity to ask questions, make statements, and give reactions?

_____10. Do you feel that the demonstration was a significant learning experience for children?

Figure 5–3. How to Evaluate a Demonstration: A Checklist

Textbooks are typically divided into a number of units, or groups of chapters. By looking over the units and the teacher's guide that accompanies the book you will find many helpful teaching ideas. You will also find that many of the suggestions can easily be applied to learning units that you devise on your own. Many teacher's guides for textbooks provide bulletin-board ideas, field-trip suggestions, lists of audiovisual materials, lists of children's books, and other helpful information that you can use to enrich your learning units.

Many teachers whom I know like to include "learning centers" in their classrooms. The content and activities in textbooks can provide you with ideas for learning centers that can foster discovery. Indeed, you could probably prepare a science curriculum that had such learning centers as the principal medium of instruction and textbooks as supplementary resources. If you are unfamiliar with the construction of in-class learning centers, see Chapters 7, 10, and 13 of this book, which contain numerous learning-center ideas as well as plans for sample centers.

Children discover through direct experience, but they can also make discoveries through audiovisual materials. You can use the teacher's guides of textbooks to locate films, filmstrips, records, and audio tapes that are appropriate for the age level of the children you teach. By studying the teacher's guide before beginning a particular unit you may be able to identify a variety of useful audiovisual materials that can be rented or purchased. You may tend to think of AV materials as being suited principally to large-group instruction, but this is not always the case. I know some teachers who have taught their children to use basic AV equipment on their own, and in this way to make some discoveries with their own eyes and ears.

At the end of most textbook units you will find a list of ideas for long-term science projects. You can encourage children to select some of these projects as personal research activities to be carried out during the school year. Done at home or in school, they will give children the experience of working at a series of related activities over an extended period.

In order for children to pursue their curiosity about phenomena that they learn about through hands-on activities, they need reading materials. With advance planning on your part you can identify units and chapters in available textbooks that relate to your curriculum. Reading about science can be a valuable learning experience for children. Their acquisition of some fundamental terms and definitions in textbooks has the additional benefit of providing them with the background they will need in order to use other reference books to find answers to questions that come to mind. The child who is reading about science and learning vocabulary while carrying out hands-on activities will be in a good position to follow the trail of his or her interests wherever they lead.

Textbooks can also give you and the children an underlying structure of content and experiences that will provide continuity during the school year and from year to year within a school. They can help build a solid foundation from which the child can be continually encouraged to reach out and learn more and more. Textbooks can be a meaningful aid to you and the children. The extent to which they lead to discovery learning will in the final analysis depend very much on you.

DISCOVERY–BASED CURRICULUM MODELS: AN IMPORTANT RESOURCE FOR YOU

An artist striving for excellence can study great paintings of the past. A musician who wishes to compose a masterpiece can listen to the recorded works of Brahms or Beethoven. Whom can you turn to for inspiration and ideas if you wish to achieve excellence by creating a classroom environment that encourages children to make discoveries? Were there teachers before you who devoted themselves to the pursuit of such a goal and were successful in reaching it? The answer is, of course, yes.

Unfortunately, such teachers were, and are, so busy in the day-to-day world of planning for, teaching, and caring for children that their successes tend to be known only within their school. Most teachers have very little time to even think about writing articles or giving speeches about their successes. Very few have any feasible way to share their wonderful ideas with anyone except those few fortunate colleagues who happen to work in the same building or school system. Indeed, a sad thing about excellence in teaching is that it is very difficult to capture it so that others can benefit.

Fortunately there are curricular materials that can provide you with a gold mine of useful ideas as you strive toward excellence. I like to refer to such curricula as curriculum models. They are not perfect by any stretch of the imagination, but they are good examples of what can be accomplished by teachers who wish to foster discovery-based learning.

There are three elementary science curricula that in my opinion serve as landmark developments in the history of science instruction: the Elementary Science Study, Science: A Process Approach, and the Science Curriculum Improvement Study. Each was developed at a time when national concern for the quality of science instruction was at a peak. As a result of this concern, federal agencies joined with private nonprofit groups to develop high-quality curricular materials that emphasized the importance of having children interact with materials. The original materials have been revised numerous times and are presently available in revised form.

As a teacher of elementary science you owe it to yourself to locate copies of the original curricula or their revisions and analyze them carefully. You will, of course, find that each has its own strengths and weaknesses, and you will find that each can be an important resource for you as you develop discovery-based learning experiences for your classroom.

The Elementary Science Study

The Elementary Science Study (ESS) is a curriculum developed by the Educational Development Center of Newton, Massachusetts. It consists of classroom-tested science units that can conveniently supplement any existing school science curriculum or replace a curriculum. All units emphasize hands-on activity for children. The role of the teacher is that of a guide and resource person. The process of discovery is at the heart of every ESS unit. It is very difficult to capture on paper the spirit of ESS. Essentially, it is a very significant example of a curriculum in which the child is a relatively self-directed learner.

The content of ESS includes the earth, physical, and life sciences, and its units can be used at a wide variety of grade levels. For example, I have done portions of the unit "Batteries and Bulbs" with primary-grade, intermediate-grade, and high-school students and have found success due to the natural interest generated by the unit. I have also successfully done many other ESS units with both undergraduate and graduate students. The discovery-based nature of the materials seems to ensure high interest among the students, irrespective of their age or sophistication.

Science: A Process Approach

"At the end of the study of locomotion of animals, the children wrote a story about their experiences. One little girl wrote for the closing statement of her story: 'I wonder if when I push against the earth with my feet as I walk, I make the world turn just a little.' " Isn't this a marvelous statement? It was reported by a teacher using a science curriculum that encourages children to observe their world and make discoveries.

The curriculum that occasioned these comments has had a history of approximately twenty years, and to this day continues to influence the thinking of all those who seek ways to create curricula that encourage the development of science-process skills. The curriculum is known as Science: A Process Approach (SAPA). It originated in the 1960s, when the Commission on Science Education of the American Association for the Advancement of Science held a series of conferences that brought together scientists, educators, and administrators to consider the present and future status of science education at the elementary- and intermediate-school levels. Recommendations that emerged from these conferences resulted in the acquisition of funds from the National Science Foundation for the purpose of creating instructional materials that would stress the processes of science. The curriculum is presently being used in schools in two forms: the original SAPA and a revision known as SAPA II.

The Science Curriculum Improvement Study

The University of California at Berkeley was the site for the development of an elementary science curriculum that emphasizes the following three-step teaching/learning strategy:

1. Exploration: The child explores materials with little guidance from the teacher.
2. Invention: The teacher supplies a definition and term for a new concept.
3. Discovery: The child discovers a new application for the concept.

Known as the Science Curriculum Improvement Study (SCIS), this curriculum was developed by a group of individuals with various interests and abilities. As with SAPA, funds were provided by the National Science Foundation. The original SCIS is presently found in elementary schools, as are two revisions—SCIS II and SCIIS.

CLASSROOM ORGANIZATION AND MANAGEMENT
FOR DISCOVERY LEARNING

"Don't smile until Christmas" is a phrase that summarizes the conventional wisdom on the fostering of appropriate classroom behavior. In my work as a teacher and teacher educator, I have encountered some individuals who apparently believe this so strongly that they are able to refrain from smiling for the entire school year! These people must manage to get all their smiling done in July and August. I have a vision of thousands of teachers and principals whiling away their summers by smiling. I imagine their response to the question "What did you do all summer?" to be "Well, I managed to get a lot of smiling done; now I'm set for another year."

I will not attempt to provide an elaborate treatise on maintaining appropriate classroom behavior. If you are able to achieve this goal when you teach social studies, reading, math, or any other subject, you will find the same success in teaching science. If you have problems with classroom "control," the doing of science activities will not automatically solve your problems or make them worse. There are, however, some steps you can take that will help things go more smoothly for you and the children as they engage in science activities. I have seen more teachers produce discipline problems than I have seen children cause them. Appropriate classroom behavior is not hard to achieve. It just requires attention to a few common-sense matters.

Distributing Materials

The attack of a school of piranha on a drowning monkey is a model of tranquility compared with a group of twenty children each trying simultaneously to acquire a magnet from a tote tray containing ten of them. I have often been in science classrooms where the teacher's lack of awareness of appropriate distribution methods caused behavior problems. In order to distribute materials effectively, you will need to devise techniques that are appropriate for your setting. Two or three children can, for example, distribute materials to all the learning groups. Another technique is to have one child from each group come forward to acquire needed materials. Regardless of the procedure you employ, try to avoid having all the children simultaneously trying to get what they need.

Providing Work Space

"Please make him (her) stop bugging us or I will wring his (her) neck."

This is a rather common classroom request (threat) among children involved in science activities. One way to diminish this type of problem is to give learning groups some work space. To accomplish this is difficult if you have a small room, but you should try anyway. Movable bookcases, room dividers, and similar objects should all be pressed into service to give groups of children some semiprivate work space. Science activities provide ample opportunities for social interaction among group members. There is little need for groups to interact with one another, for such contact is often counterproductive.

If you have the opportunity to design the classroom space for science in a new elementary school, you may be able to create an environment that truly supports an emphasis on the doing of activities by children. Since such an opportunity will occur very rarely during your teaching career, though, you may wish to focus your attention on how to use traditional classroom space in ways that will be of maximum benefit to you and the children you teach.

The most important element of science work space is a flat surface. If you have any opportunity to select furniture for your classroom, try to acquire tables and chairs instead of conventional desks. The typical classroom desk for children is designed for *writing* and not for doing science activities. To compensate for the presence of desks with slanted tops you will need to acquire tables, build your own tables, or use the floor as the place for science activities.

Some teachers find that the inflexibility presented by the traditional desks can be overcome by placing tables along the periphery of the room. Students can then carry out their science activities on the tables and utilize their desks during other instructional activities.

Wherever possible, rollers (wheels) should be placed on cabinets, room dividers, portable chalkboards, and bookcases. This will allow you a great deal of flexibility in rearranging classroom space to meet the physical requirements of particular science activities. For example, you will want to have some science activities done by children working in groups. This can proceed more readily if you create "private" space for each group.

Providing Clear Directions

> "I didn't know what I was supposed to do with the ice cubes, so I put them down her back."

Children (and adults as well) seem to get into trouble when they do not understand what they are supposed to be doing. Problems arise in the classroom when children do not understand what your expectations are. If you can learn to announce these expectations clearly and simply, you will find that misbehaviors decrease.

If the science activity children are going to do requires procedures or materials that they are unfamiliar with, you will need to "model" their use (except, of course, when the objective of the activity is the "discovery" of how to use particular materials or procedures). *Children who do not know how to read a meter stick will as a result of frustration use it more like a baseball bat than like a device for making linear measurements.* By simply taking a few minutes to teach children how to use materials and equipment, you can make the process of discovery more pleasant for yourself and for them.

Eliminating Boring Activities

> "Oh no, it's the old paper-mâché-around-a-balloon bit."

Each year teachers who do not plan carefully wind up having children do activities that they have done before. A child who has made a model of the earth by placing paper-mâché around a balloon in previous years may have a tendency to utilize distributed materials in rather creative ways. *The flight characteristics of balloons and the molding of paper-mâché into models of interesting portions of the human anatomy will be but two unplanned discovery activities that will occur if children are bored with this earth-model activity.*

A good procedure to follow early in the planning of activities for learning units is to determine whether the children have done science activities before. Checking with their teachers from previous years is a good way to do this. A boring activity can produce a more lively classroom than you expected.

Figure 5–4. (*Source:* United Features Syndicate, © 1980 United Features Syndicate)

GOING FURTHER

On Your Own

1. Reflect upon the science activities you experienced as an elementary-school child:
   a. Specifically, what activities do you remember? Why do you think you remember them?
   b. If you do remember activities, were they carried out by individual children or by groups? What do you think motivated the teacher's decision in this respect?
   c. When the activities were done, were there any specific problems with work space, classroom behavior, or the availability of science materials?
   d. Would you say that your teacher or teachers encouraged discovery learning?
2. Select a chapter in a conventional elementary-school science textbook that contains some science activities. Develop a strategy for using the activities and text materials as the basis for a group of discovery-based lessons. How does your strategy compare with the more conventional use of chapters in science textbooks?
3. Make a sketch showing your vision of an ideal classroom in which to teach science. Label the various special areas in your classroom. Note in particular the location and arrangement of classroom seating and work space. What advantage does your ideal classroom have over a conventional elementary-school classroom? To what extent could you use your ideas for classroom organization in a conventional classroom?
4. This chapter included a discussion of three curriculum models that had a strong discovery-based approach. How could you use some of the ideas in these curricula to create an ideal curriculum for children at the grade level you are most interested in? Be specific and focus upon:
   a. The content you would stress
   b. The concepts you would stress
   c. How the curriculum would reflect the teaching style you would use.
5. Make a list of three or four "discipline problems" you have either observed or experienced in an elementary-school classroom. For each problem consider the following:
   a. To what extent could the teacher have avoided it? How many persons did it ultimately involve?
   b. Would you say the problem was a major one or a minor one?
   c. What would you say was the cause of the problem?
   d. If you were the teacher, what measures would you take to avoid a recurrence of the problem?
   e. Could the problem have been handled better by the teacher? If so, how?

On Your Own or with Others

6. With others, role-play the *best* and *worst* science demonstration you have ever observed. What factors contributed to the quality (or lack thereof) of each? If you are doing this activity by yourself, respond in writing.
7. Select a topic commonly covered in elementary-school science, and create five questions the teacher could use to help children make discoveries in this field of study. Also, try to think of a demonstration on the topic with which the teacher could raise questions among the children that could lead to discoveries.

8. Formulate your position on each of the following statements. If you are working in a group you may wish to have a mini-debate, various members of the group adopting extreme positions.
   a. Discovery learning uses up valuable classroom time.
   b. Textbooks cannot be used with discovery-learning techniques.
   c. By asking questions you can slow down a child's thought processes.

TEACHER TALK: SPRINGBOARDS FOR DISCUSSION

- "Science is a child-centered activity in our school. It should be a place where the child finds out how things work for himself. It should be fun. Asking 'Why' is important and seeing 'how' is essential. . . . In science we try to expose them all to the same concepts and don't ability group. It is the one academic place where we are all together."

- "[looking at the book] Finding out 20 percent of the air is oxygen. That's no challenge. Why not just tell them. You shouldn't just have to do an experiment for everything, only if it excites them or triggers them off."

- "Reading about yeast does not equal making bread."

- "Exposure is important. A kid will become aware and will know he's heard something before when it comes up again. I teach kids the thrill of seeing things. During sharing time one boy told me of seeing a red fox. His eyes sparkled. He wanted to share it with us. This is a science observation, an awareness of the wild creatures, where they see them. We'll look up the common ones, the number of babies, the food they eat, where they live. We spend more time on the things they see."

- "A 'dead giveaway' to our unsure attitude toward social studies and often science . . . is the number of films or film strips we use and show in science and social studies. Too many teachers show films and call it science."

SUMMARY

One way to help children make discoveries about their environment is to ask questions that lead them to think more critically. The types of questions we ask and the manner in which we ask them has a great deal to do with how well a child learns. We can sometimes provoke questions in a child's mind with demonstrations that pique his or her curiosity. There are many ways in which science textbooks can be used to encourage discovery learning. The textbooks themselves and the accompanying teacher's guide can provide basic content, numerous science activities, and many ideas that the creative teacher can use to develop a learning environment that fosters discovery. An additional, very valuable resource for teachers interested in encouraging discovery learning are various federally funded projects devoted to the elementary-science curriculum. Three such projects are discussed in this chapter.

SUGGESTED READINGS

BAILEY, G. D., "Learning How to Self-Critique Using Audiotape and Videotape in Teacher Self-Assessment," *Educational Technology*, 21, no. 2(February 1981), 41–45.

BENNET, L. M., "Science Corners, Mysteries Areas, Etc. . . . for Elementary Science Teaching," *School Science and Mathematics*, 81, no. 4(April 1981), 303–306.

BETHEL, L. J., and K. D. GEORGE, "Classroom Control," *Science and Children*, 16, no. 5(February 1979), 24–25.

COBB, V., "A Science Lesson Out of Anything," *Instructor*, 90, no. 9(April 1981), 44–48.

COBLE, C. R., and P. B. HOUNSHELL, "Science Learning Centers," *Science and Children*, 16, no. 1(September 1978), 11–13.

DeROSE, J. V., D. LOCKARD, and L. G. PALDY, "The Teacher Is the Key: A Report on Three NSF Studies," *Science and Children*, 16, no. 7(April 1979), 37–41.

DYRLI, O. E., "Should We Scrap Lab Centered Science Programs?" *Learning*, 9, no. 7(February 1981), 34–39.

EAKIN, J. R., and R. KARPLUS, *SCIS Final Report*. Berkeley Science Curriculum Improvement Study, University of California, Berkeley, 1976.

EVANS, M. W., "Opening Resource Centers," *Science and Children*, 16, no. 4(January 1979), 24–25.

KIRSCH, M. G., "Building a School Greenhouse from the Grassroots Up," *Teacher*, 96, no. 8(April 1979), 45–47.

KIZER, F. D., "Design for Safety," *The Science Teacher*, 46, no. 6(September 1979), 23–24.

KRUMBOLTZ, J. D., and L. DUCKHAM-SHOOR, "Discipline: Reward Direction Not Perfection," *Learning*, 8, no. 1, 154–159.

LEVITT, T. C., *Managing Inappropriate Behaviors in the Classroom*. Reston, Va.: Council for Exceptional Children, 1978.

National Science Teachers Association, *Safety in the Elementary School Classroom*. Washington, D.C., 1978.

NEVENDORFFER, M. J., and E. ROMNEY, *The Elementary Science Study: A History*. Newton, Mass.: Educational Development Center, 1973.

WELCH, F. C., and J. D. HALFACRE, "Ten Better Ways to Classroom Management," *Teacher*, 96, no. 2(October 1978), 86–87.

chapter 6

How Can I Help Handicapped and Gifted Children Get the Most out of Science?

You and I . . .
we meet as strangers, each carrying a mystery
  within us.
I cannot say who you are; I may never know
  you completely.
But I trust that you are a person in your own
  right,
possessed of a beauty and value that are the
  Earth's
richest treasures.

So I make this promise to you:
I will impose no identities upon you, but
  will invite you

to become yourself without shame or fear.
I will hold open a space for you in the world and
  defend
your right to fill it with an authentic vocation.
For as long as your search takes, you have my
  loyalty.[1]

The time that we have with each child who steps through our classroom doorway into our care is but a fleeting moment—so brief that we are seldom able to use our talents to the fullest to respond to the numerous ways in which individual children differ from one

[1]Theodore Roszak, *Person/Planet: The Creative Disintegration of Industrial Society* (New York: Doubleday, 1978). Copyright © 1977, 1978 by Theodore Roszak. Reprinted by permission of Doubleday & Company, Inc.

Figure 6–1. (*Source:* Used with permission of SAVI/SELPH [Science Activities for the Visually Impaired/Science Enrichment for Learners with Physical Handicaps] © 1980 by the Regents of the University of California. SAVI/SELPH materials are available from the SAVI/SELPH Project, Lawrence Hall of Science, University of California, Berkeley, California 94720.)

another and from ourselves. Sadly, children who differ greatly from the mythical average child have not always been welcomed into our midst.

Potential cancer cures, hydrogen bombs, the energy crisis, and heart transplants are parts of a reality that exists for *every* person. *All* adults need to become scientifically literate. This means that the child with a handicapping condition, the average child, and the gifted and talented child each need an appropriate education in science.

This chapter will help you respond to children who for one reason or another have special needs. I hope that it will prepare you to say to every child who takes that first step into your classroom, "Hello. I'm glad you are going to be in my class."

RESPONDING TO THE SCIENCE NEEDS OF HANDICAPPED CHILDREN

Teaching Science to Children with Visual Impairments

THE SCIENCE CURRICULUM

Visually impaired children do not need a special classroom. Does that sentence surprise you a bit? Think about it. Why would a visually impaired child *not* be expected to learn any of the content, processes, or attitudes that make up your science curriculum? The fact is that visually impaired children should experience the same science curriculum as their agemates. Remember, a visual impairment affects only the *manner* through which knowledge enters a child's mind; it should not in any way affect the *nature* of the knowledge we select for the curriculum.

If we do not modify the curriculum, then what do we do for visually impaired children? The answer is straightforward: we modify equipment and materials so that the visually impaired child can garner the same learnings as his or her classmates. In your classroom, learning occurs as a result of the child's processing of information, attitudes, and values acquired through reading

Figure 6–2. A blind child discovers the structure-function of a flower. (*Source:* Hadary Model Demonstration Program, The American University, Washington, D.C.)

materials, science activities, audiovisual materials, and classroom discussions. The visually impaired child needs opportunities that will provide the same information in a way that does not require his or her sight.

SCIENCE READING MATERIALS

If you expect the children in your classroom to read science textbooks, science-related fiction and nonfiction, children's literature, and resource books, then you must develop strategies to help visually impaired children have the equivalent experience. One convenient method is to have sighted agemates with good oral-reading skills systematically audio-tape books, chapter sections, newspaper stories, and any other printed materials that you will be using with the entire class. This would be a very appropriate ongoing *class* project in which children take turns preparing instructional materials for their classmates with vision impairments. This type of peer-group activity has a tremendous potential for transforming just another classroom into a learning community.

Children with visual impairments should be expected to repay their classmates by using their own unique talents and abilities. Remember that young Ricky or Lisa may be visually impaired, but this does not and should not restrict their ability to participate in science fairs, talent shows, or school-wide spelling bees, seek the classroom "presidency," or conduct the class in holiday band or choral presentations.

Another strategy you can use to enable visually impaired children to process printed matter is to have the school purchase large-type books, "talking" books, or Braille books (if the visually impaired children have Braille reading skills). Here is one major source of such materials: American Printing House for the Blind, 1839 Frankfort Avenue, Box 6085, Louisville, Kentucky 40206.

SCIENCE ACTIVITIES AND EQUIPMENT

The science teacher who uses reading and writing as the sole means of instruction will give all of his or her children a handicap. "Normal" children and children with handicapping conditions both suffer from one-dimensional teaching. The teacher who uses a full range of multisensory techniques in the regular classroom will be responding to some of the special needs that exceptional children may have. A visual impairment is a handicap only if the teacher uses sight-related instruction to the exclusion of other modes of learning.

In thinking about the carrying out of hands-on experiences by visually impaired children, you should be aware that about 80 percent of these children are not totally blind. Many of the legally blind children that you will work with in your teaching career will have some residual vision. That is, they will be able to distinguish light from dark areas and differentiate shapes. To capitalize on this residual vision you will need to talk with the child, his or her parents, and perhaps his or her physician. In this way you will have information to use when you modify science activities to ensure that the child is acquiring the maximum benefit from them.

One easy way to foster the observation process and at the same time take advantage of a visually impaired child's abilities is to have the child dictate observations into a small cassette tape recorder during science activities. By doing this you will be able to teach visually impaired children the importance of systematically keeping track of their observations. The taping procedure will also help the visually impaired child understand that you hold him or her as accountable as the remainder of the class for making and maintaining observations.

Adapting Science Materials and Equipment. Here is a challenge for you: how would you have a blind child observe a fish in an aquarium? Since most aquarium fish are not noisy creatures, the problem might seem insurmountable—but is it? Consider this classroom dialogue:

"How does the fish feel?" asks the teacher.
"It feels like lemon pie."
"Does it have a neck?"
"No."
"What holds its head on?"
"Its body holds it on."
Sighted children cluster around the blind child and encourage him to find the fish. As he feels around he comments, "The fish is on the bottom because he wants to hide."
"Pick up the fish," orders one of the sighted children.
The blind child starts to pick up his inner aquarium.
"No, the fish," says the sighted child.
"But I have to do it this way," he explains, "I have to empty the water out first."[2]

By simply adapting a classroom aquarium by placing an inner plastic aquarium containing drilled holes in it, the teacher enables visually impaired children to observe fish. The child learns to lift and tip the inner aquarium until most of its water drains into the larger aquarium. The fish becomes trapped in the water that remains at the bottom of the inner aquarium. It is then in a position to be thoroughly observed by the visually impaired child—a pleasant educational experience for the child, if not for the fish.

In this case a simple adaptation made the impossible possible and a blind child was able to have the experience of observing a fish. This incident illustrates

[2]Actual in-class dialogue reported in "Joining In," *SCIS Newsletter*, no. 30 (Fall 1977), 3.

Figure 6–3. A blind child with a deaf partner experimenting to find which objects float and sink. (*Source:* Hadary Model Demonstration Program, The American University, Washington, D.C.)

that a child's most severe handicap is the difficulty the teacher has in seeing a way through a seemingly insurmountable problem. Perhaps Shakespeare put it best when he gave Caesar these words: "The fault, dear Brutus, lies not in the stars but in ourselves." As teachers we must transcend the apparently difficult or insoluble problems associated with helping children with handicapping conditions and simply find a way.

Our efforts to accommodate the needs of these children will be rewarded in many ways. The child with a handicap will learn, and his or her "normal" peers will gain some very important knowledge and attitudes about children who seem different. Witness this report of an observed classroom interaction:

> One of the groups is growing plants and measuring their growth. Some blind children measure with cardboard strips and, by touch, compare their length and strips cut in previous weeks. Another blind child drags a magnet across a tray covered with iron filings. With her fingers she feels the cluster that has accumulated on the magnet: "Can you make your magnet do this?" she asks, pushing it toward her classmates. One of the student teachers reports that the blind children in his class have no trouble keeping up with the sighted. In comparing tap water and distilled water only the blind students could feel a difference and then shared this information with their sighted classmates.[3]

Many science activities for children emphasize the measurement of elapsed time, length, volume, mass, or weight. All of these tasks can be accomplished by visually impaired children who are Braille readers. All you need to do is ensure that your children have access to equipment that has braille markings. If your school does not have such equipment, it is your responsibility to notify school officials that it needs to be purchased. An eleventh commandment for regular classroom teachers who work with handicapped children should be "Do not be meek in your demeanor as you go forth to make requests for special materials." Such materials must be available for children with handicapping conditions: it is a matter of federal law, not local whim.

Teaching Science to Children with Hearing Impairments

As a regular-classroom teacher you will probably have very few totally deaf children in your classroom during your teaching career. Mainstreamed children with hearing impairments range from those who do not require a hearing aid to the relatively few who cannot hear at all. Most totally deaf children who are mainstreamed will probably have been taught to be skilled lip readers and will also be adept at sign language. If you have totally deaf children in your classroom, it would be well worth your while to enroll in one of the many short courses on "signing" offered by major universities, hospitals, and centers for communication disorders.

Hearing impairments in children have a variety of causes, including congenital defects, respiratory diseases, and infections of the tonsils, adenoids, or ears. Some children may experience temporary hearing impairments as a result of colds, flu, or allergic reactions. As a teacher you should act quickly if any of your children complain of earaches: contact the school nurse, doctor, or parents during

[3]*Ibid.*, p. 5.

the school day so that the child can be examined. Many permanent hearing impairments are the consequence of untreated ear infections. The continuing cycle of colds, sore throats, and flu that elementary children experience provide many opportunities for potentially permanent hearing impairments. With care, teachers and children can avoid these impairments.

As with children with other physical handicaps, the presence of a child with a hearing impairment does not automatically necessitate an adjustment of the curriculum. Your approach to teaching science in a classroom with a hearing-impaired child should capitalize on the adaptive behaviors that the hearing-impaired child has already acquired.

Hearing-impaired children can derive great benefits from multi-sensory and hands-on approaches to science. Your principal challenge in helping them do so will be to provide written or pictorial directions for activities and assignments for these youngsters. This can be accomplished in a variety of ways. Activity directions can be written on the chalkboard, task cards can be developed, and the steps in a science activity can be acted out by you or by the hearing-impaired child's classmates prior to a science experience. In the upper elementary grades you can foster student cooperation in your classroom by having various children take notes from your oral directions and then share them with hearing-impaired students.

The child should, of course, be seated somewhere in the room where he or she has an excellent view of you. The child will need such an unobstructed field of vision in order to search for visual cues to supplement any information that you transmit orally. As you carry out demonstrations, explain content, or give directions, try to keep your head oriented so that the child can read your lip movements and facial expressions. It will also be useful if you remind the child's agemates to do the same when communicating with their hearing-impaired peers.

Once again, you will need to capitalize on the many multi-sensory activities that should be part of any science curriculum. The hearing-impaired child as well as his or her classmates will learn most effectively when experiences reach them through a variety of sensory channels.

When working with a hearing-impaired child, be careful not to form incorrect assumptions about the child's intellectual abilities as a result of listening to his or her speech. A hearing impairment, of course, bears no relationship whatsoever to basic intellectual ability. The inability of a hearing-impaired child to articulate properly is simply a speech problem resulting from an inability to fully hear oral language. The child lacks a "model" for the words he or she attempts to use. By encouraging a hearing-impaired child's oral responses you will provide him or her with self-confidence and increased practice in articulation.

Teaching Science to Children with Physical Impairments

As with other handicapping conditions, children's orthopedic impairments range from mild to severe. They may be congenital, or they may have resulted from accidents or diseases that affected muscles, bones, or joints. The essential functional problem of an orthopedically handicapped child is his or her difficulty in grasping objects, moving, stopping, or remaining steady. Some of the children in your classroom may have conditions that require crutches, prosthetic devices, or wheelchairs. The principal learning that *you* will acquire as you help integrate children with physical handicaps is simply that these children are neither brighter nor duller than anyone else.

"The most important factor to learn in interacting with the physically handicapped is that they are people just like you and I. So what if their body doesn't work when they want it to, *they* have learned to live with that problem. They have no choice. We must learn to live with that, too, and not feel sorry or try to overprotect children because of their differences."[4]

This description of the posture we should take as teachers of science reminds us that we must get over our prejudices toward children and youth with physical handicaps. We must continually be aware of any tendency we may have to focus on the external physical child instead of the internal thinking and feeling child.

The physically handicapped child may differ from his or her agemates in mobility, but not in mental ability or emotions. What we need to do first as we prepare to work with physically handicapped children in the science classroom is become aware of what they *can* do. You will probably find that they can do most of the things expected of their agemates. You may have to make a few minor modifications in the classroom itself. For example, you may need to arrange seating so that a child in a wheelchair can have ready access to all parts of the room. You may also need to see that a child with a disability that slows his or her walking rate has a work space close to science materials that the children are expected to obtain and use.

Common sense will serve you very well as you work with children who have orthopedic problems. A child's handicap can be turned into an asset by a teacher who wishes to capitalize on the opportunities it provides for building a feeling of community through the interaction of the child and his or her agemates. The child with a handicap can provide other children with numerous opportunities to

[4]Judy Hoyt, "Adapting Science to Disabled Learners," in *Science Education and the Physically Handicapped*, ed. Helenmarie H. Hofman and Kenneth S. Ricker (Washington, D.C.: National Science Teachers Association, 1979), p. 163.

Figure 6–4. Focus your attention on the internal thinking and feeling child. (*Source:* Photo by Educational Facilities Lab. From H. Hoffman and K. Ricker, *Science Education and the Physically Handicapped.* Washington, D.C.: National Science Teacher Association, 1979, p. 9.)

practice helping skills. Your patient work with all the children in your class toward developing a physical and social environment that benefits the physically impaired child will also reap benefits for the child without observable handicaps. The most important of these reciprocal benefits is the opportunity to grow up without acquiring the negative attitudes that some adults have about persons with physical impairments. By helping children interact positively with their peers who are visibly different, we remove a handicap from the "normal" child—that of an additional lifelong prejudice.

Teaching Science to Children with Emotional Problems

Some children display behaviors that interfere with their ability to function or with their personal and social development. The problems that these children may pose depend on a wide variety of factors. They may have little self-confidence, they may be frightened easily, they may be depressed, they may be disobedient or defiant, or they may simply spend their time daydreaming. The emotionally disturbed child acts the way he or she does for a reason. Unfortunately, that reason may have eluded even the most skilled school psychologist or psychiatrist. The causes for inappropriate behavior probably lie outside your ability to remediate them; what *is* within your purview is the nature of the child's present classroom environment.

Science activities can serve an important therapeutic function for emotionally disturbed children. They enable them to manipulate and control variables, thereby giving them a unique opportunity to operate in responsible ways. If children can find success through such activities, they will gain self-confidence and pride in accomplishment. You may not be able to remedy the emotional problems of such children, but you will be able to create an environment that can enhance feelings of self-worth.

Seriously emotionally disturbed children will probably not join the mainstream of school activities for the entire school day. In many cases, they will have been placed in school resource rooms with specially trained teachers. For some portion of the school day, however, they should and probably will join their agemates in more normal settings. As a "regular"-classroom teacher of science, you should help your children welcome and encourage any emotionally disturbed children that join the class for a portion of the day. Remember, children with emotional problems need ever increasing contact with children who display appropriate behavior—in other words, they need good role models. Some teachers are concerned that their "normal" children will learn inappropriate behavior from a mainstreamed child with emotional problems. Where this occurs, the probable reason is that the teacher himself or herself has been unable to create a classroom environment that values and affirms productive and appropriate social behavior.

TEACHING GIFTED CHILDREN

Who Are They?

The so-called normal child may strain your patience and knowledge with the simple question "Why is the sky blue?" The gifted child will ask a question that reveals a far different level of thought: "Why is the sky?" Gifted children sometimes make their presence known to us.

Who are the gifted? They are the children who by virtue of environmental or hereditary factors possess talents and abilities that distinguish them from their peers. They seem to learn quicker, retain longer, and possess analytic abilities that make them the easily recognizable "stars" of our classrooms. They are the children who come to school knowing the names of the planets, having an understanding of the sun as the ultimate energy source, and possessing curiosity about the inner workings of mechanical apparatus. As they move through childhood and our school systems they leave a path strewn with disassembled alarm clocks, organized collections of natural or human-made objects, and frustrated teachers and parents who have attempted to respond to their persistent and penetrating questions about the world around them.

There are many gifted children in our schools. The following definition may help you identify them:

> . . . children capable of high performance, including those with demonstrated achievements or ability in any one or more of these areas—general intellectual ability, specific academic aptitude, creative or productive thinking, leadership ability, visual and performing arts, or psychomotor ability.[5]

It is estimated that between 3 and 5 percent of the school-age population fits this definition. If the children in your school are grouped into classroom heterogeneously, it is likely that you will have at least one gifted child to work with.

Each time you work with children you should be aware of some of the characteristics of giftedness so that you respond appropriately to special talents and needs:

Early use of advanced vocabulary. Most children at age two make sentences like: "There's a doggie." A two-year-old who is gifted might say, "There's a brown doggie in the backyard and he's sniffing our flowers."

Keen observation and curiosity. A gifted child might pursue lines of questioning such as, "What makes Scotch tape sticky on one side and smooth on the other?" "How can they make a machine that puts on the sticky part without getting the machine all gummed up?" "Why doesn't the sticky side stay stuck to the other side when you unroll the tape?" A gifted child will also observe details. At a very young age the child might remember where all the toys go on the shelf and replace everything correctly.

Retention of a variety of information. Gifted children amaze parents and teachers by recalling details of past experiences. For example, one six-year-old returned from a trip to the space museum and reproduced an accurate drawing of a space rocket he had seen.

Periods of intense concentration. A one-year-old gifted child might sit for five minutes or more listening attentively to a story being read to an older brother or sister. Older gifted children can become totally engrossed in a book or project, becoming oblivious to the events happening around them.

Ability to understand complex concepts, perceive relationships, and think abstractly. Although an average four-year-old looks through a picture book of baby and mother animals with interest, a gifted four-year-old is more likely to observe concepts such as how much animal mothers and babies look alike except that the baby is smaller. Or, if a fifth-grade

[5]Dorothy Sisk, *What If Your Child Is Gifted?* (pamphlet available from the Office of the Gifted and Talented, U.S. Office of Education, 400 6th St., S.W., Room 3835, Washington, D.C. 20030).

class were told to write a paper on what it's like to be poor, most of the children would write, "I would be hungry" or "I wouldn't have enough money." A gifted fifth-grader would tend to view the problem more abstractly and might write something like: "Being poor would only be a problem if others were not poor. If everyone else had very little money, then we would all have less to spend and things would be cheaper."

Strong critical thinking skills and self-criticism. Gifted children evaluate themselves and others. They notice discrepancies between what people say and what they do. But they are usually most critical of themselves. For example, a gifted child who has just won a swimming race might complain, "I should have beat my time by at least one second."

Characteristics of children gifted in other areas. Children gifted in visual and performing arts or psychomotor skills will display many of the characteristics just cited as common to intellectually gifted children. In addition, such creatively or physically gifted children demonstrate their talents early. A visually gifted child might draw a man riding a motorcycle while classmates are still struggling to put nose, eyes, and mouth in right places in drawing a face. Overall, children who have special creative abilities differ from intellectually gifted children in many ways. They are likely to have one or more of these characteristics: a reputation for having wild and silly ideas or ideas that are off the beaten track, a sense of playfulness and relaxation, a strong tendency to be nonconformist and to think independently, and considerable sensitivity to both emotions and problems.[6]

Gifted children are probably our greatest natural resource. They have the potential to contribute the ideas, products, and procedures that will undoubtedly have a great effect upon the quality of life on our planet in the future. The educational nourishment they receive within the classroom will be a significant factor in determining whether this potential will ultimately be fulfilled or frustrated. Let us turn, then, to some strategies we can employ to ensure the fullest development of the talents and abilities of the gifted children in science.

How Can I Provide for Their Special Needs?

Your classroom can be a garden in which each gifted child can blossom. Science can provide such children with unique opportunities to design and carry out explorations of their environment. The challenge is to keep them growing and blossoming, since they will move very quickly through the planned learning experiences you provide for the full class. You will need to find ways to extend and enrich the "normal" science activities so that gifted children do not become bored. There are two types of enrichment experiences for gifted children that you should consider: day-to-day enrichment activities and challenge projects.

DAY-TO-DAY ENRICHMENT ACTIVITIES

Here are some activities you might wish to use in a school whose science curriculum includes a K–6 textbook series:

1. Secure single copies of books at advanced grade levels from two or three publishers of science texts and use them as supplementary resources for gifted children. Also, have

[6]*Ibid.*

supplementary science-activity books from the school library temporarily placed in your classroom.

2. Identify the portions of these books that deal with topics included in your science curriculum for the year.

3. Locate science activities in these books that bear upon the topics you are going to cover in the science curriculum.

4. Have a conference with your gifted children each time the class begins a new unit of work. During these conferences:

   a. Agree upon the specific enrichment activities in the nonclass textbooks that these children will carry out in addition to their regular science activities.

   b. Make lists of any special materials that will be needed.

   c. Establish a schedule of progress-review meetings.

5. Establish the ground rules for carrying out the enrichment projects. You will need to answer such questions as these:

   a. When will the gifted children do the activities?

   b. What will be the tangible products (charts, notes, drawings, etc.) of their work?

   c. How will their experience be shared with the class?

   d. Who is responsible for acquiring the materials needed?

   e. Which activities or parts of activities can be done before school, which can be done after school, and which at home?

6. Find ways to continue encouraging the children who participate in enrichment activities.

CHALLENGE PROJECTS

Gifted children are a special joy to teach since they are usually able to function rather independently. You will find that they do not require specific directions for every science activity they carry out. This capacity for independent, self-directed work is well suited to long-term science projects. I call such activities challenge projects. Here are a few examples:

Can You Make:

A sundial and use it as a clock?

A model wind-speed indicator?

A water filter using sand and pebbles that will clean up muddy water?

A compound machine from a group of simple machines?

A working model of a fire extinguisher?

A simple battery-operated electric motor?

A balance that really works?

A clay contour map of the school grounds?

Challenge projects can enrich a child's science experiences either by extending them to other facets of the topics being studied or by encouraging an indepth study of a particular topic and more of a challenge for a gifted child's intellect. Long-term projects can have a strong read-about, think-about, and write-about emphasis through reports, or a heavy emphasis on science research through activities that require careful observations over long periods.

Figure 6–5. Gifted children are usually able to function quite independently. (*Source:* Hugh Rogers, Monkmeyer)

Regardless of the format employed in such long-term projects, they should all commence with teacher-student conferences in which the principal focus is the child's interest in and capacity to undertake potential projects. Conferences provide an opportunity for both you and the child to communicate clearly with respect to your expectations about the manner in which special projects and activities are carried out.

OTHER TEACHING TECHNIQUES

As you teach and encounter more and more gifted children you will continually add to your repertoire of teaching techniques that can help you respond to their special needs and interests. The following techniques can serve as points of departure:

1. Have gifted children prepare and do some of the classroom demonstrations of phenomena that you would normally do yourself.
2. Provide gifted children with specific work and storage space in order to encourage long-term science projects.
3. Have gifted children become responsible for helping you secure, construct, or organize science materials to be used by the class.
4. Encourage gifted children to read science-fiction books and science biographies as replacements for or supplements to normally required book reports.

5. Review television program schedules with gifted children to encourage the viewing of special programs with science content.
6. After school, take gifted children to visit with scientists, engineers, or other persons with science-based careers in the community.
7. Encourage gifted children to make slides, transparencies, videotapes, or films of science phenomena or demonstrations.
8. Encourage gifted children to take some leadership in the writing, directing, and producing of science-oriented plays, "TV" shows, or puppet shows (for young children) to be presented in the classroom or for a larger audience.

The science classroom can provide gifted children with many different opportunities, and it will provide *you* with many opportunities to stretch your intellectual and imaginative abilities to the fullest. You will find that the experience of helping gifted children fulfill their potential is an extremely enjoyable part of teaching.

GOING FURTHER

On Your Own

1. Identify a science activity that you would do with children. How would you adapt that activity to meet the special needs of a child with a visual impairment and a child with a hearing impairment?
2. Write a sample letter to the parents of a hearing-impaired child that describes ways in which they could help their child make observations of science phenomena (for example, violent weather and changes in the seasons). Write a similar letter to the parents of a child with a visual impairment.
3. Develop a list of science experiences you might have a visually impaired child carry out during a nature walk through a wooded area. What advantages would there be to having all children carry out the same activities as the visually impaired child? How could you encourage and enable the visually impaired child to keep track of observations made on the nature walk?
4. Write a sample letter that you could use to establish communication among yourself, a scientist living in the community, and a gifted child with a strong interest in science. In the letter highlight the benefits that would accrue to both the child and the scientist.

On Your Own or with Others

6. Role-play the following situations with your learning-group peers. When you are done, discuss each situation.
   a. Parent/teacher conference regarding a gifted child whose parents are dissatisfied with your response to the child's special abilities
   b. Same as above except that the child in question has a handicapping condition
   c. A conference in which the teacher encourages the parents of a physically handicapped child to allow the child to participate in a class field trip to a water-treatment plant.

   If you are doing this activity by yourself, write a brief description of what you predict would take place in each of these three conferences.

7. Interview the parents of a gifted child to determine when and how the child's special abilities become apparent, their response to this discovery, and the school's response. Also, ascertain whether the child has a special interest in some particular area of science.
8. Brainstorm a list of at least ten steps a teacher could take to ease the transition of a child from a special-education classroom into a regular classroom in which science is taught. In what ways could the list vary for a child with orthopedic problems and a child with emotional problems?

TEACHER TALK: SPRINGBOARDS FOR DISCUSSION

- "High achievers learn in spite of you. . . . that's what high achiever means: he has gotten more than what has been offered on the average. The easiest thing in the world to teach is subject matter. That means the kid is ready and able. The fact is that by the end of our school year most of our kids aren't ready or able for most of our instruction; they have dropped out, drifted down to the bottom groups, or are doing badly in the top ones."

- "I feel science and social studies give us the one place in academic schooling where the lowest kid can really participate in class. There are so many things that can be done that are fun for children of all ages, abilities. It is vital that we keep science and social studies informal in a school that homogeneously groups in reading and mathematics."

- "Dumbest idea [grouping by achievement levels] ever perpetrated on schools. Fewer levels are better levels. The idea of a *level* is stagnation for starters. There is no such thing as a level. There are adults who need to figure out some way to meet the challenge of different kids. So, we invent the idea of a level. Pretty soon we say it enough that it becomes real. . . . what we have to get around to here pretty soon is what good are these ideas, levels, and can we show that they serve anything more than teacher convenience."

SUMMARY

Children with handicapping conditions should participate as fully as possible in the science activities that take place in classrooms. Your response to the special needs of these mainstreamed children will require an understanding of various handicapping conditions and the development of a variety of ways to help these children learn science.

Gifted children in your classroom will also have special needs. The science curriculum for such children should include various enrichment activities, challenge projects, and other opportunities for them to use their unique talents and abilities. Various techniques for working with gifted children were discussed in this chapter.

SUGGESTED READINGS

AWKERMAN, G., and P. TELLER, "Mess Management for Gifted Students," *Science and Children*, 16, no. 6(March 1979), 10–11.

BOYER, E. L., "Public Law 94-142: A Promising Start," *Educational Leadership*, 30, no. 5(February 1979), 298–301.

DAVIS, P. A., "Teaching Partially Sighted Children," *Teacher*, 98, no. 7(March 1981), 39–41.

GLICK, H. M., and M. SCHUBERT, "Mainstreaming: An Unmandated Challenge," *Educational Leadership*, 38, no. 4(January 1981), 326–327.

HOFFMAN, H., and K. RICKERS, eds., *Science Education and the Physically Handicapped*. Washington, D.C.: National Science Teachers Association, 1979.

KATZ, G., and S. BUSHNELL, "Meeting Special Needs through Environmental Education," *Teaching Exceptional Children*, 11, no. 3(Spring 1979), 110–113.

KNUTSEN, L., "Teaching Fifty Gifted Science Units in Two Easy Steps," *Science and Children*, 16, no. 6(March 1979), 51–53.

KUHN, D. J., "Giving the Gifted Their Due," *The Science Teacher*, 46, no. 2(February 1979), 32–34.

MOLLICK, L. B., and K. S. ETRA, "Poor Learning Ability . . . Or Poor Hearing?" *Teacher*, 98, no. 7(March 1981), 42–43.

OVERMIRE, R., "Providing Materials for Handicapped Visitors to Museums and Zoos," *Teaching Exceptional Children*, 13, no. 3 (Spring 1981), 126–129.

PASSOW, A. H., "The Nature of Giftedness and Talent," *Gifted Child Quarterly*, 25, no. 1 (Winter 1981), 5–10.

PINI, R. A., "Planetarium Presentation for Deaf Students," *Science and Children*, 17, no. 1 (September 1979), 41–42.

PRYT, M. C., "Helping Scientifically Gifted Students," *Science and Children*, 16, no. 6 (March 1979), 16–17.

WHITMORE, J. R., *Giftedness, Conflict and Underachievement*. Boston: Allyn & Bacon, 1980.

part 2

The Earth and the Cosmos

METHODS, CONTENT, DISCOVERY ACTIVITIES, AND DEMONSTRATIONS

chapter 7

How to Plan and Teach Earth/Space-Science Learning Units

THE DAY THE DINOSAUR CAME TO SCHOOL

The learning unit on community helpers was going quite smoothly. Sarah Marshall was proud of the way the children had become involved in their study of the various roles of the people who worked in the community. As a matter of fact, a skit on the topic was developed by the children and presented to the other classes at their grade level. (Sarah, of course, wasn't sure that the other teachers' enthusiasm for sending their children to see the skit was due totally to their interest in the subject.)

This particular morning the children were at their desks working busily on group reports about the community helpers. Sarah walked around the room visiting with the groups. The children seemed to be enjoying looking up various occupations in the reference books they had borrowed from the school library. Suddenly two of the children, Anne Marie Bukowsky and Lamar Johnson, materialized at her side. As Anne Marie tugged at her elbow Lamar asked, "Mrs. Marshall (although she was unmarried and preferred

Figure 7–1.

Ms., the children always called her Mrs.), what about the dinosaurs?" She thought to herself, "Dinosaurs? What do they have to do with community helpers?" She patiently asked Anne Marie and Lamar, "What dinosaurs? I thought you two were writing about what a *mayor* does." "We were," they answered. "But we were looking up 'mayor' in the encyclopedias and couldn't find anything. Then we looked up 'dictator,' since the headline on the newspaper we read for current events said 'Mayor Westlake Accused of Being a Dictator by the Eastside Community Group.' While we were looking up 'dictator' we found 'dinosaur.' What about the dinosaurs?"

At this point the group she was visiting began agreeing with Anne Marie and Lamar: "Dinosaurs, let's do some work on dinosaurs." Good-naturedly the other work groups in the room began a chant of "Dinosaurs, Dinosaurs, DI—NO—SAURS!" After calming the groups down, Sarah said she would think about doing a unit on dinosaurs later in the school year.

"Dinosaurs, Dinosaurs, Dinosaurs" was etched in her memory. The chant echoed through Sarah's mind as she left the building that evening. She felt happy that the children were interested in the topic, but she wasn't really sure she had the time or energy to carry out such a unit.

The next day she walked into the classroom and noticed that except for some giggling it was rather subdued. Suddenly a large green shape emerged from behind a bookcase. It was an old bed sheet on which was painted a green, fire-breathing dinosaur. She could make out the lumpy forms of two children under the sheet, and she noted that Anne Marie and Lamar were not at their desks. She joined in the laughter as the lumpy dinosaur waddled down one of the aisles toward her desk. As she hugged the friendly dinosaur she realized that a unit on dinosaurs had just begun.

BASIC CONCEPTS FOR EARTH/SPACE-SCIENCE UNITS

Dinosaurs don't come to school each day. But a child's interest in exotic things always does. The earth/space sciences have much to offer you as you plan for your science teaching. From this area of science you can select many topics that are almost certain to grab the attention of the children you teach. Just think of the possibilities: volcanoes, tornadoes, thunder, lightning, the exploration of the planets and the stars, and, of course, an opportunity to look backward in time to the dinosaurs. All this and much more is available to you when you develop earth/space-science units. The only real difficulty is choosing from such an exciting array of possibilities.

You can easily develop your own list of interesting, if not exotic, earth/space-science concepts that you can refer to as you develop units. Elementary-science textbooks, professional books, and school-curriculum descriptions can all be quite helpful. To help you get started, I have constructed a list of earth/space-science concepts you may find useful. Please keep in mind that the list is not intended to exhaust all the possibilities; it is simply a place to begin.

1. The earth is about five billion years old.
2. The earth is composed of a variety of rocks and minerals.
3. Some evidence of the many physical changes that have occurred over the earth's history are found in rocks and rock layers.
4. The study of fossils found in rocks can tell us much about the various life forms that have existed on earth.

5. Many species of animals and plants have become extinct. Our only knowledge of their existence comes from the study of fossils.

6. Various forces change the earth's surface, such as weathering, erosion, and mountain building.

7. The climate of the earth has changed many times over its history.

8. Weather is a description of the conditions of our atmosphere at any given time.

9. The energy we receive from the sun is a principal factor affecting our weather.

10 Weather instruments are used to assess and predict our weather.

11. The water cycle, a continuous change in the form and location of water, affects the weather and life on our planet.

12. Our solar system includes the sun, our star, and nine planets.

13. The sun is one of many billions of stars in the Milky Way galaxy.

14. Rockets, artificial satellites, and the space shuttle are all devices that enable humans to explore the characteristics of the planets in our solar system.

15. The exploration of the planets has so far not revealed the presence of life on any planet other than earth.

16. Some rockets have been launched that will eventually leave our solar system and reach the vicinity of the stars.

17. The natural resources of our planet are limited.

18. The quality of the earth's water, air, and soil is affected by human activity.

19. Water, air, and soil must be conserved or life as we know it will no longer be able to continue on earth.

20. The responsibility for preserving the quality of water, air, and soil rests with individuals, governments, and industries.

PROCESS SKILLS FOR EARTH/SPACE-SCIENCE UNITS

The study of earth/space-science units will provide you with many opportunities to help children develop science-process skills. This section consists of a brief list of science-process skills and earth/space-science activities that you can use to foster the development of these skills. You may wish to consider these process skills and activities and then develop your own activities for the full list of science processes presented in Figure 1–5.

Observing

Identify rocks and minerals on the basis of color, shape, and hardness.

Name various weather phenomena, such as thunder, lightning, and tornadoes.

Identify and name the planets of the solar system by looking at magazine pictures of them.

Describe how air quality changes as one visits various places in the community.

Classifying

Group the rocks in a collection according to their colors.

Group a variety of observed clouds into categories.

Group water samples taken from various water sources according to their clarity.

Group the causes of air pollution into two categories: (1) natural sources and (2) human sources.

Communicating

Describe how the surface of the earth changes as a result of the forces of nature.

Describe the variety of clouds observed over a seven-day period.

Construct a map showing the path of a recent hurricane.

Make a poster showing three ways in which water could be conserved in a school.

Using Numbers

Count the number of grains in a thimbleful of sand.

Place a collection of rocks in order from the smallest to the largest.

Locate two places on a weather map that have the same temperature.

Using an alphabetical list of planets and their distance from the sun, place the planets in order from closest to the sun to farthest from it.

Inferring

Make an observation of soil eroding at some location in the schoolyard, and then make an inference about the cause.

Make an inference about the cause of a thunderstorm at the end of a hot day.

Make an observation of the moon's surface from a photograph; then make inferences about the causes of craters.

Predicting

Make a prediction about tomorrow's weather from an observation of today's weather.

Make a prediction about the size of a dinosaur from a photograph of a fossil dinosaur leg bone.

Make a prediction about the effect of falling drops of water on the surface of soil in a flat metal pan.

Make a prediction about the exact time the sun will set tomorrow.

A SAMPLE LEARNING CENTER IN DETAIL

Our Earth in Space

OBJECTIVES

Children will classify a set of pictures into one of four seasonal categories.

Children will note the movement of the sun by marking shadows on the floor at regular intervals.

Children will illustrate the seasonal changes on mural paper.

Children will study a globe and note land masses, water, and where they live.

OUR EARTH IN SPACE

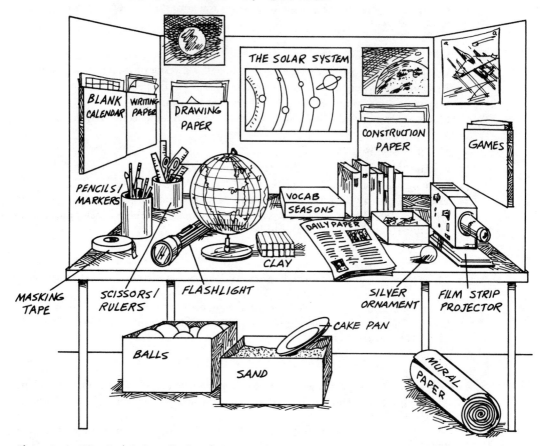

Figure 7–2. "Our Earth in Space"—Sample Learning Center

Children will observe and record the phases of the moon for a month.

Children will observe and illustrate the path of the sun through the sky over a day.

Using a globe and a flashlight, children will study how day and night are caused by the rotation of the earth.

Using a flashlight, children will observe the difference in the size and brightness of a light as it moves closer to and farther away from the observer.

Children will make a simulation of the apparent light of the moon.

Children will build models of the nine planets.

Children will design, construct, and label a mural of the solar system.

Using a photograph of the moon's surface, children will build a model surface from wet sand.

Children will make and label constellation patterns on construction paper.

After viewing a filmstrip on an appropriate topic, children will dramatize a space scientist's report on that topic.

Children will match space vocabulary words to corresponding photographs.

While playing a game, children will use space-related vocabulary words.

SCIENCE PROCESSES EMPHASIZED

Observing
Using space–time relationships
Inferring
Classifying

MATERIALS NEEDED

Writing paper and pencils
Construction paper, scissors, markers
Modeling clay
Silver stick-on stars
Globe
Flashlight
Filmstrip projector
Filmstrips on the topic
Library books on the topic
Various sizes of balls
Masking tape
Blank calendars
Large mural paper
Silvery Christmas ornament or ball of crumpled aluminum foil
Bucket of sand, large cake pan
Magazines to be cut up
File folder, file cards, clear adhesive plastic
Daily newspaper

DIRECTIONS FOR THE TEACHER

Set aside an attractive space in your classroom for this center. Decorate the walls and any other available space with posters and pictures of anything relating to space—in particular, a photograph of the surface of the moon, a photograph of our earth taken from space, and a chart of the solar system. Try to locate the center in a place where the students can turn out the lights when necessary. Allow space for working with clay, viewing filmstrips, and making large murals. Arrange a library section with books about the sun, seasons, earth, stars, planets, and solar system that are appropriate to the ability levels of the group.

Chase the Shadows! On a sunny day have the children mark the movement of the sunny patches in the room or any sunny location. At half-hour intervals, have the children mark the edge of the sunny patch with a piece of masking tape and record the time on the tape. Make the following activity card:

---

1. Find a patch of sunlight on the floor of your room early in the morning.
2. Put a piece of tape on the edge of this sunny patch and write down the time on the tape with a marker.
3. Every half-hour add a new piece of tape to the edge of the sunny patch and record the time.
4. What happened? Why?

Globe Exploration. With a piece of tape, paper, or clay mark the place where you live on the globe. Place the globe in the center for the children to explore. Make this activity card:

---

1. Look at the globe carefully.
2. Find the pieces of land.
3. Find the water.
4. Is there more land or more water?
5. Find where we live.
6. Have you traveled anywhere? Can you find that place on the globe?
7. Do you think the world is very big?

Seasons Mural. Have the children draw or paint a mural showing the seasonal changes in your city or town.

---

1. Divide the paper into four sections.
2. Draw or paint a picture of what your city looks like in winter, spring, summer, and autumn.

Seasons Mix-Up. Collect magazine pictures depicting the four seasons. Paste these pictures on cards and cover the cards with clear adhesive plastic. Make four heading cards: "Spring," "Summer," "Autumn," and "Winter." Have the students sort and classify the pictures and place them under the proper heading. Place these cards in a small box or large envelope, and label it with the title of the activity and the following directions:

1. Spread out the heading cards.
2. Sort the pictures of the seasons and place them under the right heading.
3. Check your answers.
4. Mix up the cards and put them away.

The Phases of the Moon. Provide the children with blank calendars and the following directions:

1. Take your calendar home.
2. Try to observe the moon every night for a month.
3. Each night record the shape of the moon on your calendar.
4. Also, record on your calendar when you are able to see the moon during the day.
5. Use the local newspaper to collect additional information about the moon.

Variation on "The Phases of the Moon."

1. Record the daily sunrise and sunset times for a month.
2. Is the day lengthening or shortening? Why?

The Sun's Path. Have the children observe, without directly looking at the sun, the location of the sun in the sky throughout the day. Ask them to draw or paint the path of the sun on mural paper and hang the mural on the south wall of the room with the east end of the paper on the east side of the room.

1. On mural paper draw the scene outside your window (or wherever you can watch the sun).
2. Beginning early in the morning, draw on your mural the position of the sun. Be careful not to look directly at the sun. Record the time of day.
3. Every half-hour find the position of the sun and draw its position on your mural. Record each time.
4. At the end of each day hang your mural on the south wall of your classroom to share with others.

The Rotation of the Earth.

1. Find a partner.
2. Hold a globe or place it on the floor, and slowly rotate it counterclockwise while looking at the North Pole.
3. In a darkened room, if possible, have your partner shine a flashlight or a filmstrip projector on the globe from the side.
4. Watch what happens as the earth rotates.
5. How much of the earth is in light and how much in darkness?
6. Note when it is daytime and when it is nighttime in the spot where you live.

Distance and Brightness.

1. With a partner, go into a long dark corridor.
2. Shine a flashlight at your partner while standing close together, and then move away from each other.
3. Watch what happens to the apparent size and brightness of the light.
4. Fill out the following worksheet:
   a. When does the light look the largest?_____

   _____

   b. When does the light look the smallest?_____

   _____

   c. When does the light look the brightest?_____

   _____

   d. When does the light look the dimmest?_____

   _____

   e. Use what you have learned in this activity to answer this question: How can two stars of the same size and brightness appear very different to us on Earth? _____

   _____

Reflection.

---

1. Hang a silvery Christmas ornament or a ball of crumpled aluminum foil. Turn out the lights.
2. Can you see the ornament well?
3. Shine a flashlight on it.
4. Can you see the ornament well now?
5. Where does it get its light?
6. If the moon does not produce any light of its own, why does it appear bright to us?

Clay Planets. Have the students make models of the sun and the nine known planets from modeling clay, using a chart of the solar system as a guide. Students should approximate the sizes and positions of the planets and display them on a large sheet of construction paper with the appropriate labels.

---

1. Study the chart of our solar system.
2. Using clay, make a model of each of the planets and the sun.
3. Be careful to make the sizes of the planets as close to the approximate sizes on the chart as you can.
4. Place your planets on a large sheet of construction paper in the proper order.
5. Label the planets.

Variation of "Clay Planets." Collect a variety of sizes of balls from BB size to beach-ball size (ping-pong balls, tennis balls, basketballs, etc.). Arrange these as representations of the planets.

Solar-System Mural.

---

1. Take a large piece of mural paper.
2. Design and draw a chart of the solar system. Draw the orbits.
3. Cut out of construction paper the various planets and paste them on the chart in their proper places.
4. Label all interesting features on your mural.

The Surface of the Moon.

1. Study a photograph of the moon.
2. Take a large cake pan, fill it with sand, and wet the sand.
3. Try to make your sand look like the surface of the moon. You will need to build craters, mountains, rocks, etc.

Constellations.

1. Using a book or a filmstrip from the library, study the most well-known constellations.
2. Take a piece of blank paper and silver stick-on stars.
3. Make the shapes of several of the constellations and label them.

Dramatization.

1. Choose a topic in this center that interests you.
2. View a filmstrip or read a book about your topic.
3. With several of your friends, pretend you are part of a team of scientists traveling through space.
4. As you go by each object in space (a meteor, a planet, the sun, etc.) have the "scientist" who studied the object give a report on it to the class.

Vocabulary Match-Up. Collect pictures of space-related subjects. Mount these on 5-by-7 cards and cover the cards with clear adhesive plastic. On another set of cards write the terms that correspond to the pictures—weightlessness, launching pad, astronaut, galaxy, solar system, orbit, etc.

1. Spread the pictures on the table or the floor.
2. Match the word cards to the pictures.
3. Check your answers.
4. Mix up the cards and put them away.

EXTENSION IDEAS

Read and report on a topic of your choice.
Take a field trip to a planetarium.
View a space movie (for example, *Star Wars, Star Trek*, or *Black Hole*). Discuss the special effects used.
From a list of items (oxygen, food, books, clothing, and so forth) select those you would need the most for space travel.

CORRELATIONS WITH NONSCIENCE SUBJECTS

Math. Develop problems involving the distances between the planets and the sun—for example, "How far must you travel to get to Jupiter from the Earth?"

Music. Listen to a recording of *The Four Seasons* by Vivaldi.

Art. Build a planet mobile.

Drama. Write your own *Star Wars*—type space adventure and then dramatize it for your class.

EVALUATION IDEAS

Have the children fill out a form that includes the following questions:

---

1. What did you like doing the best in this center?
2. What did you like the least?
3. What would you have added to this center?
4. What was the most important thing you learned in this center?

Maintain records of which activities each child worked on in this center. Note each child's progress and his or her strengths and weaknesses.

A SAMPLE BULLETIN BOARD IN DETAIL

The Air: Who Needs It?*

OBJECTIVE

Children will cut out and sort pictures of objects that need air to work and those that do not.

*Asterisks refer to activities for young children.

LIBRARY

Figure 7–3. "The Air—Who Needs It?"—A Sample Bulletin Board

SCIENCE PROCESS EMPHASIZED

Classifying

MATERIALS

Magazines
Scissors
Stapler

DIRECTIONS FOR THE TEACHER

Show students a jar filled with air and ask them "What is inside this jar?" Pour the air out of the jar by placing it under a water-filled jar and bubbling air up into it. Then discuss the question "What can air be used for?" with the class. Children can cut out a picture for each category of use listed on the bulletin board and then staple each picture on the board to form a collage.

EXTENSION IDEAS

Place a tissue in the bottom of an empty glass. Invert the glass and submerge it in a large glass jar or tub of water. Show how air is keeping the kleenex dry.

Place one cup of water in a *clean* and *empty* metal duplicating-fluid can. Heat the can until steam appears. Remove the can from the heat and quickly screw the cap on. Observe what occurs. Discuss how air has weight.

CORRELATION WITH NONSCIENCE SUBJECTS

Language Arts. As a class, prepare on a chart a list of answers to the question "How do we know the air is there?" ("It moves the leaves," "It blows our hair," etc.) Use this list for writing creative stories and poetry.

Social Studies. Discuss such topics as air pollution and the use of the wind to produce energy.

ADDITIONAL IDEAS FOR BULLETIN BOARDS

Wind*

How do we know the air is there? Provide and display various photographs and pictures illustrating the effects of wind (for example, a collapsed umbrella, tree leaves blowing, and kites flying). Have the children make drawings of their observations of the presence of wind, and include these in the bulletin-board display. Children may wish to write stories to accompany their pictures.

Save Water*

Design a bulletin board showing a cutaway view of a typical house. Include in the diagram a bathroom, kitchen, laundry room, and outdoor hose. Prepare a set of cards listing various ideas for saving water. (Examples: "Take a short shower." "Don't leave the water running." "Don't play with the hose.") Using yarn and push pins, the children will connect these ideas to the places in the house where they should be carried out.

Shadows on the Moon

Using cutouts to represent the earth, moon, and sun, show how the earth's shadow causes the moon to appear crescent-shaped. Prepare a set of cutouts that represent the various phases of the moon, and have the children arrange them in a sequence by using information from the bulletin board. They can then check their try against an answer key.

Natural Features

Provide a set of labels for different types of lands, including grassland, mountains, hills, lakes, rivers, forests, and swamps. Provide a set of pictures showing examples of each of the categories. The children will organize the pictures under the correct headings, using push pins.

Topography

Place on the bulletin board a large topographical map that includes a key. Place cards around the map that list or show the various physical features that can be found on it. Have the children connect the cards to the map, using stick pins and yarn.

Time Zones

Place on the bulletin board a map of the world that includes the twenty-four time zones. Explain how the rotation of the earth necessitates these zones. Prepare an accompanying chart that lists a number of countries evenly spaced around the world. Given a time in their own time zone, children will calculate the comparable time in each of these countries and compare their results with an answer key.

Compost

Prepare a bulletin board that shows the various processes evident in the production of compost. Use drawings or cutouts of the basic components of compost and compost-bin construction—concrete blocks, wire mesh, leaves, manure, vegetable garbage, grass clippings, soil, water, lime, etc. Have the children arrange these materials on the bulletin board with push pins so that they depict the proper construction of a compost pile.

SAMPLE FIELD TRIPS

The Earth's Surface

When studying the earth's surface with a group of intermediate-grade students, you can illustrate many of the concepts by taking a trip to an area where the earth has been eroded. The following activities are meant to accompany a visit to a site where a stream has cut its path, but with adaptations they could be used with a trip to a beach or a construction site as well. The services of a geology student, naturalist, or extension-service agent would be an asset but are not necessary for a successful trip.

Before going, obtain road maps and topographical maps of the area. State-government agencies, office-supply stores, and camping stores are possible sources for the topographical maps. Aerial photographs and land-use maps will be useful too. By studying and comparing the maps, students can work on direction, latitude and longitude, key-reading skills, and the combining of information from several maps. Learning about various soil and rock types and the geologic history of the region can begin here. Using the maps, students can draw routes ahead of time and predict which areas will be interesting to explore. Setting up a stream table will give students experience with stream flow and erosion. Encourage them to compare the speed of water on the inside and outside of curves. If you plan on doing soil and water sampling at the site, practice in school first; kits are available in hardware and gardening stores.

At the site, have several tasks to be accomplished and make sure students know what they are expected to investigate and report on. Whether each student does each task will depend on the size of the group, the time available, and the number of tasks. Students should have notebooks, magnifying glasses, and something to carry samples in. The tasks can include testing soil and water, collecting soil and rock samples, observing and drawing layers revealed by stream erosion, verifying observations made at the stream table, and carrying out map activities. A geologic scavenger hunt and simple orienteering using the maps and compasses are enjoyable activities for the entire group.

Presenting topic reports, making displays of collected items, preparing charts showing test results, and working further with stream tables are among the post−field trip activities. Showing pictures or a filmstrip of a totally different area and having students create their own geologic narration is an interesting method for evaluating learning.

The Weather Station

A field trip to a weather station can be adapted to any age level, but it is especially suitable in the primary curriculum. Weather stations or equipment can be found at airports, colleges, some high schools, some TV and radio stations, and at various state agencies. Be sure to find out what equipment is used ahead of time so you can familiarize your class with it. Contact the person who will be showing you around to let him or her know the abilities and interests of your students and to find out what background information you can give the students about the place you will be visiting.

Discussing the weather is a regular activity in primary classrooms. Expand this activity to cover information on instruments used in measuring and predicting weather. The differences among the seasons and weather around the world can be brought out, and the term *climate* introduced. Types of clouds and precipitation can be covered. Many teaching aids are available for this study: filmstrips, recordings of weather sound effects, photographic series, and flannel-board kits are a few. Don't overlook the many excellent children's books with weather themes. Snowflake patterns and rainbows are just two of the art-in-weather activities you can do. The newspaper weather map should be displayed and interpreted, and the class could watch TV weather shows, keeping a record of the accuracy of the predictions.

On the way to the station have the class make statements about the day's weather. The tour should include an explanation of the instruments and procedures used at the station. Brief discussions of short- and long-range forecasting, the use of satellites in weather prediction, and the interdependence of weather stations can follow the tour. There should be ample time for questions; you may want to keep a list of questions as they come up in class and bring them with you to the station.

There are many follow-up activities that can be carried out. Making some simple instruments for a classroom weather station—paper-cup anemometer, rain gauge, weather vane, barometer—will be a popular occupation. Children can give daily reports and try their skills at long-range forecasting. This is an opportune time to help students consider the impact of weather on their lives, especially its psychological, economic, and recreational effects. Weather oddities and disasters fascinate many people. Older students can explore the wisdom of the many weather sayings (such as "Red sky at night, sailor's delight") by keeping records over a period of time. Considering the future of forecasting and the consequences of weather control are lead-ins to writing activities, and examining myths that supposedly explain weather can lead to more writing. Weather study can be a multi-disciplinary unit that builds on students' interests while developing their skills and creativity.

ADDITIONAL IDEAS FOR FIELD TRIPS

The Earth's Surface

Visiting a jeweler gives children the opportunity to see what is done with some of the earth's more beautiful minerals. Many jewelers have special viewing equipment that can introduce children to crystal structure and light refraction. The origin of various stones, mining methods, polishing, and setting design are additional topics the jeweler will have information on.

While not common in all areas, quarries, caves, and mines are often equipped to offer field trips. A cement manufacturer, a local gravel or sand pit, or any industry using minerals is worth investigating.

A trip to a potter's or sculptor's studio can begin discussion about the sources of the materials used, techniques for shaping, how to preserve the finished product, and elements of design. The in-class follow-up should include a chance for the children to work with the materials or to try out on more pliable materials some of the techniques they observed.

The Air

Many factories have added air-pollution controls to meet federal standards. A trip to one of these factories can be very interesting. A similar trip would take you to the nearest auto mechanic or car dealer to observe automobiles being fitted with a variety of pollution-control devices.

Many states have mobile pollution-monitoring stations, and large cities have stationary equipment that measures air quality. A visit to these stations and the opportunity to make simple testing equipment for school use (such as vase line-covered cards to collect airborne pollutants) are a meaningful combination.

The Earth in Space

Visiting a planetarium, viewing the stars at an observatory, and using a hobbyist's telescope are unforgettable but hard-to-arrange experiences. We can create our own viewing opportunities with a large appliance box, a flashlight, and a coffee can. Nails can be hammered through the bottom of the coffee can to make holes in the pattern of a constellation. A child enters the box, shines the flashlight through the can, and observes the "stars" on the ceiling of the box.*

Communications play an important role in space exploration and travel. A field trip to a TV or radio station can help children learn about wave frequencies, transmission, the effects of sunspots, and the earth's atmosphere. Learning about future developments in communications would be especially interesting to older children.

Time is determined by the movement of bodies, but on earth we often use more arbitrary measures. A visit to a clockmaker can make children aware of how we keep track of time. Before going, look at photographs of some historical time pieces—candle clocks, water clocks, sundials, and so on.*

Conservation of Natural Resources

Most children are aware of pollution but do not realize their role in creating and controlling it. Traveling to an area where refuse ends up, such as a dump, sewage-treatment plant, or auto-salvage company, can point out the fact that pollution is everyone's problem.*

A forester or nursery worker can be an excellent contact for discussing renewable resources and the need for carefully managing them. Some lumber, paper, and furniture companies have developed reforestation techniques and might be able to provide you with information about them before you visit such a person.

If your area is fortunate enough to have a recycling center, a field trip is a must. Learning what materials are collected, how they are reused, and what the savings are in terms of energy and materials could result in a class recycling project upon your return to school.

chapter  8A

The Earth's Surface, Atmosphere, and Weather

CONTENT

THE EARTH'S SURFACE

The children in the photograph on this page look like they are about to do some mischief. They are not. They are simply trying to cope with the lingering effects of a geologic event that reminded us of how little we know about the earth on which we live, the fragility of its surface, and the atmosphere that surrounds it. The eruption of Mt. St. Helens in the state of Washington and continuing volcanic activity in that part of our continent and elsewhere on our earth shake our assumptions about the peacefulness of nature. They remind us that we may take too much for granted in our day-to-day lives. The children in the photograph are not wearing masks in preparation for mischief making; they are simply trying to breathe.

The Earth Today

The earth beneath our feet consists of various layers. The crust on which we live, work, and play is a relatively thin shell, ranging from 11 kilometers (about 7 miles) to 32 kilometers (20 miles) in thickness. Under the crust is a region about 2870 kilometers (1780 miles) deep. This layer is known as the mantle. The central portion of the earth is the core. The outer core extends from the mantle to a depth of 5060 kilometers (about 3140 miles). The inner core has a depth of 2680 kilometers (1680 miles).

We probably know more about the crust of the earth than we do about the remaining layers. The rocks of the upper crust are, of course, solid (except for those being formed from molten material that reaches the crust). Most of the rocks

Figure 8A–1. (*Source:* Wide World Photos)

of the lower crust and the upper mantle are also solid. Little is known about the inner and outer cores of the earth. It is thought that the inner core may consist of molten iron. The outer core may also be a mass of molten material, but it is thought to be less dense than the inner core. The high pressure within the inner core seems to be characteristic of a solid. Perhaps, then, we can visualize a solidlike inner core surrounded by a liquidlike outer core.

The origin of the magnetic field that surrounds the earth is largely unexplained. Many scientists believe it is produced by the properties of the inner core and the movement of the materials within the outer core. They reason that the movement of these metallic materials may generate electric currents that in turn create the magnetic field.

Gradual Changes in the Earth's Surface

The crust of the earth has undergone many changes over the years. The mountains, valleys, oceans, and continents that we are familiar with have not always occupied their present locations. Changes in the earth's surface seem to result from two processes. External forces such as weathering and erosion wear down the surface, and internal forces resulting from heat and pressure build mountains and cause movements within the crust.

In order to understand the changes that have occurred in the earth since it was formed, scientists have developed a time scale. The largest division of this scale is the era. The name of each era refers to the type of life that existed then. The four eras of geologic time and the approximate beginning of each are as follows:

Cenozoic Era	70,000,000 years ago
Mesozoic Era	225,000,000 years ago
Paleozoic Era	600,000,000 years ago
Precambrian Era	4,500,000,000 years ago

The three "recent" eras have been divided into periods, and the periods of the most recent era have in turn been divided into epochs.

THE PRECAMBRIAN ERA

The Precambrian era represents about 90 percent of all geologic time. Rocks dating from Precambrian time have been changed to such a degree over their history that it is about impossible to tell how they were formed. Most of the earliest Precambrian rocks have been covered over. There are, however, some places where they are exposed. The largest of these areas stretches from South Africa to Arabia. Smaller areas can be found in Canada, the United States, South America, Australia, Scandinavia, and Siberia. The Precambrian rocks found in these locations were probably the base of the earth's earliest mountains. Years of erosion and weathering have worn their upper portions away. Precambrian rocks contain extremely valuable deposits of iron, nickel, uranium, gold, and silver.

THE PALEOZOIC ERA

During this era great changes occurred on the earth's surface. Various mountain chains were formed and later destroyed. Sheets of ice covered much of the land mass in the Southern Hemisphere. Various seas and oceans formed in the Northern Hemisphere. It is thought that the land mass formed in the Southern Hemisphere was the earth's original continent. Over time this continent drifted northward. As the covering of ice on this original continent melted, the level of the ocean surrounding it rose. Many changes occurred as the land masses of North America emerged from the oceans. Great troughs developed, sediment accumulated, mountain chains were uplifted and later destroyed, seas evaporated and left behind great salt deposits, swampy areas that were to become coal deposits developed along the land and the sea: in short, the North American continent began to form.

THE MESOZOIC ERA

During the Mesozoic era North America took on many of the surface characteristics that we are familiar with today. An ancient chain of mountains in the east was uplifted once again to form what we know as the Appalachian Mountains. The Rocky Mountains and the Sierra Nevada were also created during this era. The middle portions of the United States and Canada, formerly at the bottom of the sea, began to rise. Eventually these areas became an almost level plain. As they rose, the water from the sea drained off as rivers and streams and carried away exposed rocks and other materials eroding from the Rocky Mountains. Much of this material was deposited at the edge of what we now know as the Gulf of Mexico. The levels of the seas dropped during this era and the climate became cooler. As the shallow seas began to dry out many organisms that depended on the seas and swampy areas became extinct. An era had come to an end.

THE CENOZOIC ERA

In recent years geologists have determined that the outer surface of the earth can be viewed as consisting of at least six major units or plates. The movement of these plates has caused many changes on the surface of our planet. During the Cenozoic era, their movement and crashing into one another uplifted mountains and caused an increase in volcanic activity. Thick layers of lava covered large areas of western North America. Late in the Cenozoic era great climatic changes began. Glaciers at the polar regions began to spread toward the Equator. These ice sheets changed the surface of the earth that was in their path. Glacial ice at one time or another covered the land between the Appalachian Mountains and the northern Rockies. Those areas of New York, northern New Jersey, and New England east of the Appalachians were also covered with glacial ice. As the glaciers receded in South Central Canada, rivers flowing northward became blocked with ice. The damming caused by the ice led to the formation of a very large lake. When the ice dam melted, most of this gigantic lake disappeared, yet hundreds of smaller lakes and one large lake (Lake Winnepeg) remain to this day. The Great Lakes were also formed by glacial action.

Perhaps the most spectacular change that seems to be occurring on the surface of the earth is the drifting of the continents. It is now believed that all the continents that we know today as distinct land masses were once joined together. The apparent proof for this is the similar rock structures in the west coast of Africa and the east coast of South America. Many other rock structures common to two or more continents have been found.

Violent Changes in the Earth's Surface

EARTHQUAKES

An earthquake is a violent shaking or a gentle rolling felt at the earth's surface. Millions of earthquakes happen each year. Many are not observed because they occur in remote areas or under the sea. Earthquakes that do occur near populated areas can cause a great deal of damage: buildings and bridges may topple, injuring or killing many people. Very large earthquakes at the ocean bottom can cause vibrations that travel through the sea as gigantic waves. When these waves reach shore considerable damage may occur.

The rocks that make up the crust of the earth are continually subjected to pushing and pulling forces. Sometimes these forces become so great that rock layers break, producing the vibrations that we know as earthquakes. Most of the ruptures, or faults, in the crust lie under the surface. Some, such as the San Andreas Fault in California, are visible.

The energy released from the breaking apart of rock layers travels away from the fault as *seismic waves*. The specific location at which the waves are produced is known as the earthquake's *epicenter*. Geologists can learn a great deal about earthquakes from the waves that reach energy-measuring instruments located at various places on the earth's surface. These instruments are known as *seismographs*.

Earthquakes tend to originate where new mountains, sea trenches, or volcanoes have been formed. Regions that have a great deal of earthquake activity are known as earthquake belts. Almost 95 percent of all earthquakes occur in either the circum-Pacific belt (from the west coast of South America, the United States, and Canada to eastern Asia) or the Alpide belt (from Burma to southern Europe).

VOLCANOES

On August 24, A.D. 79, the apparently extinct volcano Vesuvius[1] suddenly exploded, destroying the cities of Pompeii and Herculaneum. Vesuvius had been quiet for hundreds of years; its surface and crater were green and vine-covered,

---

[1]The discussion of volcanoes beginning on this page was excerpted with minor modifications from *Volcanoes*, a pamphlet prepared by the U.S. Geological Survey, U.S. Department of the Interior. This pamphlet (stock number 1976-211-345/59) is available for purchase from the Superintendent of Documents, Government Printing Office, Washington, D.C. 20402.

and no one expected the explosion. Yet in a few hours volcanic ash and dust buried the two cities so thoroughly that their ruins were not uncovered for more than 1600 years!

Molten rock below the surface of the earth that rises in volcanic vents is known as *magma*, but after it erupts from a volcano it is called *lava*. It is red-hot when it pours out of the vent, but it slowly changes to dark red, gray, or black as it cools. If lava erupts in large volumes, it flows over the surface of the earth. Generally, very hot lava is fluid, like hot tar, whereas cooler lava flows more slowly, like thick honey.

All lava as it comes to the surface of the earth contains dissolved gas. If the lava is a thin fluid, the gas escapes easily. But if the lava is thick and pasty, the gas escapes with explosive violence. Gas in lava may be compared with the gas in a bottle of soda pop. If you put your thumb over the top of the bottle and shake it, the gas separates from the pop and forms bubbles. When you remove your thumb, there is a miniature explosion of gas and pop. The gas in lava behaves in somewhat the same way. It causes the terrible explosions that throw out great masses of solid rock as well as lava, dust, and ashes.

The violent separation of gas from lava may produce rock froth, called *pumice*. Some of this froth is so light that it floats on water. In many eruptions the froth is broken into small fragments that are hurled high into the air in the form of volcanic ash (gray), cinders (red or black), and dust.

Geysers and hot springs, such as those in Yellowstone National Park, are generally found in regions of volcanic activity. Rainwater sinking into the ground is heated by hot rocks, and the hot water and steam rise to the surface along fissures and cracks in the rocks. Sometimes geysers and hot springs are called dying volcanoes, because they seem to represent the last stage of volcanic activity as the magma in the earth cools and hardens.

Rocks and Minerals

ROCKS

A stone hops and skips its way across the quiet surface of a sun-warmed woodland pond, making exactly four jumps into the air. On the shore a child carefully searches for another very special stone—one that will "five-jump" its way across. The stone must be flat, disc-shaped, smooth, and of course able to be held comfortably and firmly in the child's hand. There are many ways to spend part of a summer afternoon; searching for special stones and skipping them across a pond is probably one of the better ones.

The special stones are not easy to find, for they are partially hidden in the soil. Their essential qualities are invisible to everyone except the child who is searching for them. To everyone else they are simply rocks. To the child they are treasures. They serve a purpose. The fact of their existence allows the child the freedom to do something. A rock is only a rock to someone who has no sense of its larger meaning. Rocks are much more than what they seem at first glance. Indeed, they provide us with many of the things that make possible an enjoyable and productive life. From rocks come the soils that nourish plants; the minerals we use

Figure 8A–2. Some Igneous Rocks (*Source:* William A. Andrews et al., *Soil Ecology.* Englewood Cliffs, N.J.: Prentice-Hall, Inc., 1973. Used with permission.)

for nutrients, fertilizer, adornment, and raw materials for manufacture; and, of course, the special stones that skip across the surface of a quiet pond on a hot summer day.

Igneous rocks are formed from the heating or cooling of melted materials in the earth. The word *igneous* comes to us from a Latin word that means "coming from fire." Igneous rocks on the surface of the earth are exposed to the elements of the hydrosphere and atmosphere. Such agents as water, wind, and temperature changes cause the chemical and physical breakdown of igneous rocks, a process known as *weathering*. The particles and pieces of igneous rock that are removed by weathering are moved from place to place by the wind, water, and in some cases glaciers. This movement is known as *erosion*. Much weathered matter is washed into streams and rivers and eventually transported to the oceans. Thus, matter that was originally inland igneous rocks is deposited in layers at the water's edge to form beaches, or, more commonly, settles in layers on the ocean floor.

Sandstone

Shale

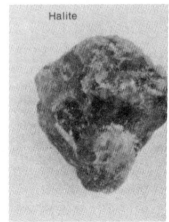

Halite

Figure 8A–3. Three Sedimentary Rocks (*Source:* William A. Andrews et al., *Soil Ecology*. Englewood Cliffs, N.J.: Prentice-Hall, Inc., 1973. Used with permission.)

Material from igneous rocks that is transported to the oceans is known as *sediment*. Over a long period of time, layers of sediment may become pressed together. Such layers eventually become *sedimentary* rocks. This type of rock can be formed from particles that were originally part of any other type of rock.

When rock is heated or pressed together for a long time it can change. Such rock is known as *metamorphic* rock. Fashioned deep within the earth, metamorphic rocks are formed from igneous or sedimentary rocks. The term *metamorphic* comes from Greek words that mean "change" and "form."

Slate

Schist

Gneiss

Figure 8A–4. Three Common Metamorphic Rocks (*Source:* William A. Andrews et al., *Soil Ecology*. Englewood Cliffs, N.J.: Prentice-Hall, Inc., 1973. Used with permission.)

At the edge of a swiftly moving mountain stream a solitary prospector swirls a pan filled with water and sand. With each careful circular movement some water and sand flow out of the pan and into the stream. The prospector does not see what leaves his pan but only what remains. His fixed gaze, arched back, and tightly knit brow reveal his intense concentration. He does not hear the chatter of nearby birds, the echoes of a far-off logging tractor, or the rush of the stream. He is totally focused on the remnants at the bottom of the pan. He gives the pan one quick final swirl, and a few golden flecks materialize right before his eyes. He has found gold. A slight grin breaks across his weather-beaten face. Once again he has found gold.

The tiny particles of gold have taken a long path. At one time they were part of rocks high up on the mountainside. The action of water and wind broke them free of the rocks and brought them into the uppermost reaches of the mountain stream. The swiftly moving water carried them on a twisting and turning path to the place where the prospector managed to uncover them.

Gold, silver, and platinum are well-known and highly valued substances found in the rocks of the earth's crust. They are examples of minerals—naturally occurring chemical elements or compounds. Rocks are combinations of minerals. Many mineral compounds include oxygen and another element found in abundance in the earth's crust—silicon. These compounds are known as silicates.

There are a variety of silicates, among them quartzes, feldspars, and micas. Quartz consists of one silicon atom for every two oxygen atoms. It is a very hard mineral since its atoms are tightly joined. Feldspars commonly contain aluminum-oxygen and silicon-oxygen combinations of atoms. In some feldspars, sodium, calcium, or potassium replaces the aluminum. Feldspar is a softer mineral than quartz. Micas are groups of silicate minerals whose atomic patterns cause them to be easily separated into thin sheets. *Biotite* and *muscovite* are two minerals that are micas.

Silicates are not the only minerals found in the earth's surface. There are also ores—rocks that contain quantities of useful metal—and gems—crystals that have an unusual color and the ability to reflect light from their many faces, or facets. Other nonsilicate minerals are calcite, gypsum, halite, and fluorite. Sulfur and graphite are nonsilicate minerals that are elements. An element is a substance composed of just one type of atom.

How Can Minerals Be Identified? Scientists are able to identify the minerals in rocks by performing laboratory tests. Each mineral has a variety of identifying characteristics, including color; streak—the color it leaves when it is rubbed against a piece of porcelain; luster—the property of reflecting, bending, or absorbing light; the form of its crystals; cleavage and fracture—how it splits or breaks apart; its relative weight; and hardness—how easily it can be scratched. Figure 8A–5 shows the hardness of common minerals as determined by a measuring system known as Mohs' hardness scale. As you can see from this chart, you can easily determine the hardness of a mineral by scratching it with common materials.

In addition to the common characteristics noted above, a mineral may display some special properties, such as magnetism—being attracted to a magnet; fluorescence—glowing under ultraviolet light; phosphorescence—glowing after an ultra-

mohs' hardness scale		some common materials and their place in the hardness scale		
hardness	mineral	hardness	common material	comment
1	Talc	about 2.5	Finger nail	Will scratch gypsum with difficulty but will not scratch calcite.
2	Gypsum			
3	Calcite			
4	Fluorite	about 3	Copper	Scratches calcite; will also be scratched by calcite.
5	Apatite			
6	Feldspar			
7	Quartz	about 5 to 5.5	Glass	With difficulty scratches apatite; is also scratched by apatite.
8	Topaz			
9	Corundum			
10	Diamond	about 5.5 to 6	Knife Blade	Will scratch feldspar with difficulty.
		about 7	File	Will scratch quartz with difficulty.
Explanation: A given mineral will scratch those minerals above it in the table and will be scratched by those below it.		about 9	Silicon Carbide	With difficulty will scratch corundum; will be also scratched by corundum.

Figure 8A–5. The Mohs' Hardness Scale and the Place of Some Common Materials in It (*Source:* Ramon E. Bisque, Harold Pratt, and John F. Thompson, *Earth Science: Patterns in our Environment.* Englewood Cliffs, N.J.: Prentice-Hall, Inc., 1975. Used with permission.)

violet light that has been shining on it is turned off; and radioactivity—giving off rays that can be detected by a Geiger counter.

The Parade of Life: The Story in the Rocks

FOSSILS

Today life exists virtually everyplace on earth. At this very moment microscopic organisms are floating in the air you breathe, deep in the oceans creatures are swimming about carrying out their life processes, and in California giant sunlit sequoia trees are producing food from water and carbon dioxide. The earth contains billions of living things, which display amazing variety in both their appearance and their behavior. However, life as we know it has apparently changed a great deal over the five billion years in which the earth has existed. Fortunately, there is a record of the type and quantity of living things that have lived on earth—a record maintained in the rocks.

We are certain that long ago dinosaurs lived in Utah, that great mammoths lived in Canada, and that swampy forests once stretched across parts of Pennsylvania and Illinois. We are certain because we have found evidence of their existence in the rocks. The evidence that tells us the story of life is in the form of fossils.

Fossils are created in a variety of ways. Since dead plants and animals usually decay quite rapidly, it is only the harder parts of their bodies that are preserved. This explains why teeth, shells, bones, and woody tissues are all commonly found fossils. If plant or animal remains are covered by a protective material soon after death, the likelihood of fossilization increases. For example, the remains of creatures that live in the water fall to the bottom of the lake or sea floor, where soft mud and sand stirred by water currents may bury them. Fossils that form in such environments are preserved in the sedimentary rocks that have been created by the deposition of materials.

Fossils are seldom found in igneous rocks, since the process by which such rocks are formed would tend to destroy any fossilized remains of living things. However, windblown ash from volcanic activity may settle on animal or plant material and provide a protective covering that increases the likelihood of fossilization. Yellowstone National Park in Wyoming contains fossilized remains of forests that were covered by volcanic ash and dust.

Some unfossilized remains of plants and animals that lived millions of years ago have been found. At least one mammoth has been discovered preserved in ice. Natural mummies have also been found. Amber, a fossilized plant resin, has served as the final resting place for a variety of small plants and animals.

Tar pits are the source of beautifully preserved animal bones. The La Brea tar pits in the Los Angeles area are probably the most well-known source of bones of animals that lived thousands of years ago. Apparently, the animals became stuck in these natural tar pools. The tar has acted as an excellent preservative and has provided scientists with excellent specimens of plant and animal life.

The hard portions of animals such as bones or shells are typically fossilized as a result of the presence of water containing compounds that replace the hard portions with other minerals. Typically, shells that were originally calcium carbonates may be completely replaced during the fossilization process.

Some fossils are found in the form of molds or casts. For example, seashells that are buried in mud and sand may eventually dissolve in the water. The cavity

Figure 8A–6. This reconstruction of an American Mastodon becoming entrapped in a La Brea tar pool captures the anguish of that moment in time. Fossilized remains found in the La Brea tar pools have provided us with a great deal of information about early life on our continent. (*Source:* Abruscato.)

Figure 8A–7. On display at the La Brea Museum, this reconstruction of saber-toothed tigers and their cubs is based on the fossilized remains of this extinct species. What creatures will people be able to see only in museums a few hundred years from now? (*Source:* Abruscato.)

that is left may preserve the outline of the shell and its surface. Minerals from ground water may settle in this mold and eventually form a cast of the original shell.

The earliest humanlike creature seems to have appeared about four or five million years ago. Fossils dating to that time have been found in Africa. Over that period humans developed into their present form. Modern humans—that is, creatures that would appear to us to be very much like ourselves—have probably existed for about 100,000 years. Our present physical and mental capabilities mark us as a species with an enormous capacity to both adapt to diverse environments and change environments to fit our needs.

THE DINOSAURS

What Did They Look Like? Few members of the parade of life offer as much fascination to children and adults as the dinosaur. Dinosaurs were air-breathing animals who ranged in size from that of chickens to that of whales. Their body forms varied considerably from species to species: Some walked on two feet, others on four; some had horns, others had talons, and still others were distinguished by large teeth. Some dinosaurs were meat eaters and others were vegetarians.

Tyrannosaurus was a dinosaur that reached a length of 14 meters (about 47 feet), weighed more than an elephant, had teeth that were 8 to 15 centimeters (about 3 to 6 inches) long, huge feet, powerful claws, and relatively small, grasping "animal hands." It spent most of its time on land, moved about on two legs, and was a meat eater.

Brontosaurus was a large, amphibian, and probably vegetarian dinosaur. It walked on four legs and had a very large and long neck. Fossil evidence of a brontosaurus over 21 meters (about 67 feet) long has been found in Colorado.

Figure 8A–8. In this painting the artist has depicted a ferocious *Tyrannosaurus* attacking a *Triceratops*. Notice the small dinosaur in the foreground trying to get away before the action begins. (*Source:* Atlantic Richfield Company.)

Like the other dinosaurs, brontosaurus and its vegetarian relatives eventually became extinct. Scientists are not sure why this happened, but conjecture that their huge bulk made it difficult for them to move to new environments as changes occurred in their natural habitat.

Stegosaurus was about 6.5 meters (21 feet) long, moved about on four limbs, and had a small head and brain and a large, curved, armor-plated back. The armor consisted of a double row of upstanding plates over the full arch of the back and two or more spikes on a powerful tail that was an effective weapon for warding off attackers. Although its brain was small, stegosaurus had a large nerve center in its pelvis that controlled the muscles of the tail and the rear legs.

Triceratops was one of a group of horned dinosaurs. Its huge head was approximately one third its entire length. On its head were one small horn and to large ones. Its bony crest apparently protected its neck. Triceratops was 7 meters (about 22 feet) long and was a vegetarian.

Why Did They Become Extinct? There is much debate over this question. The fossil evidence reveals that the peak of the dinosaurs' development occurred near the end of the Cretaceous period in the Mesozoic era. What happened to the various species of dinosaurs is one of the continuing mysteries that scientists hope to solve eventually. Some scientists suggest that catastrophes such as earthquakes and volcanoes killed the dinosaurs. This theory does not explain why *only* the dinosaurs would have been destroyed: other life forms obviously survived such events. Changes in climate may have changed the vegetable and animal life upon which dinosaurs fed. If this was the case, however, some species of dinosaurs should have survived, since there were places where such climatic changes did not occur. Perhaps one of the children you teach will someday develop a theory that satisfactorily explains the extinction of the dinosaur.

THE EARTH'S ATMOSPHERE AND WEATHER

The atmosphere, that thin layer of air surrounding the earth, is continually changing. When we use the term *weather* we are really describing the condition of our atmosphere at a given time. That condition changes from day to day. Daily weather reports tell us in specific terms how hot, cold, windy, dry, wet, sunny, or cloudy it is. Some people confuse the meaning of *weather* and *climate*. The difference between them is not difficult to understand. Weather is the day-to-day changes in the atmosphere. Climate is the total effect of these changes in a particular region.

There are many causes of changes in the weather. Principal among them is the sun. The earth receives almost all its heat energy from the sun. This energy causes many changes in the atmosphere, including the warming of air and its subsequent upward movement, the evaporation of water into the atmosphere, and the movement of air we call wind. These changes all play a part in determining the extent and type of precipitation (rain, snow, hail, sleet) that reaches the earth's surface. Storms are violent weather changes.

Scientists who study the weather and predict weather changes are called meteorologists. Every county has meteorologists who gather weather data from a variety of sources, summarize it, place it on a weather map, and then make predictions. Information is recorded on weather maps by means of various symbols. Figure 8A−9 shows weather maps for a two-day period and an explanation of the symbols used.

Water in the Atmosphere

We drink it, wash with it, raise crops with it, and depend on it for our survival. Water is a necessary ingredient for all life on this planet. Fortunately, we are blessed with an abundant supply of this life-giving, colorless, odorless, and tasteless substance. An invisible ocean of it surrounds the Earth. This water in the air is part of a process we call the water cycle. This process involves the evaporation of water from streams, rivers, ponds, lakes, and oceans; the movement of the water vapor into the atmosphere; and the eventual condensation of the vapor into clouds and precipitation.

One of the tasks of a meteorologist is to compare the amount of moisture in the air to the maximum amount of moisture the air could hold at that temperature. The resulting percentage is the *relative humidity*. When the relative humidity is high we usually feel uncomfortable, since the air contains a great deal of moisture and the evaporation of our perspiration is slowed down. The evaporation of perspiration is one of the principal ways in which our bodies lose heat. Anything that retards the process will make us feel warm and uncomfortable.

When the temperature in the air drops to a certain point, the water vapor in the air can no longer be held by it. Air at this temperature is *saturated*. The temperature at which a given body of air becomes saturated is the *dew point*.

At the surface of the earth, water enters the air by evaporation. The sun's energy warms this air and carries it and the water vapor it contains upward. As air rises in the atmosphere it cools. When the rising air is cooled to its dew point,

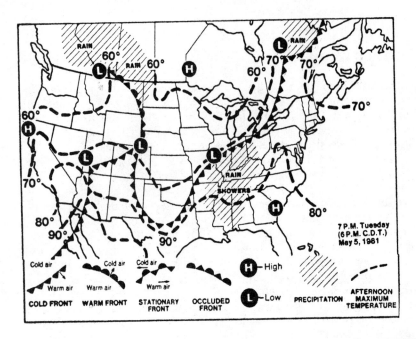

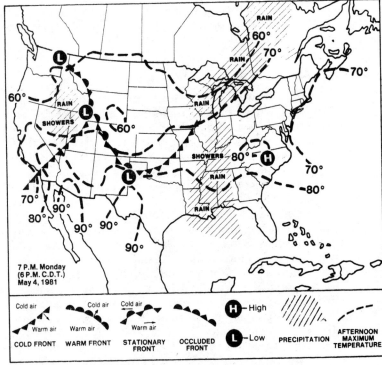

Figure 8A–9. The Daily Weather Map for Two Successive Days (*Source: The New York Times.*)

condensation may occur. Drops of water are formed when enough molecules of water vapor accumulate around and become attached to a particle of dust in the atmosphere. Billions of tiny droplets of water form the weather phenomenon we call a cloud. Clouds have been classified by meteorologists according to their appearance from the ground.

CLOUDS

Clouds[2] are visible evidence of moisture in the air. The moisture may be in the form of liquid water droplets or ice crystals, or both. The type of cloud is an indicator of the stability of the atmosphere in which it forms. Stratiform (layered) clouds indicate generally stable conditions that change rather slowly. Clouds with cumuliform (vertical) development indicate a degree of instability in the atmosphere which produces rapid changes in the clouds. Because of these indications, weather forecasters find it most helpful to have accurate descriptions of the clouds at each weather-observing site. Since clouds are continuously growing or decaying, they appear in an infinite variety of forms. However, it is possible to define a limited number of characteristic forms generally observed all over the world into which clouds can be broadly grouped.

Low clouds include fog, stratus, stratocumulus, cumulus, and cumulonimbus. The average heights of their bases range from the surface up to 1980 meters (about 6500 feet). Low clouds are usually made up entirely of water droplets, and are usually quite dense.

Middle clouds include both altocumulus and altostratus, and the average heights of their bases range from 1980 to 7000 meters (about 6500 to 23,000 feet). They are made up of water droplets, ice crystals, or both—usually both—and they exhibit considerable variation in density. In a dense water-droplet cloud a pilot in flight may be able to see only a few feet, whereas in an ice-crystal cloud visibility may be as much as a mile.

High clouds are the cirrus, cirrocumulus, and cirrostratus. Their bases are generally above 5030 meters (about 16,500 feet). They are always made up of ice crystals and vary greatly in density. A distinguishing feature of cirriform clouds is the halo they produce around the sun or moon as a result of refraction of the sunlight or moonlight shining through the ice crystals. Lower clouds (altostratus) containing water droplets exhibit the solar- or lunar-corona phenomenon rather than the halo.

Clouds exhibiting great vertical development constitute another major category. This category includes all the low cumulus clouds except the fair-weather cumulus and stratocumulus. The cumulonimbus, or "thunderhead," is in a category by itself because it may extend from the very lowest to the very highest levels of the atmosphere and during its life cycle may produce nearly all the other cloud types.

[2]The discussion of clouds beginning on this page was excerpted with minor modifications from *Clouds*, a pamphlet prepared by and available from the Environmental Science Service Administration, U.S. Department of Commerce, Washington, D.C. 20013.

Figure 8A–10. This cumulonimbus cloud has a distinctive anvil top. (*Source:* U.S. Department of Commerce, NOAA.)

The Condensation of Water Vapor

Water vapor in the atmosphere is returned to the earth in a variety of ways. Some of it leaves the atmosphere as a result of condensing on the earth's surface. A great deal of it leaves by first condensing in the atmosphere and then falling to the earth. Both processes play central roles in the water cycle and nourish the earth with water.

SURFACE CONDENSATION

Air that is close to the ground may come in contact with surfaces that can cool it to its dew point. Moisture in the air that is in direct contact with cold surfaces may condense into droplets of water. This type of surface condensation is known as dew. The tiny droplets of water found clinging to plant stems and leaves on a cool morning are the result of the condensation of water vapor.

If the air temperature is low enough to cause the water vapor to change directly from a solid, frost may form on surfaces. Frost is not frozen dew, but rather ice crystals formed directly from water vapor.

PRECIPITATION

Water vapor that condenses in the atmosphere and falls to the earth is called precipitation. Rain is moisture that falls to the earth as a liquid. The rain that reaches the earth has many effects. Some simply falls into bodies of water. Rain that falls to the ground can eventually be used by plants and animals. Rainwater can penetrate the surface of the earth and become part of the total water supply available to a region. When rainfall is so heavy that most of it cannot pass through the surface, the excess unabsorbed water may cause streams, rivers, and lakes to overflow their banks.

If the temperature is low enough, water vapor can change to snow. A snowflake is usually a six-sided, lacy-patterned product of the direct change of water to a solid. Large snowflakes result from the combination of smaller snowflakes. Surprisingly, snow that falls to the ground can have the beneficial effect of insulating the soil below from cold temperatures. The lack of a good snow cover can freeze soil to great depths and destroy plant roots. This remarkable protective function results from the numerous pockets of air trapped within a blanket of snow. These air pockets effectively retard the loss of heat from the earth below to the much colder air that lies above the snow cover. Snow, of course, also causes many problems for transportation. The removal of snow from roads and railroads involves great effort and expense.

Hard, rounded pellets of ice or ice and compacted snow are called hail. If you cut a hailstone in half you will see that it consists of concentric layers. Hail is a phenomenon associated with thunderstorms. Water droplets caught in a strong updraft of warm, moist air may be carried into cloudy regions where the temperature is quite low. At these altitudes they acquire a coating of ice and solidify. They may then fall to a lower cloud region and gather a coating of water. Another strong updraft may carry the hailstones back up to a region of lower temperature. The ultimate size of the hailstones depends on many factors, including the number of times this up-and-down cycle is repeated. Eventually the hailstones become so heavy that no updraft can carry them, and they fall to earth.

Some meteorologists think that hail is formed by a much simpler process: water droplets fall through below-freezing layers of air and pick up extremely cold water, which is transformed into layers of ice. Although the precise way in which hail is formed may be under question, its destructive effects are agreed upon. Large hailstorms can beat down crops, break tree branches, destroy roofs, shatter glass, and injure animals and humans.

Sleet is a form of precipitation that has a different meaning to meteorologists than it does to the general public. Sleet is the term used by meteorologists to describe small particles of clear ice that were originally raindrops. It results from the passing of the rain drops through a layer of cold air. In everyday life we commonly use the term to describe a mixture of rain and snow.

What Instruments Are Used to Observe the Weather?

Meteorologists use a variety of instruments to observe the weather. The pressure of the air above us is measured with a barometer. The wind vane is used to determine the direction of the wind at the earth's surface. Wind speed is measured with an anemometer, an instrument consisting of a set of cups mounted so that they can easily be rotated by the wind. The amount of moisture in the air is determined by a hygrometer. The amount of moisture that reaches the ground as precipitation is measured by rain and snow gauges.

The characteristics of the air high above the earth are commonly determined by the use of radiosondes. These are miniature radio transmitters to which are attached a variety of weather instruments. Radiosondes are carried aloft by balloons or small rockets. Data gathered by the instruments are transmitted back to earth by the radio transmitter.

In recent years weather satellites have greatly improved the accuracy of weather forecasts. Their photographs of the clouds over the earth's surface reveal a great deal about weather phenomena. Such satellite photography, when used with information about air temperature, atmospheric pressure, and humidity, is of great assistance to meteorologists as they develop their weather forecasts for a particular area.

Violent Weather: The Storms

THUNDERSTORMS

Thunderstorms[3] are generated by temperature imbalances in the atmosphere. They are a violent example of convection—the upward and downward movement of air. The cooling of cloud tops, or the warming of the cloud base, puts warmer, lighter air layers below colder, denser layers. The resulting instability causes convective overturning of the layers, with heavier, denser layers sinking to the bottom and the lighter, warmer air rising rapidly.

On the ground directly beneath the storm system, strong gusts of cold wind from the downdraft and heavy precipitation (rain or hail) typically mark the storm. Tornadoes may be associated with especially violent thunderstorms.

Lightning. Lightning is an effect of electrification within a thunderstorm. As a thunderstorm develops, interactions of charged particles produce an intense electrical field within the thundercloud. A large positive charge is usually concentrated in the frozen upper layers of the cloud, and a large negative charge along with a smaller positive area is found in the lower portions.

The earth is normally negatively charged with respect to the atmosphere. But as the thunderstorm passes over the ground, the negative charge in the base of the cloud induces a positive charge on the ground below and for several miles around the storm. The ground charge follows the storm like an electrical shadow, growing stronger as the negative cloud charge increases. But air, which is a poor conductor of electricity, insulates the cloud and ground charges, preventing a flow of current until huge electrical charges are built up.

Lightning occurs when the difference between the positive and negative

---

[3]The discussion of thunderstorms beginning on this page was excerpted with minor modifications from *Thunderstorms*, a pamphlet prepared by the U.S. Department of Commerce. This pamphlet (stock number NOAA/PA 77027) may be purchased from the Superintendent of Documents, Government Printing Office, Washington, D.C. 20402.

charges—the electrical potential—becomes great enough to overcome the resistance of the insulating air and to force a conductive path that will allow current to flow between the two charges. The potential can be as much as 100 million volts. Lightning strokes proceed from cloud to cloud, cloud to ground, or, where high structures are involved, from ground to cloud.

Thunder. Thunder is the sound produced by explosive expansion of air heated by a lightning stroke. When lightning is close by, the thunder sounds like a sharp crack. More distant strokes produce growling and rumbling noises, a result of the sound being refracted and modified by the turbulent environment of a thunderstorm. Because the speed of light is about a million times that of sound, we see a lightning bolt before the sound of the thunder reaches us. This makes it possible to estimate the distance (in miles) to a lightning stroke by counting the number of seconds between lightning and thunder and dividing by five.

TORNADOES

Consider the following report of the course of a tornado:

> At 4:29 P.M., the tornado roared into the Southwest corner of the city, took a Northeast path through homes, apartments, an industrial area, across Interstate 80, into the crowded business area, and lifted on the north side in Benson Park at about 4:59 P.M. It was 600 yards—550 meters—wide, packed 150–200 mph—240–320 kph—winds, and traveled about 9 miles—15 km—on the ground. Officials estimate 31,000 people lived or worked in the 200-block area that caught the full fury of the storm. When it was all over, there were 3 dead, about 200 injured, and more than 2,000 homes, apartments, or businesses destroyed or damaged.[4]

Their time on earth is short, and their destructive paths are small. But the march of a tornado through a populated area leaves a path of terrible destruction. In seconds it can transform a thriving street into a ruin and hope into despair.

Tornadoes are short-lived local storms containing high-speed winds usually rotating in a counterclockwise direction. These are often observable as a funnel attached to a thundercloud. The funnel is initially composed of nothing more than condensed water vapor and is itself a cloud. However, when it reaches the ground it usually picks up dust and debris, which eventually darken the entire funnel. Tornado damage can occur on the ground even though the visible funnel does not seem to reach ground level.

Tornadoes occur in many parts of the world. But no area is more favorable to their formation than the Great Plains and Gulf Coast of the United States and in these areas no season is free of them. Normally, the number of tornadoes is lowest in December and January and at its peak in May. The months of greatest frequency are April, May, and June.

---

[4]*Tornado*, pamphlet prepared by the U.S. Department of Commerce, National Oceanic and Atmospheric Administration, National Weather Service, January 1978 (stock number 003-018-00085-7). Superintendent of Documents, U.S. Government Printing Office, Washington, D.C. 20402.

WINTER STORMS

In September the sun leaves the Northern Hemisphere, its perpendicular rays drifting south of the Equator. Until the sun's return in March, polar air rules the northern continental atmosphere, pushing back the tropical warmth of summer. It is autumn, then winter, a season broken by intervals of fine weather and by the seasonal parade of winter storms[5]—snow-dumping, ice-covering, blood-chilling paralyzers of cities, trappers of travelers, takers of life, destroyers of property.

Snowstorms. The word *snow* in a forecast, without a qualifying word such as *occasional* or *intermittent*, means that the fall of snow will probably continue for several hours without letup. There are a variety of terms used by meteorologists to describe winter storms. They include: heavy snow warnings, snow flurries, snow squalls, blowing and drifting snow, drifting snow, blizzards, blizzard warnings, severe-blizzard warnings, travelers' warnings, and stockmen's warnings.

Freezing Rain, Freezing Drizzle, and Ice Storms. Freezing rain or freezing drizzle occurs when surface temperatures are below 0°C (32°F). The moisture falls in liquid form but freezes upon impact, resulting in an ice glaze on all exposed objects. The occurrence of freezing rain or drizzle is often called an *ice storm* when a substantial glaze layer accumulates. Ice forming on exposed objects generally ranges from a thin glaze to coatings of two or three centimeters (about an inch), but much thicker deposits have been observed.

Ice storms are sometimes referred to incorrectly as *sleet storms*. Sleet can be easily identified as frozen raindrops (ice pellets) that bounce when hitting the ground or other objects. Sleet does not stick to trees and wires, but in sufficient depth it does cause hazardous driving conditions.

The terms *ice storm, freezing rain*, and *freezing drizzle* warn the public that a coating of ice is expected on the ground and on other exposed surfaces. The qualifying term *heavy* is used to indicate an ice coating whose weight will cause significant damage to trees, overhead wires, and the like. Damage will be greater if the freezing rain or drizzle is accompanied by high winds.

Cold Waves. Cold waves are another common form of winter storm. A *cold-wave warning* indicates an expected rapid fall in temperature within a twenty-four-hour period that will require substantially increased protection to agricultural, industrial, commercial, and social activities. The temperature falls and the minimum temperatures required to justify cold-wave warnings vary with the season and with geographic location. Regardless of the month or the section of the country, a cold-wave warning is a red-flag alert to the public that during a forthcoming forecast period a *change to very cold weather will require greater-than-normal protective measures.*

[5]The discussion of winter storms beginning on this page was excerpted with minor modifications from *Winter Storms*, a pamphlet prepared by the National Oceanic and Atmospheric Administration, U.S. Department of Commerce. This pamphlet (stock number NOAA/PI 70018) may be purchased from the Superintendent of Documents, Government Printing Office, Washington, D.C. 20402.

HURRICANES

There is nothing like hurricanes[6] in the atmosphere. Even seen by sensors on spacecraft thousands of miles above the earth, the uniqueness of these powerful, tightly coiled storms is clear. They are not the largest storm systems in our atmosphere, or the most violent, but they combine those qualities as no other phenomenon does, as if they were designed to be engines of death and destruction.

In our hemisphere they are called *hurricanes*, a term that echoes colonial Spanish and Caribbean Indian words for evil spirits and big winds. The storms are products of the tropical ocean and atmosphere, powered by heat from the sea and steered by the easterly trades, the temperate westerlies, and their own fierce energy. Around their tranquil core, winds blow with lethal velocity, the ocean develops an inundating surge, and, as they move ashore, tornadoes may descend from the advancing bands of thunderclouds.

Hurricanes have a single benefit: they are a major source of rain for the land beneath their track. Perhaps there are other hidden benefits as well. But the main consequences for people are hardship and tragedy.

Tomorrow's Weather

The weather here tomorrow is very likely to be much the same as the weather someplace else today. The reason for this is that changes in the conditions of the atmosphere (the weather) tend to move in regular patterns above the earth's surface. As a result, the most important tool that the weather forecaster has is the weather map. He or she studies the most recent weather maps and tries to predict both the strength of the disturbances observed and their path. The forecaster also studies the map to see where and how new disturbances are being formed.

Meteorologists in North America know that in the middle latitudes the upper air moves from west to east. Storms tend to enter from the west, pass across the middle of the continent, and move toward the North Atlantic.

The weather that is likely to affect a local area is predicted on the basis of the larger-scale weather movement. More specifically, the meteorologist's prediction is based on an interpretation of the data gathered at weather stations and recorded on the weather map. The map itself is created by first recording symbols representing pressure, temperature, humidity, wind direction, wind velocity, and cloud types. The meteorologist then fills in the map by drawing in lines called *isobars* that connect regions of equal pressure. By studying the isobars and the other information on the map, the meteorologist identifies regions of the atmosphere that have approximately the same characteristics. The masses of air in these regions are the key weather producers: their movement creates the clouds and storm systems that may come into or form in an area. The regions where the air masses move internally with one another are called fronts. By studying the formation and movement of

[6]The discussion of hurricanes beginning on this page was excerpted with minor modifications from a pamphlet prepared by the U.S. Department of Commerce. This pamphlet (stock number NOAA/PA 76008) may be purchased from the Superintendent of Documents, Government Printing Office, Washington, D.C. 20402.

fronts and combining such information with geographic features of the local area *and* the present local weather, the meteorologist can make a weather forecast.

Daily forecasts are of immediate interest to us since the weather has a substantial affect on our lives. Long-range forecasting, however, is possibly of greater general significance. It is extremely important, for example, to the success of farmers and livestock producers. The quality, availability, and prices of the foods we purchase depend to no small measure on the ability of farmers and ranchers to plan for their crops and livestock. The length of a growing season, for example, is a critical factor in the size of a crop. With good long-range forecasting farmers can delay harvests, knowing when crop-endangering weather will probably occur. Among other things, the National Weather Service prepares weekly and monthly estimates of temperatures and rainfall amounts that can be expected. These projections indicate to farmers and ranchers (and to the rest of us as well) how close to normal the weather conditions will be within a region.

In making a long-range forecast the meteorologist first prepares a weather map for the coming month that contains lines showing air-pressure predictions. These predictions take into account historical weather data for the region during that month. The air pressures for previous years are then adjusted on the basis of current information about such things as storm systems, snow cover, land temperatures, and ocean temperatures. Along with these factors meteorologists consider the relationship beween the present flow of air in the upper atmosphere and the present surface weather. The results of all these variables is a long-range weather forecast for the region.

SUMMARY OUTLINE

I. The earth consists of various layers; the outermost layer is the crust.

    A. The crust of the earth has undergone numerous gradual and violent changes during the earth's history.

    B. The crust of the earth is composed of a variety of rocks, minerals, and soils.

    C. Fossil evidence of life forms that existed in various periods of the earth's history has been found.

II. The atmosphere is a thin layer of constantly moving air that surrounds the earth.

    A. Water vapor in the atmosphere sometimes condenses to form clouds.

    B. Some water vapor in the atmosphere condenses and falls to earth as precipitation.

    C. Barometers, anemometers, and hygrometers are some of the instruments used to measure weather phenomena.

    D. Thunderstorms, winter storms, tornadoes, and hurricanes are examples of violent weather phenomena.

    E. Scientists are able to make both short-term and long-term weather forecasts.

chapter

The Earth's Surface, Atmosphere, and Weather

DISCOVERY ACTIVITIES
AND DEMONSTRATIONS

DISCOVERY ACTIVITIES

How Do Layers of Sediment Form?*

OBJECTIVE

The children will make a model that displays the production of layers of sediment.

SCIENCE PROCESSES EMPHASIZED

> Observing
> Experimenting
> Communicating

MATERIALS FOR EACH CHILD OR GROUP

> Large glass jar
> Source of water

*Asterisks refer to activities for young children.

Figure 8B–1. A Rock Magician (*Source:* J. Abruscato and J. Hassard, *The Whole Cosmos Catalog.* Santa Monica, Calif.: Goodyear Publishing Company, Inc., p. 48. Used by permission of Goodyear Publishing Company.)

Soil
Pebbles
Gravel
Sand

MOTIVATION

This is a good activity to do before the children begin studying how various rocks are formed. In particular it will give the children an opportunity to see how the materials carried by water settle out to form layers of sediment. These layers of sediment may eventually form sedimentary rocks. To motivate the children simply display at the front of the room or at a learning station all of the materials listed above. Ask the children to guess what this activity will be about. After some initial discussion, focus their attention on the soil, pebbles, gravel, and sand. Ask them to think about what would happen if a stream carrying these earth materials suddenly slowed down. This should get them thinking about the dropping of the materials carried by the stream and their settling into layers. When the discussion reaches this point, group the materials that they need for the activity.

DIRECTIONS

1. Have each group of children place equal amounts of soil, pebbles, gravel, and sand in the large glass jar. They should adjust the quantities so that only about one third of the jar is filled with the materials.
2. Have the children fill the jar the rest of the way with water.
3. Have the children shake the jar so that all the earth materials are thoroughly stirred up in the water.
4. Ask the children to let the materials settle out.
5. Have the children observe the settling out of the various earth materials in layers. When this is accomplished have them make drawings of their layers. Then engage the class in a discussion of the results of the activity.

KEY DISCUSSION QUESTIONS

1. Which of the earth materials settled to the bottom of the jar first? *The gravel.*
2. How can you explain the results that you had in the activity? *The large pieces of gravel settled first because they were heavier than the other earth materials. The heaviest materials at the bottom and the lightest materials at the top.*
3. What types of rock are formed from layers of earth material that settle out of water? *Sedimentary.*

SCIENCE CONTENT FOR THE TEACHER

When water moves across the surface of the earth it picks up tiny rocks, pebbles, grains of sand, and soil and carries them along. This flow of water and earth materials eventually reaches streams, rivers, and the ocean. These bodies of water carry along the particles of earth they have received, which are known as sediment.

Whenever a flow of water is slowed, some of its sediment is deposited. Layers of sediment pile up under the water, and after hundreds of years have passed, the weight of these layers may have become so great as to turn the bottom layers of soil into rock.

EXTENSIONS

Science. You may wish to have one group of children repeat the activity, this time with larger jars and larger quantities of sediment. You will probably need to help them stir the sediment thoroughly. This larger jar can then be used as a permanent display of the layering of sediments.

Science/Social Studies. Some children may be encouraged to do some research on the effect of moving water on farmland. The loss of topsoil to moving water is a significant threat to agriculture. With their research these children will find that there are many government agencies that assist farmers who are trying to protect their soil from erosion.

How to Make a Fossil*

OBJECTIVES

The children will create a fossil of a sample of plant material.
The children will explain the process by which fossils are produced in nature.

SCIENCE PROCESSES EMPHASIZED

Hypothesizing
Experimenting
Communicating

MATERIALS

For Each Child or Group

Aluminum-foil pie plate
Plastic spoon
Plaster of paris
Water
Vaseline
Assortment of plant materials, including portions of a carrot, a leaf, and a twig

For the Teacher

2 or 3 real fossils
Reference books that display pictures of a variety of fossils

MOTIVATION

Display the fossils and have children make observations of their characteristics. Then have the children discuss how the fossils might have been formed. Tell the children that they will be creating their own fossils during this activity.

DIRECTIONS

1. Have the children first coat each portion of plant they will be using with a thin layer of Vaseline.
2. Now have the children mix the plaster of paris with water in the bottom of the pie plate until they obtain a thick, smooth mixture.
3. Have the children gently press the plant material into the upper surface of the plaster of paris. They should now set the plaster aside to dry and harden.
4. Bring the children together for a group discussion. Emphasize that what they have done represents *one* way in which fossils are formed: that is, the settling of rock material and minerals carried by water upon plant or animal material, producing an imprint when the organic material decays.
5. When the plaster is dry the children will be able to observe a permanent imprint in it when they remove the plant material.
6. Establish a display of the reference books showing the pictures of fossils. Have the children look at them and hypothesize about how the fossils were formed.

KEY DISCUSSION QUESTIONS

1. Have you ever found any fossils or seen any on display? If so, what were they like and where did you see them? (*Answers will vary.*)
2. The fossils you made are known as *molds*. How could a scientist use a mold fossil to make something that looked like the object that formed the mold? *He or she could use something like clay to press against the mold fossil. The surface of the clay would take the shape of the original plant material.*

SCIENCE CONTENT FOR THE TEACHER

A fossil is any preserved part or trace of something that lived in the past. Leaves, stems, bones, and even footprints have been preserved as fossils. Some fossils are formed when water passing over and through portions of animal or plant remains deposits minerals that replace the original materials. In other cases animal and plant remains are buried in sediment and then completely washed away. An imprint of their shape is left in mud, and if the mud hardens and turns to rock the imprint can be preserved. This type of impression is known as a mold. The activity above provides children with an opportunity to replicate this latter type of fossilization.

EXTENSIONS

Science. You may wish to encourage some children to do an activity that extends their knowledge of fossil molds to fossil casts. They can replicate the formation of a cast fossil by mixing plaster of paris outdoors and filling in animal tracks with it.

Science/Art. You may with to encourage some children to become involved in making mold fossils of a variety of vegetable surfaces, using a separate small disposable container for each. These children can then arrange their fossils on a sheet of heavy cardboard with an assortment of magazine pictures of the vegetables used to form a collage that displays their work.

Quakes and Shakes: An Earthquake Watch

OBJECTIVE

The children will be able to locate those regions of the earth that have more earthquake activity than other regions.

SCIENCES PROCESSES EMPHASIZED

Interpreting data
Making a hypothesis

MATERIALS FOR EACH CHILD OR GROUP

This is a long-term activity in which children plot data from current government information regarding earthquakes during the year. Thus, you will need to order the *Preliminary Determination of Epicenters: Monthly Listing* (from the Superintendent of Documents, Government Printing Office, Washington, D.C. 20402. An annual subscription costs $10.00.).
World map with latitude and longitude marked
Access to an atlas
Paper
Pencil

MOTIVATION

Ask the children if any of them has ever been to a part of the country that has a lot of earthquake activity, such as San Francisco. If so, have them discuss anything they may have heard about earthquakes from persons who live there. If no one has visited an area where earthquakes occur, you may wish to engage the children in a discussion about earthquakes. Stress their cause and possible hazards. Explain that scientists are able to study information about previous earthquakes to predict the general location of future earthquakes. Tell them that they will be working with some of the very same information that scientists use. Then display the collection of epicenter charts and the world maps.

DIRECTIONS

1. Give a map and copies of the epicenter charts to each child or group. Explain to the children that the information on the charts shows where scientists believe the source of an earthquake was. Then explain this information. Although there is a lot of information on each chart, the children should work only with the date, time of eruption, latitude, longitude, region, depth, and magnitude. Explain that magnitude indicates the strength of the earthquake.

2. Have the children refer to an atlas to find the specific location of each earthquake and then mark their copy of the world map with a symbol for it. They should plot all earthquakes with a source from 0 to 69 kilometers deep with one symbol, 70 to 299 kilometers with another symbol, and more than 299 kilometers with a third symbol.

3. When they are done with this, ask them to gather more information.

4. When they have recorded data from epicenter chart you may wish to have a discussion of the patterns they observe.

5. Have the children maintain their maps for a few months and repeat the activity each time you receive a monthly epicenter chart.

KEY DISCUSSION QUESTIONS

1. Do you see any patterns on your map that tell what parts of the earth seem to be the source of most earthquakes? Where are these places? *Yes, along the western portion of the Pacific Ocean, from the Mediterranean Sea across Asia, and along the west coast of North and South America.*

2. What problems do you think are caused by earthquakes? *Answers will vary. Some may include comments such as the following: those that break apart the land can cause buildings to fall; those that move parts of the ocean floor can cause great waves.*

SCIENCE CONTENT FOR THE TEACHER

An earthquake is the shaking of the ground caused by the breaking of underground rock layers. The vibrations at ground level are sometimes strong enough to do structural damage to buildings and threaten life. The shaking of the ocean floor can produce gigantic waves that roll across the ocean. Scientists record the presence of an earthquake with an instrument known as a seismograph. To pinpoint the source of an earthquake's vibrations, scientists gather data from seismographs all over the world. This source, or epicenter, is thought to be directly above the place where the initial rock fractures occurred—the focus of the earthquake. When the locations of epicenters are plotted on a map, they roughly mark the places on the earth where crustal plates grind against each other.

EXTENSIONS

Science/Social Studies. Some children may wish to do research to find out what the effects of the San Francisco earthquake of 1906 were. They will be able to find pictures in encyclopedias showing how the city looked after the earthquake. Ask the children to predict what effects the earthquake had on community life after the earthquake and then after a few years had passed.

Science/Language Arts. Some children may be encouraged to read accounts of the devastation caused by various major earthquakes and create letters that might have been written by survivors describing what had occurred.

How to Find the Dew Point

OBJECTIVE

The children will find the temperature at which the water vapor present in the air condenses.

SCIENCE PROCESSES EMPHASIZED

Observing
Gathering Data
Interpreting

MATERIALS

Empty soup can with one end cut out
Outdoor thermometer that will fit in the soup can
Supply of ice cubes
Rag

Figure 8B–2.

MOTIVATION

Begin a discussion with the children about the invisible water vapor present in the air by having them present any evidence they may have observed about the presence of water vapor. They will probably share such observations as the steaming up of mirrors in bathrooms and the steam that seems to come out of their mouth when they breathe on a cold day. Tell the children that water vapor is present in the air, but is usually not observed because the air temperature is sufficiently high to keep the water vapor a gas. As a gas, water vapor is invisible. Display the equipment that will be used for this activity and tell the children that they will be using it to find the temperature at which the water vapor presently in the air will condense. In other words, the children will be determining how cold the air will have to be in order for water vapor to change from a gas to a liquid.

DIRECTIONS

1. Distribute the soup cans to the children and have them remove the labels. Then have them scrub the outside of the can (the bare metal) with soap and water and polish the surface.

2. Demonstrate the following procedure for the children. Fill the shiny can about two-thirds full of water at room temperature and place a thermometer in it. Then add small amounts of ice and stir the mixture until the ice melts. Have the children observe the outside of the can as you continue adding small amounts of ice and stirring. Eventually the outside of the can will begin to lose its shine and a layer of moisture will be observable on its surface.

3. Now have the children do this activity on their own. Ask them to keep track of the temperature on the thermometer and pay close attention to the outside of their shiny can as the temperature drops. Stress the importance of their observing the precise temperature at which the film forms on the outside of the can.

4. After the children have found the dew point inside the classroom you may wish to have them find it outside. When the children have completed the activity begin a class discussion of their results. Be sure the children understand that the drier the air, the lower the temperature must be in order for moisture to condense.

SCIENCE CONTENT FOR THE TEACHER

The air's capacity to hold moisture is determined by its temperature. The temperature to which a parcel of air would have to be cooled in order to reach the point at which it no longer holds its moisture is known as the dew point. Condensation, the change from water as a gas to water as a liquid, is usually observable in our atmosphere as dew, fog, or clouds. All these forms of condensation occur when the air is saturated with water vapor. Saturation occurs when the temperature of the air is lowered below its dew point. If the air is saturated and a surface is available on which the water vapor can condense, we can see the resulting dew, fog, clouds, or precipitation. In the activity above, the air near the outside surface of the can was cooled to its dew point. The moisture in that layer of air condensed on the available surface—the outside of the can.

KEY DISCUSSION QUESTIONS

1. Why do you think we use a *shiny* can for this activity? *It makes it easy to tell when the moisture condenses. The moisture makes the shiny can look dull.*
2. Why do you think knowing the dew point might be important to weather forecasters? *If they know the dew point they will know the temperature at which the moisture in the air will condense. Then they can more easily predict when fog, clouds, or rain will happen.*
3. Why do you think dew forms only at night? *During the night the temperature of the air falls because the earth is not receiving sunlight. Sometimes the temperature falls so low that the dew point is reached. When this happens, the moisture condenses on grass and on the leaves and branches of plants.*

EXTENSIONS

Science/Math. You may wish to have some children find the dew point with both Celsius and Fahrenheit thermometers. Afterwards they can determine through the use of conversion charts whether the number of degrees Celsius is equivalent to the number of degrees Fahrenheit.

Science. You may wish to have a group of students invent solutions to a common problem—the formation of fog on highways and airport runways. You could have this group use their new knowledge of the dew point to invent devices that would eliminate these formations. The children could make drawings of their inventions showing how they would operate on highways or airport runways.

ADDITIONAL ACTIVITY IDEAS

Taking Things for Granite: Making a Rock Collection*

Children enjoy collecting things, and rocks are relatively easy for children to collect and organize. Using egg cartons or other materials, they can design display cases for their samples. The children will be curious about the names of the rocks they collect. One way for them to identify their specimens is to check any of the common paperback field guides to rocks and minerals. These books are available at local bookstores. If your children discover rocks that are more difficult to identify, you may wish to have them visit the high-school earth-science teacher for some assistance. You might want to encourage some of the children to scrub their rocks and display them in creative ways—for example, on an assortment of tiny wooden pedestals that they make themselves. Each rock can be identified at the bottom of its pedestal. Rock collections can serve as an interesting display of your children's work in their study of the earth's surface.

Comparing Rocks*

Children can use any collection of rocks and minerals to carry out various tests that reveal similarities and differences among rocks. They can perform a rudimentary color test by comparing rocks against a painter's color chart. You can get an assortment of such charts at any store that sells household paints. Children will enjoy trying to find the color or colors that most closely approximate a rock sample.

Children can use vinegar to replicate one way in which geologists compare rocks. Geologists apply a weak acid to rocks to see if they contain materials such as calcium carbonate. These compounds fizz when acid is applied. Children can conduct the same basic test with white vinegar. They may have to put the rock samples in vinegar and then heat the vinegar in order to get a reaction. They should see bubbles forming on the surface of the rock. Any collection that contains such rocks as quartz, limestone, kaolinite (the most common constituent of clay), calcite, white marble, and chalk will provide some interesting acid tests. Ask the children to put small particles of these minerals in containers, cover each with vinegar, and make observations at twenty-four-hour intervals to see if any of the rocks are affected by the vinegar.

Children can reproduce another test used by geologists: studying the powder left behind when a rock is rubbed across interiorlike porcelain; the color of the streak helps geologists identify the rock. Children can perform this test—the streak test—by rubbing samples of various rocks across a porcelain plate.

How Does Water Get into the Atmosphere?*

Children can study the process of evaporation simply by preparing three containers of water and marking the water level in each. The containers are then placed in various locations in the schoolroom and observed on successive days. Each time the children observe the container they should mark the side of it with a marking pen so that the amount of water lost will be evident. After a few weeks the children can share their data and discuss the process of evaporation. This can lead to a larger discussion of the water cycle.

What Kind of Cloud Was That?

Each child in the class can maintain a daily log of the various types of clouds he or she observes in the sky. Prior to this activity the students should become familiar with the basic cloud types by studying textbook pictures. Encourage the children to make drawings of the clouds they observe so that their identifications can be verified. This type of activity provides an opportunity for children to learn not only to make accurate observations of phenomena but also to keep careful records—time, date, and place—of their observations. When you have a class discussion of the results of this activity be sure, then, to have the children indicate not only the observations they made but also the time, date, and place of the observations.

What Did the Old-Timer Say?

Many of the senior citizens in your community will have excellent stories to tell about severe weather they have observed over the years. A group of children could interview and possibly tape-record responses from a number of senior citizens to such questions as "What's the worst weather you can remember in this area? When did it happen? What did the people do when it happened?" An interesting variation would be to try to locate senior citizens who have traveled widely and who can share with children their stories about various extremes of climate they have observed. Among the many important goals this activity can accomplish, perhaps the most important is that it gives children an appreciation of the life experiences of the senior citizens in their community.

DEMONSTRATIONS

You've Heard of Rock Musicians, but Have You Heard of Rock Magicians?

OBJECTIVES

The children will observe a surprising characteristic of each of five rocks.
The children will describe each characteristic observed.
The children will name each of the rocks used in the demonstration.

SCIENCE PROCESSES EMPHASIZED

Observing
Communicating

MATERIALS

Samples of the following rocks: pumice, anthracite, asbestos, calcite, willemite (or any rock that will fluoresce)
Bowl of water
Sheet of paper
Matches
White vinegar, or any dilute acid
Any ultraviolet-light source (you may be able to borrow one from a high-school earth-science teacher)
Optional: bow tie, magic wand
Very optional: top hat and/or cape!

MOTIVATION

Because of the nature of this demonstration you will need very little motivation to get the children's attention. You may wish to be the rock magician. However, you may happen to have a child who would be perfect for the part! Assemble the materials and organize the classroom so that all the children will have a good view of what is to transpire.

1. The rock magician should use the above materials to demonstrate the following:
   a. The floating rock: pumice will float in water.
   b. The writing rock: anthracite will write on paper.
   c. The rock that can resist flame: asbestos fibers will not burn.
   d. The fizzing rock: a few drops of vinegar will cause calcite to fizz.
   e. The fluorescent rock: with the room darkened the willemite will fluoresce when placed under ultraviolet light.
2. Have the children write down their observations.
3. The magician should name each rock, spell it, and write its name on the chalkboard. The children thereby learn the name of each rock displayed.

KEY DISCUSSION QUESTIONS

1. Why do you think geologists are interested in the special characteristics of these rocks? *They can tell a lot about what the rock is made of if it does certain things.*
2. Why do you think the pumice floated? *It has lots of air trapped in it.*
3. Do you think the material in your pencils might be something like the anthracite? Why? *Yes, both can make marks on paper.* (*Note:* The material in pencils these days is not lead but graphite. Graphite is essentially carbon. Anthracite is also carbon.)

SCIENCE CONTENT FOR THE TEACHER

Pumice is magma (molten rock) that trapped bubbles of steam or gas while being thrown out of a volcano. When such magma solidifies, it is honeycombed with gas-bubble holes. This gives it the buoyancy to float on water.

Anthracite is a type of coal that results from the partial decomposition of plants. The carbon in the plants is the primary constituent of anthracite and other forms of coal. Carbon particles are not closely built to one another and can thus be easily fractured.

Asbestos is the popular name of the mineral chrysotile. The silky fibers of asbestos can be woven into a yarn that is used in brake linings and in heat- and fire-retardant fabrics.

Calcite is a mineral found in such rocks as limestone and marble. Geologists test for its presence by placing a few drops of a warm acid on the rock under study. If calcite is present, carbon-dioxide gas will be released with a fizz by the chemical reaction.

Willemite is a mineral that fluoresces. That is, it gives off light when exposed to ultraviolet light. Some other minerals, generally available from science-supply companies, that can be used to demonstrate fluorescence are calcite, tremolite, fluorite, and scapolite.

EXTENSIONS

Science/Social Studies. You may wish to follow this demonstration with a map or study exercise in which the children find out where the various rocks and minerals come from. They will need some earth-science reference books and an atlas.

Science. You may wish to have some children use the information gathered from this demonstration as well as from other activities involving the properties of rocks and minerals to create a detailed chart of rock and mineral characteristics.

Indoor Rainmaking*

OBJECTIVES

The children will observe the production of rain in a storm.[1]
The children will explain how the rainmaking model can represent the water cycle.

SCIENCE PROCESSES EMPHASIZED

Observing
Inferring
Explaining

MATERIALS

Hot plate or stove
Teakettle
Large pot
Ice cubes
Water

MOTIVATION

Use the materials to motivate the children for the demonstration. Ask them to suggest how the materials could be used to make a model showing how rain forms. With some discussion they will be ready to observe the demonstration and follow the path of the water. You may wish to have a volunteer assist you with the steps described below.

DIRECTIONS

1. Place water in the teakettle and begin to heat it. As the water is heating put the ice cubes in the pot.

[1]The activity on indoor rainmaking beginning on this page is based on an activity of the same name in Joe Abruscato and Jack Hassard, *The Whole Cosmos Catalog* (Santa Monica, Calif.: Goodyear, 1977), p. 66.

Figure 8B–3. (*Source:* J. Abruscato and J. Hassard, *The Whole Cosmos Catalog.* Santa Monica, Calif.: Goodyear Publishing Company, Inc., p. 66. Used by permission of Goodyear Publishing Company.)

2. When the water in the teakettle is boiling, hold the pot above the steam emerging from its spout. Have children observe the formation of water droplets on the bottom of the pot.

3. Eventually the children will see some water droplets become large enough to fall.

4. Using the questions below, discuss the rainmaking process as a model.

KEY DISCUSSION QUESTIONS

1. What do you think the teakettle of boiling water stands for in the model? *Oceans and lakes.*

2. How does water from the oceans and lakes get into the atmosphere? *The sun heats the water and it evaporates.*

3. Where are the clouds in our model? *The steam stands for the clouds.*

4. Rainmaking is part of the water cycle. What do you think scientists mean when they talk about the water cycle? *Water is always moving. Water that leaves the lakes and oceans moves into the air. Water that is in the air forms clouds and sometimes falls to the earth. Rain, snow, sleet, and wind fall onto the land and oceans. Water that reaches the land flows back into the oceans and lakes.*

SCIENCE CONTENT FOR THE TEACHER

Water on our planet is being continually recycled. The path that water takes in nature is known as the water cycle. Water that evaporates from oceans, lakes, and rivers enters the atmosphere. Precipitation forms when this water vapor accumulates around dust particles at low temperatures and high altitudes. The water then returns to earth.

EXTENSIONS

Science. Some children may be encouraged to do research to find out how precipitation other than rain is formed. They may be able to present to the class what they learn about the formation of snow, sleet, and hail.

Science/Language Arts. Some children may wish to use this demonstration of a rainmaking model as a starting point for writing poetry about the principal form of precipitation in their area. They could write their poetry on large sheets of paper suitable for display.

ADDITIONAL DEMONSTRATION IDEAS

Making and Using a Stream Table

You can simulate the action of a moving stream on a layer of rock and soil by means of a simple stream table. The table itself can be a shallow cardboard box made waterproof with an inner covering of plastic from heavy-duty garbage bags. A large baking pan could also be used for the table. Add a layer of sand to the container. Have the children observe what happens when the stream table is tilted and a continuous stream of water is directed at its upper end. Through this demonstration the children can observe how the water that forms the "stream" over the sand surface carries away sediment. You can also display various effects caused by increasing or slowing the rate of water flow.

Up, Up, and Away: Wind and Balloons*

You can demonstrate that the atmosphere is in constant movement by taking children outside to release several helium-filled balloons. You can get balloons filled with helium by locating an industry in your community that uses it. Check the classified section of your phone book for suppliers of gases, and call them to locate a manufacturer whom they supply with helium. When the balloons are filled and tied, have the children attach a plastic sandwich bag containing return-addressed postcards and a note to the finder requesting his or her name and address. To get the best results, release the balloons on various days of the week so that they are subjected to wind from various directions. This will increase the likelihood of at least some balloons reaching a populated area.

chapter 9A

The Cosmos

CONTENT

A LOOK AHEAD

HOW WAS THE UNIVERSE FORMED?

> For the scientist who has lived by his faith in the powers of reason, the story ends like a bad dream. He has scaled the mountains of ignorance; he is about to conquer the highest peak; as he pulls himself over the final rock, he is greeted by a band of theologians who have been sitting there for centuries.[1]

This is how one authority on the scientific explanation of the formation of the universe reflects on the strange coincidence between scientists' age-old search for truth and religious belief about creation. Clearly, the theory of an all-at-once creation of matter has a great deal in common with explanations of the creation of the universe found in many of the world's religions.

Recent evidence seems to indicate that the universe—all the matter and energy that exists anywhere—had a beginning. It is possible that other universes preceded the present one, but if so, all the evidence of the prior universe was

[1]Robert Jastrow, *God and the Astronomers* (New York: W. W. Norton and Co., Inc., 1978), p. 116.

Figure 9A–1.

apparently destroyed the moment our present universe was created. Although we will probably never know for sure how it all began, scientific evidence is now rapidly accumulating in support of a theory that has existed for over fifty years. This theory is known as the big-bang theory.

The big-bang theory tells us that about twenty billion years ago the universe was created as a result of a fiery explosion. This is supported by various evidence, including astronomical observations that all the galaxies (clusters of stars) known to humans have been moving apart from one another at enormous speeds. By reasoning backward from this present outward movement of galaxies, we see that all the matter of the universe was once packed together.

The theory of a big bang or cosmic explosion is also supported by a discovery made in 1965 by Arno Penzias and Robert Wilson of the Bell Laboratories. They discovered and measured the strength of faint radiation that came from every direction in the sky. The entire universe seemed to be immersed in this radiation. Measurements of the strengths and forms of this radiation coincide exactly with what would have resulted from an enormous explosion occurring fifteen to twenty billion years ago. This theory is in conflict with another theory, which Penzias and Wilson call the steady-state theory. The steady-state theory suggests that new matter is continually created in the universe as "old" matter is changed into energy.

WHAT IS THE UNIVERSE?

The universe is all the matter, energy, and space that exists. Within it are *billions* of clusters of stars. Each of these clusters, or galaxies, contains *millions* of stars, clouds of dust, and gas. The galaxy of stars that contains our sun is known as the Milky Way. The stars of our galaxy are so far from one another that measurement in kilometers (or miles) would be impossible to imagine. As a result, astronomers use a measuring unit called the light-year. A light-year represents the distance that light travels in one year. Light travels 299,792 kilometers (about 186,000 miles) in just one second, so one light-year represents a distance of 9,450,000,000,000 kilometers (about 6,000,000,000,000 miles). The Milky Way galaxy is tens of thousands of light-years in length and one eighth that distance in width. Astronomical evidence seems to indicate that our galaxy has a spiral shape. The closest star to our sun is Alpha Centauri. This star is more than four light-years away. The distance from the Milky Way to the nearest galaxy is 1,500,000 light-years. Galaxies themselves are thought to be parts of clusters of other galaxies, dust, and gas called nebulae.

CONSTELLATIONS

Ages ago people looked up at the night sky and saw that the stars seemed to be organized into patterns. Each area of the sky containing such a grouping was identified as a constellation. All the stars within such an area were considered part of the constellation. Many constellations were given names from mythology. Others were named for their apparent resemblance to familiar animals and objects. At present there are eighty-eight constellations having a name.

The easiest constellations to recognize are the polar constellations. These groups of stars are located around the North Star (Polaris). To locate the North Star, first find the constellation known as the Big Dipper. By sighting along an imaginary line between the two stars at the rim of the Big Dipper, you should be able to locate the North Star.

OUR SUN, A STAR

With all of the new solar data pouring in from spacecraft, the sun[2] is proving more complex than ever. But the answers to many questions may be hidden in the data now on hand.

On one subject, however, most scientists seem to agree: how the sun was born and how it will die. They have even calculated how much longer it has to live: five billion years as a normal, or main-sequence, star.

Astronomers hold that the sun and planets formed from an enormous contracting cloud of dust and gas. All parts of this cloud did not move uniformly. Some parts formed local condensations that eventually became our planets, moons, comets, and asteroids.

Gradually, the main cloud tended to become spherical. Gravitational contraction increased its temperature. Eventually the core temperature rose to a point where its hydrogen nuclei began to fuse. Nuclear energy then produced enough outward pressure of heated gas to balance the inward force of gravity and maintain the sun as a glowing main-sequence star. This process is believed to have begun about five billion years ago.

About five billion years from now, the sun will have depleted the hydrogen fuel in its core. Its thermonuclear reactions will then move outward where unused hydrogen exists. At the same time, the tremendous nuclear heat at the sun's core will also move outward, expanding the sun by as much as sixty times. As the sun cools by expansion, its surface color will become a deep red. It will then be a red giant—not a main-sequence star. Looming across much of our sky, it will boil off our water and air and incinerate any remnants of life.

When the sun exhausts its hydrogen fuel, it will no longer be able to withstand gravitational contraction. Eventually, it will shrink to a white dwarf, no bigger than Earth but so dense that a piece the size of a sugar cube would weigh thousands of kilograms. Eventually, after billions of years more, our sun will cool and dim to a black cinder. Only then will eternal night fall upon the solar system.

OUR SOLAR SYSTEM

Our sun, its nine planets, and associated clouds and bodies of matter make up what we call the solar system. The solar system is the place in the universe that has in its midst the planet Earth.

[2]The discussion of the sun beginning on this page was excerpted with modifications from *Our Prodigal Sun*, a pamphlet prepared by the National Aeronautics and Space Administration. This pamphlet (stock number 3300-00569) can be purchased from the Superintendent of Documents, Government Printing Office, Washington, D.C. 20402.

The Planets

After the sun condensed, planets[3] of different sizes and probably different compositions were formed at various distances from it. Electric and magnetic fields of the original nebula could have forced these newly formed planets into orbits around the central sun and spun them on their own axes.

As they condensed, the inner planets of the solar system lost lighter elements, such as hydrogen and helium, because they were too hot—as a result of their closeness to the sun—to hold these gases. Their relatively weak gravities were another cause for their loss of lighter elements. The outer planets, however, retained their hydrogen. Thus, the planets of the solar system consist of rocky inner planets—Mercury, Venus, Earth and its moon, and Mars—separated by the asteroid belt from fluid outer planets—Jupiter and Saturn, whose compositions are similar to that of the sun, and Uranus and Neptune, which may be ice giants. Pluto is thought by some scientists to be a large example of an outer belt of asteroidal bodies from which comets may be originating today. In some respects, too, it behaves as a very distant satellite of Neptune.

There are striking differences among the five inner planets, and particularly between the Earth and the others. These differences are important to our understanding of why the Earth is as it is today, and why the other planets are different despite their formation from common building blocks at about the same time.

Mercury is moonlike in some respects, a cratered world with virtually no atmosphere, but displaying evidence of volcanic activity after its formation and bombardment molding, and also showing contraction around a very dense core. Mercury, like the moon, rotates very slowly on its axis: three rotations for every two revolutions around the sun. The moon rotates once each revolution around Earth. Mars and Earth rotate quickly in close to 24 hours. Venus has a unique backward rotation of 243 days.

After the formation of the planetary bodies there appears to have been a period of planetary heating in which more dense material sank toward the center of each planet to form a core, while less dense material rose to form a crust. The moon and Mercury still show much of the ancient cratered surface on which there are some lava flows. Mercury exhibits compressive shrinkage around a cooling, iron-rich core.

Volcanic activities on the planetary bodies would release gases from their interiors: water vapor and carbon dioxide with traces of other gases. On Mercury and the moon these gases escaped into space; they were lost from Mercury because of high temperatures close to the sun, and from the moon because of its weak gravity. But on Venus, Earth, and Mars the gases were retained, so that these planets still have atmospheres.

Today, however, these atmospheres are very different. Venus has an extremely dense atmosphere of carbon dioxide, at the bottom of which the surface of the planet is hot enough for lead to melt (480°C; 900°F). On Mars the atmosphere is again predominantly carbon dioxide, but at a very low pressure, and the

---

[3]The discussion of the planets beginning on this page was excerpted with modifications from *NASA Facts*. This pamphlet (stock number 75-0-579-914) can be purchased from the Superintendent of Documents, Government Printing Office, Washington, D.C., 20402.

planet has a cold surface. On Earth the atmosphere is predominantly nitrogen with some oxygen and traces of carbon dioxide. Most of the earth's carbon dioxide has been bound with the rocks of the earth's crust as carbonates because of the presence of much water. Both Venus and Mars seem very deficient in water compared with the earth, which may be why their atmospheres are predominantly carbon dioxide. The physical characteristics of both the inner and outer planets are shown in Figure 9A−2.

Mars: A Closer Look

PHYSICAL CHARACTERISTICS OF MARS

Mars[4] is the outermost of the solar system's rocky inner planets. Mars is not a large planet: it is between Mercury and Earth in size. Its equatorial diameter is 6786 kilometers (4217 miles) compared with Earth's 12,756 kilometers (7926 miles). It rotates on its axis, as does Earth, but in 24 hours 39 minutes. So day and night on Mars are almost the same lengths of time as on Earth. The Martian day has been called a Sol by space experimenters planning expeditions to the Martian surface. A Mars year consists of 670 Sols (687 Earth days).

Mars's axis, like that of Earth, is not perpendicular to the plane of its orbit. It is tilted 25 degrees, compared with Earth's axial tilt of 23.5 degrees. So Mars too experiences seasons, as one hemisphere and then the other tilts toward the sun because of the movement of Mars around its orbit. But, because Mars's distance from the sun varies considerably during a Martian year, the Martian seasons are more complicated than seasons on Earth.

Mars is closest to the sun during spring in the planet's southern hemisphere; thus, southern-hemisphere spring on Mars is always warmer than northern hemisphere spring. Summer in the northern hemisphere is also long because Mars is moving slowly along its orbit close to aphelion (its furthest distance from the sun), but it is a cool summer. Mars receives about 44 percent more solar radiation per unit area of surface at perihelion (its closest distance to the sun) than at aphelion; surface temperatures can thus vary considerably. The south polar cap of Mars almost disappears during the hot southern-hemisphere summer, whereas the north polar cap has never been observed to disappear as viewed from Earth. Actually neither cap disappears completely: there is a small permanent cap even at the southern polar region of the planet.

SATELLITES OF MARS

Mercury and Venus do not have satellites. Earth has its unusually large moon. Mars has two very small satellites that can be observed in large telescopes at a close

---

[4]The discussion of Mars beginning on this page was excerpted with minor modifications from *Mars and Earth*, a pamphlet prepared by the National Aeronautics and Space Administration. This pamphlet (stock number 033-000-00621-7) is available for purchase from the Superintendent of Documents, Government Printing Office, Washington D.C., 20402.

	MERCURY	VENUS	EARTH	MARS	JUPITER	SATURN	URANUS	NEPTUNE	PLUTO
Mean distance from sun (millions of kilometers)	57.9	108.2	149.6	227.9	778.3	1,427	2,869	4,496	5,900
Period of Revolution	88 days	224.7 days	365.26 days	687 days	11.86 years	29.46 years	84.01 years	164.8 years	247.7 years
Rotation period	59 days	−243da. retrograde	23 hrs. 56 min. 4 sec.	24 hrs 37 min. 23 sec.	9 hrs. 50 min. 30 sec.	10 hrs. 14 min.	−15 hrs. retrograde	22 hrs. or less	6 days 9 hrs.
Equatorial diameter (kilometers)	4,880	12,104	12,756	6,787	142,800	120,000	51,800	49,500	6,000(?)
Mass (Earth = 1)	.055	.815	1	.108	317.9	95.2	14.6	17.2	.1(?)
Volume (Earth = 1)	.06	.88	1	.15	1,316	755	67	57	.1(?)
Density (Water = 1)	5.4	5.2	5.5	3.9	1.3	.7	1.3	1.7	?
Atmosphere (main components)	None	Carbon dioxide	Nitrogen, oxygen	Carbon dioxide	Hydrogen, helium	Hydrogen, helium	Helium, hydrogen, methane	Hydrogen, helium, methane	None detected
Known satellites	0	0	1	2	13	10 + 3 rings	5 + 5 rings	2	0

Figure 9A−2. The Planets of Our Solar System: Their Location and Characteristics

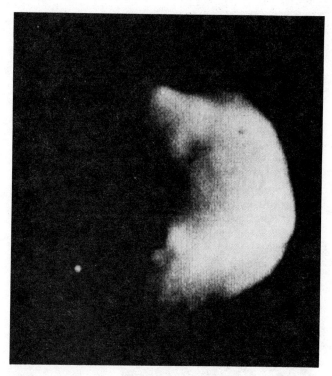

Figure 9A–3. Mariner 9 Photo of Deimos (*Source:* "Mars as a Member of the Solar System," *NASA Facts*. Washington, D.C.: U.S. Government Printing Office, 1976.)

opposition of the planet. At the 1971 opposition they appeared in a twenty-four-inch telescope as tiny spots of light almost hidden in the glare of the planet itself.

In 1610 Johannes Kepler predicted that Mars might have two satellites, on the grounds that Earth had one and Galileo had seen four satellites of Jupiter. It was a wild guess, but it probably was known to Jonathan Swift, the English satirist, who in his *Gulliver's Travels*, published in 1726, wrote of two lesser stars or satellites revolving around Mars. But these two satellites were not actually seen until 1877. Asaph Hall, their discoverer, named the two tiny worlds Deimos and Phobos (Flight and Fear, respectively) after the horses that draw the chariot of Mars.

The Martian moons revolve very close to their planet. Phobos, the inner satellite, revolves in 7 hours and 40 minutes in an almost circular orbit only 6005 kilometers (3700 miles) above the surface of Mars. The tiny, odd-shaped satellite is about 27.2 kilometers (16.9 miles) long and 19.4 kilometers (12.0 miles) wide. Deimos orbits at 23,500 kilometers (14,600 miles) in 30 hours and 18 minutes. It is even smaller than Phobos—16 kilometers (9.9 miles) long and 11 kilometers (6.8 miles) wide. From the dark appearance of these satellites and their heavily cratered and irregular shapes as seen by close-up photography from NASA's Mariner spacecraft, scientists conclude that Deimos and Phobos were formed perhaps three or four billions of years ago and possibly are captured asteroids.

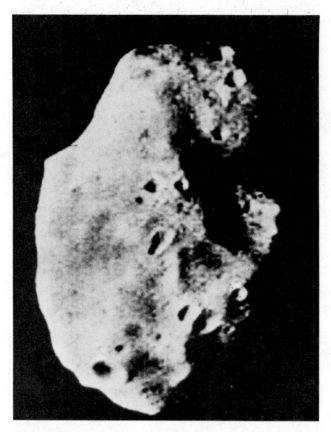

Figure 9A–4. Mariner 9 Photo of Phobos (*Source:* "Mars as a Member of the Solar System," *NASA Facts.* Washington, D.C.: U.S. Government Printing Office, 1976.)

Meteors

Meteors are masses of stone and iron from space that move through our atmosphere and sometimes strike the earth. Some have a mass of less than one gram. Others have masses of thousands of kilograms. Although many meteors enter our atmosphere, very few reach the surface of the earth. Most are simply burned up by the friction they produce as they move through the atmosphere. Some meteors are so large that part of them remains after their journey through the atmosphere. A meteor that reaches the earth's surface is known as a meteorite. Scientists have various theories about the origin of meteorites. Most think they originated in our solar system, perhaps from the band of planetlike objects between the orbits of Mars and Jupiter.

Comets

Comets are heavenly bodies that move in large orbits around the outside of our solar system. Occasionally a comet may be pulled from its normal orbit and move toward the sun. Comets are thought to be composed of solidified ammonia, carbon dioxide, and ice. This solid portion of a comet is known as its head. Comets have a characteristic tail that is formed by the evaporation of the solidified matter by energy from the sun. The tail of a comet always points away from the sun. Although comets do not produce light themselves, energy from the sun causes the material of their head and tail to give off light.

Asteroids

Between the orbits of Mars and Jupiter lies a belt of objects that are smaller than any of the planets—the asteroids. Scientists are not sure how the asteroids were formed. Some believe they are the remnants of an explosion of a planet that formerly existed between Mars and Jupiter. Others think they may just be "leftovers" from the materials that combined to form Mars and Jupiter.

Some asteroids leave their orbit and cross the paths of planets or moons. Craters observed on the moon and on Mars are probably the result of collisions with asteroids. Some craters on Earth can be explained most easily as a result of the collision of asteroids with Earth millions of years ago.

QUASARS, PULSARS, AND BLACK HOLES

Quasars[5]

A healthy quasar each year eats up as much energy as our sun will use in its entire existence.[6]

Quasars may be the same size as large stars, yet they emit energy at all wavelengths equivalent to that of a thousand galaxies and produce more energy in a given volume than any other object in the sky. They were first called Quasi-Stellar Objects when discovered in 1963 by radio astronomers because they were point sources of radio energy—starlike—instead of diffused over large areas of the sky like all previously discovered radio sources. To astronomers, finding a quasar is like finding a flashlight that shines as brightly as all the lights in the entire Los Angeles basin.[7] Understanding their energy processes could be a key link to new theories on the structure of matter itself.

Quasars are controversial objects because observations do not yet permit conclusive interpretation. They are believed to be receding at enormous velocities—up to 92 percent of the speed of light—because of the huge red-shifts of their spectral lines. Objects moving at this speed must be billions of light-years distant, near the limits of the observable universe. One newly discovered quasar,

[5]The discussion of quasars, pulsars, and black holes beginning on this page was excerpted with minor modifications from *Quasars, Pulsars, Black Holes . . . and HEAO's*, a pamphlet prepared by the National Aeronautics and Space Administration. This pamphlet (stock number 003-000-00542-3) is available for purchase from the Superintendent of Documents, Government Printing Office, Washington, D.C. 20402.

[6]Marten Schmidt, "Light-Years Past Copernicus," *Newsweek*, May 7, 1973, p. 62.

[7]*Astronomy and Astrophysics for the 1970's*, Vol. 1, Report of the Astronomy Survey Committee (Washington, D.C.: National Academy of Sciences, 1972), p. 4.

OQ 172, is believed to be the most remote recorded object in the universe. Calculated to be ten billion light-years from earth, it started sending out its energy before the sun, the earth, or the moon existed—even as stellar dust. If quasars are that remote from us, they may be among the youngest observed objects and may prove important to cosmological research by revealing what the early universe was like.

Pulsars

> During the collapse . . . the stellar matter passes from the atomic regime of condensed matter and atomic physics through the nuclear realm . . . to the still mysterious realms of elementary particles. . . . In this one collapse, the star sweeps through much of modern physics.[8]

Formed from the collapsed remnants of supernovae explosions, pulsars are extremely dense, rotating neutron stars with intense magnetic fields. They are believed to generate beams of directional energy that sweep across space like a lighthouse beacon. According to this mode, when the beam wipes across earth, it appears as a pulse.

When first formed, pulsars may spin up to 1000 revolutions per second. Their diameter is typically 19.3 kilometers (about 12 miles). When the first pulsar was discovered in 1967, the remarkable regularity of its pulse rate was initially interpreted as a meaningful signal from another intelligent civilization.

A very rich pulsating source for future investigations is Hercules X-1, a binary x-ray star that exhibits a wide variety of pulse periods and interactions with its visible companion. At least one of the pulse periods is produced by eclipses of the x-ray star by this larger companion.

Another important pulsar in the Crab Nebula has been observed in the radio, optical, x-ray, gamma-ray, and infrared regions of the spectrum. This spinning star, like the rotor in an electrical-power generator, produces most of the Crab Nebula's energy. Collapse to a neutron star converts the gravitational potential energy of the particles in the original star into kinetic energy of explosion and rotation. Squeezed by its collapse, the star explodes, blowing off the matter in its outer shell, or mantle. Next, continued collapse spins up the remnant star as it grows smaller. The detailed mechanism of this gravitational collapse is one of the major problems being studied by astrophysicists.

Black Holes

> At first glance any theory that talks of a hole in space, where time stands still so that a fraction of a second becomes eternity and where all things simply disappear from sight, would seem to belong to the more fantastic realms of science fiction. But to astronomers it is far from fantasy.[9]

Black holes are former stars that, having collapsed to an extremely dense state, have an extraordinarily powerful gravitational field. This field is so strong that no

---

[8]*Physics in Perspective*. Vol. 1, Report of the Physics Survey Committee (Washington, D.C.: National Academy of Sciences, 1972), p. 345.

[9]David Brand, "Where's the Matter?" *Wall Street Journal*, June 16, 1972, p. 1.

object, light, radio waves, or other radiation can escape to reveal the presence of the black hole.

Black holes may account for 90 percent of the content of our universe. Potentially, there are one billion black holes in our galaxy. Astrophysicists speculate that black holes may be bridges connecting one part of our universe to another. Similarly, the other violent sources that we have observed may be white holes through which this energy is surging to us.

Cygnus X-1, believed to be the first identifiable black hole, was discovered by the Uhru satellite in 1972. This black hole is the invisible but dominant component of a binary pair of stars and is shown sucking the material of its visible companion into a rotating disk. The black hole is at the center of the disk. The violence of the transfer and shredding action heats the atoms of gas into emitting x-rays at the edge of the black hole. These x-rays indirectly reveal its presence.

The total energy of the particles and radiation near a black hole is enormous. This energy is produced by the conversion of gravitational energy into radiation energy as the matter falls inward, accelerating into the hole. This mechanism is many times more efficient than nuclear fusion, which produces stellar and solar energy. A black hole converts mass to energy more efficiently than any other mechanism known in physics—except for matter-antimatter annihilation. Accordingly, black holes have been called an "ultimate" source of cosmic energy.

EXPLORING SPACE

The exploration of outer space has been made possible by the development of powerful rockets. (An explanation of the scientific principles involved in rocket propulsion may be found in Chapter 14A.) The use of rockets for space exploration began in earnest with the launching in 1957 by the Soviet Union of the first artificial space satellite—Sputnik I.

On August 17, 1958, the United States attempted its first launch of a rocket to the moon. Intended to place an artificial satellite in orbit around the moon, this mission was a failure. On July 2, 1959, the Soviet Union fired a rocket that went into orbit around the sun. A later rocket in the launch series was sent past the moon and transmitted pictures from its far side.

The moon is the only place in space that humans have visited. The first step on the moon's surface was taken by Neil Armstrong on July 20, 1969. This accomplishment was one of the many outcomes of the Apollo space-exploration program, which witnessed visits on the moon's surface by twelve astronauts in all from 1969 to 1972. As a result of their work and that of their compatriots who orbited the moon in "mother" ships, a great deal of information about the moon was gathered. In addition, 379 kilograms (about 834 pounds) of lunar rocks and other solids were returned to earth for analysis.

In 1965 both American and Soviet unmanned (unpersonned?) spacecraft flew by Mars and took pictures of its surface. In 1971 Mariner 9 was placed in orbit about that planet. The pictures it transmitted to earth showed a surface that looked as if it had been sculptured by intensive flooding millions of years ago. More detailed information about the Martian surface was gathered in 1976 by the spacecrafts Viking I and 2, which dropped small instrument packages to the surface.

Various spacecraft have been used to explore Venus. American Mariner and Soviet Venera rockets have both reached the Venusian atmosphere and transmitted information. Venera IX and X landed on the surface of Venus in 1975.

Pioneer Venus 1 was the first American spacecraft to orbit Venus. It reached the Venusian atmosphere on December 5, 1978. A few days later Pioneer Venus 2 discharged five probes toward the planet's surface. Each transmitted important information about the Venusian atmosphere before being destroyed by its heat. Soviet Venera spacecraft parachuted instrument packages to the surface of Venus in 1978. These "landers" sent information to orbiting spacecraft, which in turn reflected it to Earth.

Mariner 10 flew within 720 kilometers (about 450 miles) of Mercury in 1974. Its television cameras and scientific instruments sent back information concerning temperature, solar wind, and Mercury's surface.

Voyager 1 and 2 are rocket probes launched in 1977 to observe phenomena on Jupiter, Saturn, Uranus, and Neptune. It is hoped that one or both of these probes will be able to reach the edges of our solar system and beyond. They are expected to cross Pluto's orbit in 1989 and then escape the solar system at a speed of 62,000 kilometers (about 38,700 miles) per hour. On board each spacecraft are a phonograph record, sound-reproduction equipment, and playing instructions. The records include music, spoken languages, and common nature sounds. Also included is a plaque that shows pictures of humans and a description, in scientific symbols, of Earth, its location, and its people. The Voyager spacecraft will reach the first star in their interstellar voyage in about 40,000 years. Perhaps someone or something will interrupt them before then; find the "strange" information, equipment, and pictures; and learn about *our* planet and its people.

THE SPACE SHUTTLE

The Space Shuttle[10] is a true aerospace vehicle. It takes off like a rocket, maneuvers in orbit around earth like a spacecraft, and lands like an airplane. The Space Shuttle is designed to carry heavy loads into orbit around Earth. Other launch vehicles have done this. But unlike these launch vehicles, which could be used just once, each Space Shuttle orbiter may be reused more than 100 times.

The shuttle permits the check out and repair of unmanned satellites in orbit or their return to Earth for repairs that cannot be done in space. Thus, the shuttle makes possible considerable savings in spacecraft costs. The types of satellites that the shuttle can orbit and maintain include those involved in environmental protection, energy, weather forecasting, navigation, fishing, farming, mapping, oceanography, and many other fields useful to man.

Interplanetary spacecraft can be placed in orbit around Earth by the shuttle together with a rocket stage called the Interim Upper Stage (IUS), which is being developed by the Department of Defense. After the IUS and spacecraft are checked out, the IUS is ignited to accelerate the spacecraft into deep space. The

[10]The discussion of the Space Shuttle beginning on this page was excerpted with minor modifications from *NASA Facts: The Space Shuttle*, prepared by the National Aeronautics and Space Administration. This publication (stock number 003-000-00679-9) is available for purchase from the Superintendent of Documents, Government Printing Office, Washington, D.C., 20402.

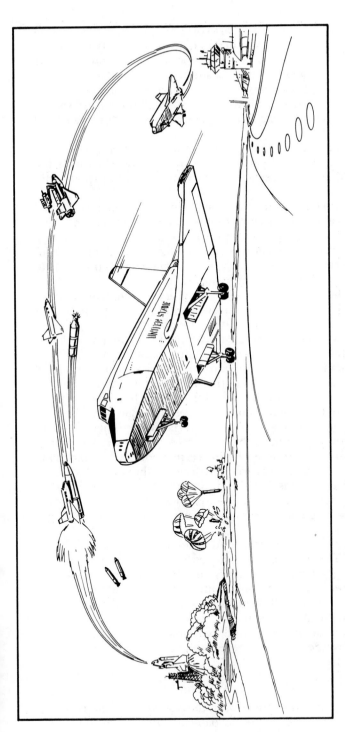

The Space Shuttle will take off vertically with a pilot and a co-pilot at the helm and two other crew members. In early operations, the Shuttle port will be at Kennedy Space Center, Florida, for east-west orbits. Later a port will be added at Vandenberg Air Force Base, California, for north-south orbits. Two solid-propellant booster rockets will supply most of the takeoff power (1). About 40 kilometers (25 miles) high, the boosters will separate (2) and descend by parachute to the ocean surface (3). There they will be recovered and returned to the launch site for re-use.

The main section of the Shuttle, called the Orbiter, will continue flying (4) on the power of its liquid-propellant engines, supplied by a large external tank. After these two sections reach orbit, the tank will separate (5) and a small rocket will cause it to re-enter and land in a remote ocean area. The Orbiter will be able to carry out space missions lasting at least seven days (6). Special materials covering its entire surface will protect the interior from the searing heat of re-entry. The Orbiter will fly horizontally like an airplane during the latter phase of descent (7) and it will land on a runway (8) near the launch site (9). As ground crews gain experience in readying it for subsequent flights, the turnaround time will be reduced to two weeks.

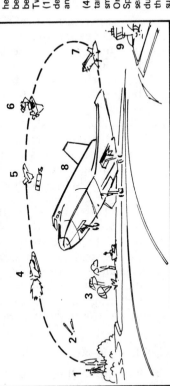

Figure 9A–5. The Mission of the U.S. Space Shuttle, from Launch to Touchdown (*Source:* NASA Office of Public Affairs, *Space Shuttle.* Washington D.C.: U.S. Government Printing Office, 1972.)

IUS also will be employed to boost satellites to earth orbits higher than the shuttle's maximum altitude, which is about 1000 kilometers (approximately 600 miles).

Unmanned satellites such as the Space Telescope, which can multiply our view of the universe, and the Long Duration Exposure Facility, which can demonstrate the effects on materials of long exposure to the space environment, can be placed in orbit, erected, and returned to Earth by the Space Shuttle. Also, shuttle crews can perform such services as replacing the Space Telescope's film packs and lenses.

The shuttle orbiter is a manned spacecraft, but unlike manned spacecraft of the past, it touches down on a landing strip. Thus, the shuttle eliminates the expensive recovery at sea that was necessary for Mercury, Gemini, Apollo, and Skylab.

The reusable shuttle also has a short turnaround time. It can be refurbished and ready for another journey into space within two weeks after landing. The shuttle can quickly provide a vantage point in space for observation of interesting but transient astronomical events or of sudden weather, agricultural, or environmental crises on Earth. Information from shuttle observations would contribute to sound decisions for dealing with such urgent matters.

The shuttle will also be used to transport into space a complete scientific laboratory called Spacelab. Developed by the European Space Agency, Spacelab is adapted to operate in conditions of zero gravity (weightlessness). It provides accommodations suitable for working, eating, and sleeping in ordinary clothing.

Spacelab provides facilities for as many as four laboratory specialists to conduct experiments in such fields as medicine, manufacturing, astronomy, and pharmaceuticals. Spacelab remains attached to the shuttle orbiter throughout its mission. Upon return to Earth, Spacelab is removed from the orbiter and outfitted for its next assignment. It can be reused about fifty times. Spacelab personnel will be men and women of many nations who are experts in their fields and in reasonably good health. They will require only a few weeks of space-flight training.

The Space Shuttle will bring within reach projects that not too long ago many considered impractical. The shuttle could carry into orbit the "building blocks" for constructing large solar-power stations that would convert the unlimited solar heat and sunlight of space into electricity for an energy-hungry world. The components would be assembled by specialists whom the shuttle would transport to, and support in, space.

The shuttle could also carry into orbit around the earth the modular units for self-sustaining settlements. The inhabitants of the settlements could be employed in building and maintaining solar-power stations and in manufacturing drugs, metals, glass for lenses, and electronics crystals. Manufacturing in weightless space can, among other things, reduce costs of certain drugs, create new alloys, produce drugs and lenses of unusual purity, and enable crystals to grow very large. Drugs, metals, glass, and crystals will be manufactured experimentally during Spacelab missions long before establishment of a space settlement.

Principal Components

The Space Shuttle has three main units: the *orbiter*, the *external tank*, and two solid rocket *boosters*. The orbiter is the crew- and payload-carrying unit of the shuttle system. It is 37 meters (122 feet) long, has a wingspan of 24 meters (78 feet), and without fuel weighs about 68,000 kilograms (150,000 pounds). It is about the size and weight of a DC−9 commercial air transport.

The orbiter can transport a payload of 29,500 kilograms (65,000 pounds) into orbit. It carries its cargo in a cavernous payload bay 18.3 meters (60 feet) long and 4.6 meters (15 feet) in diameter. The bay is flexible enough to provide accommodations for unmanned spacecraft in a variety of shapes and for fully equipped scientific laboratories.

The orbiter's three main liquid rocket engines are fed propellants from the external tank, which is 47 meters (154 feet) long and 8.7 meters (28.6 feet) in diameter. At lift-off the tank holds 703,000 kilograms (1,550,000 pounds) of propellants, consisting of liquid hydrogen (fuel) and liquid oxygen (oxidizer). The hydrogen and oxygen are in separate pressurized compartments of the tank. The external tank is the only part of the shuttle system that is not reusable.

A Typical Shuttle Mission

In a typical shuttle mission, lasting from seven to thirty days, the orbiter's main engines and the booster ignite simultaneously to rocket the shuttle from the launch pad. Launches are made from the John F. Kennedy Space Center in Florida for east−west orbits or from Vandenberg Air Force Base in California for north−south orbits.

At a predetermined point, the two solid rocket boosters separate from the orbiter and parachute to the sea where they are recovered for reuse. The orbiter continues into space. It jettisons its external propellant tank just before orbiting. The external tank enters the atmosphere and breaks up over a remote ocean area.

The orbiter then proceeds on its mission in space. When its work is completed, the crew directs the orbiter on a flight path that will take it back to the earth's atmosphere. Various rocket systems are used to slow its speed and adjust its direction. Previous spacecraft followed a direct path from space to the predetermined landing area. The orbiter is quite different. It can maneuver from the right to the left of its entry path a distance of about 2035 kilometers (about 1270 miles). The orbiter has the capability of landing like an airplane at Kennedy Space Center or Vandenberg Air Force Base. Its landing speed is about 335 kilometers (about 210 miles) per hour.

SUMMARY OUTLINE

   I. Recent evidence seems to indicate that the universe had a beginning.
  II. The universe is all the matter, energy, and space that exists.
 III. Stars are formed by the condensation of clouds of gases and end their existence when the hydrogen used in nuclear reactions within them is depleted.
  IV. The sun is a star that will use up its supply of hydrogen and come to the end of its existence in about five billion years.
   V. The solar system consists of the sun, its nine planets, and associated clouds of matter.

VI. In recent years scientists have discovered and begun studies of extraordinary astronomical phenomena, such as quasars, pulsars, and black holes.

VII. Powerful rockets have enabled us to explore outer space in a variety of ways, such as through the use of astronauts.

VIII. The Space Shuttle is a space vehicle that can return to earth and be reused in subsequent space journeys.

chapter **9B**

The Cosmos

DISCOVERY ACTIVITIES AND DEMONSTRATIONS

DISCOVERY ACTIVITIES

How to Build an Altitude Finder (Astrolabe)

OBJECTIVES

The children will construct a simple device for measuring the height of planets and stars above the horizon.

The children will measure how many degrees an object is above the horizon.

SCIENCE PROCESSES EMPHASIZED

Observing
Using numbers
Measuring

MATERIALS FOR EACH CHILD OR GROUP

Piece of cardboard 25 by 25 centimeters (about 10 by 10 inches)
25-centimeters (10-inch) length of string

Figure 9B—1. A Trip to a Strange Planet or Star (*Source:* J. Abruscato, "Creative Classroom." Reprinted from the March issue of TEACHER Magazine. This article is copyrighted. © 1978 by Macmillan Professional Magazine, Inc. All rights reserved.)

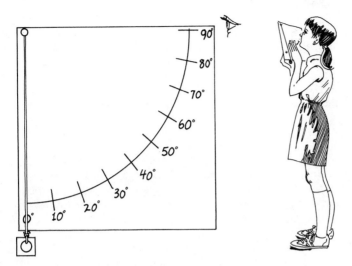

Figure 9B–2. Altitude Finder

Small weight such as a washer or nut
Protractor
Tape

MOTIVATION

Tell the children that they will be building something that has been used in one form or another for many centuries. They will be building an instrument that was invented by the ancient Greeks for finding how far above the horizon the planets and stars are. Tell the children that the scientific name for this instrument is the astrolabe but they can call it an altitude finder.

DIRECTIONS

1. Distribute a protractor to each child or group. Show the children that the protractor scale can be used to measure angles from 0° to 180°.
2. Distribute a cardboard square to each group. Have the children place a 0° mark at the lower left-hand corner of the cardboard. Have them place a 90° mark at the upper right-hand corner.
3. Have the children use the length of string as a compass to guide a pencil across an arc from the lower left-hand corner to the upper right-hand corner.
4. Now have the children divide the arc they formed by marking 10° intervals from 0° to 90°—that is, 0°, 10°, 20°, ... 90°. The protractor can be used to help mark these divisions.
5. The children should now tie the nut or washer to the string and tape the free end of the string to the upper left-hand corner of their altitude finder. The string should cross the 0° mark when the upper edge of the cardboard is held horizontally. Tell the children that they will be sighting objects along the top of the cardboard with the string on the edge of the cardboard that is farthest away from them.

6. When the children have constructed their altitude finders you may wish to take them outside to find the number of degrees that such things as chimneys, treetops, or lampposts are above the horizon. Be sure they do not try to sight the sun with their altitude finder.

7. Encourage the children to take their altitude finders home and measure the number of degrees the visible heavenly bodies are above the horizon.

KEY DISCUSSION QUESTIONS

1. Why do you think we attached a weight to the string? *To pull the string straight down.*
2. Sometimes people use the term *angle of elevation* when they use an astrolabe. What do you think that term means? *How many degrees the object is above the horizon.*
3. Does the altitude finder tell you anything about the direction the object is from you? *No.*
4. How could you find the direction? *Use a compass.* (*Note*: The next activity in this chapter can be used to help children make an instrument that measures the angle of a heavenly body from true north.)

SCIENCE CONTENT FOR THE TEACHER

The astrolabe was invented by the Greeks for observing heavenly bodies. It consisted of a movable rod that was pointed at a star or planet. The position of the rod against a circle indicated the altitude of the sun, moon, and stars. The astrolabe was eventually refined for use as a navigational tool. The sextant, a more accurate device that fulfills the same purpose, came into use in the eighteenth century. It uses a small telescope and a system of mirrors to compare the position of a heavenly body with the horizon.

EXTENSIONS

Science. You may wish to have a group of children do some research into the use of the sextant in modern sea navigation. The children should use encyclopedias to find pictures of sextants and diagrams of how they operate.

Science/Social Studies. You may wish to have a group of children do some library research to find out more about the extent to which the ancient Greeks were involved in astronomy. This group can also do research on importance of the astrolabe and sextant in the exploration of the world by seafaring countries.

How to Build an Azimuth Finder

OBJECTIVE

The children will construct a simple device that will tell how many degrees from north, measured in a clockwise direction, a heavenly body is.

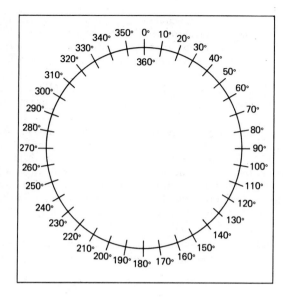

Figure 9B—3. Azimuth Finder

SCIENCE PROCESSES EMPHASIZED

Observing
Using numbers
Measuring

MATERIALS FOR EACH CHILD OR GROUP

Magnetic compass
50-centimeter (20-inch) square of cardboard
25-centimeter (10-inch) length of string
Pencil
Protractor
Straightedge

MOTIVATION

Tell the children that astronomers usually keep track of both the position of heavenly bodies above the horizon and their direction in relation to north. Write the word *azimuth* on the chalkboard and indicate that this term refers to how far an object is from north. Display the materials and begin a discussion of how they can be used to make an azimuth finder.

DIRECTIONS

1. The children should first use the protractor and pencil to draw a circle on the cardboard square. The circle should touch each side of the square.

2. Show the children that they can divide the circle into 10° units by first placing the protractor so its center measuring point is at the center of the circle. Have the children label any point on the circle 0° (north). Then have them mark off 10° positions from 0° to 360°, going in a clockwise direction and using the bottom of the protractor as a straightedge.

(*Note*: Since the protractor goes from 0° to 180°, the children should simply turn it upside down in order to continue around the circle in 10° intervals from 180° to 360° [0°].)

3. Distribute a compass to each child or group and take the children outside to use their azimuth finder to find azimuths of chimneys, treetops, and other tall objects. In order to do this they must first rotate their compass so the needle is pointing north. (You may wish to introduce the difference between true north and magnetic north at this point. Refer to the science content below for information on this subject). Next have the children align the azimuth finder so that the 0° mark is oriented to the north.

4. The children can find various azimuths by noting the number of degrees counterclockwise the object is from the zero reading.

5. Encourage the children to take their azimuth finders home to make evening measurements of the positions of heavenly bodies. They will need a flashlight to read the finders.

KEY DISCUSSION QUESTIONS

1. What would be the azimuth of a planet that was due east of you? *90°.*
2. What would be the azimuth of a planet that was due south of you? *180°.*
3. What would be the azimuth of a planet that was due west of you? *270°.*

SCIENCE CONTENT FOR THE TEACHER

One can readily find the azimuth of a heavenly body by using true north as a reference point. Navigators generally label true north as 0°, and describe the azimuth of an object in terms of the number of degrees, measured from 0° along a circle in a clockwise direction, by which its direction differs from true north. (Astronomers tend to use true south as 0°. However, for school use the 0°-north reading used by navigators is a perfectly acceptable method of measurement.)

One problem in the use of an azimuth finder is that the magnetic north measured by a compass is (except for a small portion of North America) displaced from geographic north. The amount of deviation for some representative cities is as follows:

Portland, Oregon	21°E
San Francisco	17°E
Denver	13°E
St. Paul	5°E
Atlanta	0°
Cleveland	5°W
Philadelphia	9°W
Portland, Maine	17°W

Science/Social Studies. You may wish to have a group of children do some research in geography books and then discuss the difference between geographic north and magnetic north. They may be able to use charts or maps to find the actual number of degrees by which magnetic north deviates from geographic north in their region.

Science/Social Studies. You may wish to have some children do library research on the history of astronomy. These children could find information on Egyptian, Babylonian, Chinese, and Mayan astronomy in commonly available reference books. They might also be interested in gathering pictures of Stonehenge from reference books to share with the rest of the class.

**Using Altitude and Azimuth Finders
to Follow the Motion of a Planet**

OBJECTIVE

The children will use simple altitude- and azimuth-measuring instruments to observe the motion of a planet.

SCIENCE PROCESSES EMPHASIZED

Observing
Measuring
Communicating

MATERIALS FOR EACH CHILD OR GROUP

Altitude-measuring instrument (see the first activity in this chapter)
Azimuth-measuring instrument (see the previous activity)
Chart with the following headings: observations, date, time, altitude, azimuth
Paper and pencil

MOTIVATION

Ask the children if they have ever seen planets in the evening sky. They may have observed that planets do not twinkle and in some cases appear other than white in color. Discuss with the children the importance of making observations of planets over an extended period of time so as to see patterns of motion. Indicate that this activity is going to extend over a period of months and will require them to do their observations at home.

1. Review the use of the altitude and azimuth measurers described in the two previous activities. If the children have not constructed these instruments, they will need to do so prior to beginning this extended activity.
2. Have each child prepare an observation chart.
3. Explain to the children that they should attempt to locate one planet in the evening sky and record observations at the same time each day. To help them locate a planet, first find one yourself and determine its altitude and azimuth (you can get help from any almanac that describes the location of visible planets for your area at various times of the year). Share the location of this planet with the class. Children can then try to find it on their own with their measuring devices.
4. Every few months hold a class discussion of the observations that have been made as of that time.

KEY DISCUSSION QUESTIONS

1. What planet did you observe? How did you know what planet it was? (*Answers will vary.*)
2. What problems did you have during the activity? (*Answers will vary, but may include such problems as a cloud cover obscuring the planets, precipitation making outdoor work difficult, misplacing instruments, and forgetting to make observations at the same time every day.*)

SCIENCE CONTENT FOR THE TEACHER

(See the content presented in the previous two activities.)

EXTENSIONS

Science. You may wish to encourage a group of children to carry out some long-term library research to coincide with this extended activity. These children can focus upon such topics as the astronomers Tycho Brahe and Copernicus, the invention of the telescope, and the use of modern astronomical instruments, such as the radio telescope.

Science/Social Studies. You may wish to have some children explore the resistance of society to the conclusion reached by Copernicus and Galileo that the sun is the physical center of our solar system.

Making a Model That Shows the Relative Distances of the Sun and Planets from One Another

OBJECTIVE

The children will construct a scale model showing the relative distances of the sun and planets from one another.

SCIENCE PROCESSES EMPHASIZED

Measuring
Using numbers

(*Note*: This activity provides an excellent opportunity for children to use the metric system.)

MATERIALS FOR EACH CHILD OR GROUP

9 strips of oak tag each labeled with the name of a planet
Strip of oak tag labeled "Sun"
Meter stick

MOTIVATION

Ask the children to show what they think to be the distance of the earth from the sun relative to the distance of Pluto from the sun. They can show their guess to the class by placing textbooks representing the planets at different distances from the sun. (Perhaps you can be the sun!) After various children have shown their guesses, indicate that you will be giving them some information and materials that they can use to make a scale model showing such distances.

DIRECTIONS

1. Distribute copies of the list that appears in the science content for this activity.
2. Distribute the oak-tag labels and a meter stick to each group.
3. Have each group of children use a different area of the classroom floor to place their strips of oak tag.
4. When all groups have finished, engage the class in a discussion of any surprises they had as they assembled their model.

KEY DISCUSSION QUESTIONS

1. Which planet do you think gets the least amount of the sun's energy on an equal portion of its surface? Why? *Pluto—it is farthest from the sun.*
2. If you used the distance from Mercury to the sun as 2 meters instead of 2 centimeters, how far would the Earth be from the sun? *5.2 meters.*
3. How many times farther away from the sun is Pluto than earth? *About 40 times.*

SCIENCE CONTENT FOR THE TEACHER

Relative Distances of the Planets from the Sun

Mercury	=	2.0 cm
Venus	=	3.7 cm
Earth	=	5.2 cm
Mars	=	7.9 cm
Jupiter	=	26.8 cm
Saturn	=	49.2 cm
Uranus	=	99.2 cm
Neptune	=	155.2 cm
Pluto	=	204.2 cm

EXTENSIONS

Science/Math. You may wish to have a group of children make a bar graph that displays the relative distances of the planets from the sun.

Science/Math. You may wish to have some children calculate how long it would take a spaceship leaving the earth's orbit at a velocity of 30,000 kilometers per hour (about 25,000 miles per hour) to reach each planet. They will need to locate a chart showing the actual distances of the planets from one another prior to doing this activity.

ADDITIONAL ACTIVITY IDEAS

Hello, Up There!*

Children are often interested in the moon since it is such a spectacular sight on a clear night. You can capitalize on this interest by engaging the children in a wide variety of activities related to the moon. Here are a few that you may wish to carry out.

Have the children compare the various phases of the moon. Over a period of time they can prepare a set of paper cutouts showing the crescent moon, the quarter-moon, the half-moon, the three-quarter-moon, and the full moon. They can also keep track of the days in the moon's cycle. In addition, they can draw pictures of the waxing and waning of the moon right on the calendar.

Some children can explore the causes of the phases of the moon. Have them move a rubber ball around a source of strong light and observe the areas of the ball that are lit and those that are shaded.

Children can make remarkable observations of the moon's surface simply by using a good pair of binoculars on a clear night. They can make sketches of their observations and compare them with photographs of the moon's surface. Many reference books have photographs of the moon that identify its major surface features. Children can study these and develop a good understanding of the nature of the moon's surface.

Children can develop a good understanding of the size of the moon and its distance from the earth by making scale models of the earth and the moon.

If you have many children engaged in making discoveries about the moon, it would be very helpful to bring them together at the end of their work to share what they have learned.

"Take Me to Your Leader, Earthling!"

All of us are fascinated by the possibility of life on other planets in the universe. Over the years many people have described types of life that we might encounter. One source of such descriptions that children are quite familiar with are movies and television productions about space, space travel, and life in the universe. Children can make drawings of various extraterrestrial creatures they have seen

*Asterisks refer to activities for young children.

194

Figure 9B–4. Have the children keep track of the phases of the moon. (*Source:* Lick Observatory Photograph.)

represented by these media. When they have done this you can engage them in a discussion of why a script writer created the shape and behavior of a creature in a particular way. Have the children consider the characteristics that an extraterrestrial creature shares with living things on earth. You may wish to raise an even more interesting point by asking whether it is possible for a human artist to represent an extraterrestrial creature that is unrelated to anything the artist has seen on earth. In other words, is it possible to imagine something that may be unimaginable?

Are You Fit to Fly?

A group of children may be interested in doing some library research to discover the physical-fitness activities carried out by astronauts in training for space flight.

The children should be able to find pictures and descriptions of the astronauts taking part in a wide variety of such activities. The children should also be able to find out the types of food astronauts eat on earth in preparation for their journey and the types of food they eat on board a spacecraft. Such information can provoke a lively discussion about whether the children (and you) are in good enough shape to take a space journey. Have the children also discuss whether they would be interested in participating in a voyage into outer space. You can extend this activity and class discussion by having children determine the types of physical exercises that astronauts carry out on board a spacecraft. Some of these exercises can be demonstrated by members of the class.

DEMONSTRATIONS

Moon Watcher

OBJECTIVES

Using a model, the children will observe the phases of the moon as demonstrated. The children will explain why the moon seems to change in shape.

SCIENCE PROCESSES EMPHASIZED

Observing
Communicating

MATERIALS

Small lamp with ordinary light bulb and removable shade
Orange
Paper and pencil
Signs with the names "Earth," "Moon," and "Sun"

MOTIVATION

Ask the children to describe and draw the various shapes that the moon seems to take. Have them show their drawings to the rest of the class. Ask the children if they think the moon really changes its shape. After some discussion, leave the questions unanswered for the moment. Display the materials for the demonstration and tell the children that they will be making a model of the moon in orbit around the earth that will help them understand the changes in the shape of the moon.

DIRECTIONS

1. Remove the lampshade and place the "Sun" label on the lamp. Place the sun at the center of the front of the room. Affix the "Earth" label to a child.

2. Darken the room by drawing the shades and shutting off the classroom lights.
3. Now have the child labeled "Earth" hold the moon (the orange) so that his or her hand containing it is fully outstretched. Have the child first stand so that he or she is facing the sun and holding the moon directly in line with it. The child should be about one meter (a little more than three feet) from the sun.
4. The "sun" should be turned on at this point. Have the child holding the moon describe how much of the moon's lit surface is seen from the earth. (*None of the lit surface is seen. The moon is not visible in the sky.*)
5. Have the "earth" turn sideways and ask him or her how much of the lit surface of the moon he or she can see? (*Half the lit surface. The child sees a half-moon.*)
6. Have the "earth" stand so that his or her back is to the lamp and so that the moon is about 30 centimeters (one foot) away from his or her eyes and slightly to the left of the head. Ask how much of the lit surface of the moon can be seen. (*All of it. The child sees a full moon.*)
7. Repeat the demonstration so that the crescent moon, half-moon, three-quarter moon, and full moon can all be seen.

KEY DISCUSSION QUESTIONS

1. Does the moon produce light? *No, it just reflects light from the sun.*
2. What name do we give to the shapes that the moon seems to take? *Phases.*
3. Does the moon really change in shape? Why? *No. The only thing that changes is the pattern of the light we can see bouncing off the moon.*

SCIENCE CONTENT FOR THE TEACHER

The sun shines on only half the surface of the moon. This entire lit surface is not always visible from earth. The apparent shape of the moon at any given time is really the portion of the lit surface then visible. The different portions of the surface that are lit at different times are the phases of the moon. The full moon is that phase in which we see the entire lit surface. When full, the moon appears as a round disk in the sky. We refer to the phase in which we see half the lit surface as the half-moon. The crescent moon is a phase in which we see only a sliver of the lit surface. The new moon is the phase in which none of the lit surface can be seen.

EXTENSIONS

Science. You may wish to encourage a group of children to use the lamp, orange, and other round objects to demonstrate other astronomical phenomena, such as lunar and solar eclipses, to their classmates.

Science. Some children may wish to do some library research about the exploration of the moon and the kind of information that has so far been gathered. This group of children could be encouraged to construct posters and charts to report information they have found as well as to depict those portions of the lunar surface that have been explored.

Science/Language Arts. A group of children may wish to write a short play about an incident that occurs while a group of astronauts are exploring a mysterious crater on the moon. The children could write two plays, one that is science fiction and one that is consistent with the presently available knowledge of the moon.

A Trip to a Strange Planet or Star[1]*

OBJECTIVES

Each child will take the role of a member of a space-exploration team and describe his or her imaginary adventure.

The children will explain the similarities and differences between their imaginary journey and a possible real journey.

MATERIALS

A darkened room

MOTIVATION, DIRECTIONS, KEY DISCUSSION QUESTIONS, AND EXTENSIONS

A fantasy space journey can provide a lively classroom experience that tests students' descriptive skills, stimulates their imaginations, and promotes leadership, team thinking, and sharing.

First, tell everyone that they are going on an exciting space trip. Then, divide the class into groups of three and have each group decide who will be the captain, navigator, and scientist. Ask each group to put three desks together, and have the captain, who is seated in the middle, link arms tightly with the navigator and scientist.

Next, turn out the classroom lights and tell the children that each group is its own *spaceship*. Explain that you will begin a countdown for takeoff beginning with the number ten. When you reach five, the youngsters are to close their eyes and keep them shut for the entire journey. At this point you can heighten the impact of the trip by playing a sound-effects record. Then, read the following script dramatically, pausing between statements:

"Feel your body being pushed back against the chairs. Your voyage in space has started. In a short while, you will be out of the earth's atmosphere. Can you see it getting smaller and smaller? What colors to you see? You are moving faster and faster through space. Think about how small the earth looks.

"Now look ahead. Try to imagine a tiny spot of light ahead of you. Watch it get bigger and bigger. That is the sun's light reflecting off another planet. The spaceship is getting closer and closer. Prepare for landing. Keep your eyes shut.

---

[1]The demonstration beginning on this page was excerpted from Joseph Abruscato, "Space Journey," *Teacher*, 95, no. 7 (March 1978), 102. Used with permission of the publisher. This article is copyrighted, © 1978 by Macmillan Professional Magazine, Inc. All rights reserved. Due to the unique nature of this demonstration, its motivation, directions, key discussion questions, and extensions have been integrated under one heading.

The ship will land with a slight bump; ten, nine, eight, seven, six, five, four, three, two, one, landing. Keep your eyes shut.

"The crew should be ready to open the hatch and explore the planet. Unlink your arms and imagine the crew leaving the spacecraft to explore the planet. (Pause a minute.) What kinds of things do you see? What are the members of the crew doing?

"The crew . . . Oh! The crew is in trouble. What do you think is happening? Oh, no, it's . . . It's . . . Quick! Head back to the safety of the spacecraft. Can you see yourself climbing back in? Prepare for blast-off. Link arms; ten, nine, eight, seven, six, five, four, three, two, one, blast off and head for Earth.

"You are getting closer and closer. Finally you see it. It's the size of a baseball but getting bigger and bigger. Prepare for landing. There will be a slight bump; ten, nine, eight, seven, six, five, four, three, two, one, landing. You are back home safely. Open your eyes when you are ready."

Following the "trip," ask such questions as: Where did you go? What colors did you see? What was the planet like? What did the members of the crew do on the planet? What was the danger? What was the surface of the planet like? Would you like to take a real space voyage some day?

The fantasy trip might be used to introduce a science unit. Suggest that students read books about the moon, the sun, other planets, or rocket ships as a follow-up to ideas that come up during your discussion.

The trip can also be a springboard for individual or small-group projects. Activities might include studying and listing the physical requirements for a spaceship and drawing its floor plan, or researching the physical-fitness exercises required of astronauts and then showing the rest of the class how to do them. You might ask youngsters to write short stories or poems about their feelings during their imaginary space journey and illustrate them with drawings, collages, or paintings.

With a little guidance, children can create their own fantasy trips and read them aloud to their classmates. Suggest that they begin by writing down their destination and the number of children accompanying them on the trip. Then, they create a suspenseful story about their journey. You'll enjoy many thrilling trips with your students.

SCIENCE CONTENT FOR THE TEACHER

Prior to this demonstration you should study the physical characteristics of the various planets in our solar system as well as of the stars. This knowledge will enable you to assist the children when they discuss their experience.

ADDITIONAL DEMONSTRATION IDEAS

The World's Simplest Planetarium*

To do this demonstration you will have to find out what major constellations are visible at this time of the year in the evening skies of your locale. After you have identified a few of these constellations you can prepare children to locate them on their own by building and using the following apparatus. Begin with a shoebox that has its lid taped on. At one end cut out a hole sufficiently large for you to insert the lamp end of a flashlight. Cut a rectangular window in the other end the size of a small index card. Prepare a piece of cardboard for each constellation by punching holes in it to represent the stars of the constellation. Using black electrical tape, seal one end of the box around the flashlight that extends into it. Display the various constellations by attaching the pieces of cardboard to the window of the shoebox. Have the children learn the name of each constellation, and then encourage them to search for the constellations in the evening sky.

What Causes Day and Night?*

This demonstration will help children understand how day and night are related to the earth's rotation. You will need a globe, an incandescent lamp without a shade, paper cutout in the shape of a person about 5 centimeters (2 inches) tall, and some transparent tape. Have a volunteer hold the globe and find the place on it that is closest to the location of the school. Have the children tape the cutout to that location. Using the paper figure as a reference, identify east and west on the globe and show how the rotation of the globe makes the sun appear to rise in the east and set in the west. Have the children discuss the apparent movement of the sun in the sky and the cause of day and night.

What Causes the Seasons?*

The materials from the previous demonstration can be used here as well. With the children, establish that the earth's axis is tilted in space. Hold the globe so as to show this tilt, and demonstrate the rotation of the earth on its axis. Now have a volunteer carry the globe around the lamp (the sun) so that its axis remains tilted. Have the remainder of the class form a large circle (actually an ellipse) to represent the earth's path as it revolves around the sun. You can now show that in June the Northern Hemisphere is tilted toward the sun and that this part of the earth receives intense heat. In December the Northern Hemisphere is tilted away from the sun. Show the children that the spring and fall seasons occur midway between the winter and summer locations of Earth in its orbit.

chapter 10

How to Plan and Teach Life-Science Learning Units

THE TAPPER

The walls lining the dimly lit hallway echoed Pat Williams's footsteps as she counted down the classroom numbers. Room 12, 11, 10, 9, 8. And there it was—the doorway to room 7. The classroom in which she would spend the months from September to June was right beyond the door. What would it be like? With excitement and more than a little nervousness, she opened the door. Her first quick look around the room brought a sinking feeling. Drab, drab, drab—thirty desks with firmly attached chairs facing forward, an old wooden teacher's desk, modern green blackboards, bookshelf after bookshelf of schoolbooks, and some bulletin boards swisscheesed with tack holes.

Pat walked to the front of the room and sat on the chair behind the old wooden desk. The eerie silence of the classroom lulled her into a flight of imagination about the months ahead. What would it be like teaching in this school? *Will the other teachers accept me? There are so many things the children will need to learn—what will I emphasize? What will the children be like?* Yes, the children, what would they be like?

She didn't notice the tapping sound for a

Figure 10−1.

while. Finally, a particularly loud tap broke her from her reverie and brought her back to the classroom. She turned to her right and saw the smiling face of a child at one of the windowpanes tapping with one hand to get her attention. She left her chair, walked to the window, and opened it.

"Hi, I'm Patricia Williams. I'm going to be the teacher in this room."

"I found this old bird's nest by the bushes," said the tapper.

Pat asked, "What grade are you going to be in?"

The tapper answered, "It has some pieces of blue eggshell in it."

Pat tried again. "What's your name?"

The tapper answered, "Where are the birds?"

Pat tried once again. "Are you having fun this summer?"

The tapper answered, "The birds, the little birds. Where are the birds?"

BASIC CONCEPTS FOR LIFE-SCIENCE UNITS

Children are concerned about life. They express their concern and curiosity continually and persistently. They want to know what happened to the baby birds, they want to know the name for a brightly colored creepy-crawly caterpillar they found on a leaf, and they want to know about the essence of life itself. Young children wonder whether rocks are alive, and older children wonder how life itself began. The teaching of life-science units will help you develop and extend children's curiosity, knowledge, and concern for life in its multitude of forms. This chapter will help you meet the challenge of teaching life-science units and prepare you to respond to the hundreds of "tappers" you will be meeting in the years ahead.

Well, then, where do you begin? What can you include in a unit that will help it reach out and capture the attention of the boys and girls in your classroom? What will extend and amplify children's curiosity and gently lead them to think about things they may never have thought of before? What will spark their enthusiasm and move them from questions and curiosity to the acquisition of new knowledge, skills, and attitudes? The answers to these somewhat unsettling questions will become apparent as you reflect upon the basic concepts that underlie the life sciences. It is these concepts that serve as nature's answers to your children's questions about the natural world.

There are a wide variety of concepts that can serve as the focus of a life-science unit. The following list is presented as a resource for you as you develop life-science units for children. They were written for you, the teacher, and will need to be adapted to the particular grade level or levels that you teach or will be teaching. Each of these concepts can be considered a *basic* life-science concept. Each can serve as the starting point for the development of specific concepts having a more limited focus.

1. Living things are different from nonliving things.
2. The basic unit of all living things is the cell.
3. Living things can be classified according to their unique characteristics.
4. Plants and animals are living things.
5. Living things reproduce in a number of different ways.
6. Animals and plants inherit and transmit the characteristics of their ancestors.

7. Animals and plants affect one another.
8. Living things affect their environment.
9. The environment affects living things.
10. Different areas of the earth support different life forms, which are adapted to the unique characteristics of the area in which they live.
11. Living things depend upon the earth, its atmosphere, and the sun for their existence.
12. Plants are food producers.
13. Animals are food consumers.
14. Animals get their food by eating plants or animals that eat plants.
15. The human body consists of a number of groups of organs (systems) that work together to perform a particular function.
16. The human body can be affected by a wide variety of diseases.
17. Humans affect the air, water, and land in their environment.
18. The environment affects humans.

PROCESS SKILLS FOR LIFE-SCIENCE UNITS

Do it! To learn we must act. We must taste, touch, smell, feel, see, hear—in short, we must experience. To have a better and more successful tomorrow we must first fully experience today. Similarly, if we expect children to learn we must expect them to *do*. Certainly, they must read, think, and discuss, but sooner or later they must *act*.

The action for children in life-science units occurs as they experience science activities or participate in demonstrations of science phenomena. Chapters 11B and 12B will provide you with many activities and demonstrations that you can use to help children make contact with the life sciences.

Activities and demonstrations are important in and of themselves, but they perform another very important function: they can tangibly help children prepare for life itself. Science experiences enable children to acquire skills that are transferable to their present and future life experiences. These easily transferable components of the experiences are the science-process skills.

A list of some of these skills and a brief description of practical ways in which children can be involved in process-oriented experiences appears below. You may wish to consider these process skills and activities and then develop your own list of science activities for the more complex processes listed in Figure 1–5.

Observing

Observe the characteristics of nonliving things.
Observe the characteristics of living things.
Observe the characteristics of plants.
Observe the power of the senses.
Observe the changes that organisms undergo.

Classifying

Group things according to whether they are living or nonliving.
Group organisms as plants or as animals.

Group organisms into the categories of producer, consumer, and decomposer.
Group the types of changes displayed by living things.

Communicating

Make a record of the characteristics of nonliving and of living things.
Make a record of the characteristics of plants and of animals.
Make charts that represent the characteristics of objects and of organisms.

Using Numbers

Use numbers to quantify the changes that you observe in plants.
Use numbers to quantify the changes that you observe in animals.
Use fractions and decimals to describe the changes in organisms or their environment.

Inferring

Make inferences about the causes of the following phenomena:
Change of leaf color in the fall
Pollution of air, water, or soil
Various diseases
The relationship between living things and their environment
How living things adapt to changes in their environment.

Predicting

Make an educated guess about the effects that each of the following will have on an organism or its environment:
Increased food or water supply
Decreased food or water supply
An increase in the population of one type of organism
The pollution of an organism's or a community's environment.

A SAMPLE LEARNING CENTER

I hope you have had an opportunity to visit classrooms in which teachers include in-class learning centers as instructional tools. Learning centers can serve many purposes, the most important of which is to enable teachers to help individuals and small groups of children to learn on their own. The following pages describe in some detail a life-science learning center. If you study it carefully you will discover examples of the multitude of ways in which a well-developed learning center can help children learn and enjoy science.

The Wonder Machine

OBJECTIVES

Given an incomplete drawing of the human body, students will select from the various parts the ones that are missing.

THE WONDER MACHINE!

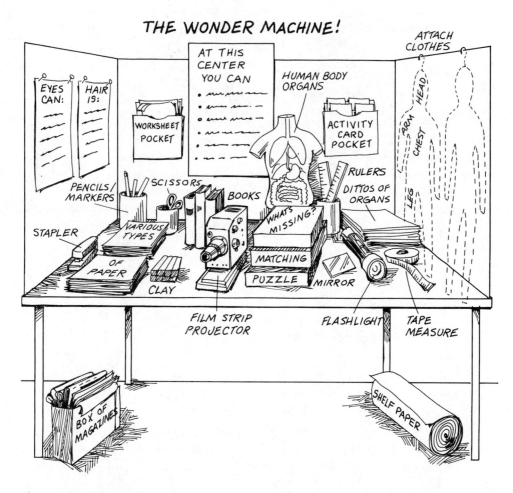

Figure 10−2. "The Wonder Machine!"—A Sample Learning Center

Given a collection of pictures of various body parts and a collection of clothing, students will match each article of clothing to the appropriate body part.

Students will identify and list the functions and characteristics of various body parts.

Students will determine various body measurements.

After reading about a body system of their choice, students will write a story describing the system.

Given a list of various organs of the body, students will group them into the appropriate body systems.

Students will trace their body outline and paste on and label various body parts.

Students will record their observations of the following simple body reactions: breathing, heart rate, and pupil response to light.

SCIENCE PROCESSES EMPHASIZED

Observing
Classifying
Measuring

MATERIALS NEEDED

Large brown shelf paper
Modeling clay
Writing paper
Drawing paper
Colored construction paper
Chart paper
Metric measuring tools
Human-body model (if possible)
Clothesline and clothespins
Small mirror
Stopwatch or a clock with a second hand
Penlight or flashlight
Magazines to cut up
Books and filmstrips on the human body

DIRECTIONS FOR THE TEACHER

You may wish to use a corner of your room for this learning center. Decorate the walls and any available bulletin boards with posters, pictures, and any brightly colored objects related to the topic of the human body. There should be floor space on which the children can roll out large mural paper and trace around their bodies. You may wish to cover part of the floor with newspapers on which the children can play with clay and use paste.

Teach the children how to make simple books having a few blank pages and a colored sheet of construction paper or a piece of wallpaper for a cover. These can be used for numerous purposes.

Prepare dittoed cutouts of internal organs on appropriately colored construction paper. Provide strips of paper for the children to use when they label body parts. Set up a clothesline with clothespins that the children can use when they display their "bodies." Children in the lower grades can label the various parts of their bodies—head, neck, wrist, ankle, etc. Older children can prepare cutouts of the internal organs, label them, and paste them on their body cutout.

What's Missing?"* On 8-by-10 cards draw about six bodies or faces with one or two parts missing. On separate cards draw the missing parts. Cover the cards with clear adhesive plastic. Have the children find and place appropriately the missing

*Asterisks refer to activities for young children.

parts. Keep the cards in a small box or envelope with the directions printed on the cover or front.

*Matching.** Draw or find pictures of:

Mittens	Hands
Hat	Head
Pants	Legs
Shirt	Chest
Shoes	Feet
Socks	Feet
Scarf	Neck
Sweater	Chest and arms

Mount these pictures on cards, cover them with clear adhesive plastic, and package them in a small box or large envelope. Write these directions on the cover:

Can you find the partner to each of these pictures?
Spread the pictures out on the floor or the table and see if you can match the piece of clothing to the part of the body it is worn on.

Variation on Matching. Use the vocabulary words in addition to or instead of the pictures.

*Worksheets.** To enable students to work independently on some of the worksheets in this center, you will need to spend time with the whole class developing the following concepts. Ask the children to brainstorm ideas. You write their ideas on chart paper. The following are typical of the charts that could be made:

Eyes can be:

Brown	Small
Blue	Green
Pretty	Laughing
Big	

Skin can be:

White	Tan
Black	Sunburned
Yellow	Wrinkled
Freckled	Brown
Sweaty	

Hair can be:

Long	Straight
Short	Messy
Blond	Neat
Brown	Curly

Feet can:
Walk
Jump
Hurt
Smell
Run

Hands can:
Hit
Write
Pick up things
Sweat
Shake
Clap

After these charts have been prepared, place them in the learning center for the children to refer to while they complete the following activities:

Do This With a Partner:

My hair is _____.

_____'s hair is _____.

My eyes are _____.

_____'s eyes are _____.

My skin is _____.

_____'s skin is _____.

Frame Sentences:

My foot can _____.

My hands can _____.

My knee can _____.

My nose can _____.

My eyes can _____.

These two activities can either be put into a worksheet or written on a separate page of a homemade book for the child to read and keep. Do not develop more than one or two concepts at a time for very young children.

*Puzzle.** Either make or find a commercially made puzzle of the human body. Depending upon the ages of your students, use a puzzle with either external or internal body parts.

"Bodies in Action" Book. Have the children cut from magazines pictures of people involved in various activities—playing tennis, eating, sleeping, walking, etc. Have the children paste the pictures into their homemade books and then write a sentence or two describing the picture. Make the following direction card:

> Make a book. Cut out pictures of people doing things and paste them one on a page in your book.
>
> Write a sentence about your pictures. You can begin your sentences with "Our bodies can ___."

*Measuring.** Provide students with metric measuring tools and have them do a worksheet similar to this one:

I am _____ cm tall.

My foot is _____ cm long.

My hand is _____ cm wide.

It is _____ cm from my knee to my heel.

It is _____ cm from my elbow to my wrist.

My waist is _____ cm around.

It is _____ cm from my elbow to my wrist.

What Happens? Help the children practice taking their pulse and observing their breathing and the reaction of their pupils to light. Prepare activity cards for the learning center similar to these:

Find Your Pulse

1. Using a stopwatch or the second hand on the clock, count how many times your heart beats in a minute.
2. Run in place for one minute.
3. Count again the number of times your heart beats in a minute.
4. Record your results on paper.
5. What happened? Why?

Observe Your Breathing

1. Breathe on a mirror.
2. What happens?
3. Record what you see.
4. Why do you think it happened?

Observe Your Partner's Pupil Response to Light

1. Find a partner.
2. Have your partner shade his/her eyes.
3. Shine a penlight into his/her eyes for a second or two.
4. Watch his/her pupils.
5. What happens?
6. Record your results.

Filmstrips. * Set up a filmstrip projector so that the children can view various filmstrips on the human body, individually or with partners.

Incredible Journey. Prepare an activity card similar to this one:

---

1. Choose one of the systems of the human body.
2. Read out the organs in that system.
3. Pretend you are the size of a microorganism and are traveling through the system.
4. Write about what you see.

Classifying. Prepare a set of cards each with one of the following words printed on it:

Heart	Blood vessels	Blood
Nose	Esophagus	Lungs
Windpipe	Nerves	Stomach
Mouth	Small intestines	Spinal cord
Brain	Large intestines	

Make the following heading cards:

> Circulatory System
> Respiratory System
> Digestive System
> Nervous System

Package the cards in a small box or a large envelope with the following direction on it:

> Group these organs under the proper body-system headings.

Poster. Make the following poster:

At This Center You Can:

1. Trace your own body, cut it out, and add a heart, lungs, etc.
2. Pretend you are an explorer and write a report of your trip through one of the systems in a human body.
3. Put together a puzzle.
4. Watch a filmstrip.
5. Take your pulse, breathe on a mirror, and watch the pupil responses in a friend's eyes.
6. Measure various parts of your body.
7. Play matching games.
8. Write stories about how bodies move.

EXTENSION IDEAS

Have students use microscopes to study the cell structure of blood cells, hair strands, and cheek cells.

Have students investigate careers related to the human body, such as being a doctor, nurse, physical therapist, trainer, or dentist.

Have students make a handprint and label it with their name. Display the identified handprints in the room. Have the students make a set of unidentified handprints. Ask the students to play detective and try to identify the owners of the mystery handprints.

CORRELATION WITH NONSCIENCE SUBJECTS

Use the books made and stories written in the learning center for reading and language-arts lessons.

Continue the development of vocabulary about the human body in reading and spelling lessons.

Write a "medical book" describing the human body.

Refine the measurement of body lengths, include measurements in inches and feet. Measure weights in pounds and ounces and in grams and kilograms if possible.

Take a field trip to a local medical school or hospital to learn more about the functioning of the human body.

Build a clay model of the human body.

Make an internal-organ mobile.

EVALUATION IDEAS

Children. Have the students fill out a form similar to this one:

What did you like to do the best in this center?
What did you like the least?
What would you have added to this center?
What was the most important thing you learned while doing the activities in this center?

Teacher. The teacher should maintain permanent records to take note of each child's progress, his or her strengths and weaknesses, and directions for future work. These records might include anecdotal records, check lists on which students have recorded the activities they have completed, and skill check lists. These records can be kept in individual folders for each child or combined in a large notebook.

A SAMPLE BULLETIN BOARD

I confess to having created some of the worst bulletin boards ever seen in a classroom. Reflecting upon the causes of my poor performance in this area of teaching, I have reached the following conclusions. First of all, I had and continue to have no artistic talent whatsoever. (Only the mercy of one of my college art professors allowed me to pass the art course required of all preservice teachers.) My poor sense of design and color led me to create bulletin boards that simply looked bad. Second, I really didn't spend much time thinking about the creation of bulletin boards. The realities of planning and teaching took so much time that bulletin boards never received much of my attention. Third, I never really understood that bulletin boards have the potential to be something that children can both look at and learn from. My bulletin boards usually took the form of a display rather than a useful teaching tool.

Fortunately for you, I have asked an extremely talented teacher (and bulletin-board maker) to help me with this section of the chapter. By studying the sample bulletin board that follows, you will gain some practical insight into the preparation of bulletin boards that you can use in teaching the life sciences. So, if you feel that you are somewhat lacking as a bulletin-board maker, the following ideas may be a great help to you.

Flower Power*

OBJECTIVE

Students will identify the various basic parts of plants and their environment.

SCIENCE PROCESS EMPHASIZED

Observing

MATERIALS

Word cards
Push pins
Construction-paper cutouts of a plant stem, plant leaves, petals, and roots, the sun, clouds, soil, and raindrops

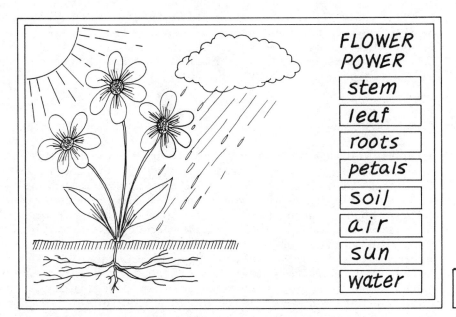

Figure 10-3. "Flower Power"*—A Sample Bulletin Board

DIRECTIONS FOR THE TEACHER

After the children have become familiar with the vocabulary on the word cards, allow them to practice identifying the cutouts. Have the students attach the word cards directly to the appropriate parts with push pins. A self-correcting key should be provided.

EXTENSION IDEAS

Collect an assortment of small seeds and some small objects that are not seeds. Have the students plant these to see which are actually seeds.

Examine a soaked bean seed with a magnifying glass to find the "baby plant."

Obtain cross sections from trees of various ages. Observe the rings and calculate the ages.

CORRELATION WITH NONSCIENCE SUBJECTS

Art. Make leaf prints by rubbing a crayon over a piece of paper that covers a leaf.

Math. Develop plant word problems such as this one: "There were ten leaves on the tree yesterday. Today there are only four. How many leaves fell off?"

Social Studies. Take a field trip to a local greenhouse. Or list the types of jobs that depend upon plants (furniture maker, grocer, nursery worker, etc.).

A SAMPLE FIELD TRIP

Ah yes, the field trips. Can they be complicated, confusing, disruptive, time-wasting, and nerve-shattering? Yes, they certainly can! But they can also be extremely worthwhile experiences for you and for the children you teach. Life-science units provide many opportunities for productive and enjoyable field trips. The remainder of the chapter consists of brief descriptions of the types of field trips you may wish to carry out with children.

Is Bread Alive?*

The origin of many common foods is so clouded in mystery that children may not realize that living things need other living things in order to survive. The typical primary field trip to a bakery takes on new meaning when used to help answer the question, Is bread alive? A trip to a grain farm, grist mill, or natural-grains stores can be used to answer this question too.

After children have developed lists of characteristics of living and nonliving things and completed several activities based on these lists, pose the question, Is bread alive? Encourage discussion of the question. The matter of ingredients will very likely arise. Read several recipes to the class (or have the students do this), and then list common ingredients (flour, salt, sugar, liquid, yeast, shortening). Next, the children can explore several of these ingredients to determine whether they are alive. Flour can be seen as wheat and then as grain going through the grinding process. Sugar can then be tasted, and its harvesting and refining processes shared with the class. Yeast, mixed with sugar and water and then gently warmed, will give off carbon dioxide. This is easily demonstrated by means of a narrow-necked jar or flask with a balloon stretched across it. The balloon will expand slightly as the yeast inside the jar or flask grows and gives off more gas. A comparison of sugar and salt could be useful in showing the differences between living and nonliving things. The function of all the ingredients in bread should be discussed. Then students can make their own bread. Volunteer parents would be very helpful at this stage.

The actual field trip can be to a bakery of any size. Encourage students to compare the methods used at the bakery with those they used in making bread in the classroom. Be sure they ask questions about the sources of the ingredients used by the bakery. Have the tour guide concentrate especially on the function of yeast.

Back in the class, you can take the study of bread one step further by growing mold on it. This step completes the food chain started with the wheat and can be used to show that participation in a food chain is a characteristic of living things.

ADDITIONAL IDEAS FOR FIELD TRIPS

Living and Nonliving Things*

Children in the primary grades sometimes give life to inanimate objects, often in delightful ways, such as by saying that rocks are grown-up pieces of sand. A unit on living and nonliving things ideally should help students be aware of likenesses and differences but allow them to retain the interpretations that their imagination leads them to. Develop lists of characteristics of living and nonliving things, and then walk through the playground or neighborhood collecting items and observations for inclusion in each category. Some items will cause much discussion when you return and try to categorize them. Creation of new categories such as "once-living" may be necessary. Display the items and have students add to the display.

Living things reproduce, and a trip to a florist or greenhouse will give children ample proof of this phenomenon. Late winter, when the coming summer's flowers are being started, is an especially interesting time to visit. Have the tour guide demonstrate several forms of reproduction—seeds, cuttings, grafts, and so on. If it is not possible to plant some seeds there and bring them back to class, have the planting equipment and materials ready for use when you return to class. Planting several buttons, rocks, and marbles in addition to the seeds will help illustrate the difference between living and nonliving things. Make sure the soil used is free of other seeds, and be prepared to discuss why some seeds did not grow.

Animals from Simple to Complex*

Many communities have humane societies that are anxious to have children become aware of the responsibilities of owning pets. A tour, question-and-answer session, and time to observe the animals should be included. Preparation could include discussion of pet care, the role of the humane society, and what to do about the population explosion among animals. Follow-up possibilities are art projects, creative writing, an animal-care awareness project for other classes, finding out about certain breeds, and a discussion of responsibility. A similar trip could be arranged to a pet shop.

Visiting a facility with many animals, such as a zoo, aquarium, or farm, is an activity for any age group, but older students will become greatly involved if properly prepared for such a visit. Students could become "experts" on one animal or phase of operation before the trip and then compare their research with what they observe during the trip. Map reading and model building are ideal preparatory and follow-up activities. The opportunity to find out what goes on behind the scenes in caring for the animals, financing the operation, and dealing with the public will make this field trip stimulating for older children.

A nearby stream, field, or park can provide an interesting field trip and materials for further classroom study. Nets from stockings and wire, plastic-cup "bug-jars," and an observation notebook will equip the explorers; an available camera could be used to gather pictures of the overall environment. Encourage students to draw and write about particularly interesting specimens they observe. Visiting the same location at different seasons of the year can provide added interest.

Ecology

An ecology unit can provide a fine opportunity to use community resources. An examination of the factors making your area suitable for growing a certain crop, manufacturing a certain product (industrial areas have reasons for being where they are), or providing a service should precede a field trip to a local agricultural, industrial, or commercial site. The follow-up should consider the effects of the business on the human and natural environment, the future development of the business, and student suggestions for improving the product and/or methods used to create it.

Where does our trash go? Many people forget about their waste once it is in the garbage can or down the pipe. A visit to a landfill, recycling center, water-treatment plant, or junkyard will make students aware of the problem of waste disposal. Brainstorming ways to cut down on household and classroom waste and a recycled-materials art project are suitable follow-ups.

The Human Body: Its Structure and Functions

Inviting someone in the medical field to talk to the children about his or her career or visiting such a person at work is a good chance to involve classroom parents. A doctor, nurse, or dentist is not the only possibility; consider also a first-aid instructor, orthopedic-device salesperson, nursing-home worker, therapist, or hospital volunteer. Remember that children like to do more than listen, so plan for active involvement as well as discussion. Learning the Heimlich maneuver, examining equipment, and practicing an exercise are all related activities that may be of interest to the children.

chapter 11A

Plants and Animals

CONTENT

THE FUNCTIONS OF LIFE

Hot patches of dust from the surface of an African plain are kicked into clouds by the plodding feet of a dirt- and dust-covered rhinoceros. As the giant, lumbering beast moves along munching plants, it frightens insects into temporarily confused flight. Some of these insects land on the rhino's body and are carried along to greener pastures as the rhino moves across the plain. The insects are not the only creatures who benefit from the rhino, for on its back also ride tick birds. As the rhino feeds on grasses and weeds, the tick birds flutter about feasting upon the newly arrived insects. The rhino, the insects, and the flapping, hungry birds are all animals. They depend on other living things for food.

There are at least eight characteristics that distinguish living things from nonliving things. We call these characteristics the *functions* of life. When a scientist observes something to determine whether it is a living thing or a nonliving thing, he or she searches for the presence of all eight characteristics. These characteristics, or functions, are:

1. The ability to respire (respiration)
2. The ability to produce, acquire, or use food
3. The ability to get rid of waste products (secretion and excretion)
4. The ability to move a variety of materials within it (transport)
5. The ability to move (locomotion)
6. The ability to respond to changes (irritability)
7. The ability to grow (growth)
8. The ability to produce more of its own kind (reproduction)

Figure 11A—1.

221

THE SCIENCE OF BIOLOGY

Biology is the science of living things. Scientists who study the characteristics of living things are known as biologists. The science of biology has many different parts:

1. Zoology: the study of animals
2. Botany: the study of plants
3. Anatomy: the study of the structure of living things
4. Physiology: the study of the functions or life processes of living things
5. Microbiology: the study of very small living things
6. Heredity: the study of how the features of living things are passed from parents to offspring
7. Evolution: the study of the origin of living things and their changes
8. Ecology: the study of the relationships among living things and their surroundings[1]

CLASSIFYING LIVING THINGS

Shark! The shout on a crowded summer beach rivets attention on a single dorsal fin cutting through the water. Terrified swimmers try to remain still, afraid to draw attention to themselves by rapid movement. The fin moves silently, less than forty meters from the shore, toward a group of swimmers. Under the surface a horizontal mouth opens to allow water to flow in and over rows of razor-sharp teeth. The shark's gills remove dissolved oxygen, and the water is expelled through gill slits. Its blood now contains the oxygen it needs to convert an upcoming meal into energy. Suddenly the dorsal fin disappears below the surface. On shore people scream, for now they do not know where the shark is. The fear of the unknown is stronger than the fear of the known. Where is it? The shark's tail fin makes a sudden powerful sweep and the torpedolike body is propelled toward an unsuspecting fish. With a quick snap of its jaws the shark has its meal. Its hunger satisfied, it turns and heads for deeper water. On the shore and in the surf, people scan the surface of the water. There is no sign of the shark. And they are left to wonder . . . where is it now?

Did the people really see a shark on this day? If so, what kind of shark was it? Were the swimmers in any real danger? Could the shark have been the rather common and harmless sand shark? Or was it a great white shark, having a length of over twelve meters (about forty feet), that just happened to see the fish before it saw the swimmers? The answer will never be known, for no one was able or willing to get close enough to examine the animal in detail. It is the details that make one

[1]Charles Tanzer, *Biology and Human Progress* (Englewood Cliffs, N.J.: Prentice-Hall, 1977), p. 8.

shark different from another. It is the details that make sharks far different creatures of the sea than dolphins. And it is the details that make one type of living thing quite different from other types of living things.

Sharks are only one of over five million different *kinds* of living things on our planet. Enough is known about them so that scientists are able to group them by their characteristics. Actually we have only been able to classify about one and a half million of the forms of life that inhabit the Earth. There are many more to be classified and many more that have yet to be discovered.

Classifying means placing a living thing in a system. When we classify living things we first group them into large kingdoms. Then we divide the kingdoms into smaller and smaller groups until we have a living thing classified with all other living things that have identical characteristics. The names of the major groupings that we use are:

Kingdom
Phylum
Class
Order
Family
Genus
Species

Each living thing can be classified according to this system. Traditionally, scientists have classified living things into one of two kingdoms—plants and animals. Some organisms possess combinations of characteristics that seem to set them apart from both plants and animals. As a result, some scientists have added additional kingdoms: Protista, for one-celled organisms that have characteristics of both plants and animals (slime molds and fungi are also in this kingdom); and Monera, for one-celled organisms that do not have a definite nucleus and reproduce asexually (bacteria and blue-green algae are in this kingdom).

In most elementary classrooms it is probably more functional to begin with a two-kingdom system as the basis for introductory discussions and activities or a three-kingdom system such as the one shown in Figure 11A–2. Note that Protista is shown as a separate kingdom. Then, when and where it might be appropriate, some children should probably be encouraged to use a more comprehensive classification system.

When a scientist classifies an organism he or she first decides whether it belongs in the animal kingdom or the plant kingdom (or in Protist or Monera). Next, the scientist decides in which phylum to place the plant or animal. This process is continued until the living thing has at least seven individual names. As an example, let's take a common grasshopper. Its seven names are:

Kingdom	Animalia
Phylum	Arthropoda
Class	Insecta
Order	Orthoptera
Family	Acridiidae
Genus	*Schistocerca*
Species	*americana*

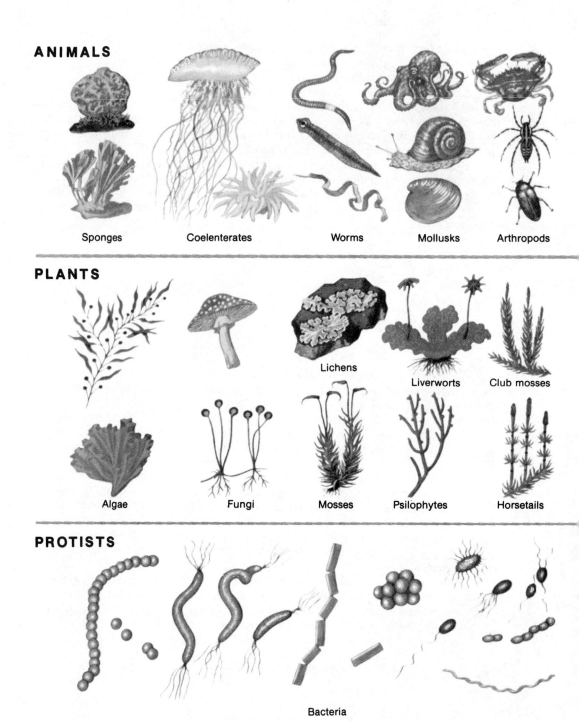

ANIMALS

Sponges Coelenterates Worms Mollusks Arthropods

PLANTS

Lichens Liverworts Club mosses

Algae Fungi Mosses Psilophytes Horsetails

PROTISTS

Bacteria

Figure 11A–2. A Three-Kingdom Classification System (*Source:* Vera Webster et al., *Prentice-Hall Life Science.* Englewood Cliffs, N.J.: Prentice-Hall, 1980. Used by permission.)

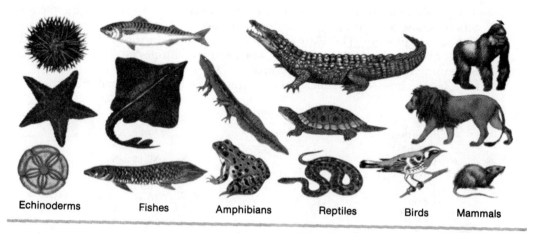

Echinoderms   Fishes   Amphibians   Reptiles   Birds   Mammals

Ferns   Gymnosperms   Angiosperms

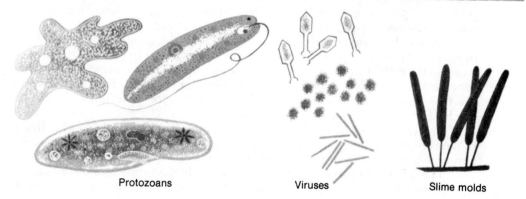

Protozoans   Viruses   Slime molds

Figure 11A-2. (*cont.*)

225

The grasshopper is an animal, so its kingdom is Animalia. Since there are so many other members of the animal kingdom, it is further classified as a member of the arthropoda phylum. There are also thousands of other arthropods, so the grasshopper is placed in the class Insecta. The process continues until the grasshopper is identified by the series of seven names.

Notice how the classification of a grasshopper and a human differ:

	Grasshopper	**Human**
Kingdom	Animalia	Animalia
Phylum	Arthropoda	Chordata
Class	Insecta	Mammalia
Order	Orthoptera	Primates
Family	Acridiidae	Hominidae
Genus	*Schistocerca*	*Homo*
Species	*americana*	*sapiens*

The use of a classification system helps scientists avoid confusion when they talk and write about living things. For example, there are many different kinds of maple trees. All are in the same kingdom, phylum, class, order, family, and genus. The different types are identified by their species name. The sugar maple is known as *Acer saccharum*: its genus is *Acer*; its species is *saccharum*. What type of maple would you guess the *Acer rubrum* to be? It is the red maple.

Although the panther, lion, and common house cat are all "cats," they each belong to a different species. They all are members of the genus *Felis*, but they have different species names. *Felis leo* is the genus and species of the African lion. Can you guess what type of cat *Felis domesticus* is?

SIMILARITIES BETWEEN PLANTS AND ANIMALS

Although there are many differences between plants and animals, there are many ways in which they are similar. For example, all plants and all animals are made up of a gelatinlike, colorless, semitransparent substance called protoplasm. Protoplasm is made up of a variety of elements, including carbon, hydrogen, oxygen, potassium, phosphorus, iodine, sulfur, nitrogen, calcium, iron, magnesium, sodium, chlorine, and traces of other elements.

Although protoplasm is found in the cells of all living things, the protoplasm in a particular type of living thing is unique to that thing. In other words, protoplasm in the cells of a porcupine enables the porcupine cells to carry on the unique functions that permit the porcupine to function as a porcupine. The protoplasm in the cells of a rosebush is uniquely able to carry on the functions that make a rosebush a rosebush.

The protoplasm of any living thing is found within tiny cells. Cells in living things contain a well-defined nucleus, which is essential to the cell's many functions and is also involved in the process of cell division.

The cells of any given living thing are not all similar to one another. Your skin cells, although they contain protoplasm and a nucleus, differ in many ways from the cells that make up the muscles of your heart. Similarly, every plant and every animal contain a variety of very specialized cells.

Any group of cells that perform a similar function is known as a tissue. A group of tissues that function together is called an organ. A group of organs that work together to perform a major function is known as a system. In plants the various cells and tissues that enable food made in the leaves to be transported to the stems and roots are called the vascular system. A plant contains many different systems. The human body is composed of a variety of systems, including a skeletal system, a muscular system, a respiratory system, a nervous system, an excretion system, and a reproductive system.

To summarize the similarities between plants and animals: both are made of cells, each of which contains protoplasm. Both contain tissues—groups of cells that work together to perform a particular function. Both contain organs—groups of tissues that function together. Both contain systems—groups of organs that work together to perform a given function.

DIFFERENCES BETWEEN PLANTS AND ANIMALS

The higher forms of plants and animals possess characteristics that allow us to distinguish between them:

Plants	Animals
Cell walls contain cellulose.	Cells are surrounded by a cell membrane that does not contain cellulose.
Organs are external to the plant's body—for example, leaves and flowers.	Most organs are internal to the animal's body—for instance, the heart and the stomach.
They produce their own food.	They cannot produce food internally.
They show little movement	Most can move freely.
No organs that have a specific excretory function.	They possess excretory organs.
They respond slowly to changes in the environment.	They can respond quickly to changes in the environment.

THE PLANT KINGDOM

An Overview of the Major Plant Phyla

Recent classification systems have grouped the organisms of the plant kingdom into two major phyla: the Bryophytes (Bryophyta) and the Tracheophytes (Tracheophyta). Bryophytes are small plants that lack conducting vessels for transporting water and nutrients. This phylum includes mosses, liverworts, and hornworts. The phylum Tracheophyta includes all vascular plants—that is, plants that have vessels for transporting water and nutrients.

Ferns, conifers, and flowering plants are all tracheophytes. Ferns do not produce true seeds. Both conifers and flowering plants are seed-producing tracheophytes. These seed-producing plants are grouped into two classes: the Gymnosperms and the Angiosperms. Most Gymnosperms do not produce flowers—they produce cones. Evergreen trees such as pines, redwoods, and spruces are all Gymnosperms. Angiosperms produce flowers. Fruit trees, rose plants, and daisies are all examples of angiosperms. The flowering plants are the most advanced form of plant life on earth and are able to survive and thrive in a wide variety of soils and climatic conditions.

The Flowering Plants: A Closer Look

THE ROOT

The roots of flowering plants typically grow under the ground. They grow all through the life of a healthy plant, continually pushing their way through soil as they absorb minerals and water. Roots have two major functions: to anchor the plant in the soil and to absorb water and dissolved minerals. The tip of the root is made of a group of loose cells called the root cap. As the root makes its way through the ground the cells of the root cap are worn away. New cells behind the root cap continue to grow and take the place of the cells that are worn away. Fuzzy hairs grow behind the root cap. Each of these root hairs is quite thin and is able to take in large amounts of water and dissolved minerals. Water that enters the root hair is transported upward through tubes in the center of the root. These tubes ultimately carry water and also dissolved minerals to the stem and leaves of the plant. Surrounding these tubes are other tubes that carry food from the leaf and stem to the root. Many roots also contain large storage cells. Food produced in the leaves and stem and transported to the root is stored in such cells.

THE STEM

The stem of a plant can be thought of as an elaborate pipeline through which a two-way flow of materials occurs. At the outside of the stem is a group of tubes that carry food produced in the leaves downward through the stem into the root. Closer to the center of the stem, as we have just seen, is a group of tubes that carries water and dissolved minerals upward to the leaves. In the center of the stem are groups of cells that store food. This region is known as the pith.

Trees are seed plants whose various tubes are made of cells that are very strong. The walls of such cells are made of a very tough material—cellulose. You are familiar with the many uses of wood, such as the production of lumber and paper.

THE LEAF

The process of food making occurs in the leaves of plants. Leaves use water and dissolved minerals, which are absorbed by the roots and carried upward by the

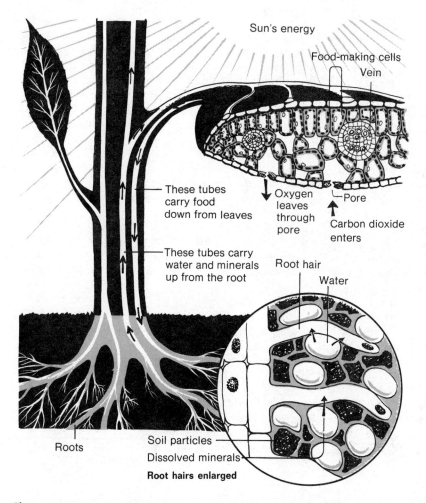

Sun's energy

Food-making cells

Vein

These tubes carry food down from leaves

Oxygen leaves through pore

Pore

Carbon dioxide enters

These tubes carry water and minerals up from the root

Root hair

Water

Roots

Soil particles

Dissolved minerals

Root hairs enlarged

Figure 11A–3. How a Green Plant Makes Food. Water enters from the root hairs. It passes up the stem to the leaves. Here it is combined with carbon dioxide from the air to make carbohydrates. Sunlight and green chlorophyll are necessary for this process, which is called *photosynthesis*. (*Source:* Charles Tanzer, *Biology and Human Progress*, 5th ed. Englewood Cliffs, N.J.: Prentice-Hall, 1977. Used by permission.)

stem, the carbon dioxide in the air, and the energy of the sun to produce food. There is a wide variety of leaf shapes, but all green leaves, regardless of their shape, contain chlorophyll, the vital substance that enables them to produce food. Leaves contain an elaborate network of tubes that carry liquid through the stalk of the leaf and to all areas of the leaf. These tubes, or veins, carry water and dissolved minerals to the leaf and then transport the food that is produced there to the stems, roots, and fruit. Some of the food produced in the leaf is stored in the leaf, but most is carried to other parts of the plant.

THE REPRODUCTIVE ORGANS
OF FLOWERING PLANTS

The principal organ of reproduction of a flowering plant is the flower. A flower in the bud stage is protected by an outer covering of sepals. Seen at the base of most flowers, sepals look like small leaves and are usually green. The parts of the flower that are most familiar to us are the petals. Petals are usually bright and possess a color and odor that attract most insects. The petals of a flower are also important in that they produce a sugary material called nectar. Insects seek out this nectar as a food source.

The reproductive organs of a flower are found within its petals. The female organ is the pistil. Some flowers have many pistils, whereas others have only one. At the base of the pistil is a swollen area called the ovary. In it are tiny ovules that can eventually develop into seeds. The ovule contains an egg nucleus that, if fertilized, can produce a new plant.

The pistil is surrounded by a group of male organs, or stamens. A stamen consists of a slender stalk with a yellow or orange pollen box on top. This pollen box, which is called an anther, contains many pollen grains. Within each grain is a sperm nucleus that can eventually unite with an egg nucleus to form a seed that can become a new plant.

Most flowers contain both male and female organs. However, some contain just one or the other. The reproduction of flowering plants is similar to reproduction in animals in that an egg nucleus and sperm nucleus must unite before an offspring can be formed.

Refer to Figure 11A–4 and note the location of the various parts of the flower. Here is a list of the principal flower parts and their function.

1. Sepals: a group of modified leaves that protect the budding flowers
2. Petals: modified leaves that attract insects
3. Stamen: the male reproductive organ of a flower
4. Pistil: the female reproductive organ of the flower

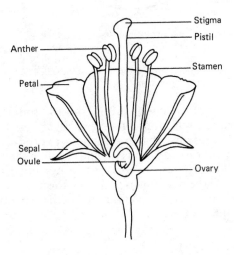

Figure 11A–4. The flower is an organ of reproduction. What is the function of each part? (*Source:* Adapted from Charles Tanzer, *Biology and Human Progress*, 5th ed. Englewood Cliffs, N.J.: Prentice-Hall, 1977. Used with permission.)

5. Ovary: enlarged egg sac at the lower end of the pistil containing unfertilized egg cells, or ovules
6. Anther: the "box" containing pollen grains at the tip of the stamen
7. Stigma: the tip of the pistil

POLLINATION

Pollination is the process through which the sperm cell in a pollen grain unites with the egg nucleus of the ovule. Pollen grains are carried to the stigma at the top of the pistil by wind, water, or insects. The bee, for example, is a principal agent of pollination. As the bee visits the flower, pollen grain may stick to its many bristles when it brushes against the stamen. If the bee then brushes against the tip of the pistil, some pollen grains may rub off its body and become attached to the stigma.

Soon after the pollen grain becomes attached to the stigma, it begins to produce a slender pollen tube that grows down through the pistil toward the ovary. If the pollen tube reaches the ovary, the sperm cells inside the pollen grain may move from the pollen grain down the tube to the ovary and eventually unite with the nuclei of egg cells. Fertilized egg cells from the ovary will divide, multiply, and eventually form seeds. Within each seed is an embryo surrounded by stored food—a tiny plant. If the seed eventually reaches moist soil, a new plant will grow.

After fertilization occurs in a flower, the ovary enlarges and its petals fall off. Fruits are enlarged ovaries that contain seeds. Apples, oranges, and even watermelons are all large, ripened, seed-containing ovaries. Animals eating such foods will excrete the seeds and indirectly assist in the germination of new plants at a distance from the original plant.

If a seed reaches a destination that provides the appropriate environment of moisture and warmth, it may eventually develop into a plant. Water entering the seed causes it to swell, and the covering of the seed—the seed coat—splits. A young root begins to grow downward from the seed, absorbing water and dissolved minerals. The stem and leaves of the embryo plant also begin to grow, but their direction is up, and eventually they break through to the sunshine above. As this occurs, the food stored in the original seed leaves is used up and the food-storage parts of the leaves—the cotyledons—begin to shrink. Eventually, the leaves of the new plant are large enough to produce food. Figure 11A-5 shows the process by which a seed develops into a plant.

Seeds are transported from their parent plants in many ways. Seeds that are part of an edible fruit are transported by the creatures that consume the fruit. The seeds of milkweed or dandelion are blown through the air on parachutes. Some fruits, such as that of the witch hazel, explode and blow out their seeds. The burdock produces seeds with tiny hooks that catch on the fur of passing animals. You may have noticed the tiny wings of the elm and maple seeds that make them appear as tiny helicopters as they fall toward the ground.

ASEXUAL REPRODUCTION OF PLANTS

Some plants reproduce in the absence of a sperm cell uniting with an egg cell. Reproduction that does not require seeds produced by the fusion of male and female cells is known as asexual reproduction. Florists and fruit and vegetable

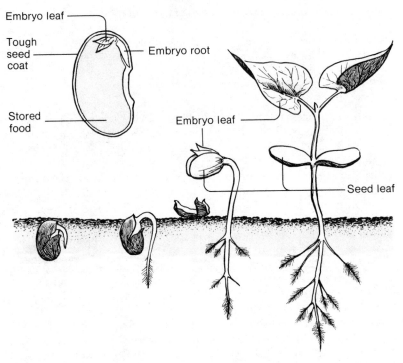

Embryo leaf

Tough
seed
coat

Embryo root

Stored
food

Embryo leaf

Seed leaf

Figure 11A–5. How a Seed Becomes a Plant (*Source:* Charles Tanzer, *Biology and Human Progress*, 5th ed. Englewood Cliffs, N.J.: Prentice-Hall, 1977. Used with permission.)

growers utilize a number of different ways to produce plants without using seeds.

Some plants, such as the begonia, can be reproduced simply from a piece of stem with leaves on it. Such a stem is called a cutting or slip. Cuttings are usually placed in water or moist sand and then kept warm. Eventually a new plant begins to form.

Other plants, such as lilies and tulips, reproduce from bulbs—large portions of stems that store food. All that is usually required in this case is warmth and moisture.

The white potato is an underground stem that contains stored food. Farmers who wish to grow new potato plants simply cut a potato into pieces and plant them. In order for a piece of potato to form a new plant, it must contain a bud, or eye. The buds of the pieces of potato eventually sprout to form the new plant.

THE PROTIST KINGDOM

The four major groups of protists are the bacteria, the protozoans, the slime molds, and the viruses. Bacteria have a cell-like structure but do not have a well-defined nucleus. Bacteria are very small in size. Some bacteria produce their own food in the manner that plants do. Others get their nutrients from other living things. The protozoans include such organisms as amoebas and paramecia. Slime molds are extremely difficult to classify as plants or animals; consequently, they also are often classified as protists. Viruses are only able to exist within the cells of other living things; as a result, some scientists consider them to be nonliving.

One-celled protozoa such as amoebas and paramecia can reproduce simply by splitting in two. This occurs only after the organism reaches a mature state. The nucleus of a protozoan begins to split first. Then the two equal parts of the nucleus thus created move away from each other within the cell, and the other material in the cell begins to separate. Eventually the original cell is transformed into two smaller cells, each having its own protoplasm containing a nucleus. This kind of reproduction is known as fission.

Paramecia are also able to reproduce by a process that resembles sexual reproduction. Two paramecia may become physically attached and exchange small portions of their nuclei. This accomplished, the paramecia separate, and then *each* begins the process of fission. This process, which is known as conjugation, seems to be a forerunner of the true sexual reproduction displayed in higher animals.

THE ANIMAL KINGDOM

An Overview of the Major Animal Phyla

There are almost one million different kinds of animals inhabiting the earth. In order to keep track of them, scientists have found it very useful to classify them into two major groups: animals without backbones and animals with backbones. Animals without backbones are called invertebrates. They include sponges, jellyfishes, starfishes, worms, mollusks, lobsters, spiders, and insects. The second major group, those with backbones, are called the vertebrates. This group includes fishes, frogs, snakes, birds, mammals, and other animals. Vertebrates and invertebrates are divided into various phyla.

The Mammals: A Closer Look

Mammals are vertebrates whose bodies are covered with hair or fur. They usually have four legs. In some mammals the fore legs and rear legs are modified to perform particular functions. For example, the fore limbs of kangaroos enable them to grasp food, whereas their strong, enlarged back legs enable them to hop.

The eggs of mammals are usually fertilized internally. Most mammals produce their young by giving birth to them. Female mammals suckle their young and care for them as they mature. The amount of time for a young mammal to mature into an adult varies greatly. Mammals seem able to teach their young to perform functions that will ensure their survival. Such functions include the ability to hunt and/or fish. Some mammals care for their young until they are fully grown and able to survive on their own.

Female opossums and kangaroos have pouches in which they place their young as soon as they are born. Bats are mammals that can fly. They accomplish

Figure 11A—6. A Young Kangaroo
and Its Mother. (*Source:* Courtesy
Australian Information Service.)

this through the use of a leathery membrane stretching between their forelimbs and hind legs. Although bats may seem to be birds, one notices that they have hair instead of feathers.

Rats, mice, beavers, and other rodent mammals have very sharp front teeth that enable them to gnaw. Rabbits and squirrels are also rodents. Some mammals, such as pigs, deer, sheep, and cattle, walk on the tips of their toes. Their hooves are really large toenails. Some hoofed mammals, among them horses and zebras, have only one hoof per foot. The giraffe is the tallest of all animals, sometimes attaining six meters (about twenty feet) in height. It is able to eat leaves that grow at the tops of trees. Meat-eating mammals are called carnivores. Their long teeth and sharp claws make them very proficient predators. The fox, the lion, and the coyote are all carnivores.

Although whales look like fish, they are really sea-living mammals. The blue whale can reach almost 30 meters (about 100 feet) in length and weigh over 140,000 kilograms (about 150 tons).

The primates, which include monkeys and apes, are the most intelligent mammals. They have the best-developed brains of all animals, fingers that are able to grasp objects, and nails instead of claws. Monkeys have long tails that help them move about on branches. The largest of all apes is the gorilla, which can weigh as much as 180 kilograms (about 400 pounds). The gorilla is able to walk upright and support itself by placing its hands on the ground. The most intelligent of all animals is probably the chimpanzee, though some people feel that a sea mammal, the dolphin, may be more intelligent than the chimpanzee and perhaps as intelligent as humans.

Men and women are very different from other animals. Nonetheless, scientists usually group the human race with the primates. Our hands can handle small objects much more easily than those of any other primate, our brain is capable of reasoning, we have fully developed communication systems, and we are able to invent and use tools and machines.

Some Examples of Animal Reproduction

FROGS

Although frogs are able to live on both land and water, they reproduce in the water. The male frog releases sperm cells over egg cells expelled into the water by the female. The egg cells are surrounded by a jellylike material and are attached to one another in long strands. The sperm cells fertilize the eggs.

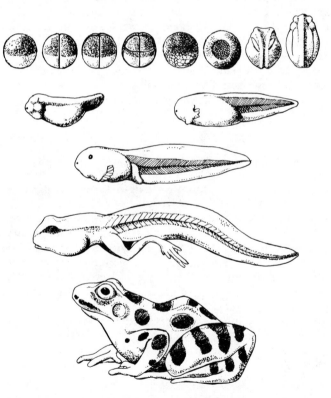

Figure 11A–7. How a Frog Develops. The fertilized egg divides into many cells. In time, as the gills disappear and the legs develop, the adult frog emerges. (*Source:* Charles Tanzer, *Biology and Human Progress*, 5th ed. Englewood Cliffs, N.J.: Prentice-Hall, 1977. Used with permission.)

After fertilization a many-celled embryo begins to develop. Eventually the embryo takes the form of a tadpole. When the fishlike tadpole is sufficiently mature, it breaks free of its jellylike envelope and swims away. The tadpole is able to absorb oxygen from water through a pair of gills in its neck.

The tadpole changes in form as time passes. Its tail shrinks, hind and front legs appear, and its gills get smaller. As the gills shrink lungs begin to form. The tadpole must now rely on air above the water's surface for oxygen. At this stage it has become a young frog.

BIRDS

Birds reproduce as a result of internal fertilization. The basic process is the same for most types of birds. The chicken will serve as a good example.

Within the body of the female chicken, or hen, is an ovary. The ovary produces the hen's egg cells. As a tiny egg cell within the ovary matures it fills with yolk. After this occurs the egg leaves the ovary and enters the upper part of the oviduct, the channel through which sperm deposited by a male chicken, or rooster, can swim. If a sperm cell that swims up the oviduct meets an unfertilized egg cell, a fertilized egg will be produced. The fertilized egg passes down the oviduct and develops an external membrane. The material that we call egg white is also added in the oviduct. As the fertilized egg, now containing both egg white and yolk, moves toward the outside world, shell glands at the bottom of the oviduct produce a hard substance that surrounds it. This shell will prevent the fertilized egg from drying out and will protect it against crushing when it reaches the outside world.

MAMMALS

Young mammals are born alive and are typically nurtured for a relatively long time by their parents. A few mammals, such as the spiny-anteater and the duck-billed platypus, resemble lower forms of vertebrate life in that they lay eggs in a manner similar to that of the birds and reptiles. As we have seen, opossum and kangaroo females have an external pocket, or pouch. Newborn animals of these species are placed by the mother in the pouch, where they are fed from mammary glands.

In mammals sperm cells enter the female reproductive system and internally fertilize an egg cell. The fertilized egg journeys to the uterus, an organ in which it will grow and develop until it is sufficiently mature to survive in the outside world. The amount of time the developing egg, or embryo, spends in the uterus is known as the gestation period.

The gestation period for a human being is about nine months. A human baby is virtually helpless at birth and takes a very long time to become fully grown. Human reproduction is a subject that requires considerable detail. It will be discussed in Chapter 12A.

SUMMARY OUTLINE

I. Living things can be distinguished from nonliving things on the basis of charistics known as functions of life.

   A. The life functions are respiration; food production, acquisition, or use; secretion and excretion; transport; locomotion; irritability; growth; and reproduction.
   B. Biology is the study of living things.
  II. Living things can be classified into groups based on their common characteristics.
   A. Living things are classified into a kingdom, phylum, class, order, family, genus, and species.
   B. Plants and animals are the traditional kingdoms. Some living things do not fit conveniently into either of these kingdoms and may be placed instead in Protist, Monera, or some other alternative kingdom.
 III. The plant kingdom includes simple plants, mosses, ferns, and seed plants.
 IV. The Protist kingdom includes bacteria, protozoans, slime molds, and viruses.
  V. The animal kingdom includes the invertebrates—sponges, hydra, jelly-fishes, corals, worms, mollusks, and jointed-leg animals—and the vertebrates.
 VI. Animals reproduce as a result of the union of male and female reproductive cells.

chapter 11B

Plants and Animals

DISCOVERY ACTIVITIES AND DEMONSTRATIONS

DISCOVERY ACTIVITIES

How Is a Kitten Different from a Stone?*

OBJECTIVE

Children will describe three ways in which a kitten (or other small animal) is different from a stone.

*Asterisks refer to activities for young children.

Figure 11B–1. (*Source:* J. Abruscato and J. Hassard, *The Whole Cosmos Catalog.* Santa Monica, Calif.: Goodyear Publishing Company, Inc. Used by permission of Goodyear Publishing Company.)

PROCESSES EMPHASIZED

Observing
Classifying
Communicating
Inferring

MATERIALS

Small animal (or a picture of a small animal)
Stone
One picture of a living thing and one picture of a nonliving thing for each child group

MOTIVATION

Keep both the kitten and the stone out of sight at the beginning of the activity. Secretly pick up the stone and tell the class that you would like them to guess what is in your hand. If they guess that it is a stone, show the stone and tell them that today's activity will teach them how a stone is different from a living thing. Now show them the kitten (or picture of a kitten) and begin the lesson.

DIRECTIONS

1. Display both the kitten and the stone so that all the children can see them.
2. Ask the children to make observations of each.
3. Make a list of their observations on the chalkboard.
4. Begin a discussion of their observations of the stone and the kitten, focusing on the difference between living and nonliving things.
5. Distribute one picture of a living thing and one picture of a nonliving thing to each child or group of children. Have them study the pictures and think about the differences between the living and nonliving things depicted in them.
6. Have the children summarize what they have learned about the differences between living and nonliving things.

KEY DISCUSSION QUESTIONS

1. What are some nonliving things you have noticed on your way to school? *Water. Sun. Wind.*
2. What are some living things you have noticed on your way to school? *Children. Plants. Animals.*
3. What are some of the living things in this classroom? *Children. Teachers. Plants.*
4. What are some of the nonliving things in this classroom? *Books. Desks. Pencils.*

SCIENCE CONTENT FOR THE TEACHER

Living things differ in many ways from nonliving things. The characteristics of living things—the functions of life—are reproduction, food production, acquisition, and/or use, growth from within, locomotion (self-initiated movement), internal transport of materials, responsiveness to stimuli, secretion and excretion of waste products, and respiration.

EXTENSIONS

Science. A field trip taken in conjunction with this activity would enable children to observe living and nonliving things in the environment.

You might use this activity to begin a discussion of the ways in which one type of living thing—plants—differ from another type of living thing—animals. This would be an excellent time for children to begin thinking about the fact that a specific living thing (such as the kitten) more closely resembles its parents in appearance than it resembles other living things.

Art. Have the children make drawings or clay sculptures of living and nonliving things they observe.

Have the children make drawings of all the four-legged and all the two-legged living things they can think of.

Social Studies. This activity is a good setting in which to help children begin thinking about the relationships of living things to nonliving things. Shelter and implements are among the uses of nonliving things that you can highlight.

You may wish to have children begin to think about and discuss how nonliving things such as volcanoes, violent weather, and landslides affect the lives of humans.

What Is a Seed?*

OBJECTIVE

The children will be able to describe a seed as something capable of growth.

PROCESSES EMPHASIZED

> Predicting
> Observing
> Recording
> Interpreting data
> Contrasting variables

MATERIALS

> Large cardboard boxes cut 2 to 4 inches tall and lined with plastic
> Soil or starting mixture (vermiculite plus soil)
> Collections of seeds and other small things ("red-hot" candy, marbles, pebbles)
> Chart paper
> One index card per student

MOTIVATION

Ask the children to bring in the seeds and other small items for some science experiments. Tell them that when the candy comes in, they will begin their study of seeds and see if the candy will grow a candy bush or tree.

DIRECTIONS

1. This experiment can be done by individuals or by the class as a whole, depending upon the amount of materials and the abilities of your students.
2. Begin by setting out samples of the small things that have been brought in. Ask the students to describe the items while you list their observations on the chart papers.
3. The children (or the class) should record in pictures and in words how each of the seeds looks at the start of the experiment. In addition, they could glue a seed to an index card. They can then use the index card as a place to record observations from the activity.
4. Some decisions need to be made regarding the number of each object to be planted and the depth of planting. Next, explain that the amount of water, light, warmth, etc., should be equal for each item. These things will be easy to control if the samples are planted in the same box.
5. The arrangement and marking of the "seeds" within the boxes will also need some attention. The children will need to know what is underneath the soil, as some of the "seeds" will not emerge from the soil during the experiment.
6. After these variables have been considered (they may or may not be placed under control), the students can plant their seeds and begin their observation of the gardens. A short period of time should be set aside each day for maintenance and data gathering. Encourage the children to keep a daily log of what they see.
7. Some children might like to peek at the seeds during the experiment. If they do this they will need to think about the number of seeds of each type that were planted and how they can make their inspection without disturbing the others. One way to observe germination without disturbing the seeds is to place moist paper toweling in a glass jar and "plant" seeds between the toweling and the glass. Such a jar will allow students to see what is going on in the soil in the boxes, but perhaps it can be kept a secret until the students have had the pleasure of digging up a few of their own seeds.
8. When a majority of the time seeds are growing, the children should dig up samples of each type of seed they have planted to see what changes have taken place. They should record their observations and then compare them with their observations of the seeds at the start of the experiment.
9. It would be useful to divide the original set of items into growers and nongrowers. With this set to examine, students should begin to investigate where the items come from and develop a general definition of a *true seed*.

KEY DISCUSSION QUESTIONS

1. In what ways are all these items alike? *They are all small.*
2. How many seeds of each type should be planted? *More than one or two, since some might die before they come up and can be seen.*

3. How deeply should they be planted? (*Answers will vary based upon gardening experience, but common sense usually prevails.*)

4. What should be done about the amount of water, sunlight, temperature, etc., that the "seeds" receive? *They should be kept the same so that all seeds have the same chance of living.*

5. What is the biggest difference among the "seeds" at the end of the experiment? *Some grow and some don't.*

6. What did some seeds become? *They grew into new plants.*

SCIENCE CONTENT FOR THE TEACHER

Seeds come in all sizes, from those as small as the period at the end of a sentence to others as big as a walnut. Shape can also vary dramatically, from round and smooth to pyramidlike. Seeds have protective shells (seed coats) that keep the embryonic plant alive. Stored food will provide the energy for the seedling to reach the soil surface and begin producing food of its own.

In order to survive, some plants produce seeds in *great* numbers, and others produce seeds with structures (such as bark and "parachutes") that enable them to disperse (move from one place to another). Some seeds even look like insects, which discourages seed-eating birds from consuming them.

Even with this great diversity, seeds differ significantly from all the nonseed items in this activity by being able to *grow* and reproduce their own kind (much to the despair of some of your candy lovers!).

EXTENSIONS

Science. Produce a poster or bulletin board of as many kinds of seeds as can be collected. These can be grouped by size, shape, or color.

Cut open different fruits and vegetables to find where their seeds are and how big they are.

Math. Show how seeds can be used as "counters," how they can be sorted into sets, and how they can be arranged in order from smallest to largest.

Who Goes There?*

OBJECTIVE

The children will be able to match pictures of common animals with the animals' footprints.

SCIENCE PROCESSES EMPHASIZED

Observing
Inferring

MATERIALS

For the teacher

Unlabeled set of animals' footprints[1]
Set of pictures of the animals for which you have footprints
Set of pictures showing the various environments in which the animals live
Set of name cards of animals

For each child or group

Construction-paper headboard (band of construction paper that will hold paper feathers)
Paper feathers of various colors

MOTIVATION

Hand out the animal pictures and headboards to groups of children. Suggest that they all pretend they are teams of animal trackers, and explain that each team will be awarded one feather for each animal they successfully track.

DIRECTIONS

1. Display a picture (or drawing) of an animal track and a picture of the environment in which the animal is likely to be found. Begin a discussion of the track and the environment.
2. After some discussion have the children try to think of the animal being described. The group members can discuss the possibilities among themselves before reaching a decision.
3. When all the teams are ready, have the chiefs hold up their team's selection of the animal in question. Encourage the groups to tell why they think their choice is the correct one.
4. Staple a paper feather to the headboard of each team that is correct. The job of being chief is then rotated to the next person in each group, and the game continues.

KEY DISCUSSION QUESTIONS

1. Which of the tracks comes from the biggest animal? (*Answers will depend on the tracks and the pictures you are using.*)
2. Which of the tracks comes from the smallest animal? (*Answers will vary.*)
3. Which of the tracks comes from an animal with claws that stick out? (*Answers will vary.*)
4. Which of the tracks belongs to an animal that can climb trees? (*Answers will vary.*)
5. Hold up pictures of various environments (for example, a treetop for squirrels and an open plain with trees in Africa for elephants) and ask which of the animals might be found in them. Ask the students to try to guess which footprint might be found in most environments. (Be sure to have the teams explain why they decided on a particular footprint.)

[1]A good source of pictures of animal tracks is the ESSS unit *Animal Tracks*, available from Webster Division, McGraw-Hill Book Co.

SCIENCE CONTENT FOR THE TEACHER

Footprints hold clues about the life and environment of the animals that made them. Very large footprints often belong to large animals or to animals that travel over soft terrain. For example, the relatively large feet of the snowshoe rabbit support its weight on snow, thus allowing it to travel well on terrain that hinders most other animals. Most animals that live on the open range have evolved smaller feet with hooves that allow them to run fast on fairly smooth, hard land. Some footprints show evidence of claws used for defense as well as climbing. Retractable claws are an obvious benefit to animals that must be able to run quickly and silently before catching their prey.

EXTENSIONS

Science. Obtain or reproduce pictures of various tracks showing something happening (for example, animals walking and then running), and have the teams determine what happened.

Have the students research the topic of fossils, especially fossilized tracks and what scientists have learned about the animals that made them.

Have the students make an answer board on which others try to match pictures of animals with pictures of their footprints.

Art. Make a set of linoleum printing blocks of various footprints, and have the children make pictures with them.

Music. Obtain sounds of the hoofbeats of a horse (a sound-effects record is a likely and easily obtained source), and have the children guess what the horse is doing and where it is going. The children can also try to hum or sing various melodies that might fit the rhythm of the hooves.

Male and Female Guppies: What's the Difference?

OBJECTIVE

The children will observe the physical characteristics of male and female guppies.

SCIENCE PROCESSES EMPHASIZED

Observing
Classifying

MATERIALS FOR THE TEACHER

Supply of guppies
Aquarium
Supply of dry fish food
Coarse dip net

MATERIALS FOR EACH CHILD OR GROUP

Male guppy
Female guppy
2 clean liter- or quart-size jars
Supply of aquarium water
Hand lens

MOTIVATION

Ask the children if they know what a guppy is. Have them describe guppies without the benefit of guppies to observe. Now display the guppies you will be using for the activity, and tell the children that they will have a chance to make very careful observations of male and female guppies.

DIRECTIONS

1. Distribute a jar containing aquarium water and a female guppy to each child or group.
2. Ask the children to observe the external characteristics of the guppy and make a drawing of it, labeling the various body parts. Encourage them to shade in parts of their drawing to show the guppy's markings.
3. Now distribute a jar containing aquarium water and a male guppy. Have the children observe the male guppy and then make a labeled drawing of it.
4. Have the children visit with other children or groups to see if their male guppy resembles other male guppies and whether their female guppy resembles other female guppies.
5. Circulate around the room and sprinkle a small amount of dry fish food on the surface of each container. Ask the children to observe the feeding behavior of the guppy.

KEY DISCUSSION QUESTIONS

1. How can you tell the difference between male and female guppies? *The female is usually larger, with a gray color and a fan-shaped fin; the male is smaller, with patches of color and a tubelike part at the base of its tail.*
2. How does the location of the guppy's mouth make it easier and safer for the guppy to feed? *It's at the top of its head, which lets it feed on surface food without having to lift its head out of the water; this makes it easier for it to "sneak up" on food.*

SCIENCE CONTENT FOR THE TEACHER

Guppies are small tropical fish. The male is smaller than the female but has a larger tail. It is also more lightly colored. The female is usually a uniform gray. The female has a fan-shaped anal fin. The male's anal fin is pointed and tubelike.

EXTENSIONS

Science. The demonstration on the birth of guppies, described later in this chapter, is a very effective follow-up to this activity.

Art. You may wish to have some of the children create larger drawings of the guppies they have observed. Drawing paper and a supply of pastels will assist them in such a project. Encourage the children to try to reproduce nature's coloration faithfully by using the appropriate colors and shades of pastels. You may wish to spray a fixative on the children's finished drawings in order to preserve them.

ADDITIONAL ACTIVITY IDEAS

What Makes Bread Rise?*

You can have children investigate the effect that yeast has on bread dough. Have the children make a mixture of nine parts of warm water to one part of sugar by weight. Mix in approximately the same weight of dry active yeast as the weight of the sugar and set the mixture aside. Within a few hours the children will be able to see that bubbles have formed in the mixture. These bubbles contain the gas that causes bread to rise. It is the same gas that is in carbonated soft drinks. The gas is carbon dioxide.

How to Grow "New" Plants from Parts of Old Ones

Children can learn about the process of asexual reproduction if they have an opportunity to grow a "new" plant from a portion of an existing plant. Many common houseplants can be used by children to produce new plants. For this activity provide each child or group of children with two or three fresh 7-to-12-centimeter (3-to-5-inch) cuttings from the stems of a begonia, geranium, or coleus. The cuttings should have one or two leaves on the stem. Have the children plant their cuttings in moist potting soil or vermilculite (a synthetic potting material available in supermarkets or garden stores). If the medium is kept moist, within two or three weeks roots will become established and new growth will be observable.

A leaf from an African violet plant can be used to produce a "new" plant. Provide the children with two or three fresh leaves from an African violet and have them plant them in the manner described above.

How Does Temperature Affect Seed Sprouting?

Children can readily observe that the sprouting of seeds is partially controlled by temperature. With baby-food jars, moist paper towels (or sponges), and bean seeds they can explore the importance of appropriate temperature. Have the children place the paper towels (or sponges) at the bottom of each of two baby-food jars. Then ask them to place three or four bean seeds on top of the toweling in each jar. The children should then label each jar with the date and their name. Have them place a lid on each jar and then store one of them in a refrigerator and the other in a dark place in the room (to control for the lack of light in the refrigerator). They should observe the contents of both jars each day. At the end of a week they will be able to observe that the beans in the jar kept at room temperature have sprouted before the beans in the refrigerator. They will also see that the beans in the cold environment grow more slowly than the ones in the warm environment.

What Living Things Are in Pond Water?

Children are usually surprised to learn that some organisms are so small as to be virtually invisible. When they think of living things they usually think of large plants and animals. A sample of pond water can provide the children with a great variety of tiny living things to observe. You can collect enough pond water for the entire class by scooping up a bucketful of water at the edge of a pond (any area that supports cattails and pondweeds will be rich in small animal and plant life).

Keep the water at room temperature and provide each child with a baby-food–sized jar of it. The children can use a strong magnifying glass to examine drops of water from their jars. If simple microscopes are available, have the children make and study slides of drops of the pond water. The children can record what they see either in pictures or notes.

The Water Flea: A See-Through Animal

This activity requires the use of a simple microscope. Even the very inexpensive microscopes available at toy stores or department stores will fill this need very well. In addition to the microscope, you will need a supply of *Daphnia* (water fleas), eyedroppers, and slides. *Daphnia* can easily be purchased from a pet store or ordered from a biological-supply company. They are excellent animals to study, since they are transparent. Using an eyedropper, children can place a water flea on their slide without a coverslip (so as not to crush the flea) and make many observa-

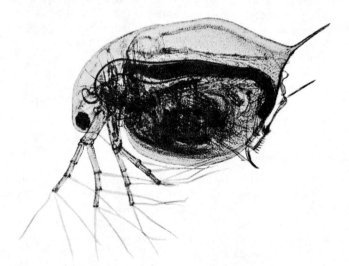

Figure 11B–2. The Waterflea (*Source:* Photograph by Carolina Biological Supply Company.)

tions of the internal systems of the animal. They should look for the beating heart, the food tube, and the kicking feet, and in some cases they may even find a sack on the back of the animal containing eggs of baby *Daphnia*.

Is a Whale a Mammal?

This activity requires that the children do some library research to discover whether a whale is a mammal. Prior to this activity you may wish to have a discussion about animals such as whales, dolphins, and porpoises. The children can easily become involved in a spirited debate if some of them argue that such animals are fish. The children can, as a result of the research, produce reports or drawings that answer the question. In the course of their work they will find that whales, dolphins, and porpoises are all mammals that have fish-shaped bodies. They will also discover that all three are air breathers and that they suckle their young. They will find that the young of these animals develop inside the mother, are born alive, and are cared for by the mother for extended periods of time.

Is a Penquin a Bird?

This activity parallels the previous one. Through research the children will find that penguins are indeed birds, and that they are good swimmers but are unable to fly. They will discover a variety of other information about penguins, including the knowledge that their body covering consists of small, scalelike feathers and that their wings are flipperlike. They will also find that species of penguins range in size from 40 centimeters (about 16 inches) to 120 centimeters (about 48 inches).

Bones and More Bones

You may wish to encourage children to bring a collection of fish or chicken bones to class. Prior to the activity they should scrub all the bones until they are clean. Boil each child's assortment in salt water to further clean them and make them easier to work with. Now have the children attempt to organize their bones so as to form part of the animal's skeleton. Provide life-science reference books that show chicken and fish skeletons. By using such illustrations as references the children should be able to identify many of the bones they have brought in.

Yogurt Making*

Provide a selection of encyclopedias, reference books, and cookbooks for the students to use to investigate and then discuss what yogurt is. After their discussion have them make some yogurt by following a recipe from one of the cookbooks. Through this experience they should learn of the helpful role that bacteria play in the production of yogurt, how a small sample of yogurt can become a culture for producing more yogurt, and how the maintenance of proper temperature is essential for the growth of the bacteria.

DEMONSTRATIONS

The Birth of Guppies*

OBJECTIVES

The children will observe the construction of an aquarium.
The children will describe the roles of male and female guppies in the reproductive process.

SCIENCE PROCESSES EMPHASIZED

Observing
Inferring

MATERIALS

Fish aquarium
Aged tap water at room temperature
Aquarium sand and gravel
Assorted fresh-water plants, including *Anarchis*, duckweed, and eelgrass
1 dip net
2 or 3 nursery traps
Small container with two male guppies
Small container with four female guppies
Thermometer
Light source (a reading lamp can be used)
Dry fish food
(*Note*: Each of the above is readily available at any pet store.)

MOTIVATION

Ask the children if they have ever seen the birth of guppies. After a discussion of any observations they have made of guppies reproducing, tell them that some day within the next few weeks they may be able to see guppies being born. Display the aquarium and the other materials listed above.

DIRECTIONS

1. Have the children observe all the materials that you have placed on display.
2. Begin assembling the aquarium by placing a 5-centimeter (2-inch) layer of sand on its floor. Plant eelgrass in the sand. Now add the aged tap water; do it gently so as to avoid stirring up the sand. Float the duckweed and *Anarchis* in the water.

250

3. Put the thermometer in the water and place the light source nearby. The light source will need to be moved back and forth during the demonstration so as to maintain the water temperature at 25°C (75°F).
4. Place the male and female guppies in the aquarium.
5. Float the nursery traps in the aquarium and sprinkle some fish food on the water's surface.
6. Maintain the aquarium over a two- or three-week period and encourage the children to make observations of any changes that occur in the shape of the female guppies. A pregnant female will develop a bulging abdomen. Use the dip net to place each pregnant female in its own nursery trap. This increases the chances that the soon-to-be-born babies will survive for the traps will protect the new guppies from hungry adult fish.

KEY DISCUSSION QUESTIONS

1. Why did we plant eelgrass and other aquarium plants in the aquarium? (*Answers will vary. They may include: So that some living things in the aquarium would have plants to eat.*)
2. What does the male guppy do in the reproductive process? *Places sperm in the female guppy.*
3. What does the female guppy do in the reproductive process? *Produces the eggs that get fertilized; has a place inside her body where the new guppies begin to develop.*

SCIENCE CONTENT FOR THE TEACHER

For this demonstration you will need to know how to assemble and maintain a simple fresh-water aquarium. The directions above provide some of the basic information. If you wish to increase the likelihood of maintaining a healthy aquarium for more than one or two weeks, it would be well worth your while to spend some time visiting with salespersons in pet stores to learn the details of raising and caring for tropical fish in general and guppies in particular. Additional materials, such as water heaters, pumps, and filters, are necessary if you wish to keep the aquarium functioning all through the year. This equipment is commonly available at pet shops.

SPECIAL NOTE

This demonstration can be used as a follow-up to the discovery activity on male and female guppies described earlier in this chapter.

The Curious Gerbils*

OBJECTIVES

The children will observe the characteristics of gerbils.
The children will provide appropriate care for gerbils in the classroom.
The children will observe the birth of gerbils in the classroom.

SCIENCE PROCESSES EMPHASIZED

Observing
Inferring

MATERIALS

Male gerbil
Female gerbil
Gerbil cage with exercise wheel, water bottle, nesting material (cedar shavings, newspaper, cloth, etc.)
Gerbil food
Supply of lettuce

MOTIVATION

Keep the presence of the gerbils and the cage supplies secret. Tell the children that today they are going to have an opportunity to meet some classroom pets. Do not divulge what kind of animals the pets are. Ask the children if they think they can be responsible for the care of some pets in the classroom. Assuming the answer is yes, proceed with the demonstration.

DIRECTIONS

1. Display all the materials for the demonstration as well as the male and female gerbils.
2. Place the nesting material and the food in the cage, and fill the water bottle. Have the children discuss the purpose of each. Also, discuss the importance of the exercise wheel.
3. Now have the children observe the male and female gerbils. Place both in the cage.
4. Discuss the importance of proper care of the gerbils. Then talk about the children's responsibility, and appropriate rules, for their maintenance.
5. If you are fortunate, within a month or two you may have a litter of gerbils. In this event, have the children observe the changes that occur as the tiny creatures begin to appear more and more like their parents.

KEY DISCUSSION QUESTIONS

1. Are gerbils mammals? *Yes. They are alive, they drink their mother's milk, and their bodies are covered with hair (fur).*
2. What do you think gerbils need in order to survive and stay healthy in the classroom? *(Answers will vary, but may include food, water, nesting material, air, exercise, and some peace and quiet.)*
3. Various other questions concerning the children's responsibilities for the continuing care and feeding of the gerbils should be asked. Such questions should focus upon what the responsibilities will be, how they should be carried out, and who will carry them out. *(Answers will vary.)*

SCIENCE CONTENT FOR THE TEACHER

Gerbils are small animals that are easy to care for in the classroom. Gerbils are covered with hair and give birth and suckle their young: they are true mammals. Young female gerbils may bear young every six to eight weeks.

EXTENSIONS

Science. This demonstration can serve as a good introduction to the general topic of caring for animals. You could easily follow it with a few days of work on caring for puppies, cats, guinea pigs, hamsters, and other animals.

Art. You may wish to have the class make drawings of both the male and female gerbil and the gerbil babies. The children can use commercially available crayonlike pastels to try and reproduce the coloring of the animals.

SPECIAL NOTE

This demonstration is a long-term classroom project that involves a very serious responsibility for the proper care of living organisms. There are many questions you must face if you embark upon it, not the least of which is what you will do with the gerbils that are born in the classroom. You will quickly run out of appropriate living space for these creatures, as they are capable of reproducing at an alarming rate. The children will undoubtedly volunteer to take excess gerbils. However, do not assume that every child who wants a gerbil to take home as a pet will be able to provide appropriate care, or that his or her family wishes to have a new addition to the household. You should also be aware that some of the children who may want gerbils will not be able to have them because they are allergic to animals. You should spend a good deal of time thinking about both the benefits and problems associated with the raising of animals in the classroom *prior* to embarking on such a project.

ADDITIONAL DEMONSTRATION IDEAS

How to Make a Spore Print

Through this demonstration children will be able to see that every mushroom contains thousands of spores. An interlude of twenty-four to twenty-eight hours is required after the demonstration has been set up. You will need an assortment of large mushrooms, construction paper of various colors, and a few bowls. You may use wild mushrooms for this activity and take the opportunity to talk to the children about the importance of *not* eating them because some species are poisonous. Mushrooms purchased in a supermarket can also be used. In either case, the mushrooms should be fully "opened" and have a large cap.

Break the stalks from the mushrooms right below their caps. Throw the stalks away and lay the caps on the construction paper, undersurface down. Cover each cap with a bowl. After a few days remove the bowls and carefully lift the

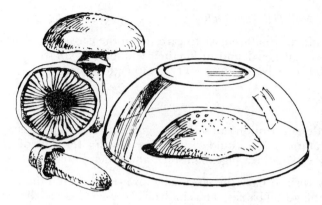

Figure 11B–3. (*Source:* J. Abruscato and J. Hassard, *The Whole Cosmos Catalog.* Santa Monica, Calif.: Goodyear Publishing Company, Inc. Used by permission of Goodyear Publishing Company.)

mushroom caps. You will be able to show the students a delicate pattern of fallen spores on the construction paper. You may wish to use this demonstration to commence a unit on nongreen plants.

Begging, Borrowing, and Showing off a Lobster*

This is a spectacular demonstration that you may wish to do during a unit on animal life. The children will be particularly excited by the appearance of this foreboding creature in their classroom. Needless to say, buying a live lobster is an extremely expensive undertaking. One way around this is as follows: Present yourself to the management of any local fresh-fish store or supermarket that sells live lobsters; explain that you are interested in borrowing a lobster to show your children and that you will need it just for a day; plead poverty. (It is best not to

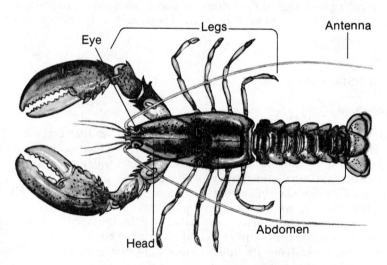

Figure 11B–4. You may wish to make a labeled drawing of a lobster such as this one for the children. (*Source:* Vera Webster et al., *Prentice-Hall Life Science.* Englewood Cliffs, N.J.: Prentice-Hall, 1980. Used by permission.)

appear hungry for lobster as you make your impassioned plea to borrow this very expensive and tasty creature. If you are convincing, you will have a live lobster to show your children. If you are unsuccessful, visit a pet shop or bait store and buy a crayfish.) Have the salesperson tape the lobster's claws shut. Keep the animal in a moist environment and hide it in a safe location in the classroom. During a discussion of shellfish (crayfish, lobsters, shrimp, and so on) produce your guest. Have the children observe the lobster, using a labeled diagram of it as a reference. *Warning*: Be sure to leave the lobster's claws taped; they are very capable of severing fingers. Return your *unharmed* and *uneaten* lobster to the fish store.

Pets on Parade*

This demonstration is particularly appropriate for young children. It may also be done with older children if you follow it up with a library research project on the various existing species of dogs, cats, tropical fish, and other animals. Invite other teachers in the school to bring any *safe* animal pets they may own to your class for part of a school day. If possible have the teachers spend some time in your classroom displaying their pets and describing their behavior, feeding habits, and other characteristics. Have your children make drawings of each animal displayed as they observe its physical features. This demonstration is an excellent opportunity for your children to view diverse animals and become acquainted with teachers who may have previously been strangers to them.

Sea Shells and Pen Pals

This demonstration can serve as the beginning of a long-term project for the entire class. You will need a strand of cultured pearls (very inexpensive ones can be bought at department stores) and a collection of sea shells. Place the shells where they are readily visible to all the children. Commence a discussion of animals with shells by introducing the amazing process by which they produce their own home (they secrete the material for the shell from a membrane known as the mantle). Display representative shells from as many of the following types of mollusks as you have in your collection: oysters, clams, mussels, and snails. Discuss the production of pearls (they are created by the secretion of the shell substance—mother of pearl—around sand grains). Display the string of cultured pearls, and give the children an opportunity to observe them.

To continue this demonstration as a full-year project, ask the children if they can think of some way to get different sea shells for the classroom collection. One suggestion you may wish to make is that they write to children who go to school in communities near an ocean. (If your community is on the West Coast, you can consider communities on the East Coast, and vice versa.) You can commence the process yourself by preparing a letter to elementary-school principals in various shoreline communities. Your own principal is likely a member of a professional organization that provides him or her with a complete roster of its membership. If you send out enough letters of inquiry, you will eventually make contact with an elementary-school teacher who is willing to commence a shell-sharing project. The potential benefits of such an activity should be obvious.

chapter 12A

The Human Body

CONTENT

Silently in the cold gray light of the dawn a runner moves briskly along the pavement. The row houses look quietly on as the rhythmic patter of footsteps echoes off their walls. Her stride is steady and firm. Her breathing is unhurried and barely reflects the strain of four miles of running. Her gaze is clear and her ears sensitive to the sounds of the neighborhood awakening. Her slightly elevated pulse rate marks the pushes and pulls of the blood coursing through her arteries, bringing oxygen and nourishment to body cells. The cells are producing energy and their by-products are being carried away by the bloodstream. The runner's body systems are functioning easily as she arrives home. Within minutes her well-conditioned body has recovered from this morning's ritual run. She feels refreshed and alive.

The four miles of minor strain have served to keep her body in good physical condition. It was not always easy to greet the dawn in this special active manner. At first it was a mere walk around the block, then a combination of walking and jogging, then longer distances as her body began to reflect its virtual hunger for exercise. Psychological benefits began to accrue as she felt her strength grow and her mind become more alert to the numerous stimuli she received

Figure 12A—1.

during the day. She began to acquire the pleasurable feeling of general well-being.

The well-functioning body matches its attributes with the enormous capabilities of the mind. The well-functioning systems of the runner's body permit her to bring her mind to bear fully on the things that matter in her life. Correspondingly it is her mind that wills her to rise early each day and run.

To understand fully how the human body is able to perform, we first need to consider its basic systems. Body systems are groups of organs that work together to carry out a particular function. For example, the heart, arteries, and veins each perform specific tasks whose combined effect is that the bloodstream is able to transport oxygen, nutrients, and waste products. The name we give to this particular body system is the circulatory system. The other basic body systems are the digestive, skeletal-muscular, respiratory, nervous, excretory, and reproductive systems. To understand them you will need to know both their structure and their functions.

THE DIGESTIVE SYSTEM

Every human action requires energy. Thinking a thought, blinking an eye, and taking a step would not be possible without energy. Energy powers every life function. The basic source of this life-giving energy is the food we eat. The process of digestion changes food from its original form to a fuel that can release energy when it reacts with oxygen. Digestion also releases and transforms proteins—the materials necessary for the building of new cells and the repair of old ones. The hamburger, french fries, and ear of corn on your plate at a late-summer picnic are much more than what they seem. They are the raw materials for the conduct of life itself. Your digestive system has the ability to change food into human cells, tissues, and organs.

Structure and Function

Digestion is the process through which the body breaks down molecules of food that are eaten and prepares them to react with oxygen to produce energy. Digestion begins in your mouth. As you chew food, glands in your mouth secrete saliva, a digestive juice that mixes with the food particles. It contains water, mucus, and a substance called an enzyme. Many enzymes are used in the process of digestion. Each breaks down a particular material found in food.

As food moves through the digestive system, enzymes continue to act on it. The organs of digestion, along with the windpipe, are depicted in Figure 12A−2. Figure 12A−3 shows where various food substances are digested and illustrates other aspects of the digestive process. The seeds of certain fruits, the cellulose in vegetables, and some meat tissues are indigestible. Such material passes into the large intestine and is eventually excreted.

Food and Nutrition

The food we eat is used in one of two basic ways by the body. Some parts of it are converted into energy, and other parts are converted into the raw material that is used to build new cells. The specific substances in foods that are necessary for life

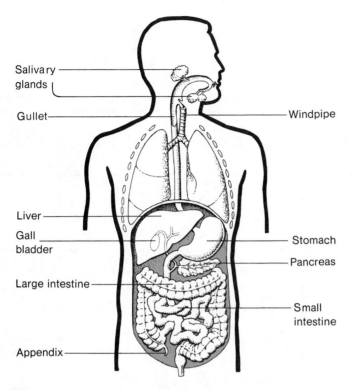

Figure 12A−2. The Human Digestive System. The system consists of a long tube through which the food passes. All along the tube, glands pour out digestive enzymes which dissolve the food. Finally, the food enters the blood through the villi of the small intestine. (*Source:* Charles Tanzer, *Biology and Human Progress,* 5th ed. Englewood Cliffs, N.J.: Prentice-Hall, 1977. Used by permission.)

have been grouped into several classes: carbohydrates (starches and sugars), fats, proteins, minerals, vitamins, and water. All these basic food substances—which are called nutrients—are necessary for health and growth. The foods we eat contain different amounts of these nutrients. Good food sources of nutrients are shown in Figure 12A−4.

WATER

Water is an essential food nutrient, since the protoplasm of your cells is composed largely of water. If these cells do not receive a sufficient supply of water, they are unable to carry out life functions. You lose a great deal of water to your surroundings by exhaling water vapor, perspiring, and discharging body wastes. Your body must replenish this lost water. The water you take in comes to you partly in the form of water that you drink and partly in the form of water contained in the foods you eat. Water is also needed to dissolve and transport other food nutrients within your body. Without water you simply cannot live.

Food substance	Place where substance is digested	Juice that digests the substance	Condition in which substance leaves stomach	Final product of digestion in small intestine
Starch	Mouth, Small intestine	Saliva, Pancreatic juice	Partly turned to sugar	Glucose sugar
Protein	Stomach, Small intestine	Gastric juice, Pancreatic and intestinal juices	Partly digested	Amino acids
Fats and oils	Small intestine	Pancreatic and intestinal juices, with the help of bile	Undigested but in liquid form	Fatty acids and glycerine
Table sugar, Malt sugar, Milk sugar	Small intestine	Intestinal juice	Undigested	Glucose sugar
Minerals	Digestion not necessary	None	Dissolved by water and acid	No change
Vitamins	Digestion not necessary	None	Unchanged	No change
Water	Digestion not necessary	None	Unchanged	No change

Figure 12A–3. Chart of the Digestive Processes (*Source:* Charles Tanzer, *Biology and Human Progress*, 5th ed. Englewood Cliffs, N.J.: Prentice-Hall, 1977. Used by permission.)

The Energy Content of Foods

The amount of energy contained in various foods is measured by the calorie. The number of calories needed by the human body varies from person to person and depends on the type of activities that the body undertakes. If you take in more calories of energy than you use, these excess calories are stored in your body. If over a long period of time you store more calories than you use, you will begin to increase in weight, since excess calories are converted into fat and stored in fat

Food substance	Good sources
Starches	Bread, cake, rice, spaghetti, potatoes
Sugars	Fruits, candy, cakes, molasses, carrots, raisins, onions
Fats and oils	Milk, butter, lard, bacon, corn, peanuts, chocolate
Proteins	Meats, fish, eggs, nuts, beans, milk, bread, corn, cheese
Minerals	
Calcium	Milk, cheese, leafy vegetables
Phosphorus	Lean meats, fish, eggs, whole-wheat bread
Iron	Liver, red meats, egg yolk, enriched bread
Iodine	Sea foods, iodized sàlt, plants grown in iodine-rich soil
Vitamins	
Vitamin A	Milk, butter, fortified margarine, fish-liver oils, yellow vegetables
Thiamin (B_1)	Pork, liver, egg yolk, whole-wheat bread, peas, beans, fruits, vegetables
Riboflavin (B_2)	Milk, eggs, liver, yeast, lean meats, vegetables, enriched bread
Niacin	Milk, eggs, liver, lean meats, peas, green vegetables, enriched bread
Vitamin C	Citrus fruits, salads, tomatoes, leafy vegetables
Vitamin D	Fish-liver oils, liver, egg yolk, salmon, fortified milk

Figure 12A—4. Various Food Substances and Their Sources (*Source*: Charles Tanzer, *Biology and Human Progress*, 5th ed. Englewood Cliffs, N.J.: Prentice-Hall, 1977. Used by permission.)

cells. If you take in less calories than you need, your body will tend to use up fat contained in fat cells and you will begin to lose weight.

Being overweight increases the likelihood of a person developing certain diseases, such as diabetes, high blood pressure, and heart disease. A person seeking to control his or her weight should do so with the advice of a physician. Various fad diets that are advertised may lack food nutrients needed to carry out life processes. Consequently, persons on such a diet may be losing weight but may also be injuring their health by depriving their body of particular vitamins, minerals, or other nutrients.

THE SKELETAL-MUSCULAR SYSTEM

Each rippling, bulging muscle of a young weight lifter straining to lift and hold a heavy weight over his head is testimony to many long, lonely hours of exercise. The constant use of his muscles has caused them to develop in a way that allows the young man to do things that seem to us superhuman. What he is able to do is, of course, not superhuman at all. His feats are simply the result of achieving some very tangible goals that he has set for himself. The young man has focused his thoughts and energies on the fullest development of his system of muscles and bones. His achievements are simply the natural outcomes of his seeking to use to the utmost the biological equipment that all of us have. To some, the weight lifter's muscular development may appear grotesque. To the weight lifter, the flabbiness and lack of vigor of the average person must certainly appear to reflect ignorance. Somewhere between the weight lifter's level of development of the skeletal-muscular system and our own lies a stage of body development that can give the average person increased strength, vigor, and vitality. It is one of the few body systems that we can directly influence and improve. Perhaps we should utilize its potential more fully.

Structure and Function

The bones and muscles of your body work together to give it form and structure. The bones provide you with support, protection for vital organs, a place in which red blood cells and some white blood cells are produced, a storage area for minerals, and surfaces to which muscles are attached. Although many people think that bones are hard and dry objects within the body, they are really alive. Their cells require food and oxygen, just as other body cells do. Bone tissue is composed of living bone cells, the products of bone-cell respiration, and deposits of minerals. Most bones in the human body originate from softer, bonelike structures, or cartilage. As you age, the cartilage present in your body when you were very young becomes strong bone.

The interior cavity of bones is filled with a soft tissue known as marrow, which contains both nerves and blood vessels. The flat bones, such as the ribs and sternum (breastbone), contain red marrow. This type of marrow produces the red corpuscles in the bloodstream and many of the white corpuscles. Yellow marrow, contained in long bones such as the leg bone, is composed mostly of fat. Most of the small bones in your body are solid. Nevertheless, they are very much alive.

A joint is a place where two bones meet. There are a variety of joints in the human body. Each provides flexibility of movement. In some joints, such as the one that connects the upper arm to the shoulder, bands of strong connective tissue, called ligaments hold the bones of the joint together.

The muscles in your body provide you with the ability to move. This results from the ability of muscle cells to contract. There are three types of muscles in your body: smooth muscle, skeletal muscle, and cardiac muscle. Smooth muscles are those that act involuntarily. For example, the muscles that line the stomach and intestinal walls and the arteries are all involuntary muscles. This means they are able to operate quickly and without the direct control of the brain.

The involuntary muscle found in your heart is called cardiac muscle. When the fibers in this muscle contract the chambers of the heart are squeezed and blood is forced out through blood vessels. If the cardiac muscle was not involuntary, your brain would have to tell your heart to beat each time blood needed to be pumped through your circulatory system.

Skeletal muscles are under our direct control. They are voluntary. Skeletal muscles attach directly either to bones or to other muscles. Tendons are bands of connective tissue that attach the ends of some skeletal muscles to bones. When a skeletal muscle such as one in your upper arm contracts as a result of a message your brain gives it, it pulls on the muscles of your lower arm. The movement of the lower arm results from the contraction of the voluntary skeletal muscle.

THE RESPIRATORY SYSTEM

In order to live you must have energy. Energy gives you the ability to perform all of your life activities. Your source of energy is the food you eat. In your body cells the molecules of the food produce energy as a result of chemical reactions with oxygen. Without oxygen the food molecules could not be broken down and energy would not be released. Carbon dioxide and water are given off during this energy-producing process. Energy is used by body cells, tissues, organs, nerves, and other body organs. This simple equation shows the process by which energy is produced in your body cells:

$$\text{food} + \text{oxygen} \rightarrow \text{carbon dioxide} + \text{water} + \text{energy}$$

Structure and Function

The oxygen your body needs in order to produce energy from food is contained in the air you breathe. Air is about 21 percent oxygen and about 78 percent nitrogen. When you inhale, both the oxygen and the nitrogen enter your lungs. The nitrogen, however, is not used by the body. The in-and-out action of your lungs is controlled by the diaphragm, a large curved muscle that lies underneath them. As the diaphragm contracts it moves downward. At the same time, the rib muscles separate the ribs and move them forward. These actions of the diaphragm and the rib muscles increase the amount of space in your chest and allow the lungs to expand.

After the air space in your chest has been enlarged, outside air pressure forces air through your nose and throat, down your windpipe, and into your lungs.

After you have inhaled air, the action of your diaphragm and rib muscles increases the pressure within your chest and pushes air out through your windpipe, throat, and nose. This occurs each time you exhale.

The windpipe is a tube that stretches from your throat to your lungs. At your lungs it divides into two branches. Each of these branches subdivides into smaller and smaller branches within the lungs. These small branches end in tiny air sacs, each of which is surrounded by tiny blood vessels called capillaries. The air sacs have very thin walls, and oxygen can pass through them and into the capillaries.

The lungs provide a way for the oxygen in the air to enter the bloodstream. Oxygen is picked up by red blood cells and carried to all parts of the body, where it reacts chemically with food to produce energy, carbon dioxide, and water. Carbon dioxide produced in the cells enters the bloodstream and is carried back to the air sacs in the lungs. There it leaves the bloodstream, enters the lungs, and is exhaled. The paper-thin walls of the air sacs are continually allowing oxygen to pass from the lungs to the bloodstream and carbon dioxide to pass from the bloodstream to the lungs.

The incomplete burning of fuels can produce carbon monoxide. This carbon-oxygen compound has one atom of oxygen for each atom of carbon in its molecules. The presence of large amounts of carbon monoxide in the air is a serious health hazard. If carbon dioxide is inhaled, it enters the red blood cells and makes them unable to absorb oxygen. As a result, the body cells are not able to produce energy. Automobile exhaust systems or furnaces that are not properly maintained can produce carbon monoxide. Laws have been passed that require furnaces and car exhaust systems to be constructed and maintained so as to minimize the amount of carbon monoxide that enters the air.

An air sac highly magnified.

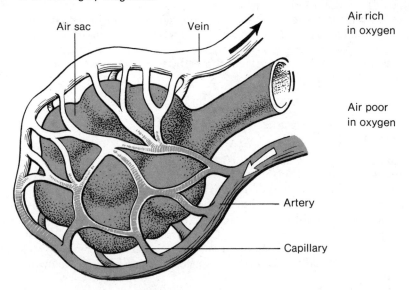

Figure 12A–5. An Air Sac Highly Magnified (*Source:* Charles Tanzer, *Biology and Human Progress*, 5th ed. Englewood Cliffs, N.J.: Prentice-Hall, 1977. Used by permission.)

THE NERVOUS SYSTEM

A happily chirping bird catches your attention during a quiet morning walk along a wooded path. You stop and turn your head in an attempt to locate the source of this early-morning joy. Your ears help focus your attention on the uppermost branch of a nearby tree. The song seems to come from somewhere behind a clump of leaves and twigs attached to the branch near the point where it emerges from the vertical tree trunk. Your eyes focus desperately on the nest in an attempt to locate the noisy feathered musician. Suddenly your eyes pick out a slight movement and come to rest on a brownish head that pokes its way over the nest top and looks directly at you. Sheepishly you apologize mentally for your intrusion and step lightly down the path.

Your sight and hearing are precious gifts that, along with your other senses, gather information about the surrounding world. The sense organs are the farthest outposts of your nervous system and are connected through a multitude of nerve pathways to your brain. It is your nervous system that permits you to see, to hear, to touch, to smell, to taste, and of course to become aware of and enjoy the existence of happily chirping birds on quiet morning walks through the woods.

Structure and Function

The nervous system consists of the brain, the spinal cord, and many nerve cells, nerve fibers, and nerves that carry messages from the brain to other parts of the body and from other parts of the body to the brain. Messages are carried by nerve impulses, chemical changes that cause electrical charges to be transmitted through the nervous system.

Twelve pairs of nerves directly connect the brain to the eyes, ears, nose, and tongue. These nerves are called cranial nerves. Branches of some of these nerves leave the head and connect with the variety of muscles and other internal organs in other parts of your body.

The principal way in which messages are sent from the brain to the body is through the spinal cord, a column of nerves that extends from the base of your brain down through your backbone. Thirty-one pairs of nerves directly connect the spinal cord with such organs as the lungs, intestines, stomach, and kidneys. These organs function without the direct control of the brain. Rather, their automatic actions are controlled by the spinal cord and other nervous-system arteries nearby.

There is another type of automatic action controlled by the nervous system—the reflex. The simplest way in which your nervous system operates, a reflex occurs when some part of the body is stimulated. You have probably seen someone demonstrate the knee-jerk reaction. If a person taps your kneecap with an object, your lower leg quickly swings upward. The tapping of the kneecap stimulates a nerve cell in your lower leg. This reaction occurs as a result of the nerve impulse traveling along nerves to the spinal cord. When the impulse reaches the spinal cord a message is immediately sent to the leg muscle, which in turn causes the jerking movement. In this and many other reflex reactions the response is not controlled by the brain. Reflex reactions are completed well before the brain is aware of their occurrence. Other reflexes are coughing, blinking, and laughing when you're tickled.

265

The sense organs, as we have noted, are the farthest outposts of the human nervous system. Specialized nerve cells in such places as the eyes and ears receive stimulation from the outside world and carry messages to the brain. Nerve cells that are capable of receiving information from the external environment are called receptors. Each of your sense organs has special receptors.

THE SKIN SENSES

Your skin is able to sense a variety of stimuli, including touch, pressure, pain, heat, and cold. Whenever a receptor is stimulated, an impulse or nerve message begins traveling along the nerve the receptor is connected to and eventually arrives at the central nervous system. Receptors for the various skin senses are distributed at different locations and different depths in the skin. The touch receptors are close to the surface of the skin. Your fingertips contain many touch receptors. Pressure receptors are deeper in the skin.

TASTE

Your ability to taste results from specialized nerve receptors on your tongue. The areas containing these receptors are called taste buds. There are specialized taste buds for each of the following flavors: sour, sweet, salt, and bitter. What you interpret as taste is actually a combination of taste and smell, for when you chew food, vapors from it reach your nose. Thus, you simultaneously taste and smell the food you're eating. You may have noticed that when you have a cold, food does not taste as good as usual. This is due to the important role of the smell of the food.

SMELL

The principal nerve that carries information about smell to the brain is the olfactory nerve. Branches of this nerve are contained in a cavity in your nasal passage. Vapor from the food you eat enters your nasal cavity, is dissolved in a liquid, and in this form stimulates the endings of the olfactory nerve.

HEARING

The ear is the principal organ through which sound waves enter the body. Sound waves enter the opening in your external ear and travel through a tube called the auditory canal. This canal ends at a membrane called the eardrum. The sound waves stimulate the eardrum, causing it to vibrate. On the other side of the eardrum exist a group of tiny bones: the hammer, the anvil, and the stirrup. These bones transmit vibrations from the eardrum to the cochlea and the semicircular canals, located in the inner ear. These organs relay the vibrations to the sensitive receptors at the end of the auditory nerve, which carries them to the brain.

SIGHT

Your eyes are sense receptors that receive information in the form of light from the external world. Light passes through a transparent covering called the cornea and enters the pupil, a small opening at the front of the eyeball. The size of the

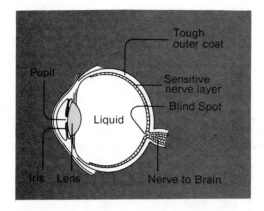

Figure 12A—6. The human eye receives information from the external environment. (*Source:* Charles Tanzer, *Biology and Human Progress,* 5th ed. Englewood Cliffs, N.J.: Prentice-Hall, 1977. Used by permission.)

pupil is controlled by the opening and closing of the iris, the colored portion of the eyeball. Directly behind the pupil is the lens, which focuses your sight. Focusing is achieved by a muscular contraction that changes the shape of the lens. Between the lens and the cornea is a watery liquid known as the aqueous humor. Within the eyeball is a thicker, transparent substance called the vitreous humor.

The structures at the front of the eyeball all serve to focus light on the retina, the rear portion of the eyeball containing light receptors. These receptors are of two types: cones and rods. The cones are responsible for color vision; the rods produce a material that helps you see in dim light. Focused light rays, or images, that reach the retina stimulate the receptors, which in turn transmit information about them to the brain, via the optic nerve. The brain, in interpreting these messages, gives us the sense we call sight.

THE EXCRETORY SYSTEM

Virtually all forms of energy production create waste by-products. The human body produces both energy and an abundance of gaseous, liquid, and solid wastes. These wastes result from both the production of energy and the process through which complex food materials are changed to simpler, more usable ones. If for some reason wastes cannot leave the body, sickness and death are certain to follow. The human body is able to rid itself of wastes by means of a very efficient group of organs.

Structure and Function

The process by which your body rids itself of wastes is called excretion. Wastes from your body's cells enter the bloodstream and are carried to specific excretory organs. The major excretory organs are the kidneys and the skin. Your kidneys lie on each side of your spine in your lower back. Each kidney is protected by a layer of fat. Waste-containing blood enters the kidneys and is divided into smaller and smaller amounts as the arteries transporting it branch out into capillaries. From these capillaries the blood flows through filters that separate the waste from the blood and combine them into urine. Urine is a liquid that contains, in addition to the body's waste by-products, water and excess mineral salts, also filtered from the blood by the kidneys. Tubes called ureters carry the urine from the kidneys to the urinary bladder. This muscular organ then expels the urine from the body through the urethra. Meanwhile, the cleansed blood exits the kidneys through the renal veins.

You may be surprised to learn that your skin is an important excretory organ. Through its pores exit water, salts, and urea, a waste that is excreted principally through the urine. The liquid that contains these body wastes is perspiration. Perspiration has a second important function: it helps control your body temperature.

There are other organs of excretion besides your kidneys and skin. Although we usually think of the lungs as the organs that enable us to secure oxygen from the air, they also assist the body in excretion. Although the liver is principally a digestive organ, it is also able to form urea and secrete it into the bloodstream. The large intestine performs an important excretory function by removing from the body the food that has not been digested by the small intestine. Solid waste that moves through the large intestine is composed largely of undigested food and bacteria. It is eliminated from the body through the anus—the end of the digestive tract. The rectum is that portion of the large intestine that lies directly above the anus.

THE CIRCULATORY SYSTEM

Right now, at this very instant, a complex system consisting of a pump and conducting vessels is trying its best to keep you alive. Its rhythmic action is constant. It operates efficiently whether you are sitting, standing, walking, running, or sleeping. You never need to switch it on, and it will not switch itself off for many years—unless you fail to provide it with appropriate exercise and nutrients. Your nose, ear lobes, eyeballs, and every other part of you depend on this elaborate internal pumping system and the life-giving fluid within its walls. It is an extraordinarily complex system, and yet so efficient and automatic that you are able to carry out the activities of living without even an awareness of its existence.

Structure and Function

The heart is the powerful pump that moves blood through your body's blood vessels. It has four chambers: a right atrium, a left atrium, a right ventricle, and a left ventricle. Blood enters this marvelous pump through the atria (the upper chambers) and departs through the ventricles (the lower chambers). It is the ventricles that pump the blood out of the heart. Between the atria and the ventricles are valves that prevent the blood from flowing backward. Once blood passes from the atria to the ventricles, it is impossible for it to return through these controlling valves. The opening and closing of the heart valves produce the sound that a physician hears when he or she uses a stethoscope to listen to your heart. The "lub-dub, lub-dub" is simply the opening and shutting of the valves. If the heart valves are damaged and blood is able to leak backward from the ventricles to the

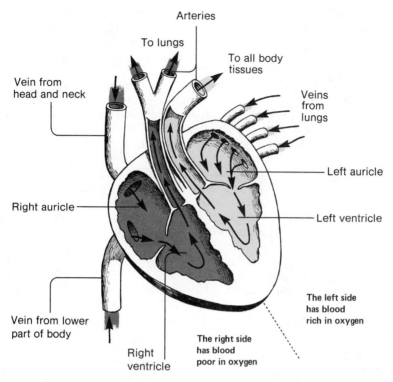

Arteries

To lungs

To all body
tissues

Vein from
head and neck

Veins
from
lungs

Left auricle

Right auricle

Left ventricle

Vein from lower
part of body

The left side
has blood
rich in oxygen

Right
ventricle

The right side
has blood
poor in oxygen

Figure 12A−7. The human heart consists of two pumps lying side by side to form a single organ. (*Source:* Charles Tanzer, *Biology and Human Progress*, 5th ed. Englewood Cliffs, N.J.: Prentice-Hall, 1977. Used by permission.)

atria, a health problem results. Physicians can usually detect this problem by listening through their stethoscope for the sound produced by blood moving in the wrong direction. This sound is called a heart murmur.

The vessels that carry blood from the ventricles to various parts of the body are called arteries. The vessels that return blood to the heart are called veins. Within the body tissues the major arteries branch out into smaller and smaller arteries and ultimately capillaries.

The right side of the heart receives blood from the body cells and in turn pumps it to the lungs. This blood contains the carbon dioxide produced by the cells as they converted food to energy. In the lungs the carbon dioxide is removed from the blood and oxygen from inhaled air is added. The oxygen-rich blood is then carried to the left side of the heart, which pumps it to the remaining organs of your body. To understand the circulatory system you must remember that the heart seems to act like two pumps. On the right side blood that contains carbon dioxide is pumped to the lungs. On the left side blood that is rich in oxygen as a result of having passed through the lungs is pumped to all parts of the body.

As blood passes through the body it picks up many things. In the capillaries of the small intestine it absorbs dissolved food, which it then carries to the liver, an organ that is able to store sugar. Other food materials in the blood are carried to the various body cells, where, in combination with oxygen, they are converted to energy. This energy production results in carbon dioxide, water, and other waste by-products. These wastes leave the cells and are carried by the bloodstream to organs that are able to rid the body of them.

Human blood contains a variety of materials. One such material is plasma, the liquid that contains blood cells. Plasma is 90 percent water and 10 percent various dissolved substances. Among the most important of these substances are the antibodies, which help your body fight diseases.

Red blood cells are another component of blood. They contain hemoglobin, the iron-rich substance that receives oxygen from the lungs and carries it to the tissue cells.

Another type of cell found in the bloodstream is the white blood cell. These cells do not contain hemoglobin. Rather, they are your body's first line of defense against infection. If you have an infection, the number of white cells in your blood increases very rapidly. White blood cells are able to surround disease-causing bacteria and kill them.

Another material in your blood is fibrinogen, which makes possible the process of clotting. If you cut yourself, substances called platelets release a chemical that causes fibrinogen to turn into needlelike fibers that trap blood cells and form a clot. It is this clotting process that allows the bloodstream to repair itself in the event of a cut. It simply restricts the flow of blood to an open cut or puncture.

THE REPRODUCTIVE SYSTEM

Think of the tiny egg cells or sperm cells within your body. They are so small that they can be seen only with a microscope, and yet they are marvelously complex. Within each reposes half of a blueprint for a new human being—who may one day contribute one of its own reproductive cells to the process of creating a new person. We are bound backward in time to our parents and grandparents—indeed to all our ancestors. We are connected with those who have preceded us by a chain of reproductive events that stretches backward over hundreds of thousands of years to people and places whose existence can only be imagined—to people who are as much a part of us as we are of them.

Structure and Function

Men and women have reproductive organs. The male organs produce male reproductive cells, or sperm. The female organs produce female reproductive cells, or eggs. Through sexual intercourse a sperm cell and an egg cell may unite to form a human embryo. The embryo has the potential for becoming a new human being.

Sperm are produced in an organ called the testis. A pair of testes are contained in a pouch called the scrotum. Since this pouch is outside the body wall, the temperature of the testes is somewhat lower than the body temperature. The production of healthy sperm cells requires the testes to function at this lower

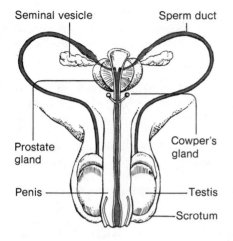

Figure 12A–8. The Human Male Reproductive System (*Source:* Charles Tanzer, *Biology and Human Progress*, 5th ed. Englewood Cliffs, N.J.: Prentice-Hall, 1977. Used by permission.)

temperature. Within each testis are numerous coiled tubes. The cells that line the walls of these tubes produce sperm. These tubes merge to form a larger tube, the sperm duct. The sperm duct carries sperm and fluids produced by other glands (Cowper's gland, the prostate gland, and the seminal vesicles) into the body and then through the external sexual organ, the penis. The penis is used to fertilize egg cells in a female.

Human egg cells are produced in a pair of ovaries in the female body. During a human female's lifetime about 500 eggs, or ova, will mature and be released by

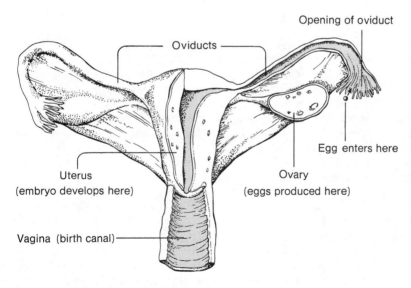

Figure 12A–9. The Human Female Reproductive System (*Source:* Charles Tanzer, *Biology and Human Progress*, 5th ed. Englewood Cliffs, N.J.: Prentice-Hall, 1977. Used by permission.)

the ovaries. Usually one ovum matures and is released at one time. A mature ovum leaves the ovary and passes into a tubelike organ known as an oviduct, where it is pushed along by hairlike projections to a large muscle-lined tube called the uterus. If the egg cell is eventually fertilized by a sperm cell, it will become attached to the uterus wall and develop into an embryo.

The vagina is a tube that connects the uterus with the outside of the body. During intercourse sperm cells placed here may swim through the uterus and reach the oviducts. If a healthy sperm cell reaches a healthy and mature egg cell, fertilization occurs. The nucleus of the female egg cell and the nucleus of the male sperm will unite to form the beginning of a new human being.

Within one week of fertilization the cell produced by the uniting of the sperm and egg cells has divided into about 100 cells. Nine months later the embryo will consist of more than 200 billion cells, each designed to carry out a particular life function.

The developing embryo gets its food through a membrane called the placenta. Food and oxygen in the mother's bloodstream pass from the uterus into the blood vessels of the placenta, and from there into the embryo by way of blood vessels in an umbilical cord. Your bellybutton, or navel, marks the place where the umbilical cord entered your body. Wastes produced by the cells of the embryo enter the embryo's bloodstream and are eventually carried by the placenta to the mother's bloodstream.

When the embryo reaches maturity birth occurs. At birth the embryo is forced out of the mother's body through the vagina as a result of contractions of the uterine wall. The umbilical cord that had connected the embryo with its mother is cut. The baby is born.

Reproduction and Heredity

Heredity is the transmission to offspring of the physical traits of their parents. Your physical traits were determined long ago. They resulted from the transmittal of hereditary information through the sperm and egg cells that united to produce you. The nucleus of that sperm cell and the nucleus of that egg cell contained material that determined your physical traits. The part of the nucleus that contains hereditary information is the gene. Genes occupy distinct places on ribbonlike structures called chromosomes. The nuclei of all your body cells contain chromosomes. The nucleus of a human sperm cell contains twenty-three chromosomes. A human egg nucleus also has twenty-three chromosomes. All other body cells, however, contain forty-six chromosomes.

When a sperm cell and an egg cell unite, the resulting cell has forty-six chromosomes. Twenty-three carry genes from the male parent and twenty-three carry genes from the female parent. The genes on the chromosomes of the first complete cell and the particular order in which they are located on the chromosome give the offspring its inherited traits.

Identical twins result when an embryo splits in two. The two halves develop into individuals who have the same physical traits. Fraternal twins are the result of two ova being fertilized by two sperm. They are simply siblings who happen to be conceived and born at the same time.

SUMMARY OUTLINE

The organs of the human body can be viewed as being part of one or more systems.

I. The digestive system converts food into energy or cell-building material.

II. The skeletal-muscular system provides the body with a shape and structure and gives it the ability to move.

III. The respiratory system secures the oxygen necessary for the conversion of food to energy and eliminates carbon dioxide.

IV. The nervous system receives stimuli and carries them to the brain, and transmits the brain's messages to various parts of the body by means of nerve impulses.

V. The excretory system rids the body of gaseous, liquid, and solid wastes.

VI. The circulatory system moves a variety of substances from place to place in the body.

VII. The reproductive system of a male produces sperm cells capable of fertilizing an ovum, the reproductive cell of a female.

chapter 12B

The Human Body

DISCOVERY ACTIVITIES
AND DEMONSTRATIONS

DISCOVERY ACTIVITIES

The Mystery Bag*

OBJECTIVES

The students will name assorted objects by using their sense of touch.
The students will match objects that they see with ones that they feel.

SCIENCE PROCESSES EMPHASIZED

Observing
Inferring

MATERIALS

Assorted objects: pencils, erasers, paper clips, rubber bands, wooden blocks, marshmallows, coins of various sizes, etc.
Boxes for containing the objects

*Asterisks refer to activities for young children.

Figure 12B—1. (*Source:* SAPA II, Module 72, p. 9. Science . . . A Process Approach II, American Association for the Advancement of Science. Used with permission.)

Large paper bags, one for each person, with two holes cut in each near the bottom. The holes should be large enough for one hand to fit through

2 large paper clips to close the top of each bag

MOTIVATION

Prepare one bag by placing an object in it. Begin this activity by placing *your* hand in one of the holes in this bag to feel what is inside. Describe it to the children. Ask if anyone has an idea of what might be in the bag. Have various children come to the front of the room to feel what is in the bag. They should place one hand in the other hole. Have each child describe what he or she feels and then make a guess about the name of the object. If the child is unable to make a correct guess, invite other children to try. After this introduction the children will be ready to receive their own bags containing mystery objects.

DIRECTIONS

1. Hand out one bag for each team of two children and a box containing a set of assorted objects to use during the activity. Let the teams decide who will go first and have that person put his or her head down and not peek. At the front of the room, hold up the type of object for the *other* team members to put into the bag. (Start the activity with an object that is easily guessed.) When this is done the tops of the bags should be secured with the large paper clips.

2. When all is ready the children who have been keeping their heads down can put one hand through each hole and feel the mystery object. During this time you can help children by directing them to feel the shape, size, and texture of the object.

3. After everyone has an idea of what the object is, they can make their guess known and see if they were right. If the children are unable to name the object, you can modify the activity and hold up an assortment of objects, having the children vote for the one they think is correct. It would also be possible to prepare an answer key with simple drawings of the objects in use. The students could circle the drawing that represents their conclusion.

Figure 12B—2. The Mystery Bag (*Source:*SAPA II, Module 8, p. 6. Science . . . A Process Approach II, American Association for the Advancement of Science. Used with permission.)

KEY DISCUSSION QUESTIONS

1. What part of the body do we use *most* often to feel things? *The hands.*
2. What are some of the things that the hands can feel? *How hot or cold things are. Whether objects are sharp, smooth, rough, soft, hard, etc.*
3. What are some things that hands can't tell? *What color an object is, how shiny or bright it is, etc.*

SCIENCE CONTENT FOR THE TEACHER

Much too often we take our sense of touch for granted, even though it is of great importance in our daily lives. Our bodies are covered with various touch organs that are sensitive to warmth, cold, pain, and pressure. They are not evenly distributed. Pressure is felt most accurately by the tip of the nose, the tongue, and the fingers. Our hands give us sense information with which we can discriminate heat, cold, pain, and pressure. In addition, the hands can grasp and manipulate objects for complete exploration and comparison.

EXTENSIONS

Science. Have students find out where various touch organs are on their bodies. Have them use some common optical illusions to demonstrate how their senses can be fooled.

Math. Place a set of rods of different lengths in the bags and ask the children to select the biggest rod, the smallest, the second biggest, etc.

Art. Build a "feely-board" collage out of materials of various textures, shapes, and sizes.

Sniff, Snuff, and Sneeze*

OBJECTIVES

The students will use their sense of smell to determine the contents of closed paper bags.
The students will be able to identify various common odors (those of an onion, vinegar, an apple, and an orange).

SCIENCE PROCESSES EMPHASIZED

Observing
Inferring

MATERIALS

Paper bags (lunch size)
25-centimeter (10-inch) length of string for each bag

Peppermint oil

Wintergreen oil

Lemon extract

Camphor oil

Plastic sandwich bags

Paper towels

Small glass jar

Vinegar

Onion

Apple

Orange

MOTIVATION

Place a small amount of one of the odor-producing substances in one of the bags. Tell the children that you have brought something special into class that you want to share. Hold up one bag tied loosely with string so that odors are able to escape but the students can't see into it. Invite the students to try to identify what it is without looking in the bag and without using their hands. If they don't catch on to using their noses, you can give them a *big* hint by smelling the air.

DIRECTIONS

1. Once all have had an opportunity to smell the contents of the bag(s) used in the motivation session, distribute the bags and strings and have the children write their names on them. Then tell them to select one of the odor-producing foods and place a small "dab" of it on a paper towel. Have them place the paper towel in the bag and tie its top with the string.
2. When the bags have been prepared, organize the children into groups of three or four. Have the members of each group share their odors and encourage them to predict what is in each bag.
3. After each child has had a chance to share his or her bag with the rest of the children in the group, the group members should choose one of their bags to share with another group in the class. The bags should be exchanged and smelled by every member of each team. Each team should discuss their observations and reach some agreement as to what is in the other team's bag. The groups can continue to trade bags until all bags are exchanged and observed.
4. Prepare sets of four plastic sandwich bags containing wintergreen oil, peppermint oil, lemon extract, and camphor oil, one essence to a bag. The liquid can be dropped on a small piece of paper towel and then sealed in the bag.
5. Hand out a set of four bags to each of the teams with the instruction to smell all of the bags and try to group them. The groups of students can arrange the odors differently, but should be able to explain their reasons for grouping them as they have. Typically they will divide the set into food smells (wintergreen, peppermint, and lemon) and a medicine smell (camphor). If the students have difficulty grouping the essences, you can direct them by asking leading questions (see the questions section).
6. For the last activity prepare sets of four paper bags containing an apple, an orange, vinegar, and an onion, one food to a bag. It might be fun to turn this activity into a

"nose laboratory exam" by setting up enough smelling stations so that each child has a place. The students would then rotate through the various stations and try to identify the odor coming from each bag. They would answer by writing a word or, if their level of writing development prohibits this, by selecting the appropriate drawing from an answer sheet.

KEY DISCUSSION QUESTIONS

1. How can we tell what is in the bag without opening it or touching it? *By smell.*
2. What are some words that can be used to describe odors? *Good, bad, strong, sour, sweet, medicine-smelling, food-smelling.*
3. How does smelling help animals survive? *By helping them track prey. By helping them sense enemies.*

SCIENCE CONTENT FOR THE TEACHER

When we smell something we sample the air by inhaling it by way of receptors deep in our nasal cavity. These receptors analyze the chemicals in the air sample with *great* precision and transmit the findings to the brain for storage. Minute odors can trigger more vivid memories than any other sense.

EXTENSIONS

Science. Obtain a cross-section model or a diagram from a biology book of the nasal cavity and have some children locate the smell receptors.

Have some children produce a series of dilutions of a substance that produces a strong odor, such as vinegar. Then ask them to determine how dilute the vinegar solution can be and still be distinguished from pure water solely by smell.

Art. Have some children produce a collage of pictures of good- and bad-smelling things. The children may be able to have portions of the collage that actually have a smell, such as pictures of flowers that have been perfumed.

How Does Smell Affect Taste?

OBJECTIVES

The children will predict the effect of the smell of a substance on its taste.
The children will observe how the ability to smell affects taste.
The children will infer the relationship between the senses of smell and taste.

SCIENCE PROCESSES EMPHASIZED

Observing
Predicting
Inferring

MATERIALS

Onion slice in a closed container
Apple slice in a closed container
White-potato slice in a closed container
5 packs of small hard candies, such as Lifesavers or Charms, each of a different flavor
2 glasses of water
2 blindfolds

MOTIVATION

After hiding the materials, engage the class in a discussion of any changes they have observed in their ability to taste foods. Some children may volunteer that when they had colds, foods lose some of their taste. Indicate to the children that during this demonstration they will have an opportunity to observe how the smell of a substance affects its taste.

DIRECTIONS

1. Have a volunteer come forward and sit at a desk or table that faces the class.
2. Tell the volunteer that he or she is going to taste five candies. Display the hard candies at this time.
3. Blindfold the volunteer and have the class predict how well they expect him or her to do.
4. Place a candy in front of the volunteer and have him or her taste it and tell its flavor. Have the class record the accuracy of the result. The volunteer should take a drink of water to rinse the taste from his or her mouth.
5. Repeat this with each of the candies.
6. Repeat the demonstration with the same child, but this time present the candies in a different order and have the volunteer hold his or her nose, thus blocking off the sense of smell.
7. Ask for another volunteer to come forward. Blindfold this child and reassure him or her that the food that will be tasted is safe to eat.
8. Now do two things simultaneously. Hold an apple slice under the volunteer's nose and hold the potato slice so he or she can take a small bite of it to chew. Have the child tell what kind of food is being eaten. Then have the child take a drink of water while keeping the blindfold in place.
9. Repeat directions 7 and 8, but this time place an onion slice in front of the child's nose and provide an apple slice for him or her to chew on.
10. Discuss the results of this demonstration with the class, paying particular attention to the relationship between the sense of smell and the sense of taste.

KEY DISCUSSION QUESTIONS

1. Were you surprised at any of the things you observed during this demonstration? Why? (*Answers will vary.*)

2. How do you think the way something smells affects its taste? *When we taste something our brain also discovers how it smells. The taste of food depends in part on how it smells.*

SCIENCE CONTENT FOR THE TEACHER

Substances must be dissolved in liquid before our sensory nerves are able to detect their presence. Our sense of taste is stimulated when we chew food substances and small particles of food dissolve in the saliva. The nerve endings in the taste buds on our tongue are stimulated by the dissolved substances and send information about them to the brain.

The nerve that carries information about smells to the brain branches into receptors that line the nasal cavities. Particles of food that enter the air as gases are dissolved in the liquids on the surface of the nasal cavities, and in this form stimulate the smell receptors. Consequently, some of the food we chew stimulates our sense of smell and some stimulates our sense of taste. When we have a cold or allergic reaction that produces large quantities of mucus in the lining of our nasal cavities, the ability of the olfactory nerve to receive smell information is greatly limited.

EXTENSIONS

Science. Some children may wish to try to uncover a relationship between what we see when we look at food and how we think the food is going to taste. These children can experiment with food colorings and prepare such foods as cookies, bread, and fried eggs in a diverse assortment of colors. They can investigate why some people may not wish to sample their cooking.

Some children may be encouraged to repeat parts of this demonstration on a larger scale to see how well the initial results hold up.

Math. You may wish to have some children maintain tables, charts, and graphs of flavor-recognition data gathered when this activity is tried with large numbers of children.

How Does Rest Affect Tired Muscles?

OBJECTIVES

The children will gather data about the number of exercises they can do within a given period of time.

The children will determine the effect of rest on the amount of exercise they can do.

SCIENCE PROCESSES EMPHASIZED

Observing and gathering data
Inferring

MATERIALS

Pencils
Paper
Charts with ten columns
Watch or clock with a second hand

MOTIVATION

Ask the children if they remember that in the lower grades their parents or teachers tried to make them rest or take naps. Have the children discuss why they thought the adults tried to get them to rest. You may wish to suggest to them that one of the reasons might have been that young children are very active and tire out quickly. Tell them that rest might give their muscles a chance to regain some strength. Indicate to the children that in this activity they will be able to find out whether rest affects how well their muscles can operate.

DIRECTIONS

1. The children will have to work in pairs during this activity. Have them acquire partners and move to a location in the room where they will be able to see a watch or a clock with a second hand. Tell the children that they will be counting the number of times they can make a tight fist and then extend their fingers in each of ten fifteen-second periods.
2. Have one member of each team do the exercise first with the partner recording the data. Have the first partner make a clenched fist with one hand and then extend his or her fingers. Have the other partner count how many times the first partner can complete this exercise within fifteen seconds. He or she should then enter the number in the first column of the chart.
3. Have all teams repeat this procedure four times, with no rest between trials. After the first partner has completed five trials, have him or her rest for ten or fifteen minutes. During this rest period have the other member of the team do the exercise.
4. After both members of each team have completed five trials have the teams repeat the activity, but this time with a minute of rest between trials. Have the partners record the data as they did before.

KEY DISCUSSION QUESTIONS

1. How did the lack of rest between trials affect the number of exercises you did in each trial? *The number I was able to do got less and less for each trial.*
2. How did resting for a minute between trials affect the results? *When I rested between trials I was able to do more exercises during the trials.*
3. How can you use what you learned in this activity? *If I want to improve how well my muscles work when I play a sport or a game, I should rest as much as possible during time-outs or between innings.*

SCIENCE CONTENT FOR THE TEACHER

Our skeletal muscles move as a result of our ability to contract them. When they contract they cause various body parts to move. The energy that produces this movement comes from food that is digested in our body. As energy is released from these foods, wastes accumulate in the muscle cells and tissues. When too much waste has accumulated, the muscle cells are no longer able to contract normally. If this occurs, we experience the common symptom of muscle fatigue. One way of dealing with muscle fatigue is simply to allow muscles to rest. This will provide an opportunity for the blood stream to remove excess wastes that have built up in the muscle tissue.

EXTENSIONS

Science. Some children may wish to do library research on various sports and games, paying particular attention to the muscles used in each. Students should determine if a particular sport or game provides rests between periods of high activity. For example, gymnasts typically do not use their muscles constantly during a competition, but have rest periods between their performances of the various activities.

Math. You may wish to have some students synthesize all the data from this activity and prepare a classroom graph showing the average number of exercises performed during each trial for both the first part of the activity (exercises without rest periods) and the second part of the activity (exercises with intervening rest periods).

ADDITIONAL ACTIVITY IDEAS

How Fast Do You Breathe?*

The children should work in pairs in this activity. Have one child observe and record the number of times his or her partner inhales in one minute while at rest. The child being observed should sit quietly without inhaling more or less than he or she would normally. Now have the children switch roles and repeat the exercise. When this is done, have one partner measure the other's breathing rate during a one-minute period *following* two minutes of jogging in place. Obviously, children with health problems that prohibit them from exercise should not have a physically active role during this activity. Have the partners switch responsibilities and repeat the data gathering. Encourage the children to compare their breathing rate in the one minute of rest without exercise with their rate in the one minute of rest following the in-place jogging. Discuss with the children the reasons for the increase in breathing rate (the body uses up oxygen at a more rapid rate during exercise, and the supply has to be replenished by inhalation; the body produces carbon dioxide at a rapid rate during exercise, and removes this waste product by exhalation).

Fingerprints: We Are All Different

You can do this activity to help children see that although each of us has a great deal in common with every other person, we are also different in many ways. One such difference is that we have unique patterns of ridges on the outer layer of skin on our hands and feet. Even identical twins have different patterns of ridges. Have the children make their own fingerprints and compare them with those of their classmates. To do this you will need to provide each child with a sheet of white paper, a soft-lead pencil, a small square of cardboard, and access to a roll of transparent tape. Have the children rub the pencil across the cardboard until they have produced a thick layer of pencil markings. Now have them press each finger on the black surface and then on the surface of the white paper. The children will need to wash their hands when they are done. Now have the children place a small amount of transparent tape over their fingerprints to preserve them. The children can then compare fingerprints with their classmates. You may be able to invite a local police officer to your classroom to discuss how fingerprints are gathered during criminal investigations and to describe the system used to classify them.

Who Are They?

This activity will involve the children in library research to discover the contributions made by a list of various scientists to such fields as disease prevention or treatment, human behavior, and improving the quality of life. Have each group of children select two or three names from this list and prepare brief reports to the class on each individual. If the children can find photographs or drawings of the scientists they are investigating, they should make poster-size drawings to use during their reports. You may wish to check your school library prior to the activity to determine the availability of information on each individual on the list that you have the children work from. Some individuals you may wish to include are Christian Barnard, Rachel Carson, George Washington Carver, Charles Drew, Percy Julian, Margaret Mead, Louis Pasteur, Jonas Salk, and Barry Commoner.

The Label Game

Have each child bring to school ten or fifteen ingredient labels from food products. Encourage the children to collect labels from a variety of foods, including canned foods, "junk foods," and cereals. Supply the children with a chart that lists common vitamins and minerals and the ways in which the body utilizes them. To play the food-label game, first select one vitamin or mineral and write its name on the chalkboard. Have the children describe what the nutrient does for the body. Then have them look through their collection of labels to determine how many of them include that vitamin or mineral as a food ingredient. Repeat this process with each common vitamin or mineral. Have the children keep track of the number of their labels that include the nutrients you specify. You can make the game a bit more sophisticated by having the children keep track of the amount of the nutrient contained in one serving of the foods represented by their labels. This activity can serve as the beginning of a discussion of the ingredients listed on food labels and can incorporate discussion about the caloric content of foods as well as about preservatives listed on the labels.

DEMONSTRATIONS

What Is Your Lung Capacity?

OBJECTIVES

The children will estimate the capacity of the teacher's lungs.
The children will measure the capacity of their teacher's lungs.

SCIENCE PROCESSES EMPHASIZED

Observing
Predicting
Measuring
Using Numbers

MATERIALS

4-liter (1-gallon) glass or translucent plastic jug
1 meter (about 3 feet) of clear plastic tubing (available for purchase in any hobby store)
Bucket that is large enough for the jug to be totally immersed in it
Source of water
Reference book that has a diagram of the human lungs and upper torso

MOTIVATION

Tell the children that today they will be observing a demonstration that will give them an idea of the amount of air that can be contained by the lungs. Display the drawing of the lungs. Ask the children to estimate how many liters of air the lungs might be able to hold. Have the children write down their prediction.

Figure 12B–3. (*Source:* J. Abruscato and J. Hassard, *The Whole Cosmos Catalog.* Santa Monica, Calif.: Goodyear Publishing Company, Inc., p. 41. Used by permission of Goodyear Publishing Company.)

DIRECTIONS

1. Involving children as assistants, commence assembling the apparatus.
2. Fill the bucket to a depth of 10 centimeters (about 4 inches) with water. Fill the jug completely with water.
3. Cover the mouth of the jug with your hand, invert the jug, and place it in the bucket. When the mouth of the jug is under water in the bucket, carefully remove your hand from its mouth. The water in the jug will remain in place. Have a child come forward to hold the inverted jug in position.
4. Place one end of the tube inside the jug, at least 10 centimeters (about 4 inches) up from its mouth. The other end of the tube is free.
5. Take a deep breath and exhale as much of the air (actually a mixture of gases) in your lungs as possible through the free end of the tube. This "air" will displace some of the water in the jug.
6. Cover the free end of the tube with your thumb and have a child cover the inverted end of the jug with his or her hand. Now extract the tube and have the child completely seal the mouth of the jug.
7. Turn the jug upright. The jug will now be partly empty. This empty region represents the amount of water displaced by your exhaled air, and therefore your lung capacity.
8. Have the children determine the number of liters of air that were exhaled by pouring water into the jug with the liter container.
9. The children can compare the resulting figure with their prediction.

KEY DISCUSSION QUESTIONS

1. How could we make a jug that would "automatically" tell us the amount of air that was exhaled? *Fill the jug with liters of water and make a mark on the outside of the jug to show where the water level is for each liter of water that is added. Then when the jug is turned upside down and used, you could measure the amount of air in it by seeing how many liters of water were pushed out.*
2. How did your prediction of lung capacity compare with the lung capacity we measured? (*Answers will vary.*)
3. What are some things that might shrink a person's lung capacity? (*Answers will vary, but may include any injury or disease that affected one or both lungs.*)

SCIENCE CONTENT FOR THE TEACHER

The lungs are body organs that bring oxygen from the air into the body and gather and expel some of the products of cellular respiration (carbon dioxide and water vapor) from the body. Each time you breathe, the diaphragm muscle (located under your lungs) contracts, enabling the rig cage to expand. This expansion in turn allows the lungs to expand to full capacity. As this occurs, air is taken into the lungs. As the diaphragm returns to its normal state, the contents of the lungs are expelled. The capacity of the lungs depends on a variety of factors, including general body size, the condition of the diaphragm and lung tissues, and the health of the respiratory system in general.

EXTENSIONS

Science. You may wish to have some children do research to find out the possible effects of smoking on lung capacity and the symptoms and causes of pneumonia and emphysema.

Some children may wish to interview the school physical-education teacher and members of the school staff who keep in good physical condition by jogging to determine what these individuals believe is the relationship of good physical condition to lung capacity.

Art. You may wish to encourage some children to make a series of large, labeled drawings that show the location and size of the lungs in a variety of animals. These children will need access to appropriate reference books in order to carry out this activity.

What Can Change Bones?*

OBJECTIVES

The children will observe two changes in bones.
The children will infer the presence of minerals and water in bones.

SCIENCE PROCESSES EMPHASIZED

Observing
Inferring

MATERIALS

Four small chicken bones
Jar of white vinegar
Alcohol or propane burner (if one is not available in your school, you may be able to borrow one from a high-school science teacher)
Paper label

MOTIVATION

Indicate to the children that you are going to do a demonstration that will help them understand what bones are made of. If the class has not yet begun studying the skeletal system, it would be appropriate to begin such a unit with this demonstration or include the demonstration at some point in the unit. Display the bones, vinegar, and burner. Ask the children to guess how these materials could be used to discover some things about bones.

DIRECTIONS

1. Display all the chicken bones so that each child in the class can observe them.
2. Place two of the bones in the jar of vinegar. Put the label on the jar and write the date on the label. Tell the children that you are putting the jar aside and will remove the bones from the jar in about a week. Encourage the children to make observations of the contents of the jar each day during the week.
3. Compare the flexibility of the two remaining bones by bending each slightly.
4. Now heat one of the bones over the burner. Be sure the room is well ventilated, since the heating of the bone will produce some strong odors. After the bone has been dried out by this process, allow it to cool. Now try to bend this bone again. If it has been thoroughly dried out, it will now easily break in two.
5. After a week has passed, retrieve the bones that were placed in the vinegar. Show the children that these bones bend very easily.

KEY DISCUSSION QUESTIONS

1. How did heating affect the bone? *The heated bone broke easily.*
2. How were the bones that were placed in vinegar changed? *They could be bent very easily.*

SCIENCE CONTENT FOR THE TEACHER

Vinegar is a weak acid that is able to react with the calcium in bones. Calcium gives the bones of the skeleton the strength to support weight. Bones contain living cells as well as minerals such as calcium. Heating a bone drives off the water contained in the cells. The drying out of bones results in brittleness.

EXTENSIONS

Science. Some children may be encouraged to do research to determine which foods provide the body with minerals such as calcium. They may also wish to investigate why children have a greater need for calcium than adults.

You may be able to acquire some "before" and "after" x-rays of bone fractures from an orthopedic surgeon. Have the physician point out the location of the fracture and the region in which calcium was replaced as the fracture healed. You can share this information with the class when you display the x-rays.

Art. You may wish to have some of the children do research on the ways in which artists use knowledge of bone structure in animals and humans to produce paintings and sculptures.

ADDITIONAL DEMONSTRATION IDEAS

How Is Your Reaction Time?

Here are two quick demonstrations you can use during a unit on the nervous system. For each one have two or three children come to the front of the room to

Figure 12B–4. Testing Reaction Time with a Dropped Penny (*Source:* J. Abruscato and J. Hassard, *The Whole Cosmos Catalog.* Santa Monica, Calif.: Goodyear Publishing Company, Inc., p. 44. Used by permission of Goodyear Publishing Company.)

participate. The remainder of the class can replicate the demonstrations as activities after you have worked with the volunteers.

Have a volunteer extend his or her hand with the thumb and forefinger separated. Hold a meterstick by one end so that the other is between the volunteer's thumb and forefinger. Tell the volunteer that you will be letting go of your end of the meterstick and ask him or her to catch it with his or her thumb and forefinger. The distance that the meterstick drops before it is caught is an indication of the volunteer's reaction time. Repeat this with other volunteers.

Hold a penny above the outstretched hand of one of the volunteers. Tell the volunteer to try to move his or her hand away from the penny as it falls. Hold the penny at various distances above the child's hand. When your hand is close to the child's, it will be very difficult for the child to move his or her hand away before the penny hits it.

Testing Your Smeller*

Children have varying sensitivities to smells. In this demonstration you will be able to show that there are some odors they can easily detect and others that are more difficult. This demonstration also provides an opportunity for you to show that particles of substances spread into the air. You will need small amounts of perfume, ammonia, oil of peppermint, and oil of citronella. Open one bottle and pour a few drops of the liquid on a saucer. Tilt the saucer to spread the liquid over its surface. Ask the children to raise their hands when they notice the odor from the liquid. Repeat the demonstration for each liquid.

What Is in the Food We Eat?

Prepare a classroom display of a variety of food wrappers and a display of advertisements for various foods. Have various children come forward to look at the display of food wrappers to see if they can find a list of what each food contains. In particular ask the volunteers to try to locate information about the food value present in each product—for example, how much protein, fat, and carbohydrates it contains. Now have the class focus its attention on the food advertisements. Initiate a discussion about how well food advertisements represent the products being sold.

How Good Is Your Memory?

This demonstration can help children learn how focusing their attention on something to be memorized can help them remember it more easily. Prior to class place twenty common objects in a cardboard box. When class begins, distribute a sheet of paper to each child. Without telling the children that the demonstration deals with memory, dump the contents of the box on a tabletop. Simply show each object to the class and replace it in the box. When you are done, ask the children to list the objects they remember. Now repeat the demonstration, but this time have each member of the class make up a silly sentence that includes the name of one of the objects. After the objects have been returned to the box, have the children list them once again. Following the demonstration discuss various ways in which the children can improve their memory (for example by repetition, by using as often as possible the words, numbers, or whatever they are trying to remember, and by focusing their attention and shutting out distracting influences when they are studying).

part 4

The Physical Sciences

METHODS, CONTENT, DISCOVERY ACTIVITIES, AND DEMONSTRATIONS

chapter **13**

How to Plan and Teach Physical-Science Learning Units

THE LETTER

Her throat was hoarse, her eyes itched, and her feet ached. It had been one of those very long school days. Earlier in the afternoon two of her children had been sent home after they complained about upset stomachs—apparent victims of a minor flu epidemic that was progressing through the school. Beth had barely made it to the end of the day. On the way out of the building she stopped in the main office to check her mailbox. In it was a letter printed with the familiar purple ink of the school copying machine. The heady odor of duplicating fluid told her mind and stomach that the letter had been prepared very recently. She began to read it:

Dear Elizabeth:

You will recall that last year our elementary-science curriculum committee recommended that we revise our entire elementary-science curriculum this year. In order to accomplish this each teacher will be a member of a subcommittee responsible for making recommenda-

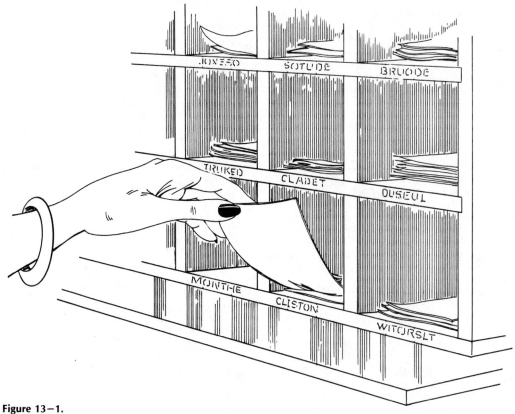

Figure 13–1.

tions about various parts of the curriculum. I would like to ask you to serve on the subcommittee that will review the physical-science units that are presently in the curriculum.

Each subcommittee should be prepared to make recommendations concerning the appropriateness of various units, activities, and materials to the full Elementary Science Curriculum Review Committee within three months. I would like to thank you in advance for your contribution to this very important effort.

Cordially,

Margaret Stephanson

Margaret Stephanson
Elementary School Curriculum Coordinator

At the bottom of the page she found a hand-written note: "P.S. Beth, would you mind being the chairperson for the subcommittee? Your principal and I both feel that you would be terrific for the job. Thanks. Margaret."

A wry smile crossed Beth's face as she thought about her consistent avoidance of, and lack of interest in, physical science in high school and college and the marvelous irony of being appointed chairperson of a subcommittee that was going to focus on physical-science units. She shook her head, tucked the letter in the pile of papers under her arm, and walked out the door.

Whether or not you enjoyed learning about atoms, molecules, and energy, you will find that physical-science topics will make up a substantial portion of any curriculum or textbook series that you are likely to work with.

If you enjoyed working with magnets, pushing on levers, playing with tuning forks, and making light bulbs light, you are going to have a lot of fun observing your children becoming involved in the very same activities. If you didn't enjoy physical sciences, you will have a chance to see them freshly through the eyes of your children.

BASIC CONCEPTS FOR PHYSICAL-SCIENCE UNITS

If you spend a little time browsing through elementary-science curriculum materials or science textbooks you will notice a variety of topics dealing with the physical sciences. Some of the basic concepts that underlie much of the physical-science material in curricula or texts are shown below. You can use this list to identify groups of concepts that can serve as the framework for learning units you may develop.

1. Matter is anything that takes up space and has weight.
2. Matter is found in three basic forms: solid, liquid, and gaseous.
3. All matter in the universe attracts all other matter in the universe with a force that depends on the amount of matter in objects and the distance between them.
4. The amount of matter in an object is known as its mass.
5. The weight of an object results from the mutual attraction between it and the earth.
6. Matter can be classified on the basis of readily observable characteristics, such as color, odor, taste, solubility, and how well it conducts electricity. These characteristics are known as physical properties.
7. Matter can interact with other matter to form new substances. The characteristic way in which one kind of matter interacts with other kinds of matter can be described by its chemical properties.
8. Substances consist of very small particles known as molecules.
9. Molecules are made of smaller particles known as atoms.

10. Atoms are composed of three smaller particles called protons, neutrons, and electrons. (These building blocks of atoms are composed of yet other particles.)
11. Atoms differ from one another in the number of protons, neutrons, and electrons they have.
12. Some substances are composed of only one type of atom. These substances are known as elements.
13. In ordinary reactions between substances, matter is neither created nor destroyed, but only changed in form. (This is the law of conservation of matter.)
14. An object that is at rest or moving at a constant speed will remain in its present state unless acted upon by an unbalanced external force.
15. Acceleration is the rate at which an object's velocity changes.
16. The amount of acceleration that an object displays varies with the force acting on the object and its mass.
17. Whenever a force acts on an object, an equal and opposite reacting force occurs.
18. The flight of an airplane results from the interaction of forces causing lift, thrust, and drag.
19. Energy, the capacity to do work, manifests itself in a variety of forms, including light, heat, sound, electricity, the energy of motion, and nuclear energy.
20. Energy may be stored in matter by virtue of its position or condition. Such energy is known as potential energy.
21. Under ordinary circumstance energy can neither be created nor destroyed (This is the law of conservation of energy.)
22. In modern times, the law of conservation of matter and the law of conservation of energy have been combined to form the law of conservation of matter plus energy, since it has been found that under certain conditions matter can be changed into energy and vice versa.
23. The energy resulting from the conversion of matter to energy is known as nuclear energy.
24. The amount of fossil fuel that remains in the earth is limited.
25. Energy can be conserved in a variety of ways, including the use of more efficient mechanical and electrical devices and more effective barriers to heat loss and gain.
26. The diminishing supply of available fossil fuels may be compensated for by the increased utilization of energy sources such as wind, water, and synthetic fuels.

PROCESS SKILLS FOR PHYSICAL-SCIENCE UNITS

The study of matter and energy provides children with many opportunities to develop science-process skills. This section consists of a brief list of process skills and activities that can be used to foster them. You may wish to use this list as a starting point for developing your own cross-referenced list of process skills and activities. A full list of science-process skills appears in Figure 1–5.

Observing

Describe objects on the basis of their physical properties: color, size, hardness, etc.
Construct a system for grouping objects on the basis of their physical characteristics.
Distinguish between warm and cold objects on the basis of how they feel.
Identify which of two sounds is louder/softer and higher/lower.

Describe the characteristics of solid, liquid, and gaseous matter.

Describe changes in the color, shape, size, and state of a quantity of matter.

Describe a device that can change wind power to electricity.

Classifying

Classify human activities as to whether they are energy wasters or energy savers.

Construct a system for classifying a sample of matter as a solid, a liquid, or a gas.

Group simple circuit diagrams on the basis of whether they represent series or parallel circuits.

Classify a group of statements gathered through interviews with adults as for or against the use of nuclear power to produce electricity.

Communicating

Use the word *force* as the term for a push or pull applied to an object.

Give an example of one of the ways in which the position of an object on a table can be described.

Construct a bar graph that shows the number of each of six types of simple machines seen during a visit to a garage.

Give an oral report about a passive-solar house visited during a field trip.

Describe in writing the characteristics of various materials that can be used to insulate a building.

Make a poster showing three alternative energy sources observed in books, in films, or during field trips.

Using Numbers

Count the number of airplanes of various types observed during a visit to an airport.

Place a collection of toys in order from those that require a lot of energy to operate to those that require less energy.

On a chart showing the amount of electricity used by the school each month, locate the months in which the most and the least electricity was used.

Using brochures gathered during field trips to automobile agencies, place the automobiles observed in order from those that use the most energy to those that use the least.

Inferring

Make an inference that may explain why matter can change in state.

Make an inference about the efficiency of a particular simple machine.

Given an operable flashlight, make an inference about the components of the circuit within the flashlight.

Predicting

Make a prediction about the amount of electricity that will be used by the school this month, based on the amount of electricity used in previous months.

After studying the sources of electrical energy and the amount of electrical energy used by a community, make predictions about the likelihood of alternative energy sources being employed to produce electricity.

Using a graph showing the amount of fossil fuels consumed each year and the amount of fossil fuels that remains in the earth, predict the number of years within which we will run out of fossil fuels.

Make predictions about the amount of gasoline used per mile for a variety of automobiles by looking at photographs, and then compare the predictions with government statements about gas mileage for each automobile.

A SAMPLE LEARNING CENTER IN DETAIL

Energy Conservation

OBJECTIVES

Using a felt board, students will dramatize the adventures of "Mr. Waste Energy" and "Miss Conserve Energy."

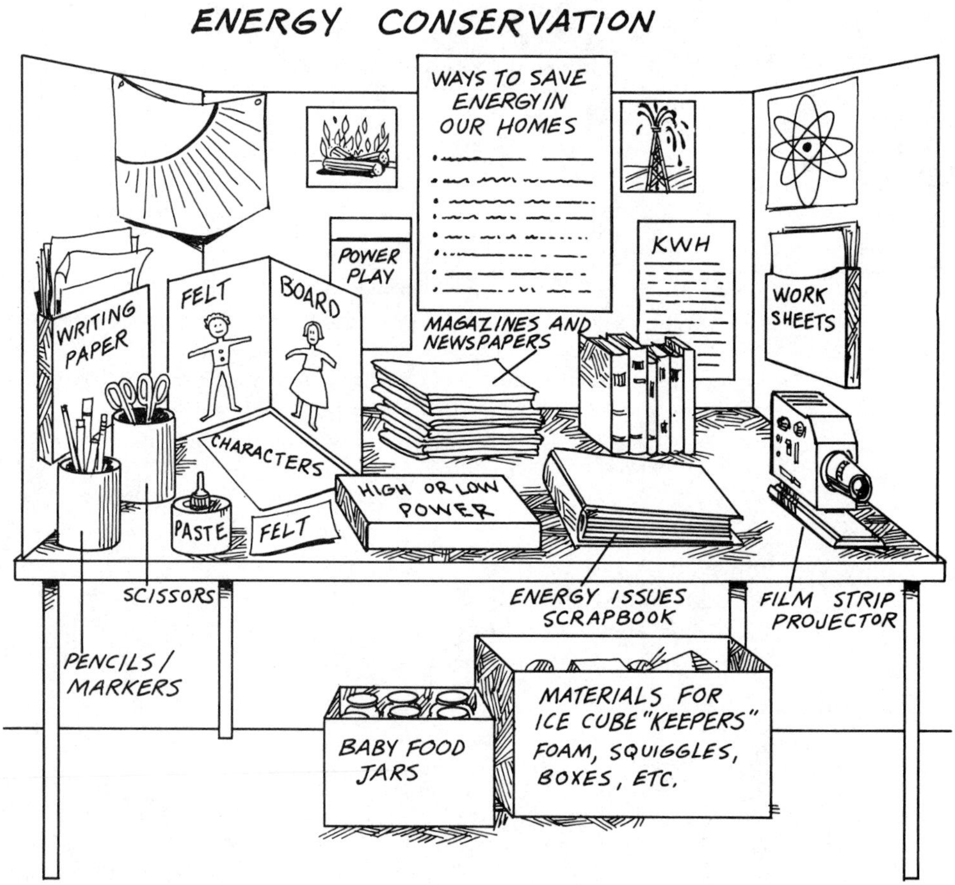

Figure 13–2. "Energy Conservation"—Sample Learning Center

Students will select from pictures of appliances those that are energy wasters and those that are energy-efficient.

Students will produce a scrapbook of newspaper and magazine articles on energy-related topics.

Students will develop a list of energy-saving techniques they can employ in their own homes.

Utilizing information found in the school library, students will prepare and present a news-style report on current energy topics.

Students will conduct an experiment in which they test the effectiveness of various types of insulation.

Students will prepare a collage depicting the various energy sources.

Students will determine the relative amount of energy used by common household appliances.

SCIENCE PROCESSES EMPHASIZED

Experimenting
Communicating

MATERIALS NEEDED

Current newspapers and magazines
Paper, pencils, paste
Graph paper
List of kilowatt-hours used per appliance
Pieces of foam and other insulating materials
Baby-food jars
Ice cubes
Felt board and felt
Chart paper and markers
Filmstrip projector
Library books on energy conservation
Filmstrips on energy conservation
Magazines to cut up
Clear adhesive plastic
Die
2 tokens

DIRECTIONS FOR THE TEACHER

Set aside an attractive area in your classroom for this center. Decorate the wall and any other available space with posters, pictures, and other brightly colored objects related to the topic. Allow space in this center for writing, game-playing, dramatizing, and constructing activities. Assuming that the needs and interests of each child in these physical-science activities will be sufficient, have the children sign up to work on one activity per day in the center for a half-hour.

Felt Board. Make or have the students make figures out of paper or cardboard. Glue strips of felt to the backs of the figures, and give them names such as "Mr. Waste Energy," "Miss Conserve Energy," and "Wise Watt Owl." Have the children invent and dramatize the adventures of these characters and their friends.

Worksheet. Put a list of the kilowatt-hours used per appliance on a chart. Then prepare a worksheet similar to this one:

---

1. Which appliance uses the most energy? _____
2. Which appliance uses the least energy? _____
3. Which uses more energy per hour, a refrigerator or a freezer? _____ Why do you think this is so?
4. How much energy would you save by hanging clothes on a clothesline instead of using the dryer for a half-hour? _____
5. If electricity costs four cents per kwh, how much money would you be saving by hanging the clothes on the line as in problem 4? _____
6. If your parents' car gets twenty miles per gallon and the roller-skating rink is two miles from your house, how much gas would you save if you walked instead of rode to the ring every Friday night for four weeks? _____

Similar problems may be substituted or included, depending upon the levels of ability and the interests of your students.

*Matching Box.** Build this game by cutting pictures from magazines of various appliances used in the home. Paste the pictures to cards and cover them with clear adhesive plastic. Write the titles "High Energy Users" and "Low Energy Users" on separate cards. Using the kwh chart for reference, students are to place the pictures under the proper headings. Place the directions for this game in the box or envelope in which the game is stored. Answers may be written on the back of the pictures for self-checking.

Ice-Cube Race. Challenge the students to build the best ice-cube "keeper." Provide foam, styrofoam packing squiggles, ice-cream buckets, styrofoam cups, small boxes, and any other available source of insulation. Allow students to design and build individually an insulated container of some sort. Have each child place a standard-size ice cube in a baby-food jar and then his or her container around it. The container should be designed in such a way that the top can be lifted every three minutes in order to check the amount of melting. Students should record the amount of time it took their ice cube to melt completely. The student with the longest melting time is the winner. The various insulators can be kept on a shelf for later discussion of their insulating properties. Make a direction card similar to this one:

*Asterisks refer to activities for young children.

Enter the Great Ice Cube Race!

1. Use any or all of these materials to build the best ice-cube keeper.
2. Design your ice-cube keeper so that you can open it every three minutes to check on the melting of your ice cube.
3. Place an ice cube in a baby-food jar and then place the jar in your keeper.
4. Keep track of the amount of time it takes your ice cube to melt. Check it every three minutes until it is completely melted. Write down the starting and ending times. How long did it take to melt?
5. Record your time on the chart next to your name.
6. Good luck!

Scrapbooks. Have the students collect articles from current newspapers and magazines on energy issues such as nuclear power and the heating-oil shortage. Students can then paste these into scrapbooks for the rest of the class to read. Students should update the scrapbooks throughout the course of study. Prepare an instruction card like this one:

1. Read newspapers and magazines daily.
2. Cut out any articles about an energy topic.
3. Paste these articles into a scrapbook for others to read.

Ways-to-Save-Energy Chart. Ask the children to list on a chart all the ways they can think of to save energy in their own homes and at school.

Ways to Save Energy in Our Homes

Turn off the lights.
Close doors.
Turn off the TV.
Etc.

Students can role-play various situations, such as turning off the TV and quickly closing the outside doors.

Model News Report. Have the students inventory the school library and prepare lists of books and other materials on the sources of energy. Then ask the students to prepare a news-type program to present to the class on one of the major sources of energy. Prepare an instruction card similar to this:

1. Go to the library.
2. Find all the books and filmstrips you can on the *sources* of energy.
3. Choose one source of energy that interests you.
4. Prepare a TV news program to present to the class about your topic.

*Power Play!** Build a race-track–type game in a file folder (for easy storage) and cover it with clear adhesive plastic. Provide a die, two tokens, and a set of "chance" cards that say:

You walked to the store today—move ahead 2 spaces.
You left the TV on—go back 3 spaces.
You left the front door open—go back 3 spaces.
You helped hang clothes on the line—move ahead 3 spaces.
You turned down the thermostat—go ahead 2 spaces.
You took a 15-minute shower—go back 2 spaces.
You asked your Dad to drive you to the movies—go back 2 spaces.

Write the following directions on the folder:

1. This game is for two players.
2. Roll the die, and move the number of spaces indicated.
3. If you land on a "chance" space, draw a card and follow the directions.
4. May the best "energy saver" win!

*Filmstrips and Collages.** Set up a viewing space in the center and allow the children to choose a filmstrip on energy conservation or on the sources of energy. Have the students prepare a collage depicting energy-conservation techniques or sources of energy, using the filmstrip as background information. Students may use their own drawings or pictures cut from magazines for the collage.

EXTENSION IDEAS

Using a thermometer and their ice-cube keepers, students can record and graph the cooling times of various items, such as hot water.

Students can design a simple solar collector and test its effectiveness.

Students can develop alternative-energy bulletin boards that compare the energy output of various types of fuels.

Students can interview the head custodian of the school to determine what he is doing to cut energy use in the school, and then report to the class.

CORRELATION WITH NONSCIENCE SUBJECTS

Language Arts. Students can write the script for the "Felt Board" activity or create some other dramatization.

Students can categorize and alphabetize the books and filmstrips they found on energy conservation.

Math. Students can calculate the amount of solar energy striking the roof of the school.

Students can convert the kwh-per-appliance figures into dollars and cents. Additional word problems can be invented by the students.

Social Studies. Students can find on maps the locations of nuclear-power plants, hydroelectric dams, oil-producing states, and other energy-related structures or areas.

Art. Students can build mobiles of alternative sources of energy.

EVALUATION IDEAS

Students. Have the children fill out a form similar to this one:

What did you like to do the best in this center?
What did you like the least?
What would you have added to this center?
What was the most important thing you learned at this center?

Teacher. Maintain a check sheet of students participating in the center and which activities they did. Maintain records of each child's progress, weaknesses, and strengths, and the directions the child needs to take in future work on this topic.

A SAMPLE BULLETIN BOARD IN DETAIL

Matter and Its Composition

OBJECTIVES

Students will classify objects, drawings representing the three states of matter, and characteristics into the following categories: solids, liquids, and gases

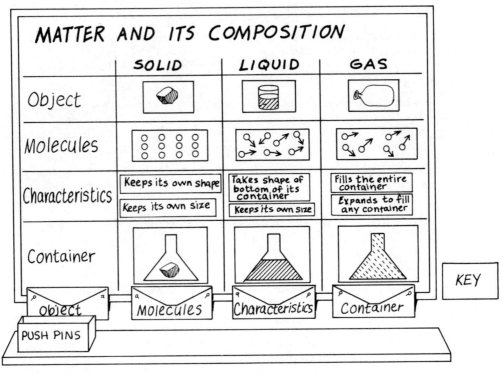

Figure 13–3. "Matter and Its Composition"—A Sample Bulletin Board

SCIENCE PROCESSES EMPHASIZED

Classifying
Communicating

MATERIALS

Cards with the following objects attached to them: rock, plastic vial with colored water, and inflated balloon
Drawings of a flask containing a solid, a flask containing a liquid, and a flask containing a gas
Cards listing characteristics of each of the three states of matter
Manila envelopes
Push pins

DIRECTIONS FOR THE TEACHER

Discuss with the students how to make a solid a solid, a liquid a liquid, and a gas a gas. Demonstrate that matter can change from one state to another by melting ice and boiling water.

Have the students place the cards or pictures in their appropriate places on the bulletin board. Students can check their work by referring to an answer key.

EXTENSION IDEAS

Investigate the different types of precipitation and how they form.

Make a thick paste of cornstarch and water. Explore its characteristics.

Have children observe how a spot of rubbing alcohol placed on the back of their hands changes in form.

CORRELATIONS WITH NONSCIENCE SUBJECTS

Language Arts. Play "Twenty-one Questions" with the children. Start by telling them "I'm thinking of a _____." Encourage students to use characteristics of the states of matter in making their guesses.

Physical Education. See how many students can fit inside a one-meter square on the edge of the gym floor.

SAMPLE FIELD TRIPS

Forms of Energy*

Many young children are fascinated by the telephone. A trip to the local phone-company office will be a memorable science lesson having many language-arts, geography, and art applications. When you make the initial contact find out what the facility contains; repair services are often in a different location and could be considered for a separate field trip.

Before going the students need to understand what sound waves are and that electrical energy, not sound waves, pass along telephone wires. On the playground or in a hallway let the children try out telephones made of tin cans and various lengths of string. They will notice the weakening of the sound as the string gets longer, and they will find it unsuccessful. Having illustrated the problems of sending sound waves over long distances by means of nonelectric media, you need to show how the sound waves are connected to electrical energy. Using a sample phone, which is provided by many phone companies, take apart the mouthpiece and then the earpiece and explain the different parts. If possible, look at the interior workings of the body of the phone also. Caution students that such exploration should not take place without parental supervision and that it can damage the phone. Check the children's corner of your library for books on telephone-company careers and stories that mention use of the telephone; these can be useful before and after the trip.

Your phone-company visit will vary with the size of the facility and the interests of your students. Areas to consider for exploration include phone-company careers, how long-distance and overseas calls are made, how records of calls are kept, styles of phones, and the latest advances in communication technology. A tour of the facility can include information on some of these topics delivered at appropriate places in the tour.

There are many posttrip activities. Children can make a class and emergency-number directory to practice writing and alphabetizing skills. Using information from the trip and the school library, the children can deliver a career-education program to another class. Children can practice dialing and using practice phones to role-play real-life situations—asking a friend over, finding out information, making an emergency call, and so on. Phone wires come in many colors; if you were able to get some odds and ends, the children can use them to make and display wire sculptures or mobiles. Children can use area codes in studying the location of different states. A phone-company field trip—the preparation, actual visit, and follow-up—will tie into a unit of sound, energy, or careers and help primary-school children understand how a device that we so often take for granted works.

Forces, Motion, and Machines

The study of friction can be the basis for various field trips. Contact the showroom of a car, boat, airplane, or snowmobile dealership or the service area of a train station, garage, or airport to arrange the excursion. Let the host know that students will be interested in how the design of the vehicle minimizes air friction and surface friction. An explanation of the propulsion system and transmission can be included. With a little imagination you could also accomplish these aims at a bicycle, ski, surfboard, or skate shop.

There are a myriad of pre-field trip ideas to choose among, depending upon the age and interests of the students, the focus of the unit, and the destination. Some simple friction experiments such as timing a drop of water as it runs down slanted surfaces of varying textures (metal, wax paper, foil, plastic wrap) or sliding wooden blocks over various surfaces can be done. These can be followed up by looking at advertisements to see how vehicles are designed so as to reduce friction from air, water, or the road surface. With older students this would be the appropriate place to mention Newton's laws of motion and the idea of perpetual motion. By looking at drawings and pictures of transportation vehicles, they can become familiar with individual parts that influence direction (rudders, elevators, ailerons) or speed (sails, gears, transmission). They can also do research to find out how government regulations affect vehicle design.

The actual field trip should have a balance of lecture and demonstration. The host may start by showing the vehicle and discussing the design, how it reduces friction, and how it was tested. If improvements are still being made, encourage the host to point this out. The engine, transmission, and other parts of the vehicle that influence speed and direction should be pointed out and briefly explained. If pertinent, the importance of properly inflated tires can be explained.

A natural follow-up is for students to draw diagrams and then build models of what they have seen or what they propose to be an improved vehicle design. A list of ways that vehicle owners can improve vehicle performance would also be an appropriate follow-up.

Conservation of Energy

Home owners are often willing to show their residence, especially if there is something unique about it. Look around the community for a building that was constructed or retrofitted to save energy. One with an active or passive solar system, windmill, off-peak-power heat-storage system, or underground design would be especially interesting. Installers of alternative energy systems and contractors would be good sources for information on energy-efficient building techniques and places to visit.

Preparation will depend on the building to be visited and whether you are interested in solar heating or cooling, but some activities are suitable in all cases. For example, children can see the desirability of south-facing windows for heat by observing how the sun affects various classrooms. Reminding students about the temperature inside a closed car on a hot day will illustrate the greenhouse effect. You can demonstrate the necessity for insulation by putting hot water or an ice cube in a styrofoam-lined box and comparing its temperature change over time with that of a similar substance left uninsulated. Children can discover the heat-retention capacity of various materials by placing them in strong sunlight and then taking their temperature at intervals after bringing them indoors. Materials of different colors can also be tested in this way.

The trip to the site should include a tour, an explanation of the energy-saving features, and demonstrations of energy-saving equipment, if any. A chance to ask the home owner about pros and cons as well as costs and savings of the system could be included. It might also be worthwhile to visit a building under construction and then return to see the finished product.

After the study and tour children can be encouraged to look at the school and their own homes for energy-efficient features as well as areas where improvement is needed. Designing on paper and then building a model of an "ultimate" energy-saving building will interest many. A display of ways to save energy would help educate the whole school. There are many excellent films and materials available (some free) from government and private sources on this topic. Today's children are sensitive to the concept of energy conservation, for recent energy-related events have received a great deal of attention.

ADDITIONAL IDEAS FOR FIELD TRIPS

Matter and Its Composition

Many industries (plastics, paper, film processing, paint, drugs, etc.) use chemicals extensively. The yellow pages are a potential source for locating such an industry. Before visiting, give the students an idea of the products made and the processes involved. While there be sure to ask the sources of the chemicals used and the destinations of the products so that you can relate the learnings to geography. Problems with chemical waste could also be discussed at the site.

Cooking causes a chemical change, so a visit to a kitchen can be a helpful experience during a physical-science unit. The food-packaging industry relies on chemicals to preserve flavor, freshness, and appearance. A trip to a dairy, bakery, or any food-processing plant will fit into a chemistry unit. The children can read the ingredients labels of the company's products to find out where the raw materials come from.

Forms of Energy

To give intermediate-grade students more awareness of the sources of the energy they use, visit a place where energy is generated. The installation can be as complex as a dam or power plant or as simple as a home windmill. Students should be familiar with the operations of a generator, battery, and dynamo before going. How to read a meter, what off-peak power is, and how much energy various appliances use are topics that might be covered during the visit.

A carillon or organ can be the basis for an informative field trip if you are studying sound. Before going, experiment with the vibration of air and materials to produce sound. When you return, have the class create their own instruments out of straws, plastic tubing, bottles, funnels, and other found materials.*

A lighting-store trip can help clear up confusion about many electrical terms—*watts, volts, lumens, incandescence, fluorescence*, etc.—and give students some design information too. When you return, have students design lighting fixtures of appropriate intensity and style for different rooms and purposes.

Forces, Motion, and Machines

Primary-age students will be wide-eyed during a visit to a heavy-equipment supplier or a construction company. Seeing the equipment, hearing what it can do, and looking for simple machines (gears, levers, wheel and axles, inclined planes, pulleys) within the equipment will keep students stimulated.*

Taking a group to a high-school physics lab would enable them to see demonstrations performed by the high-school physics teacher and also work with equipment not available in most elementary schools. The physics teacher may be willing to involve high-school students in several small-group activities. The use of force in body conditioning can be illustrated by a trip to a health club or weight-training room. The machines themselves will fit in with the unit, and a demonstration and talk on body conditioning by a coach or trainer will be an interesting addition.

Conservation of Energy

Home appliances have saved human energy for years, and they are now being designed to save electrical energy as well. During a field trip to an appliance store students can learn about microwave ovens, insulation, energy-saving switches on refrigerators, power-saver cycles on dishwashers, and other energy-conserving innovations. Discussion afterwards can include what appliances are really necessary and whether we would rather save energy or time.*

Rising transportation costs have hit school districts that transport children especially hard. If your children are bussed to school, a trip to the district's bus-maintenance center can illuminate this situation and the fuel-conservation measures that are being used. Questions could include: Does the district do its own repairs? Is gasoline purchased in bulk? Are the buses kept well tuned? Are bus routes arranged so as to diminish travel? The manager can lead a tour and answer these and other conservation questions the children may have.

Alternative-energy stores, particularly those selling wood-heating or solar-heating products, are burgeoning. Visiting one of these for a tour and demonstration of new products will raise student's awareness of alternate energy sources and show them ways to become more energy self-sufficient.*

chapter 14A

Matter and Motion

CONTENT

Imagine owning your own strap-on rocket that would enable you to fly like the test pilot in the first picture of this chapter. Ah, how nice to be able to leave the pull of the earth and simply fly.

Wouldn't it be great fun to commute from place to place by strapping on your rocket and flying? Someday it may be commonplace to begin a trip to visit a friend by first flying over to your nearest rocket-fuel station, saying "Fill it up," and then flying to your destination. "I'm so glad you dropped in" would become an expression of welcome that finally had meaning!

Our ability to accomplish such amazing things as flying through the air or more mundane things such as cooking a meal in a slow-cooking "crock-pot" depends on the technology available to us. The technology of this century has enabled us to make "progress" at an astounding pace. We can have full-color photographs in a minute; we have drugs that can prevent or cure illnesses; we have automobiles, airplanes, unbelievable weapons of destruction, and, wonder of wonders, electric toothbrushes. The rapid pace of technological development is a direct result of our increased knowledge of the nature of matter, our ability to release energy from it, and our ability to predict and control the motion of objects.

In this chapter you will be learning what matter is thought to be, how one type of matter can be converted into another type, and how matter behaves when it is put in motion. The chapter will take you from atoms to rockets with various stops along the way.

Figure 14A–1. (*Source:* Developed by Bell Aerospace Textron of Buffalo, New York 14240. Rights now owned by Williams Research Corp. of Walled Lake, Michigan.)

311

Silly-Putty, "ring-around-the-collar," and a pistachio ice-cream cone all have something in common. They are all *matter*. Anything that occupies space and has weight is matter. The earth, the planets, the sun, and everything else in our universe that has weight and occupies space are composed of matter. This definition allows us to distinguish matter from energy. Electricity, light, sound, heat, and magnetism are all considered forms of energy. Energy, in turn, is defined as the capacity to do work. Matter and energy are related. Under very special circumstances matter can be changed into energy and energy can be changed into matter.

Scientists have found that all matter in the universe exerts an attraction on all other matter in the universe. This attraction exists regardless of the location of the matter. This force of attraction is called gravitation. The matter in this book is exerting an attractive force on you and you are exerting an attractive force on the matter in the book. The strength of this attraction depends on the amount of matter in both you and the book and the distance you are from the book. The force that the earth itself exerts on matter we term weight. The weight of an object is a measurement of the extent to which the earth pulls on the object and the object pulls on the earth.

There are many different types of matter in objects. The earth itself is a vast storehouse of various types of matter. Figure 14A−2 lists some of the common types of matter found in the earth's crust. The specific types of matter represented in this chart are known as elements. Next to each element on the chart is a symbol scientists use when they refer to the element. These elements are usually found in combination with one another in the earth's crust. The minerals that make up the rocks we see are composed of combinations of elements as well as some uncombined elements.

Physical Changes

A cold, crystal-clear icicle receives morning light from the sun and begins to change. Slowly a tiny, glistening droplet forms at its tip. In a classroom a child accidentally steps on the teacher's very last piece of colored chalk and grinds it into

Element	Symbol	Classification	Per cent by Weight
Oxygen	O	colorless gas	47.3
Silicon	Si	nonmetal	27.7
Aluminum	Al	metal	7.9
Iron	Fe	metal	4.5
Calcium	Ca	metal	3.5
Sodium	Na	metal	2.5
Potassium	K	metal	2.5
Magnesium	Mg	metal	2.2
Hydrogen	H	colorless gas	0.2
Carbon	C	nonmetal	0.2
All others			1.5

Figure 14A−2. Composition of the Earth's Crust (*Source:* Milton O. Pella, *Physical Science for Progress*, 3rd ed. Englewood Cliffs, N.J.: Prentice-Hall, 1970. Used by permission.)

a powder. A child motivated to draw a "happy face" breathes on a cold mirror, instantly creating a thin film on its surface. Immediately tiny fingers sketch the eyes and mouth of the happy-face smile. All these changes in matter are physical changes. The matter has undergone a change, but the original substance remains. Some of the water in the solid icicle has changed to a liquid, the original chalk stick has become smaller particles of chalk (although in a considerably less useful form), the water vapor exhaled by the child has become the tiny droplets of water that formed the canvas for the happy-face drawing. No new substances were produced in any of these cases. They were all physical changes.

We commonly speak of the various types of matter on our planet as being solids, liquid, or gases. These forms of matter are known as states or phases of matter. Rocks and soils are solids. Water may be found as a solid, a liquid, or a gas. Matter can be changed from one state to another relatively easily. The state that matter is in can be determined by observation. A solid has a definite shape. A liquid takes the shape of its container. Both solids and liquids have a definite volume: they occupy a certain amount of space. Gases take the shape of their container, but they also expand to fill all of the container. Thus, gases do not have a definite volume: their volume is the volume of their container.

We can describe matter by its physical properties. We can describe it, first, as being solid, liquid, or gaseous. We can also describe its color, how hard or soft it is, the extent to which it dissolves in liquid, and whether it is easily stretched or broken. Another specific physical property of matter is its density. To find the density of something we can simply divide its weight by its volume. Density may also be found by dividing mass by volume. Units of mass, such as grams and kilograms, represent the amount of matter in something. On the other hand, you will recall, units of weight represent a gravitational attraction for that matter. Density is more commonly measured as mass per unit of volume and is expressed in grams per cubic centimeter.

Chemical Changes

A chemistry teacher holds a piece of magnesium with tongs and places the lustrous metallic substance in the flame of a Bunsen burner. Bright light is produced, and the metallic magnesium changes to a white powder. The burning of the magnesium produced a new substance: the white powder magnesium oxide. Changes resulting in substances that differ from the original substance are known as chemical changes.

Some types of matter are capable of uniting with one another to form very different types of matter. This characteristic is known as a chemical property of matter. The rusting of iron and the burning of wood or paper are examples of matter combining and changing to new forms of matter. We can describe these changes in many ways. However, to fully understand the chemical properties of matter it will be helpful to think about specific chemical changes. The roasting of a marshmallow and the phenomenon of fire are two good examples.

THE ROASTING OF A MARSHMALLOW

A marshmallow is made of sugar. Sugar is a combination of elements—a compound. It contains carbon, hydrogen, and oxygen. You've probably noticed that when you heat a marshmallow over an open flame the surface of the marshmallow turns dark. The heat added to the sugar is causing chemical changes, among them the breakdown of sugar into its chemical elements—carbon, hydrogen, and oxygen. The dark material on the outside of the marshmallow is carbon. Hydrogen and oxygen leave the heated marshmallow in the form of water. In short, the heating of the marshmallow causes some of the sugar in it to break down into its constituent elements. The sugar has exhibited a chemical change.

FIRE

The flickering candles atop a birthday cake, the ring of blue flame on a stovetop, and a raging forest fire are all examples of a rapid chemical change that gives off both light and heat. In each case three things are present: (1) a material that will burn (a fuel), (2) oxygen, and (3) something that heats the fuel to a temperature at which it will burn. The temperature at which a fuel will begin to burn is known as its kindling temperature.

All common fuels contain carbon. When these fuels burn, various chemical changes occur. One such change is the combination of oxygen atoms with carbon atoms to form the gas carbon dioxide. If there is insufficient oxygen, however, the very dangerous gas carbon monoxide is released. During combustion (another word for burning), oxygen in the air also combines with the hydrogen contained in the fuel to form water vapor. Since a characteristic of burning is the rapid combination of oxygen atoms with the atoms of other elements, chemists call burning rapid oxidation.

A fire can be extinguished in various ways. Fire fighters often spray burning materials with foam or water in order to place a barrier between them and the air. When we use the expression "smothering the flames" we are really talking about the removal of oxygen from the vicinity of the fuel. Another action that will extinguish a fire is the cooling of the fuel below its kindling temperature. Fire fighters often use water to lower the temperature of a fire's fuel. A third action that will stop burning is the removal of fuel. A good example of this is the cutting down and removal of trees that are in the path of a forest fire.

HOW COMMON FIRE EXTINGUISHERS WORK

Commercial soda-acid extinguishers[1] are usually metal tanks that hold a solution of baking soda in water. Above this solution inside the tank is a bottle of sulfuric acid. To use the extinguisher, one tips it upside down so that the acid mixes with the soda solution. The chemical reaction that occurs produces a salt, carbon-dioxide gas, and water. The carbon dioxide and water are then sprayed on the fire. The soda-acid extinguisher should not be used on electrical fires, since the liquid in the tank is a good conductor of electricity and the user could be electrocuted.

Dry-Chemical Extinguishers. These are available in sizes from 1 to 14 kilograms (about 2.2 to 30 pounds). A dry-chemical extinguisher is shown in Figure 14A−5 (p. 316). Extinguishers of this type contain a specially processed

[1] The discussion of fire extinguishers beginning on this page was adapted with minor modifications from Milton O. Pella, *Physical Science for Progress* (Englewood Cliffs, N.J.: Prentice-Hall, 1970), pp. 119−121.

Figure 14A–3. Soda-Acid Fire Extinguisher (*Source:* Courtesy Walter Kidde, Division of Kidde, Inc.)

powder that is forced out of the tank by compressed air or nitrogen or by a cartridge of carbon dioxide under pressure. Some of them have one device for delivering the stored gas into the tank of powder and another one for controlling the spray of the dry chemical as it comes out of the tank.

Dry-chemical extinguishers can be used for propane-gas fires and other very hot fires. They may also be used to extinguish fires in electrical equipment. The chemicals they use, however, may be difficult to clean out of motors and delicate electrical equipment, and may cause permanent damage. This type of extinguisher allows the operator to approach close to the fire because the cloud of powder offers protection from the heat.

Carbon-Dioxide (CO_2) Extinguishers. These are available in sizes from 1 to 9 kilograms (about 2.2 to 20 pounds). A CO_2 extinguisher is shown in Figure 14A–5. The tank is made of heavy metal and is filled with liquid carbon

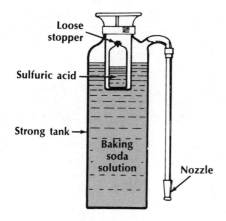

Figure 14A–4. Figure Diagram of the Components of a Soda-Acid Fire Extinguisher (*Source:* Milton O. Pella, *Physical Science for Progress,* 3rd ed. Englewood Cliffs, N.J.: Prentice-Hall, 1970. Used by permission.)

Figure 14A—5. On the left is a dry chemical extinguisher. The fire extinguisher on the right contains liquid carbon dioxide under pressure. (*Source:* Courtesy Walter Kidde, Division of Kidde, Inc.)

dioxide under high pressure. When the extinguisher valve is opened, the liquid carbon dioxide is released. When it comes in contact with air it expands and immediately turns into a gas. This gas is heavier than air, and its rapid expansion causes it to get into every crack—and even behind obstructions—and smother the fire. Carbon-dioxide extinguishers can be used to extinguish gasoline, oil, grease, and paint fires. They can also extinguish fires in live electrical equipment without damaging it.

Elements, Compounds, and Mixtures

Chemical elements such as carbon, hydrogen, and oxygen are the basic building blocks of all matter. An element is a substance that cannot be separated into simpler substances by chemical changes. This means that the carbon, hydrogen, and oxygen released from the heating of the marshmallow cannot be broken down any further by ordinary methods.

Table salt is a compound composed of the elements sodium and chlorine. Its chemical name is sodium chloride. Elements and compounds can be written in a chemical shorthand, or formula. The formula for table salt is NaCl. This combination of symbols indicates that there is one part sodium (Na) and one part chlorine (Cl) in salt.

Scientists who study the chemical composition of matter are known as chemists. Chemists around the world use the chemical shorthand to describe the changes that occur in matter. The chemical shorthand tells us what elements are in a substance and the proportion of each. In the example above, sodium chloride is seen to consist of one part of sodium combined with one part of chlorine. The formula H_2O stands for a combination of two parts of hydrogen and one part of oxygen. If we were able to look very closely into the matter contained in a glass of water, we would see that the compound water really consists of a number of small particles. Each of these particles of water consists of two parts of hydrogen and one part of oxygen.

A molecule is the smallest particle in a compound. If we broke down a molecule of water, we would produce hydrogen and oxygen. These parts of a molecule are called atoms. When we write the chemical formula H_2O we are indicating that a molecule of water contains two atoms of hydrogen and one atom of oxygen. When we write CO_2 we are saying that one molecule of carbon dioxide contains one atom of carbon and two atoms of oxygen. The number written below the line in the formula tells us how many atoms (if more than one) of the preceding element are present in the molecule.

Not all combinations of elements form compounds. The principal test is whether or not the various substances can be easily separated from one another. For example, if you were to mix a small amount of sand with a small amount of salt, no chemical change would occur. In fact, if you had the patience and a strong lens, you could probably separate the two materials. It would take a long time, but it could be done, since the salt and sand do not chemically unite with each other. Any such combination of materials that can be separated from one another is known as a mixture. The air we breathe is a mixture of various gases. The soil we walk on is a mixture of various rocks and minerals.

MOLECULAR THEORY

Scientists have reached various conclusions about the components of matter and their behavior. Among them are the following:

1. Matter is made up of small particles called molecules.
2. Spaces exist among the molecules.
3. The molecules of matter are in constant motion.

Changes in the state of matter can be explained by the motion of molecules. Solids have a definite shape because their constituent molecules are arranged in a pattern. But although they stay in this pattern they also vibrate. If heat is applied to a solid, the rate at which its molecules vibrate becomes so fast that they break away from one another in the pattern. If we add sufficient heat, the solid melts and becomes a liquid. By adding heat we can cause many solids to change to liquids. If we add even more heat, the molecules in the liquid may move fast enough to escape from the surface of the liquid and enter the air. These molecules have gone from the liquid state to the gaseous state—the process known as evaporation.

If we take the heat from gas, its molecules may slow down sufficiently for them to form a liquid. If we take away more heat, the molecules may begin forming the patterns in which they exist in their solid state. To take an example of the reverse process, by heating water in its solid state we can observe its transformation into water and finally into water in its gaseous state (water vapor).

The molecular theory of matter can be used to explain the expansion and contraction of matter. When the speed of the molecules in matter increases, they bump into one another more and tend to spread apart. Expansion of matter thereby occurs. If heat is removed, the molecules move more slowly and tend to come closer to one another. When this occurs matter contracts.

CHEMICAL EQUATIONS

Chemists use chemical equations to describe chemical changes in matter. Let's see how this is done. If we place a clean iron nail in a solution of copper sulfate, a chemical change will occur: the iron nail will become coated with a reddish covering. This red coating is copper. As this occurs, the blue color of the copper-sulfate solution becomes less intense. In the chemical change that occurs, iron in the nail changes places with some of the copper in the copper sulfate. The equation that describes this reaction is as follows:

$$Fe + CuSO_4 \longrightarrow FeSO_4 + Cu$$

Fe represents iron. $CuSO_4$ represents copper sulfate. The arrow means "forms" or "yields." On the right side of the arrow are the products of the chemical change. They are $FeSO_4$ (iron sulfate) and Cu (copper). Notice that the number of atoms on each side of the arrow is the same. No atoms are gained or lost during a chemical reaction.

THE PARTS OF AN ATOM

Even though no one has ever seen an atom, scientists have a pretty good idea of atomic structure. Much is known about the way in which atoms interact with one another as well as the way in which they absorb and release energy. With this knowledge scientists have constructed a model of what they believe an atom to be. Diagrams of this model show subatomic particles as distinct objects. Keep in mind that protons, neutrons, and electrons are not really the round objects they are depicted to be in such diagrams. The equivalence of mass and energy makes it extremely difficult to think of any bit of matter in an atom as having such permanence. Although diagrams do not really represent the real world of atoms, they can help us understand atomic interaction. Figure 14A−6 consists of a model of six different atoms, their electrons placed in shells. A shell is an energy level on which an electron exists within an atom.

The center of an atom is called its nucleus. This is the place where protons, heavy particles having a positive electrical charge, and neutrons, heavy particles having no electrical charge, are found. It is the protons and neutrons that make up most of the atom's weight. Electrons are negative electrical charges that move rapidly around the nucleus. They seem to move in circular or elliptical orbits. Electrons have only 1/1877 the weight of a proton. Atoms are electrically neutral. That is, they contain as many positive charges (protons) in their nucleus as there are negative charges (electrons) around the nucleus. The hydrogen atom does not have any neutrons. It consists of one proton and one electron. The helium atom consists of two protons and two neutrons in the nucleus surrounded by two orbiting electrons.

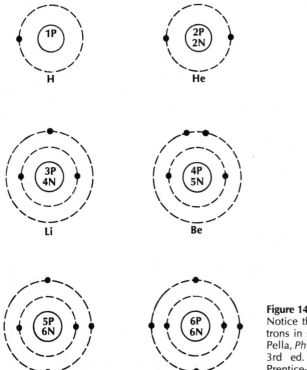

Figure 14A−6. Models of Six Atoms. Notice the placement of the electrons in shells. (*Source:* Milton O. Pella, *Physical Science for Progress,* 3rd ed. Englewood Cliffs, N.J.: Prentice-Hall, 1970. Used by permission.)

The atomic number of an element is the number of protons it contains. The atomic weight of an element is the weight of its protons plus the weight of its neutrons. An element's atomic weight is also determined in relation to the weight of a carbon atom, which is defined as being 12 units. A hydrogen atom has about 1/12 the weight of a carbon atom. Therefore, hydrogen has an atomic weight of about one. Magnesium is about twice as heavy as carbon; its atomic weight is 24. The atomic weights of various elements are shown in Figure 14A−7.

Some atoms of an element have a slightly higher weight than most atoms of the element. These atoms are known as isotopes. For example, the most common sulfur atom has an atomic weight of 32. However, some sulfur atoms have an atomic weight of 36. Both types of atom are sulfur atoms, since they have an atomic number of 16. The average atomic weight of sulfur atoms is about 32.1. The 0.1 results from the sulfur atoms that have slightly different atomic weights. These isotopes of sulfur have the exact chemical properties of the element sulfur. Their physical properties, however, may differ from the physical properties of the predominant sulfur atoms. Hydrogen is found in nature in at least three different forms—hydrogen 1, hydrogen 2, and hydrogen 3. These isotopes are represented in Figure 14A−8.

By studying the drawings of hydrogen isotopes you will note that most hydrogen atoms have one proton and one electron. Hydrogen 2 is an isotope that

Aluminum	27.0	Nitrogen	14.0
Calcium	40.1	Oxygen	16.0
Carbon	12.0	Phosphorus	31.0
Chlorine	35.5	Potassium	39.1
Copper	63.5	Silver	107.0
Hydrogen	1.0	Sodium	23.0
Iron	55.8	Sulfur	32.1
Magnesium	24.3	Zinc	65.4
Mercury	200.6		

Figure 14A−7. Atomic Weight of Some Elements (*Source:* Milton O. Pella, *Physical Science for Progress,* 3rd ed. Englewood Cliffs, N.J.: Prentice-Hall, 1970. Used by permission.

has one proton, one electron, and one neutron. Hydrogen 3 is an isotope that has one proton, one electron, and two neutrons. The atomic weight of hydrogen represents the average weight of all hydrogen atoms, including the isotopes.

ATOMS AND NUCLEAR ENERGY

The energy we get from burning a fuel comes from a chemical reaction. In a chemical reaction, some of the electrons of the various atoms involved may be exchanged or shared. Energy can also be released through the nucleus of the atom. Such release of energy is brought about not by an ordinary chemical change, but rather as a result of a change in the nucleus of the atom. Atoms of some elements, such as radium and uranium 235, are naturally radioactive. A radioactive atom is one that is unstable: it has the potential to break up spontaneously. When radioactive atoms break up, they throw off some of their particles and also a great deal of energy. The energy that is given off is known as radiation. It is a very powerful form of energy. Materials that are radioactive are too dangerous to be handled directly, since they may discharge rays that can damage human cells. This special property of radioactive materials is used by doctors who treat cancer patients. Focused radiation can destroy cancer cells. Unfortunately, healthy cells may also be destroyed in the process.

Some isotopes of uranium break down spontaneously, releasing energy and particles of matter that form radium. The radium nucleus can break down further to form a stable atom of lead. The amount of energy released in this process can be

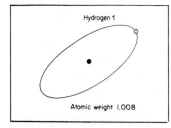 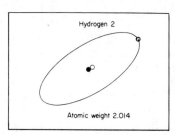 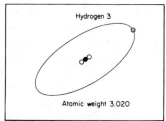

Figure 14A−8. Hydrogen Isotopes. Most hydrogen atoms have one proton and one electron. Heavy hydrogen-2 isotope has one proton, one electron, and one neutron. Heavy hydrogen-3 isotope has one proton, one electron, and two neutrons. (*Source:* June E. Lewis, Irene C. Potter, *The Teaching of Science in the Elementary School,* 2nd ed., © 1970, p. 136. Reprinted by permission of Prentice-Hall, Inc., Englewood Cliffs, N.J.)

calculated by multiplying the amount of matter that is seemingly destroyed (actually it's converted to energy) by c (the speed of light) squared. If one gram of matter is changed directly to energy, the amount of that energy is equal to the amount produced by the burning of about 3000 tons of coal. When scientists control these nuclear reactions, they harness great amounts of energy. A controlled flow of chain reactions occurs in nuclear-power plants. In detonated atomic bombs, on the other hand, uncontrolled chain reactions take place.

Matter can also be changed by a different type of nuclear reaction—fusion. In this process, just as in the fission process, small amounts of matter are changed to large amounts of energy. The sunlight that reaches you each day as well as the light from the other stars in the universe is all produced by nuclear fusion. An example of nuclear fusion is the combination of hydrogen nuclei to form helium and energy. Hydrogen bombs operate as a result of fusion. At the present time controlled fusion has been accomplished only in the laboratory.

MOTION

"How long till we get there?" That question commonly punctuates long family drives to distant destinations. It is usually asked by children over and over again, irrespective of the frequency of the parents' response. On long drives there seems to be only one other group of words that is said more frequently by children—the declaration of an urgent need to visit a rest room. The driver, if he or she is patient enough, will try to give the child a response to both the question of arrival time and the expression of urgent physiological need, a response that is based on the speed of the automobile, its present location, and the location of the destination, or, of course, of a rest room.

The distance traveled by an automobile in a given unit of time is called its speed. The units commonly used to express the speed of automobiles are kilometers per hour and miles per hour. When we specify the direction in which an object is traveling as well as its speed, we are using a scientific quantity called velocity.

We can use our knowledge of speed to determine how long it will take for an object to get from place to place. Since speed is the distance divided by the time, we can multiply the speed of the object by the time available to find how far we will travel in that time. For example, a car traveling at 50 kilometers per hour (about 30 miles per hour) for three hours will travel a distance of 150 kilometers (about 90 miles) in an hour.

In order to answer the child's question about how long it will take to reach a destination, the driver can calculate as follows. If the driver knows that the destination is 100 kilometers (about 60 miles) away and the average speed during the journey will be 50 kilometers per hour (about 30 miles per hour), he or she can divide the speed into the distance, thereby determining that the journey will take about two hours.

We call changes in velocity acceleration. An automobile speeding up or slowing down is accelerating. The rate of acceleration is equal to the change in velocity divided by the time it took for the change. If your car is stopped at a red light and then gains a speed of 50 kilometers per hour (about 30 miles per hour) in

10 seconds, traveling in a straight line, the change in velocity is 50 kilometers per hour and it occured in 10 seconds. Therefore, the rate of acceleration of the car is 5 kilometers per hour per second (about 3 miles per hour per second).

Since scientists define velocity as both speed and direction, an object that moves with constant speed yet changes direction is accelerating. For example, a racing car traveling around a racecourse at a constant speed is accelerating, since its direction is constantly changing.

The earth's gravitational pull causes falling objects to accelerate at the rate of 9.8 meters per second per second (32 feet per second per second). This means that they change their speed 9.8 meters per second (32 feet per second) during each second they fall. Strictly speaking this rate applies to objects falling through a vacuum, since the presence of air retards the acceleration of objects that have a large surface area compared with their mass (such as feathers).

Newton's Laws of Motion

Have you ever blown up a balloon, held its end shut, and then released it to watch it rocket around a room? You may not have realized it, but you were demonstrating a phenomenon described about three hundred years ago by Isaac Newton. His observations of the motion of objects led him to reach conclusions that we now refer to as laws of motion. Newton's three laws of motion help us explain the motion of objects that are subjected to forces.

Newton's first law of motion states that an object at rest will remain at rest and a body moving with a constant velocity in a straight line will maintain its motion unless acted upon by an unbalanced external force. This law is sometimes called the law of inertia. It tells us that in order to change the position of objects at rest, we must apply a force to them. Similarly, if we wish to change the velocity of an object, we must apply a force. To move a golf ball from the grass of a putting green to the hole, the golfer applies a force with his or her putter. To increase the speed of an automobile, we cause the engine to increase the forces that turn the wheels. To slow down a bicycle that is moving along at a constant velocity, we apply frictional forces by using the brakes.

Newton's second law of motion states that the amount of acceleration produced by a force acting on an object varies with the magnitude of the force and the mass of the object. If the force on an object is increased and no mass is added to or taken away from the object, the object's acceleration will increase. Specifically, this law tells us that an object will accelerate in the direction in which an applied force is acting, and that the acceleration will be proportional to the applied force. For example, when we begin to push or pull a child in a wagon that was stationary, the wagon moves in the direction of the push or pull and increases its acceleration as the force we apply increases.

Newton's third law of motion states that for every action there is an equal and opposite reaction. This section began with the example of a blown-up balloon darting about a room. The balloon illustrates Newton's third law. The air escaping from the balloon moves in one direction; it is the action force. The balloon moves in the opposite direction as a reaction to the action force. Another example of this law often occurs when a person driving an automobile finds that he or she has a flat tire. The subsequent kicking of the flattened tire in frustration is the action force. The immediate pain in the foot is the result of a reaction force acting upon the foot.

Jet and Rocket Engines

Jet airplanes and space rockets are designed to capitalize on Newton's third law of motion. Both utilize engines that discharge hot gases in one direction (an action force) so as to produce thrust (a reaction force). In both engines chemical energy is changed to the energy of motion.

The jet engine uses kerosene fuel to heat air that is taken into the engine. The products of the combustion of kerosene reach a high temperature and pressure and leave the rear of the engine. This produces the reaction force, or thrust. The turbojet is a commonly used jet engine. Turning compressor blades take in air through the front of the engine and force it into the combustion chamber. At this point kerosene is sprayed into the air and ignited. The hot exhaust gases expand and move out the back of the engine, turning the turbine blades in the process. The turbine blades are connected to the compressor blades and cause them to turn and bring in more air.

The rocket engine is designed to operate in outer space, in the absence of air. This lack of oxygen means that the fuel that is burned must be provided with oxygen from some other source such as tanks of liquid oxygen carried near the engine. Some rocket fuels do not require oxygen. Instead, they use a chemical known as an oxidizer.

Flight

"Just pull the yellow oxygen mask toward you . . . Now cover your mouth and breathe normally." Each time a flight attendant says that prior to takeoff, I begin to wonder. How exactly do you breath *normally* when an aircraft is having a serious problem that may soon give it the aerodynamic characteristics of a rock? Have you ever had a similar thought?

I know that air travel is one of the safest forms of transportation. I know that intelligent, competent pilots and navigators are in charge. I know that modern aircraft have elaborate communication systems, redundant safety systems, and many other reassuring characteristics. Yet everytime I hear that flight attendant say "Breathe normally," I start to wonder why I have strapped myself into the seat of a multiton aircraft that is going to take me for a five-hundred-mile-per-hour ride at forty thousand feet above the earth's surface. I understand the physics of flight, but I am still astonished that this lumbering mastodon is somehow going to become airborne. It is most amazing.

What causes an airplane to rise? The answer is the force called lift. Wings are shaped so that air going across their upper surface moves at a higher velocity than the air going across the bottom surface. This causes a region of low pressure to form above the wing as it moves through the air. The air pressure below the wing is greater than the air pressure above the wing, causing an unbalanced upward force.

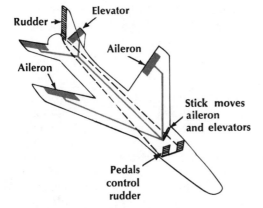

Figure 14A–9. The Controls That Can Change an Airplane's Direction of Motion (*Source:* Milton O. Pella, *Physical Science for Progress*, 3rd ed. Englewood Cliffs, N.J.: Prentice-Hall, 1970. Used by permission.)

The lifting force on a wing can be varied in several ways. For example, the faster a plane moves, the more lift is created. The angle that the front of the wing makes with the oncoming air also affects lift. This angle is known as the angle of attack. In fixed-wing aircraft the pilot varies the angle of attack by using movable portions of the wing called wing flaps, or ailerons. Extending the wing flaps also increases the surface area of the wing. A larger surface produces more lift than a smaller surface.

As we have noted, the forward motion, or thrust, of a jet aircraft is a reaction force to hot exhaust gases expelled from the rear of the engine. Propellor-driven planes, on the other hand, move forward because of the propellor, which is designed very much like a miniature wing. The pressure on the rear surface of the propellor pushes the plane forward.

"It's a drag" is an expression I've sometimes heard my students use (about other courses, of course). Pilots also use the term *drag*. Drag is a force that retards the forward motion of an aircraft. It results from the friction between the air and the surfaces of the aircraft.

The direction in which an airplane moves is controlled by the pilot's use of the ailerons, elevator, and rudder. The elevator (the movable flap on the horizontal part of the tail) causes the aircraft's nose to move up or down. The rudder (the movable flap on the vertical portion of the tail) causes the nose of the aircraft to move left or right. The ailerons change the lift on the wing surfaces. The pilot uses all these surfaces in combination to turn the plane.

SUMMARY OUTLINE

I. Anything that occupies space and has weight is matter.

    A. A change in matter from one state (phase) to another is a physical change.

    B. A change in matter that produces a new substance is a chemical change.

II. Matter exists as elements, compounds, or mixtures.

    A. Molecular theory is used to explain a variety of changes in matter.

B. Chemical changes in matter can be described with chemical symbols and equations.

C. Atoms are composed of smaller particles.

D. Under special conditions, portions of the matter in an atomic nucleus can be converted to energy.

III. Matter can be caused to move from place to place.

A. Newton's laws of motion enable us to predict how the motion of an object will change as a result of the application of a force.

B. The motion of jet planes and rockets can be explained by Newton's third law of motion, the law dealing with action and reaction forces.

C. Airplanes fly as a result of two forces: lift and thrust.

chapter 14B

Matter and Motion

DISCOVERY ACTIVITIES
AND DEMONSTRATIONS

A LOOK AHEAD

Discovery Activities

Secret Messages and Chemical Changes

Matter and Changes*

Pendulums

Additional Activity Ideas

From Gas to Liquid*

Giving Paper a Lift

The Quarter and the Paper Clip

Heat and the Fizzer

Plane Parts

The Salt Pendulum*

Demonstrations

Teacher on Wheels: Action and Reaction Forces

How Does an Earth Satellite Get Placed in Orbit?*

Additional Demonstration Ideas

From Liquid to Gas*

From Sugar to Carbon: A Chemical Change*

Action and Reaction

Water from a Flame

Making an Automatic "Balloon-Blower-Upper"

DISCOVERY ACTIVITIES

Secret Messages and Chemical Changes

OBJECTIVES

The children will observe physical and chemical changes.
The children will describe the characteristics of physical and chemical changes.

SCIENCE PROCESSES EMPHASIZED

Observing
Communicating
Making a hypothesis

MATERIALS

For each child or group

Access to a small container of freshly squeezed lemon juice
Cotton swab
Sheet of white paper
Iron nail
Plastic container of water
A few sheets of paper toweling

Figure 14B–1. Observing Secret Messages and Chemical Changes (*Source:* SAPA II, Module 17, p. 5. Science . . . A Process Approach II, American Association for the Advancement of Science. Used with permission.)

For the class

3 or 4 desk lamps with incandescent 100-watt light bulbs

Roll of masking tape

Small clear plastic containers (such as disposable glasses), each containing copper-sulfate solution; there should be one for each group

Note: The containers of copper sulfate will remain in a central location under your supervision, and not be moved to the desk tops. The children will place their iron nail in the container and simply observe the changes. At the end of the activity you should be responsible for disposing of the solutions. At no time should the copper sulfate be handled by the children.

MOTIVATION

This activity should be done following activities or discussion on physical changes. Ask the children to review the characteristics of a physical change with you. Now discuss the possibility that some changes may result in the production of new substances. Indicate that the children will be doing some activities that may help them think about such changes.

DIRECTIONS

Part I

1. Distribute the lemon juice, cotton swabs, and paper. Have the children write "secret" messages on their paper, using the swabs and lemon juice.
2. The children should allow their paper to dry. Have them make and record observations of the lemon-juice patterns on the paper.
3. The children should now exchange messages and take turns heating them over the reading lamps. This should be done under your supervision.
4. Have a discussion in which you ask the children whether they thought a physical or chemical change occurred.

Part II

1. Distribute an iron nail to each group. Have the children clean the nail with the paper towels.
2. Have the children make a small identifying tag out of masking tape for their nail and affix it to the top of the nail.
3. The children should bring their nail to one of the containers of copper sulfate, place it in the solution, and make observations every few hours (if this is convenient) or every time they have science class.
4. After some changes have occurred, have a discussion of whether the changes observed were physical changes.

KEY DISCUSSION QUESTIONS

1. When the secret writing became visible, do you think that there was a physical change?

No, the lemon juice changed to something else. It got darker; we probably couldn't make it turn back into lemon juice.

2. What were some changes you observed after the iron nail was placed in the blue liquid? *The blue color of the liquid got less; red stuff started to cover the nail.*

3. Do you think you saw a physical change? *No. Some new things formed. The color of the liquid changed, and the red stuff wasn't there when we started.*

SCIENCE CONTENT FOR THE TEACHER

When matter undergoes a physical change it merely changes in form. Physical changes are usually easy to reverse. In contrast, this activity shows two chemical changes. In the first case, heat added to the lemon juice causes the formation of molecules that absorb light, giving the juice a dark color. In the second case, copper that was part of the solution left the solution and accumulated on the surface of the nail as iron from the nail entered the liquid. The iron reacted with the copper sulfate to form a new substance—iron sulfate. The copper atoms that left the solution were observed in their metallic form on the surface of the nail.

EXTENSIONS

Science. You may wish to have some children observe an additional chemical change. They can wedge some steel wool into a small glass, moisten it, and invert it in a pan of water. There should be an air space between the steel wool in the inverted glass and the water. Within a few days the children will be able to observe the formation of rust on the steel wool—a chemical change.

Science/Language Arts. Activities such as this one can provide children with greater sensitivity to the concept of change. The acquisition of sensitivity to a variety of changes in the environment can serve as an important first step in writing experiences that focus on change. You may wish to have the children write rhymed and unrhymed poetry about the changes they observe in the world around them.

Matter and Changes[1]*

OBJECTIVES

The children will identify a substance as a solid or a liquid.
The children will describe changes in the color, shape, size, and state of samples of matter.

SCIENCE PROCESSES EMPHASIZED

Observing
Communicating

[1]The activity on matter and changes beginning on this page was adapted from "Change," Module 17 in *Science: A Process Approach II* (Lexington, Mass: Ginn, 1975).
*Asterisks refer to activities for young children.

MATERIALS

For each child or group

One ice cube

One paper towel

One cube of modeling clay 2.5 centimeters by 2.5 centimeters by 2.5 centimeters (about 1 inch on edge)

One cube of butter the same size as the cube of clay

Three saucers

Paper and pencil

For the class

Access to a sink with a hot-water faucet

For the teacher

One ice cube

One glass

MOTIVATION

Tell the children that you are thirsty and that you are going to have a drink of water. Display the ice cube in the glass and pretend to drink from the glass. Ask the children why you are having trouble getting a drink. The children will indicate that the ice cube will have to melt before you can have water to drink. Have the children discuss whether an ice cube is really water. Suggest that ice cubes might be made of "smush," a clear solid that changes to water. After some discussion of ways in which they could check to see if there is such a thing as "smush," begin the activity.

DIRECTIONS

1. Have the children heat each plate under the hot-water faucet and then place the cube of butter, the cube of clay, and the ice cube on them.
2. Have the children make comparisons of the size, shape, and color of the substances.
3. The children should keep a record of the changes that occur.
4. After the butter and ice cubes have changed in form commence a class discussion of the states of matter, using the following questions to focus the children's thinking.

KEY DISCUSSION QUESTIONS

1. Which cubes were solid when you started the activity? What changes did you observe? *All three. The butter and the ice cubes started to melt.*
2. Did the color or shape of the cubes change? *The color didn't but the shape did.*
3. What would happen if we put the saucers in a freezer before the activity? How would the changes have been different? *The butter and ice cubes would not have melted as fast.*
4. What do you think caused the changes? *Heat.*

SCIENCE CONTENT FOR THE TEACHER

Matter is commonly found in one of three forms or states: as a solid, as a liquid, or as a gas. In this activity three substances that display the essential observable characteristics of solids are observed as heat from the air in the room and pre-heated sources cause a change in state. The flow of energy from these sources causes the smaller particles (molecules) that the substances contain to increase their motion. In the case of the butter and the ice cube this increased energy causes the molecules to begin to flow past each other, and melting is observed. The change is a physical change because the substance remains the same but simply changes in form.

EXTENSIONS

Science/Art. You may wish to have some children make drawings of various changes, such as an icicle melting, water in a pond freezing, and a pond drying up during the summer.

Science/Physical Education. Some children may wish to make drawings of various sports that utilize water or ice. The children can discuss their drawings with the class and consider what would happen if the water depicted in them magically changed to ice or vice versa.

Pendulums

OBJECTIVES

The children will predict the effect of changing the string length and mass of a pendulum bob on the motion of the pendulum.
The children will measure the effect of changing the string length and mass of the bob on the motion of the pendulum.

SCIENCE PROCESSES EMPHASIZED

Observing
Predicting
Measuring

MATERIALS FOR EACH CHILD OR GROUP

Horizontal wooden support at least a meter (about 40 inches) long
4 screw eyes fastened along the length of the support
Spool of heavy-duty twine
4 sticks of modeling clay
Stopwatch
Metric ruler

Figure 14B–2. Children can design and perform experiments with a variety of pendulums. (*Source:* J. Abruscato and J. Hassard, *The Whole Cosmos Catalog.* Santa Monica, Calif.: Goodyear Publishing Company, Inc. Used by permission of Goodyear Publishing Company.)

MOTIVATION

Display the materials and ask the children to try to guess what they will be learning about in the activity they will be doing. Tell them that today they will be making some predictions and then doing an activity to check their predictions.

DIRECTIONS

1. Have one member of each group be responsible for making the pendulum bob from the clay and attaching it to string. Have another child be responsible for using the stopwatch. The children should switch roles during the activity.
2. Begin by having the children predict how changing the length of the string will affect the time it takes for the pendulum to make one complete forward-and-backward movement. Use the term *period* to represent this amount of time.
3. Ask the children to make the bob from half a stick of clay. Explain that *bob* is a general name for any object hanging from a pendulum string.

4. Have the children start with a one-meter length of string and shorten it by ten centimeters (about four inches) during each of the five trials. In starting the pendulum movement, always move the bob ten centimeters (four inches) to the left of its stationary position before releasing it.
5. The children should find the time of one back-and-forth movement by completing five such movements and then dividing by five.
6. The group members should then check their predictions.
7. Have the children repeat this procedure, this time using three different bobs—made of one quarter, one half, and three quarters of a stick of clay. Maintain the string lengths at one meter (about forty inches). The children should predict the period of each of the three pendulums, and then check their predictions against their observations.

KEY DISCUSSION QUESTIONS

1. Did you predict that the length of the string would affect the period of the pendulum? (*Answers will vary.*)
2. What did you observe when just the length of the string was changed? *The length of the string does affect the period. The longer the string, the longer the period.*
3. Did you predict that the mass of the bob would affect the period of the pendulum? (*Answers will vary.*)
4. What did you observe when just the mass of the bob was changed? *Changing the mass of the bob does not change the period of the pendulum.*

SCIENCE CONTENT FOR THE TEACHER

A pendulum is a weight, or bob, suspended from a fixed point that is able to freely swing back and forth. The period of a pendulum is the time it takes for the bob to make one complete back-and-forth swing. Galileo discovered that the period of a pendulum is independent of the mass of the bob and depends only on the pendulum's length.

EXTENSIONS

Science. You may wish to ask the children if they would predict that the period of a pendulum depends on how far the bob is released from the point at which it is hanging straight down. They can then conduct an activity to check their prediction. (The period remains the same regardless of the position from which the bob is released.)

Science/Social Studies. This activity is an excellent opportunity for having the children become aware of Galileo. You can read a brief biography of Galileo in a reference book and then have the children do some social-studies activities that focus on him. For example, they can make a time line and mark on it the time of Galileo's life as well as such events as the discovery of America, the American Revolution, the launching of the first space satellite, and the first moon walk. The children could also locate Italy on a world map and find the town (Pisa) in which Galileo made his observation of the swinging pendulum.

ADDITIONAL ACTIVITY IDEAS

From Gas to Liquid*

Children can observe the change in state from gas to liquid by causing water in the air to condense. Each child or learning group will need a supply of crushed ice and a shiny metal container. They should polish the outside of their container with a towel and observe the surface. Then have the children add crushed ice to the containers and again observe the outside surface. In a short time a thin film of water will appear on the can. This phenomenon occurs because the cold can lowers the temperature of the surrounding air to the dew point. The dew point is the temperature at which water vapor in the air condenses.

Giving Paper a Lift

This activity can be done during a unit on motion to help children understand the phenomenon of lift. Give the children a sheet of paper each and have them hold it at two adjacent corners. They should then raise the paper in front of their mouth, directly *under* their lower lip. The upper surface of the paper should resemble the shape of the top surface of an airplane wing. Have the children steadily blow across the top of the wing surface. They will observe the paper rise as a result of the lift produced on the wing.

The Quarter and the Paper Clip

Children can observe that gravity causes falling objects to change in velocity at the same rate by simultaneously dropping a quarter and a paper clip from their desk top. To ensure that both are dropped at the same time, have the children place each at the table edge. They can slide a plastic ruler into them and gently push both over the edge in one stroke. The children will observe that both objects hit the floor at the same time.

Heat and the Fizzer

Children can safely investigate the effect of heat on a chemical reaction by dropping half an Alka Seltzer tablet in glasses of ice water, warm water, and hot water. The children will know that a chemical reaction takes place in each glass because of the appearance of a new substance—a gas (carbon dioxide). The rate of fizzing in the three glasses is a good indication of the speed of the reaction.

Plane Parts

You may wish to purchase enough small wooden or plastic model-airplane kits so that each learning group has one model to build. This is a long-term activity that children can work on a few times a week and whenever they have free time. When the children are finished have them label the parts of their model. A class discussion could then be held dealing with the location and function of such airplane parts as the propeller, ailerons (wing flaps), wing, tail, elevator (the movable flap on the horizontal part of the tail), and air rudder (the movable flap on the vertical portion of the tail).

The Salt Pendulum*

You can have children design and use a pendulum that will create beautiful salt patterns. They will need to make cone-shaped containers to serve as their salt-containing pendulum bob. They will also need a supply of string, a supply of salt, a horizontal support, and sheets of dark paper. The children may wish to observe the effects produced when the bob is suspended by the different arrangements of string shown in Figure 14B–3. The children can preserve some of their patterns by spreading glue over the paper that receives them.

DEMONSTRATIONS

Teacher on Wheels: Action and Reaction Forces

OBJECTIVES

The children will observe that an action force applied in one direction produces a reaction force in the opposite direction.
The children will predict the direction and magnitude of reaction forces.

SCIENCE PROCESSES EMPHASIZED

Observing
Predicting

MATERIALS FOR THE TEACHER

A pair of roller skates or a skateboard
Length of board 25 by 3 by 49 centimeters (about 10 by 1 by 40 inches)
12 large marbles
Old textbooks of assorted sizes (or large beanbags)

MOTIVATION

Simply indicate to the children that you intend to get on roller skates or a skateboard to demonstrate action and reaction forces—that should be sufficient motivation!

Figure 14B–3. Children can produce interesting art work with the salt pendulum. (*Source:* J. Abruscato and J. Hassard, *The Whole Cosmos Catalog*. Santa Monica, Calif.: Goodyear Publishing Company, Inc. Used by permission of Goodyear Publishing Company.)

DIRECTIONS

1. Place the board on the floor. Stand on the board and have the children predict what will happen to it when you jump off one end of it. Then jump. Nothing will happen to the board. Tell the children that although they didn't observe anything happen to the board, your action of jumping from it caused a reaction force to be applied to it. However, the board didn't move because of the friction between the floor and the board.

2. Ask the children to predict what would happen if you repeated your jump but reduced the friction between the floor and the board. Now place as many of the marbles as you have under the board. Spread them out so that they support all parts of the board. Step on the board gently so that you do not disturb the marbles under it. Now have the children observe what happens when you jump off one end of the board. They will see the board move in the opposite direction.

3. Now put on the roller skates or step on the skateboard. Have a volunteer hand you some old textbooks. Ask the children what they predict will happen if you throw a textbook from your perch on wheels. Now execute a rapid underhand throw of the textbook to an awaiting container. (If the thought of throwing old textbooks around in this manner bothers you, simply substitute large homemade beanbags.)

4. Vary the number of books or beanbags and the direction and speed with which they are thrown. Have children make predictions prior to each demonstration of action and reaction.

KEY DISCUSSION QUESTIONS

1. When I threw the book while I was standing on the skateboard (roller skates) what was the reaction and what was the action? *The action was the book being thrown. The reaction was your movement in the other direction.*

2. What happened when I threw the book faster? *You moved in the other direction faster.*

3. Jet and rocket engines work because of action and reaction. What is the action and what is the reaction when these engines operate? *The hot gases going out the back of the engine is the action. The plane or rocket moving forward is the reaction.*

SCIENCE CONTENT FOR THE TEACHER

This demonstration serves to illustrate Newton's third law of motion, although it is unnecessary to refer to it as such. This law tells us that for every action there is an equal and opposite reaction. For example, when we apply a force to the earth as we try to take a step, a reaction force pushes our body forward. Similarly, any time we apply a force to an object a reaction force is produced. This law of nature can easily be taken advantage of to produce motion in any direction. A jet engine causes an airplane to move foward as a reaction to the action force produced when hot gases are expelled from the rear of the engine.

EXTENSIONS

Science. You may wish to have a group of children follow up this demonstration by attempting to build a device that will launch small objects in one direction and display a reaction force in the other direction.

Many toy stores sell plastic rockets that are launched as a result of the rearward movement of water out their back end. The rocket comes with a small pump that is used to fill the rocket with water. A small group of children might wish to demonstrate (under your close supervision) the launching on the playground of such a rocket.

Science/Physical Education. Some children may wish to extend their knowledge of action and reaction forces by trying to identify athletic events that depend on these forces. For example, they might identify diving from a diving board (the action is the downward jump on the board; the reaction is the upward propelling of the diver).

How Does an Earth Satellite Get Placed in Orbit?*

OBJECTIVES

The children will observe a model of the launching of a rocket and the placement of a satellite in orbit.
The children will identify the forces that are at work during the launching process.
The children will infer the causes of the forces.

SCIENCE PROCESSES EMPHASIZED

Observing
Inferring

MATERIALS

Tennis ball firmly attached to a one-meter (one yard) length of string
Magazine pictures of various satellites that have been placed in orbit
Globe
Small model rocket ship

MOTIVATION

Display the magazine pictures of the satellites and engage the children in a discussion of how satellites are placed in orbit. Solicit their ideas about why satellites remain in orbit after they are launched. Now display the materials and explain to the children that you will be making a model that will help them understand the various phases of the process of launching and orbiting a satellite. Explain that the model is a word model and that they will have to use their imagination. Indicate that the props you will use will help them understand what happens when satellites are launched.

1. Hold the rocket so the children can see it. Place it on the surface of the globe. Indicate that a satellite is usually placed in the nose cone of the rocket that will launch it into orbit. Show the satellite being launched by lifting the rocket from the earth's surface. Explain that the exhaust gases are expelled from the back of the rocket and that this causes the rocket to move forward.

2. Explain that as the rocket moves upward it must counteract the force of gravity pulling on it. Show the rocket turning as it places the satellite in orbit.

3. Now use the tennis ball on the string to show how the satellite stays in orbit. Whirl the ball around your head with about one meter (about one yard) of string extending from your hand to the ball. In this model the string attached to the tennis ball represents the earth's pull on the satellite. The reaction force that is produced on the forward-moving satellite acts outward and counteracts the effect of gravity. Since the inward force is counterbalanced by the outside force the satellite is weightless.

KEY DISCUSSION QUESTIONS

1. Have you ever seen a satellite launched on television? What were some of the things you noticed? (*Answers will vary.*)

2. Does the rocket stay attached to the satellite when the satellite is put into orbit? *No. It falls to earth and the satellite keeps moving ahead.*

3. What keeps pulling the satellite downward? *Gravity.*

4. Why does the satellite keep moving forward? *If you start an object moving it keeps moving unless something slows it down. In space there are no air particles to slow the satellite down.*

SCIENCE CONTENT FOR THE TEACHER

A ball thrown perfectly horizontally from the top of a tall building follows a curved path as it falls to earth. How far it travels from the building before it strikes the earth depends on how fast it was thrown and how high the building is. An object thrown forward at a speed of 7800 meters per second (about 25,600 feet per second) at a height of 160 kilometers (about 100 miles) would not return to earth. Instead, it would follow a curved path around the earth. Inertia would carry it forward, and the attraction of the earth's gravitational field would keep it continually bending toward the earth's surface.

Satellites remain in orbit as a result of a balance between the pull of gravity inward and a reaction force outward. The scientific names for these forces are centripetal (inward) and centrifugal (outward). The satellite orbits the earth because the inward and outward forces produce a balance.

EXTENSIONS

Science. This demonstration would provide a good starting point for an extensive study of recent rocket and satellite launchings. You may wish to have a group of children do library research to gather information on recent launchings and inform the class of upcoming space-exploration activities.

Science/Social Studies. You may wish to talk to the children about the financial cost of space exploration. A class discussion could focus on whether the costs are justified when compared with the short-term and long-term benefits. Children can be sensitized to the limitations of a society's resources and the difficult decisions that must be made to ensure that they are used wisely.

ADDITIONAL DEMONSTRATION IDEAS

From Liquid to Gas*

You can demonstrate the change of a liquid to a gas with a small saucer and some inexpensive perfume or cologne. Pour some of the perfume into the saucer. Be sure that the children observe that it is a liquid. Then have the children indicate when the odor reached them. Ask if they could see the perfume travel. This is a good demonstration with which to begin a unit on the states of matter.

From Sugar to Carbon: A Chemical Change*

Have the children observe you place a layer of sugar on the bottom of an aluminum-foil pie plate. Then heat the pie plate over a candle flame, concentrating the heating on various parts of the bottom of the plate. If you heat one part of the plate sufficiently, the children will be able to see the results of a chemical change at that location: the sugar will turn brown and eventually black as a result of the heat.

Action and Reaction

You can use an inflated balloon to demonstrate Newton's third law (which essentially states that for every action force there is an equal and opposite reaction force). Upon releasing the balloon, children will observe that it moves forward—a reaction to the action of the air rushing out. The flapping around of the neck of the balloon causes the air to be expelled in various directions and lack of a streamlined shape to the balloon causes its flight path to be erratic.

Water from a Flame

You can show that water is one of the products of the chemical reaction that occurs when a candle burns. Hold a jar over a burning candle so that no additional air can reach the candle flame. The flame will eventually go out. When this occurs, have the children observe the inside of the jar. They will notice a film of water and some blackening of the glass. The water was produced during the burning of the wick and wax. The blackening consists of carbon released during the reaction.

Making an Automatic "Balloon-Blower-Upper"

You will need an empty soft-drink bottle, a round party balloon, some white vinegar, and baking powder for this demonstration of a chemical change. Prior to the demonstration inflate and deflate the balloon a number of times to weaken the rubber. Fill about one-fourth of the bottle with vinegar. Then fill the balloon so it is about one-eighth full of baking soda. Have the children move a safe distance away. Now attach the neck of the balloon to the top of the bottle without dropping any of the baking soda into the vinegar. The balloon should be hanging over the side of the bottle. Now hold the bottle at arm's length and tip the contents of the balloon into the vinegar. The gas (carbon dioxide) that is produced during the reaction will partially inflate the balloon.

chapter 15A

Energies and Machines

CONTENT

A LOOK AHEAD

How Energy Is Transferred

Electrical Energy
Static Electricity
Current Electricity
Using Electricity

Sound Energy

Light Energy
The Reflection and Refraction of Light
Light, Prisms, and Color

Heat Energy

Machines
Simple Machines

Summary Outline

"Psssst. Drop your pencil from the desk top at exactly 9:07. Pass it on." A little mischief is about to take place and a substitute's teaching day is going to quickly take a turn for the worse. It's a very old prank, but it will work well once again. At precisely 9:07 twenty-five pencils begin an accidental fall from desk tops to floor and innocent faces gaze about waiting for the substitute's reaction.

I'll bet that when you were a young conspirator in the old drop-the-pencils-on-the-floor routine you didn't realize that you were also demonstrating an important scientific phenomenon—the process of energy change. Let's say that the substitute teacher outsmarted your class by not reacting to the tap, tap, tap of the pencils, and the class decided to try a repeat performance. Follow the energy changes as you recycle the prank.

HOW ENERGY IS TRANSFERRED

When you lift a dropped pencil from the floor to the desk top you do work and you use energy. Your body uses some of the energy that you acquired by eating food and changes it to a useful form. This energy enables you to move, grasp, and lift. It may surprise you to learn that when you pick up the pencil some of the energy that you use in the process is transferred to the pencil. The pencil that now rests on the desk top can do work! That's right. It has become a source of potential energy. The energy you used in picking it up gives the pencil potential energy because of its new position. It is higher above the earth than it was before. If you dropped the pencil from table height, you would hear a sound when it hit the floor. That sound is produced when the potential energy of the falling pencil is converted to the energy of motion.

Energy of motion is also called kinetic energy. The amount of kinetic energy of an object is equal to $\frac{1}{2}mv^2$ (one half of the object's mass times its velocity squared). As the pencil falls it moves faster and faster, continually gaining kinetic energy. When it hits the floor its acquired kinetic energy causes the floor and itself to vibrate, producing a sound wave (a vibration that moves through the air). The pencil and the floor also heat up slightly. The original potential energy of the pencil was transformed into sound energy and heat energy.

The ability of energy to change its form is the basis of a very important scientific law—the law of conservation of energy. This law simply states that energy is neither created nor destroyed. Whenever we use energy we only change its form. Energy is not used up. It may be changed to a less useful form, but it still exists. In the example of the pencil being picked up, placed on a table, and dropped again, some of the sun's energy was stored in food, your digestive and cellular-respiration processes released some of this energy, and you used this energy to lift the pencil. The pencil acquired potential energy, and as it fell it displayed increasing kinetic energy. The kinetic energy was changed to heat and

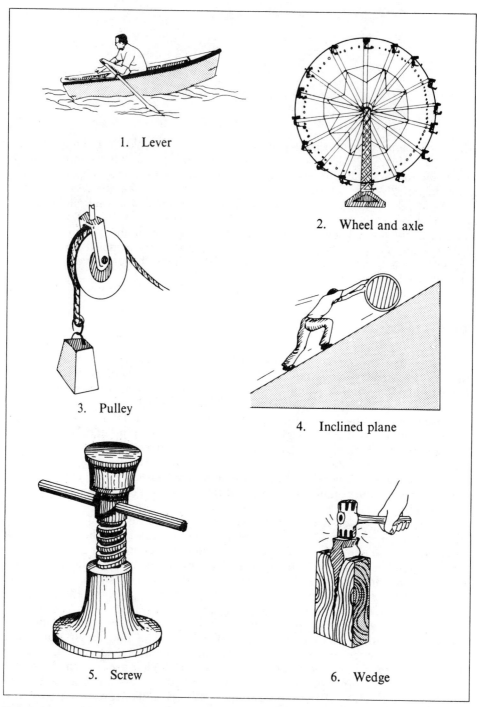

1. Lever

2. Wheel and axle

3. Pulley

4. Inclined plane

5. Screw

6. Wedge

Figure 15A–1. The Six Simple Machines (*Source:* Ewen, Nelson, Schuster, McFadden, *Physics for Career Education,* © 1974, p. 248. Reprinted by permission of Prentice-Hall, Inc.)

sound. It is at least theoretically possible, if difficult in practice, to recapture this heat and sound energy and reuse it. All the energy you used to pick up the pencil still exists. It has just changed to other forms of energy.

In this century Albert Einstein proposed that energy and matter were related. Indeed, he stated that they can be considered one and the same, since each can be converted to the other. His equation $E = mc^2$ does not really contradict the law of conservation of energy, since mass can be viewed simply as stored energy. Scientists now tell us that instead of saying that energy is never used up, we should say that the total amount of energy and mass in the universe is never used up. The interchangeability of mass and energy has resulted in the use of a more general law than either the law of conservation of energy or the law of conservation of mass. Now it is generally agreed that we should think in terms of a law of conservation of mass and energy.

There are various forms of energy available for our use. They include electricity, sound, light, and heat.

ELECTRICAL ENERGY

The bright flash of lightning jumping across the dark night sky and the subdued light coming from a desk lamp are both produced by electrical energy. They are similar to each other in that the source of their energy is electrons. There are two types of electricity: static electricity and current electricity.

Static Electricity

Kissing a person with braces on his or her teeth becomes more interesting as a result of static electricity. Lightning, a spark jumping from your fingertip to a metal doorknob, and the sticking together of articles of clothing that are removed from a clothes drier are considerably less interesting phenomena that I could have used in the opening sentence of this section. But somehow I thought I might hold your attention with the example I chose. (It really is dealt with in this section, so don't let your attention wander.) In order to understand all these occurrences of static electricity you will first need to recall some of your knowledge of the characteristics of atoms.

An atom consists of protons, neutrons, and electrons. Each proton has one unit of positive energy. Each electron has one unit of negative charge. Neutrons have no charge. Atoms normally have the same number of electrons as protons. Consequently, the positive and negative charges cancel each other out. As a result, atoms usually have no charge; they are considered neutral.

If an electron is removed from a neutral atom, the atom is left with a positive charge. If an electron is added to a neutral atom, the atom acquires a negative charge. When certain materials are rubbed together, electrons are transferred from one surface to the other. One surface gains electrons and acquires a negative charge. The other surface, having lost electrons, is left with a positive charge.

When a surface has acquired a strong negative charge, the extra electrons may jump to a neutral or positive object. A spark is a rapid movement of a number of electrons through the air.

You may have had the exciting adolescent experience of kissing a boyfriend or girlfriend with braces and being shocked by a spark. This phenomenon, sometimes confused with true love, can also be explained as a result of static electricity. Electrons were probably inadvertently rubbed from the fibers of a rug or other floor covering by the soles of the "kisser" or "kissee," giving that person's body a surplus negative charge. The extra charge was delightfully removed by the spark jumping from the negatively charged person to the neutrally charged person.

Lightning is a giant spark that sometimes occurs when clouds that have acquired a charge suddenly discharge electrons. The rapid outward movement of the air heated by the lightning ball causes the sound wave that reaches our ears as thunder.

Current Electricity

I live in a suburb, and my doorbell seems to never stop ringing. Sometimes it's an Avon lady, sometimes it's someone who wants my opinion of a new air-cleaning product (thinking that I'm not clever enough to figure out that the large case he has in hand contains a vacuum cleaner), sometimes it's a neighborhood adolescent who wants me to sponsor him or her in running, dancing, roller skating, or bike riding on behalf of a worthy cause. (I make the pledge for a certain number of miles or hours of the activity, and the child collects it by ringing my doorbell afterwards.)

Every time my doorbell rings I get grumpier, and sometimes in a weak moment I curse Benjamin Franklin, Thomas Edison, and my local electric company all in one breath. Electrical energy has given us many wonderful things, but the doorbell is one of those devices that I would just as soon not have. As a matter of fact, I sometimes disconnect it.

We are living at a time when electricity is a necessity and not a luxury. Occasional electrical blackouts bring the activities of people in busy cities to a grinding halt: traffic lights don't work, elevators stop wherever they happen to be, heating and cooling equipment stops functioning, lights in homes, apartments, and businesses go out, and food in refrigerators begins to rot. Electricity has become so much a part of our lives that we take it for granted until the moment we are without it. It has taken on this overpowering importance because it is an excellent and convenient form of energy. It can easily be converted to heat, to light, and to sound. It can also be used to operate electric motors that cause objects to move.

Electrons that move through a wire make up a current. Electron current that moves in just one direction is termed direct current. Electricity from dry cells (batteries) is direct current. Current that changes direction is known as alternating current. The electricity we purchase for home or industrial use is alternating current.

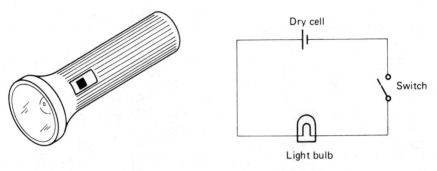

Figure 15A−2. (*Source:* Ewen et al., *Physics for Career Education,* © 1974, p. 248. Reprinted by permission of Prentice-Hall, Inc.)

Using Electricity

WHAT IS A CIRCUIT?[1]

Figure 15A−2 is a diagram of a circuit that a simple flashlight uses. An electric circuit is a loop in which electrons carrying electric energy may be transferred from a suitable source to a place where they do useful work, and then back to the source. Energy is stored in the dry cell. When the switch is closed, energy is transmitted to the light and the light glows.

Compared with static electricity, current electricity is the flow of energized electrons through an electron carrier called a *conductor*. The electrons move from the energy *source* (here, the dry cell) to the *load* (the place where the transmitted energy is turned into useful work). There they lose energy.

There are a variety of sources of electrical energy. In the circuit in Figure 15A−2 a dry cell is the source. Chemical action within the cell increases the energy of some electrons. These electrons leave the negtive (−) pole, travel through the circuit, and lose some of their increased energy to the wire and load. Their energy reduced, the electrons return to the positive (+) pole of the dry cell. The amount of energy given to electrons by a source is measured in volts.

A conductor carries or transfers electrical charge to a load (here, the flashlight). Conductors are substances that have large numbers of free electrons (electrons that can move freely throughout the conductor). Copper is a good example of a conductor. As high-energy electrons from the dry cell pass through the conductor, they collide with other electrons in the conductor and impart their energy to them. These electrons then carry the energy farther along the wire until they collide with and relay the energy to still other electrons. In this way energy is transferred through the wire.

Substances that do not allow electrons to pass readily are called *insulators*.

---

[1] The discussion of circuits that begins on this page was excerpted with minor modifications from Dale Ewen et al., *Physics for Career Education* (Englewood Cliffs, N.J.: Prentice-Hall, 1974), pp. 247−305.

Common insulators are rubber, wool, silk, glass, wood, distilled water, and dry air. A small number of materials, such as the elements silicon and germanium, are classified neither as conductors nor as insulators. The importance of these *semiconductors* is that under certain conditions they allow current to flow only in one direction. Semiconductors are a valuable component of transistors.

At the load, electrons lose energy. This lost energy is converted to other forms of energy, such as heat and light. The amount of resistance that a load offers to the flow of electrons is measured in ohms. An electric motor is a load that converts electrical energy into kinetic energy.

The flow of electrons through a conductor is called *current*. We could count the electrons passing a certain point during a certain amount of time in order to determine the rate of flow, but this is impractical because the number is so large (about 10^{18} electrons per second).

To have a workable unit of electric charge, scientists have defined the charge on 6.25×10^{18} electrons as one *coulomb*. The *ampere* is a measure of current. It is equal to the flow of one coulomb of charge past a given point in one second.

There are two basic types of circuits: series and parallel. A fuse in a house is wired in series with the house circuits' outlets. The outlets themselves are wired in parallel.

An electrical circuit with only one path in which the current can flow is called a *series* circuit. Figure 15A–3 shows a series circuit.

An electrical circuit with more than one path for the current is called a *parallel* circuit.

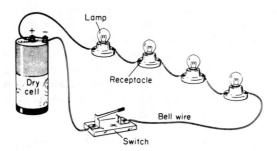

Figure 15A–3. An Electric Circuit containing Lamps Wired in Series (*Source:* June E. Lewis, Irene C. Potter, *The Teaching of Science in the Elementary School*, 2nd ed., © 1970, p. 226. Reprinted by permission of Prentice-Hall, Inc., Englewood Cliffs, N.J.)

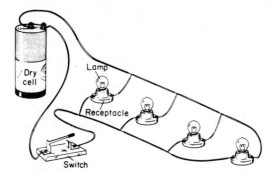

Figure 15A–4. An Electric Circuit containing Lamps Wired in Parallel (*Source:* June E. Lewis, Irene C. Potter, *The Teaching of Science in the Elementary School*, 2nd ed., © 1970, p. 226. Reprinted by permission of Prentice-Hall, Inc., Englewood Cliffs, N.J.)

The current in a parallel circuit is divided among the branches of the circuit. How it is divided depends on the resistance of each branch. Since the curent divides, the current from the source is equal to the sum of the currents through each of the branches.

MAGNETS, GENERATORS, AND MOTORS

Many devices that use or produce electrical energy depend on the relation of magnetism and electric currents. Motors and meters are based on the principle that electric currents in wires behave like magnets. Generators produce electrical current due to the movement of wires near very large magnets.

Certain kinds of metal have been found to attract iron, steel, and some other metals. Metals that have this ability are said to be magnetic. Deposits of naturally magnetic iron ore have been found. This ore is called lodestone.

Artificial magnets can be made from iron, steel, and alloys such as permalloy and alnico. Materials that can be made into magnets are called magnetic materials. Most materials, such as wood, aluminum, copper, and zinc, are nonmagnetic.

Suppose a bar magnet is suspended by a string so that it is free to rotate. It will rotate until one end points north and the other south. The end that points north is called the north-seeking pole, or just the north (N) pole. The other end is the south-seeking pole, or south (S) pole.

If the north pole of another bar magnet is brought near the north pole of this magnet, the two like poles will repel each other. On the other hand, the south pole of one magnet will attract the north pole of the other. In other words, like magnetic poles repel each other; unlike magnetic poles attract each other.

A magnet lines up along a north-south axis because of the attraction exerted by the magnetic poles of the earth. The earth has a south magnetic pole that attracts the north pole of a magnet and a north magnetic pole that attracts the south end of a magnet.

A compass is simply a small magnetic needle that is free to rotate on a bearing. The needle's north pole always points to the south magnetic pole of the earth.

There is a magnetic field near a magnetic pole. The existence of this field can be detected with the use of another magnet, as described before. By moving a small compass around the magnet the magnetic field can be observed. Scientists call the lines of force in a magnetic field *flux lines*.

A generator is a device that causes electrons to move within a conductor. This is accomplished by moving the conductor through a magentic field's flux lines. The amount of current produced by a generator can be increased by increasing the rate at which the flux lines are cut or by increasing the strength of the magnet. A generator will also function if the conductor is stationary and the magnets are moved. The source of the energy that causes the movement of the magnet or the conductor in commercial generating stations is likely to be fossil fuels, nuclear fission, or moving water.

An electric motor consists, in its simplest form, of a coil of wire wrapped around a metal core suspended between the north and south poles of a permanent magnet. Electricity is passed through the coil of wire and causes it to become an electromagnet. As a result it gains polarity: it has a north pole and a south pole.

Since the north pole of the coil will be repelled by the north pole of the permanent magnet, the coil will turn. By continually changing the direction in which the current flows through the coil, one can continually change the location of the coil's north and south poles. Consequently, the coil's north and south poles will always be near the north and south poles of the permanent magnet. The coil spins as its ends are repelled. Washing machines, electric fans, and other appliances are all able to convert electrical energy to kinetic energy by means of electric motors.

SOUND ENERGY

Have you ever slept under a roof that brought to your ears the peaceful rat-tat-tat-tat of an early-morning rain shower? Each droplet makes its arrival known with a distinctive sound. Sounds affect us in many different ways. The purring of a kitten brushing against your leg may make you feel wanted. The chirping of hungry baby birds as they extend their opened beaks for a morsel of worm brought by their mother may make you feel joyful as you think about nature. The uproarious and chaotic sounds of sanitation workers waking up your neighborhood with an early-morning symphony of bangs, crunches, screeches, and shouts may make you start your day with a bit of anger in your heart. You may even have the urge to create some sounds yourself by opening a window and shouting out some of the more colorful phrases in your vocabulary at the players in the garbage-can orchestra.

All sounds, whether they come from a garbage-can orchestra or a gentle rain on a rooftop, are produced by vibrating matter. A vibrating object receives energy from a source and transfers energy to a medium, such as air. The medium carries the energy away from the vibrating object.

A vibrating tuning fork is a good example of a source of sound waves. When a tuning fork is struck, its prongs move back and forth rapidly. When a prong moves in one direction it presses together the air ahead of it. This pressed-together air is known as a compression. As the tuning fork moves in the opposite direction it causes a portion of air to pull apart. This area is known as a rarefaction. The movement of each prong back and forth alternately produces compression and rarefaction. A sound wave is a disturbance in a medium that is caused by a vibrating object. A full sound wave consists of one compression and one rarefaction. Sound waves travel in all directions from their source. In other words, you can hear the sound of a tuning fork whether your ears are above it, to the side of it, or below it.

When a sound wave travels through a medium such as air, its compression and rarefaction cause particles within the medium to vibrate and transfer the energy of the wave to adjacent particles of the medium. The particles return to their original position, but the disturbance in the medium—the sound wave—moves.

The sounds we hear have various characteristics. The highness or lowness of a sound is its pitch. The pitch of a sound depends on the number of complete vibrations that the vibrating object makes in one second. This rate of vibration is known as the frequency.

The wavelength of a sound wave is the distance between the centers of two rarefactions. The amount of energy contained in a wave is interpreted by our ears as the loudness or softness of a sound. The loudness, or intensity, of a sound is measured in decibels.

Sound waves require a medium for their transmission. They cannot travel through a vacuum. They travel most rapidly through solids and least rapidly through gases. At a temperature of 0°C sound travels at a speed of 340 meters per second (about 1090 feet per second) in air. In water, sound travels at about 1420 meters a second (about 4686 feet a second).

When sound waves strike a barrier they are reflected. Reflected sound waves from large objects such as buildings or mountains are known as echoes. Although echoes are interesting to hear, they can be very distracting if you are attempting to speak in a room that has surfaces that produce them. Many classrooms are fitted with sound-absorbing tile or draperies. Much research is being done to design and develop other such surfaces and materials.

LIGHT ENERGY

At this very moment light[2] is being reflected from this page and is entering your eyes. It is moving at the extraordinary speed of 300,000 kilometers per second (about 186,000 miles per second) and is carrying a great deal of information with it. In particular it conveys images of the shapes of the print on the page. Your brain assembles the images that reach your retina in a way that gives them meaning. If you are lucky enough to be leisurely reading this book out of doors, the source of the light reflecting from the page is the sun. If you are reading indoors, the light is probably originating from a lamp.

There are two types of light sources: luminous and nonluminous. The sun, the stars, and light bulbs are luminous light sources. They are light producers. This book is considered a nonluminous light source since it is a reflector of light. The moon, this book, and most of the objects around you could not be seen in a totally darkened room. They can be seen only when light from a luminous source reflects from their surface. Whether an object is luminous or nonluminous depends on the substance of which it is made and the conditions to which it is exposed. For example, a piece of paper is nonluminous. But if the paper is set on fire it becomes luminous. As it burns, the energy contained in its molecules is released as light energy. Light energy is commonly produced by the transformation of chemical, heat, or electrical energy.

The scientific name for an ordinary light bulb is an incandescent lamp. The light bulb produces light energy as a result of an electric current passing through a tungsten filament. Incandescent lamps are great energy wasters, since only 5 percent of their electrical energy is converted to light. The other 95 percent is released as heat energy.

A fluorescent light bulb is able to convert electrical energy to light energy more efficiently than an incandescent bulb. Twenty percent of the electrical energy that reaches it changes to light energy.

[2]The discussion of light energy beginning on this page is based on William A. Andrews et al., *Physical Science* (Scarborough, Ont.: Prentice-Hall of Canada, 1976), pp. 380–437.

Nuclear explosions are yet another source of light energy. The conversion of matter to energy in such an explosion results in large quantities of heat as well as light. The sunlight that reaches us each day is produced by the conversion of matter to energy in the sun. The process by which this conversion takes place, in the stars as well as in our sun, is nuclear fusion.

The Reflection and Refraction of Light

Light[3] reflected from a nonluminous object carries information about the shape, color, and texture of the object's surface. Objects that have smooth, shiny surfaces, such as mirrors, reflect light in a special way: they reflect light that forms images. By looking in a mirror you can see a reflection that is your own image. Light that strikes a mirror rebounds from the mirror at an angle that is equal to the angle at which the original light ray struck the mirror. Scientists measure these angles from a perpendicular drawn at the point where the light strikes the mirror's surface.

When light travels from one medium to another it may change in direction. This bending of light is known as refraction. A lens has the ability to bend, or refract, light. Lenses that are thicker in the middle than at their ends are known as convex lenses. Lenses that are thinner in the middle than at their ends are concave lenses.

Convex lenses are also known as converging lenses. They have the ability to bring parallel rays of light to a point in space. This point of convergence is called the focal point. Light that enters a converging lens is bent toward the thicker part of the lens. The focal length of a lens is the distance from the center of the lens to the focal point. A convex lens can be used to form an image on a screen. Such an image, which is called a real image, is formed when an object producing light rays (or reflecting them) is on one side of the lens at a distance greater than the focal length. The real image will appear on a screen held on the other side of the lens.

Figure 15A–5 shows a real image being formed by means of a convex lens. Notice that the image is inverted. This inversion can be illustrated by a diagram showing the path taken by rays entering the lens from the ends of the object.

A convex lens can also produce an image that can be seen but not placed on a screen—a virtual image. Such an image is erect, and larger than the object. If you have ever used a magnifying glass (more properly called a hand lens), you have seen a virtual image. This type of image is formed when an object is placed nearer to the lens than the focal length. You see the image only when you look through the lens at the object.

[3]The discussion of right reflection and refraction that begins on this page is based on "Lenses and Intensity," in Milton O. Pella, *Physical Science for Progress* (Englewood Cliffs, N.J.: Prentice-Hall, 1970), pp. 325–333.

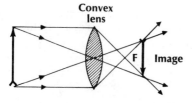

Convex lens

F   Image

Figure 15A–5. Note the inverted real image being formed by this convex lens. (*Source:* Milton O. Pella, *Physical Science for Progress*, 3rd ed. Englewood Cliffs, N.J.: Prentice-Hall, 1970. Used by permission.)

Parallel rays of light that enter a concave lens are bent toward the thicker part of the lens. As a result, concave lenses are diverging lenses: they spread out light. Concave lenses form *only* virtual images, the sizes of which are smaller than the corresponding objects.

Light, Prisms, and Color

Have you ever been surprised to see an array of colors projected on a wall or ceiling as a result of sunlight passing through a crystal glass? This band of colors is called a spectrum. Some pieces of glass are specially made to enable scientists to separate sunlight or artificial white light into a spectrum. A triangle-shaped piece of such glass is called a prism. Figure 15A−6 shows how a prism can be used to create a spectrum. The colors that are formed each represent a component of white light. The lens is used to ensure that the rays entering the prism are parallel. (*Note*: For elementary-school classroom use the lens is not crucial.)

HEAT ENERGY

A double dip of rich chocolate ice cream on a crisp sugar cone can quickly cool you off (and fatten you up) on a hot summer afternoon. It tastes good and, at least psychologically, makes us feel cooler. If for some strange reason you decided to look at the ice-cream cone instead of eating it, you would start to see the effect of heat energy on the ice cream.

The phenomenon of melting can be a good starting point for understanding heat energy and how it effects change. Heat flows from the hot surrounding air to the colder ice cream, causing an increase in the temperature of the ice cream, a lowering of the temperature of the surrounding air, and the immediate need for a napkin. The temperature of a substance is a measurement of its tendency to transfer heat to, or absorb heat from, another substance. A thermometer measures the average energy of motion of the molecules of a substance. Temperature is measured in degrees. There are two temperature scales in wide use by people around the world: the Celsius, or centigrade, scale and the Fahrenheit scale.

The Celsius thermometer shows the temperature at which water freezes as 0° and the boiling temperature as 100°. The Fahrenheit scale shows the temperature

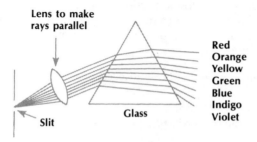

Figure 15A−6. White light is made up of light of many colors. (*Source:* Milton O. Pella, *Physical Science for Progress*, 3rd ed. Englewood Cliffs, N.J.: Prentice-Hall, 1970. Used by permission.)

at which water freezes as 32° and the boiling temperature as 212°.

Since it is virtually impossible to add up the individual energies of motion contained by the millions of molecules found in even a very small amount of matter, heat must be measured indirectly. We do this by measuring its effect on matter. The standard unit of heat is the calorie, the heat required to raise the temperature of one gram of water one Celsius degree. Since this is a very small amount of heat, the kilocalorie—one thousand calories—is a more practical unit. The energy contained in foods is expressed in kilocalories.

In the English system of measurement the British thermal unit, or BTU, is the standard unit of heat. It is the amount of heat required to raise the temperature of one pound of water one degree Fahrenheit.

MACHINES

One very important use of energy is that it gives us the ability to use machines to do work. To understand how simple machines operate, you first need to understand what a force is. In its simplest terms a force is a push or a pull. Machines enable us to increase a force, increase the speed of an object, change the direction in which a force is acting, or change the place where a force is acting. Machines work by changing one form of energy to another.

Simple Machines

You may not realize it, but the seesaw in a schoolyard is a simple machine. It is a type of lever. Wheelbarrows and fishing poles are also levers. Levers are not the only simple machines. Others are the wheel and axle, the pulley, the inclined plane, the screw, and the wedge. They are shown in the drawing that opens this chapter. All other machines (which are known as compound machines) combine at least two simple machines.

Regardless of the type of machine we study, we are always concerned with two forces—the effort and the resistance. The effort is the force we apply. The resistance is the force we overcome. We are also concerned with the amount of resistance that can be overcome by the application of a given effort. In scientific terms this quantity is known as the mechanical advantage. There are various ways of calculating the mechanical advantage of a machine. In many cases we can simply divide the resistance by the effort.

When we use a simple machine we put energy into it. Not all of this energy goes into moving the resistance: some is lost to friction. The efficiency of a machine is a comparison of the work done by the machine (or the energy put out by the machine) with the work (or energy) put into it. Here is a summary of the basic characteristics of simple machines.

1. There are six simple machines: the lever, wheel and axle, pulley, inclined plane, screw, and wedge.
2. Simple machines are mechanical devices.
3. In each simple machine an applied force (*effort*) moves a load (*resistance*).

4. Most simple machines have a *mechanical advantage*. The mechanical advantage of a simple machine is a mathematical relationship between the effort and the resistance. Mechanical advantage is written MA (See also items 7 and 8 in this list.)

5. Because of its mechanical advantage, a simple machine *magnifies* the effort exerted on it so that the effort *seems* larger. The effect of a simple machine's mechanical advantage is that a small effort can move a large resistance.

6. Simple machines are able to move the resistance through a distance called the *resistance distance*. They do this by exerting an effort through a distance called the *effort distance*.

7. Each simple machine has a mathematical formula by which (*disregarding friction*) its mechanical advantage can be figured.

8. The general formula for figuring the mechanical advantage of a simple machine is stated in either of two ways:

   actual mechanical advantages (AMA) = resistance (R) divided by effort (E)

   ideal mechanical advantages (IMA) = effort distance (ED) divided by resistance distance (RD)

   The second formula will reveal the mechanical advantage that would exist if no friction was present).[4]

Crowbars, shovels, hammers, fishing poles, and oars are all levers. All levers, regardless of their shape, have three parts: a fulcrum, an effort arm, and a resistance arm. There are three types, or classes, of levers. In Figure 15A−7 note the location of the effort, resistance, and fulcrum in each type.

A wheel is a lever that can be moved in a complete circle around its fulcrum. The fulcrum of a wheel is called the axle, and it is at the center of the wheel. The wheel and axle form a simple machine. Examples of wheel and axle are the windlass, water wheel, doorknob, pencil sharpener, screwdriver, windmill, and potter's wheel.

When an effort force is applied to the larger wheel, a larger force is produced at the axle. However, the large resistance that is lifted is moved very slowly. When effort is applied to the axle, speed and distance are gained. To find the ideal mechanical advantage of a wheel and axle, divide the radius of the wheel by the radius of the axle.

A pulley is a grooved wheel that turns loosely on an axle. The grooved wheel and axle do not turn together. The grooved wheel is called a sheave. The frame in which it rotates is called the block. Pulleys may be either fixed or movable. Figure 15A−8 (p. 357) shows examples of each. A fixed pulley does not travel with the resistance; a movable pulley does. A block and tackle is a combination of a fixed pulley and a movable pulley. The mechanical advantage of a pulley can be calculated by dividing the effort distance by the resistance distance, or by dividing the resistance by the effort. The ideal mechanical advantage of a pulley system can be determined simply by counting the number of supporting ropes.

An inclined plane is a flat surface that is raised at one end. Ramps, slopes, and stairs are inclined planes. A resistance can be *moved up* an inclined plane to a desired height *with less effort* than it can be lifted directly to the same height. The

[4]Excerpted with minor modifications from June Lewis and Irene Potter, *The Teaching of Science in the Elementary School* (Englewood Cliffs, N.J.: Prentice-Hall, 1970), pp. 246−251.

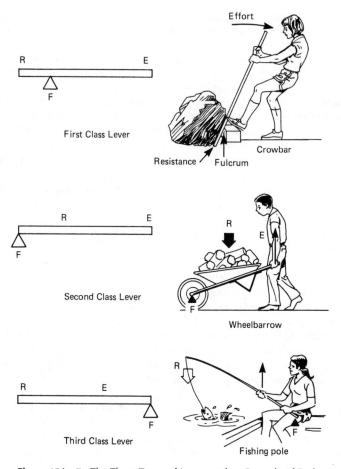

Figure 15A−7. The Three Types of Levers and an Example of Each

ideal mechanical advantage of an inclined plane can be found by dividing the length of the inclined plane (the effort distance) by its height (the resistance distance).

A screw is a twisted or rolled-up inclined plane. Some common screws are a wood screw, a bolt, a screw jack, a brace and bit, and an auger. Screws are used to lift objects, to hold objects together, and to carry things from place to place. The rotary motion of a turning screw is changed into a straight-line motion by a lever, which is needed to turn the screw. The ideal mechanical advantage of a screw is the distance the effort moves divided by the distance the resistance moves (the distance between the threads of the screw, or its pitch).

A wedge is a double inclined plane. Some common wedges are knives, needles, axes, can openers, and cold chisels. Wedges are used to pierce, split, cut, and push apart things. Effort is needed to move the wedge into the resisting object. The ideal mechanical advantage of a wedge can be calculated by dividing its length by the thickness of its widest end.

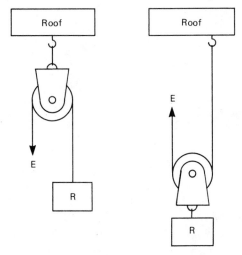

Roof

E

R

Fixed Pulley

Roof

E

R

Movable Pulley

Figure 15A–8. A Fixed and a Movable Pulley

SUMMARY OUTLINE

    I. Energy can be changed from one form to another.

  II. Electricity is a form of energy that results from the storage or movement of electrons.

     A. Static electricity is produced by an imbalance between the positive and negative charges on the surface of an object.

     B. Current electricity is produced when charges flow through a conductor.

 III. Current electricity can be used in various ways.

     A. A source of current, a conductor, and a load (a device that converts electricity to some other form of energy) can be combined to form an electrical circuit.

     B. A magnetic field is produced around a current.

       1. Motors convert electrical energy to kinetic energy.

       2. Generators produce electricity by moving a conductor across a magnetic field, or vice versa.

  IV. A sound wave is produced in a medium by the vibration of an object.

   V. Light energy reaches our eyes from luminous and nonluminous sources.

  VI. The heat energy contained by a substance is the total kinetic energy possessed by the atoms or molecules of the substance.

 VII. Machines are devices that enable us to increase a force, increase the speed of an object, change the direction of a force, or change the location of a force.

chapter **15B**

Energies and Machines

DISCOVERY ACTIVITIES
AND DEMONSTRATIONS

DISCOVERY ACTIVITIES

Using a Thermometer[1]*

OBJECTIVES

Using a color-coded thermometer, the children will be able to tell the difference between the temperature in one place and the temperature in another place.

Using a color-coded thermometer, the children will be able to tell the difference between the temperature at one time and the temperature at another time.

SCIENCE PROCESS EMPHASIZED

Observing

[1]The activity beginning on this page is based on ideas in "Temperatures," Module 5 in *Science: A Process Approach II* (Lexington, Mass.: Ginn, 1975).
*Asterisks refer to activities for young children.

dry cell

lampholder

Figure 15B–1. Experimenting with a Simple Circuit (*Source:* SAPA II, Module 70, p. 4. Science . . . A Process Approach II, American Association for the Advancement of Science. Used with permission.)

MATERIALS FOR EACH CHILD OR GROUP

1 Celsius thermometer, minus 20° to 110°, that has been color-coded by wide-tip marking pens or with strips of colored construction paper as shown in Figure 15B−2.

MOTIVATION

Prior to the activity provide two areas in the room where the air temperature will be significantly different. You might be able to accomplish this by locating the vent that carries warm or cool air into the room, or by bringing to the room a small toaster oven that can be turned on during the activity.

Point out the two areas to the children and ask them to indicate which is probably warmer. Tell them that in this activity they will be measuring how hot or how cold places are.

DIRECTIONS

1. Have the children take turns holding their hands a safe distance from the source of warmth and then holding them where the air is colder.
2. Now distribute the color-coded thermometers. Show the children that their thermometers contain a red liquid in the glass tube. Indicate that the height of the red liquid tells how warm or how cold a place is. Have the children take the thermometer to various places in the room to see if the height of the red liquid changes. They should keep track of what color band the liquid reached.
3. Have a class discussion of the measurements the children made. This activity is for young children, so the focus should be on which color the red liquid reached.
4. On another day have the children repeat their reading of the thermometer at the same locations to see if there are changes.

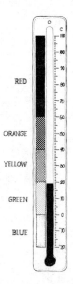

Figure 15B−2. (*Source:* SAPA II, Module 5, p. 4. Science . . . A Process Approach II, American Association for the Advancement of Science. Used with permission.)

KEY DISCUSSION QUESTIONS

1. What do we call this (hold up the thermometer)? *Thermometer.*
2. What does it measure? *How warm or cold things are.*
3. If the red liquid reached "yellow" when it was in (state a location) and "green" in (state another location), which place was warmer? *The first place.*

SCIENCE CONTENT FOR THE TEACHER

The red liquid in household thermometers is alcohol that has been dyed. The silvery liquid found in some thermometers is mercury. The volume of these liquids expands and contracts depending on the energy of motion of the molecules of the medium in which the liquids are placed.

Celsius thermometers are marked in degrees centigrade. Fahrenheit thermometers are marked in degrees Fahrenheit. The freezing point of water is 0°C or 32°F. The boiling point of water is 100°C or 212°F.

EXTENSIONS

Science. This activity is designed for young children and does not require them to measure the actual temperature. For some children it might be quite appropriate to follow this activity with a brief lesson on how to read degrees of temperature and then have them repeat the activity without the color coding.

Science/Social Studies. Display a world map or globe and attach to it colored stickers (use the same color code as in the activity) that represent temperature readings for major cities, as reported in a newspaper. Have a group of children pronounce the names of the cities that you have identified with stickers. The children can start thinking and talking about the locations of parts of the world that are cold and parts that are warm.

Simple Circuits

OBJECTIVES

The children will assemble a simple series circuit.
The children will assemble a simple parallel circuit.
The children will describe the similarities and differences between a series circuit and a parallel circuit.

SCIENCE PROCESSES EMPHASIZED

Observing
Experimenting
Communicating

3 bulbs
3 bulb sockets
2 dry cells, size D
Switch
8 pieces of insulated bell wire, each 2.5 centimeters (about 1 inch) long and stripped at
its ends

MOTIVATION

This activity should follow a class discussion about the nature of simple circuits and
the functions of various circuit components. Display the materials and make a
schematic drawing on the chalkboard of a three-lamp series circuit and a three-
lamp parallel circuit, like the ones shown in Figure 15B–3. Have a general
discussion of how the circuit diagrams are alike and different. Keep the discussion
open-ended and at an appropriate time begin the activity.

DIRECTIONS

1. You may wish to have half of the work groups construct a series circuit and the other
   half construct a parallel circuit. If you happen to have double the amount of equipment listed above, you can have each group construct both circuits.
2. Have the children light the bulbs to demonstrate how their circuits operate. Suggest
   that they make observations of what occurs when one bulb is removed from each type
   of circuit.
3. Allow the children time to make observations and then have a class discussion about
   how the circuits are the same and how they are different.

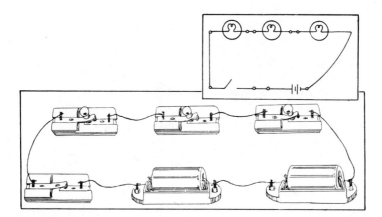

Figure 15B–3. A Series Circuit (*Source:* SAPA II, Module 64, p. 7. Science . . .A
Process Approach II, American Association for the Advancement of Science.
Used with permission.)

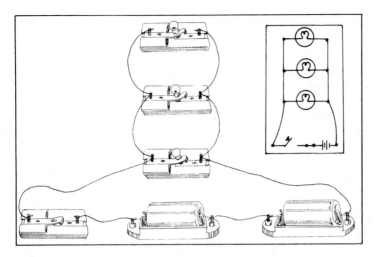

Figure 15B–4. A Parallel Circuit (*Source*: SAPA II, Module 64, p. 7. Science . . . A Process Approach II, American Association for the Advancement of Science. Used with permission.)

KEY DISCUSSION QUESTIONS

1. What do the symbols in the circuit diagram stand for? (*See Figure 15B–3.*)
2. How is the path of the electrons different in the two circuits? *In the series circuit all the electrons go through all the bulbs. In the parallel circuit they split up: some go to each bulb.*
3. What happened when you took one lamp out of each type of circuit? Why? *In the series circuit the other bulbs went out. In the parallel circuit the other bulbs got a little brighter. The series-circuit bulbs went out because there was a gap (a break) in the circuit, so the current stopped. In the parallel circuit the electrons stopped going in one path and joined the electrons going through the other paths. The bulbs got brighter because they had extra current going through them.*

SCIENCE CONTENT FOR THE TEACHER

Circuits can be represented by diagrams and symbols like those shown in Figure 15B–3. In a series circuit all the electrons go through all the bulbs (or other resistances) in it. A gap, or break, at any place in the circuit will stop the flow of current through the entire circuit. A defective bulb, a loose connection, or a break in the wire will all stop the flow of current. If the voltage is large enough, electrons may jump across gaps in the circuit, a phenomenon evidenced as a spark.

In parallel circuits the current divides. Some of it flows through each resistance. If a resistance is removed from such a circuit, the current that would normally have flowed through it is distributed to the remaining resistances.

EXTENSIONS

Science. If you have access to a small electric motor, you may wish to have a group substitute it for various lamps in the circuits to determine the effect of a running motor on the brightness of the bulbs.

You may wish to have one or two groups combine their resources and make elaborate circuits. In particular, challenge these children to make a circuit that is partly parallel and partly series.

Science/Social Studies. You may wish to have a group of children observe one of the bulbs more closely to see if they can follow the path that the electrons take. This could be the beginning of some library research on the scientists who invented the incandescent bulb—Thomas Edison. Have the children focus their attention on how life in this century was affected by Edison's many inventions.

Language Arts. Some of the children might be encouraged to write about what a typical day in their life would be like if Edison had not invented the light bulb, the "talking machine" and other devices.

Electrical Conductors and Nonconductors

OBJECTIVES

The children will distinguish between materials that conduct electricity and materials that do not.
The children will make hypotheses about characteristics of conductors.

SCIENCE PROCESSES EMPHASIZED

Experimenting
Making a hypothesis

MATERIALS

For each child or group

Dry cell, size D
Dry-cell holder
Flashlight bulb
Flashlight-bulb holder
3 pieces of insulated bell wire, each about 25 centimeters (10 inches) long

For the class

Roll of aluminum foil
Assortment of 2.5-centimeters (1-inch) lengths of base wire of various thicknesses
Box of paper clips
Sharpened pencils
Box of toothpicks
Box of crayons
Box of steel nails

MOTIVATION

This activity should follow activities or class discussions about the characteristics of simple circuits. Ask the children to describe the function of the wire used in circuits. They will indicate that the wire serves as the path for electrons. Now display the materials and indicate that the children will be finding out whether the electrons can pass through them.

DIRECTIONS

1. Have each child assemble a simple circuit, like the one shown on the chapter-opening drawing. The exposed ends of two of the wires (one from the dry cell and one from the bulb holder) will serve as probes to be touched to the materials to be tested.
2. Ask the children to first check that this "tester" works by briefly touching the exposed ends together. If the dry cell is fresh, the bulb is in working condition, and all the connections have been properly made, the bulb should light.
3. Have the children make observations of whether or not the various materials are good conductors of electricity. They should then manipulate each material to see if those that are conductors share similar characteristics.
4. When the children are done, have them make hypotheses that could be used to distinguish electrical conductors from nonconductors.

KEY DISCUSSION QUESTIONS

1. Which of the materials were good conductors of electricity? *Aluminum foil, paper clips, wire pieces.*
2. Which of the materials did not conduct electricity? *Toothpicks, crayons.*
3. Was there anything that conducted electricity but conducted it poorly? *The lead (graphite) in the pencil.*
4. What are some hypotheses that you made? *Metals conduct electricity. Materials that bend without breaking conduct electricity.*
5. What are some other activities you could do to test your hypotheses? *(Answers will vary.)*

SCIENCE CONTENT FOR THE TEACHER

Substances that allow the movement of charges with relatively little resistance are known as conductors. Materials that do not allow charges to pass through them are insulators. There are no perfect conductors, since all materials offer some resistance to the flow of charges. Metals are better conductors than nonmetals. Metals differ in conductivity. The following metals are arranged from highest to lowest conductivity:

Silver	Platinum
Copper	Tin
Aluminum	Steel
Tungsten	Lead

Science. Some children may wish to invent activities that will reveal whether good electrical conductors are also good conductors of heat.

Some children may wish to modify their tester circuit so that the entire apparatus can be packaged in a small cardboard box. The tester should have two probes extending from the side and the light bulb extending from the top.

Science/Social Studies. The children can relate this activity to social studies if you can locate maps of regions of the world that are sources of the various metals used in this activity. To identify these regions, the children can use an encyclopedia and look under headings such as "Copper" and "Aluminum."

The Ink-Lined Plane

OBJECTIVES

The children will construct a simple device that can be used to measure forces.
The children will use their force measurer to find how an inclined plane makes work easier

SCIENCE PROCESSES EMPHASIZED

Experimenting
Measuring

MATERIALS

For each child or group
Force measurer
Piece of cardboard 25 by 12 centimeters (about 10 by 5 inches)
3 paper clips
Rubber band
Inclined Plane
1-meter (40-inch) length of board
String
Small box of paper clips, crayons, or chalk
5 books

For the class
Wood wax and cloth for polishing the board

MOTIVATION

Start this activity with some humorous word play. Do not display any of the materials prior to the activity. Tell the children that today they are going to work with an "ink-lined plane." Don't write the words on the blackboard. When you say the phrase space the words as shown. Tease the chldren a bit by telling them that one year you had a child who thought you said "ink-lined plane" (say it exactly as you said it before). The children should be a little puzzled. Now show what the imaginary child made by making a paper airplane and drawing some lines across it. Tell the children that the child was really confused until you wrote the phrase on the chalkboard. Ask them to guess what you wrote on the board.

When they have done this, bring out the materials. Write "inclined plane" on the chalkboard and discuss the characteristics of an inclined plane. Tell the children that in this activity they will first make a device that measures forces and then use it to see how an inclined plane makes work easier.

DIRECTIONS

1. Have each child or group of children make a force measurer like the one shown in Figure 15B–5. By hanging small objects from the paper clip at the bottom rubber band, the children can measure the relative amount of force acting on the object. (The scale divisions in Figure 15B–5 are arbitrary.)

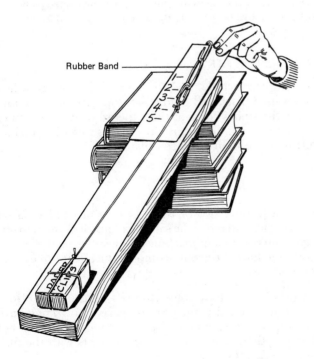

Figure 15B–5. How to Use a Force Measurer

2. Now have the children assemble the inclined plane by elevating one end of the board and placing three books under it. The children should wax the board until its surface is smooth.

3. Have the children determine how much force is needed to lift the box of paper clips from the tabletop straight up to the high end of the board. They will need to tie a string around the box and attach the string to the paper clip hanging from the bottom of the rubber band on the force measurer.

4. The children should then compare this measurement with the force needed to move the paper-clip box to the same height by means of the inclined plane. They should pull the box up the length of the board, parallel to the surface of the board, after they have attached the force measurer to one end of the paper-clip box.

5. Have the children experiment with various loads and inclined-plane heights; then hold a class discussion of their results.

KEY DISCUSSION QUESTIONS

1. Which required less force, pulling the load straight up or moving it along the sloping board? *Moving it along the board.*
2. Why do you think people use inclined planes? *You can move heavy objects up without applying a lot of force.*
3. Show the children that the distance the load moves vertically is the load distance, or resistance distance, and that the distance along the sloping board is the effort distance. Now ask the children how the effort distance compares with the load distance. *The effort distance is longer.* (This question helps the children see that inclined planes require that the small effort force move over a long distance.)

SCIENCE CONTENT FOR THE TEACHER

The inclined plane is a simple machine used to move heavy objects to heights. Ramps used to load boxes on a truck and roads that slope upwards are inclined planes. An inclined plane multiplies force at the expense of distance, since the effort force must move further than the distance the load is raised. Steep inclined planes require more effort force than less steep planes.

EXTENSIONS

Science. You may wish to have two or three groups of children assemble inclined planes of various slopes and move the same load up all of them to observe the increased force needed on the steeper machines. If possible, secure a toy truck with wheels that roll easily and have the groups compare the effort forces required to move it up the various slopes.

Science/Math. You may wish to have some children measure the effort distance and load distance of an inclined plane and compare them. Then have the children make the inclined plane steeper and repeat their measurement of effort and load distance. They can then repeat their measurements with the inclined plane in more steep and less steep positions.

ADDITIONAL ACTIVITY IDEAS

Strange Shadows*

You can have children experiment with some of the relationships between the position of a light source and the shadows[2] cast by an object by engaging them in some shadow making. You will need to borrow the school's supply of slide projectors so that each learning group will have a strong light source. They will also need a large sheet of white poster board or other material that can serve as a screen. Make copies of hand positions for various shadows and distribute them to the children for reference. As the children make various shapes have them explore such questions as, Where is the darkest part of the shadow? How does moving your hand closer to or further from the light source affect the size of the shadow? How does the screen affect the shadows?

Building an Electromagnet

Children can observe the relationship between magnetism and electricity by constructing a simple electromagnet. Each learning group will need a 1.5-volt dry cell, 25 centimeters (about 10 inches) of insulated copper wire, and a large nail or bolt. You may wish to prepare the lengths of wire in advance, since each will have to be stripped of its insulation at the ends. Have the children wind the wire around the nail and then connect one end of the wire to the dry cell. Have them check the magnetic properties of the electromagnet at this point by trying to pick up various materials with it, such as a piece of chalk and a paper clip. Now have them connect the other end of the wire to the dry cell to see if they have created an electromagnet. They should try to pick up the same materials as before. The children can find out if the number of turns of wire around the nail affects the strength of the magnet they made.

The No-Frills Telephone*

Children can easily construct a working telephone out of a paper cup and string. Each child or learning group will need two paper cups, access to a spool of very strong sewing thread or thin string, a sharpened pencil, and two toothpicks. The pencil is used to poke a very small hole through the bottoms of the cups. The thread is pushed through this hole and looped around the center of a toothpick placed horizontally in the bottom of the cup. This is done for each cup. When the thread is stretched tightly the toothpick anchors it inside the cup. Working in pairs, the children can stretch out the thread until it is taut and then communicate with each other. When one child is speaking into a cup the second child will be able to hear the voice by holding the other cup to his or her ear. The children can experiment with various lengths of thread and may even be able to invent a string-telephone party line.

---

[2]The activity on shadows that is discussed on this page is based on "Dark Shadows," an activity in Joe Abruscato and Jack Hassard, *The Whole Cosmos Catalog* (Santa Monica, Calif.: Goodyear, 1977), p. 77.

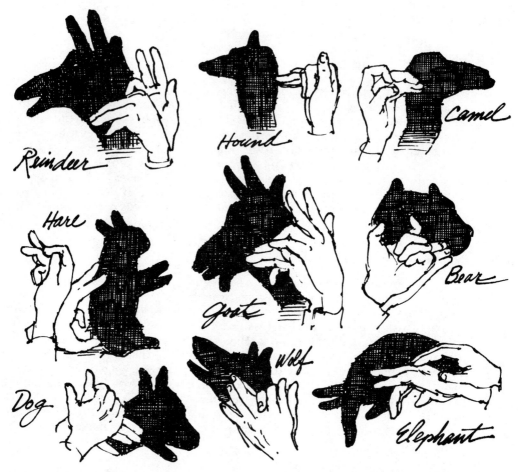

Figure 15B–6. Hand Positions for Various Animal Shapes (*Source:* J. Abruscato and J. Hassard, *The Whole Cosmos Catalog.* Santa Monica, Calif.: Goodyear Publishing Company, Inc. Used by permission of Goodyear Publishing Company.)

DEMONSTRATIONS

You Could Hear a Pin Drop: The Conduction of Heat[3]

OBJECTIVES

The children will observe the relative heat-conduction ability of various materials.

The children will make a hypothesis concerning the nature of objects that conduct heat.

The children will predict which of three objects will conduct heat the fastest.

[3]This demonstration is an adaptation of a portion of "Conduction and Non-Conduction," Module 70 in *Science: A Process Approach II* (Lexington, Mass.: Ginn, 1975).

SCIENCE PROCESSES EMPHASIZED

Observing
Making a hypothesis
Predicting

MATERIALS FOR THE TEACHER

Candle
Safety matches
Container of water to extinguish matches
5 steel pins
Glass, steel, and brass (or aluminum) rods of equal thickness
Chalk stick
Old metal fork
Long, narrow chip of pottery
Support stamp and burette clamp (see Figure 15B–7)
Watch with second hand

Note: This demonstration will require the lighting of a candle by *you* and manipulation of the candle flame by *you*. Appropriate safety measures should be observed.

MOTIVATION

This demonstration should follow a class discussion about energy and heat as a form of energy. Display all the materials and indicate that you will be doing a

Figure 15B–7. (*Source:* SAPA II, Module 70, p. 7. Science . . . A Process Approach II, American Association for the Advancement of Science. Used with permission.)

demonstration that will help the children learn some things about how well various materials conduct heat. Select a responsible child to be your assistant. Explain how you are going to perform this demonstration, emphasizing the following procedures: You are going to attach a pin near one end of each rod with a dab of wax. By heating the end of each rod and measuring the time for the wax to melt and the pin to fall, the class will be able to note which materials were the best conductors of heat.

DIRECTIONS

1. You will first need to fasten a steel pin to a dab of wax placed 4 centimeters (about 1.5 inches) from the end of each of the three rods. Do this by lighting the candle, allowing it to burn for two minutes, and then rolling the rod in the pool of wax beneath the candle flame so that wax accumulates 4 centimeters from the end of the rod. Briefly heat the head of a pin in the flame and press it into the wax.
2. Repeat this procedure for the test objects (the fork, the piece of pottery, and the chalk).
3. Place a rod in the burette clamp as shown in Figure 15B–7 and lower the clamp so that the end of the rod is about 1 centimeter from the tip of the flame.
4. Have your assistant time how long it takes for the pin to drop.
5. Repeat steps 3 and 4 for the other two rods and have the class make observations. Then have them make a hypothesis about the type of material that conducts heat the best.
6. Display the test objects and have the children predict which will be the best heat conductor. Repeat steps 3 and 4 with each object.

KEY DISCUSSION QUESTIONS

1. What are some objects that are good conductors of heat? *Pots and pans.*
2. Which rod was the poorest conductor? *Glass.*
3. What is a hypothesis you could make about heat conductors? *Metals are good conductors of heat.*
4. What test object did you predict to be the best conductor of heat? *The metal fork.*

SCIENCE CONTENT FOR THE TEACHER

The carrying of heat by a solid is called conduction. Heat energy is transferred through a conductor as a result of the increased movement of molecules at the point on the object where heat is applied. The increased motion of these molecules causes adjacent molecules to increase their energy.

In this activity the glass rod will be the poorest conductor. The best heat conductor among the metal rods will be the aluminum one, followed by the brass and then the steel.

EXTENSIONS

Science. You may wish to have some children do some research to find out how the transfer of heat in air takes place. They should focus their investigation on the term *convection.*

You may wish to have some children bring in samples of kitchen utensils that have both a good conductor and a bad insulator (for example, a stirring spoon with a metal end and a wooden handle).

Science/Math. You can extend this demonstration by fastening pins at regular intervals along each rod. Then the children can time how long it takes the heat to travel down the rods to release each pin. This data can then be graphed, with "time for the pin to drop" on the vertical axis and "distance from the place" on the horizontal axis.

Making Work Easier: Using Fixed and Movable Pulleys

OBJECTIVES

The children will predict how a fixed pulley and a movable pulley can be used to make work easier.

The children will observe the effect of using various pulley arrangements to move loads.

The children will compare the required effort force and the direction of the effort force used in lifting loads with various pulley arrangements.

SCIENCE PROCESSES EMPHASIZED

Observing
Measuring
Predicting

MATERIALS

Spring scale
String
Rock that has about 100 grams of mass
Single fixed pulley
Single movable pulley
2 screw hooks
Horizontal wooden supports

Note: Prior to the demonstration you should insert the screw hooks into the wooden support.

MOTIVATION

Display the pulleys and ask the children if they have ever seen one being used. Discuss various uses of pulleys and then display the rock. Tell the children that pulleys make work easier and that they will observe this during the demonstration. Have a volunteer come forward to assist you.

DIRECTIONS

1. First have your assistant weigh the rock by tying a piece of string around it and attaching it to the spring scale. Write the weight on the board. Be sure that the children understand that the rock is the load to be moved with the pulleys. Place the fixed pulley on the horizontal board.
2. Now have the children predict what the effect of using a fixed pulley will be. Have your volunteer carry out the demonstration and have the children compare their predictions with the actual result.
3. Using a movable pulley, repeat step 2.
4. Using a fixed pulley and a movable pulley, perform step 2 again.
5. Have the children compare the distance moved by the effort in step 4 with the distance moved by the load.

KEY DISCUSSION QUESTIONS

1. How does using a fixed pulley make work easier? *You can apply the effort force in a different location.*
2. How does using a movable pulley make work easier? *You use less force to move the load.*
3. About how much less effort do you need to raise a load with a movable pulley? Why? *You need about half as much. The load is held up by the hook and by the person holding the other end of the string.*
4. How does using a movable pulley and a fixed pulley make work easier? *You use less force than the load's weight. The fixed pulley lets you change the direction of the effort force.*

SCIENCE CONTENT FOR THE TEACHER

Pulleys are simple machines that enable us to multiply the effect of an effort force or change the direction in which the effort force is applied. A fixed pulley performs the latter function. For example, a fixed pulley at the top of a flagpole makes it possible to move a flag upward by pulling downward on the rope attached to the flag. A movable pulley attached to a load can ideally halve the effort needed to move the load. Friction, of course, diminishes the pulley's efficiency. When a movable pulley is used to lift a load, the effort force must move further than the distance the load is lifted.

EXTENSIONS

Science. If you can acquire additional pulleys, you can assemble more elaborate machines. A movable-and-fixed pulley arrangement (block and tackle) can be used to show how loads can be moved by quite small effort forces.

Science/Math. You can have children gain an understanding of the amount of energy lost to the overcoming of friction by comparing the actual mechanical advantage of the pulley (found by dividing the load by the effort) with the ideal mechanical advantage (found by dividing the load by the number of supporting strands).

ADDITIONAL DEMONSTRATION IDEAS

The Wooden Xylophone*

A good way to help young children understand the relationship between vibrations and sounds is to construct a wooden xylophone that can produce notes. The best approach is to acquire the materials described below and construct the xylophone on your own. This way you will be able to make the appropriate tuning adjustments. Then disassemble it and store it for use during a unit on sound. You will need a saw, 2 meters of heavy twine, and doweling to use as a striker. The crosspieces of the xylophone are cut from a 4-meter length of wood that is 2 centimeters by 4.3 centimeters (commonly sold as 1 inch by 2 inch). This wood should be a softwood without knots. Make the crosspieces by cutting the wood into these lengths: 50.8, 48.3, 45.0, 44.2, 41.7, 39.1, 36.6, and 34.1 centimeters. Arrange the crosspieces from the longest to the shortest. The points of attachment should be located one fourth and three fourths of the distance across the wooden pieces.

The No-Frills Guitar*

This demonstration will enable you to show children some of the variables that affect the pitch and loudness of a vibrating string. You will need a package of rubber bands of various thicknesses, a board about 50 centimeters (about 20 inches) long, some nails, and a hammer. To demonstrate that pitch increases as the tension on a string increases, you can mount the same size of rubber band over pairs of nails placed various distances apart on the board and then pluck each one. To demonstrate the cause of loud sounds, show the children that the loudness of the sound from a vibrating string depends on how far the string is displaced before it is released.

If you wish to make this demonstration a bit fancier, you can use actual guitar strings, stretching them across the board by connecting them to screw eyes anchored in the wood. Then, by turning the screw eyes you can increase and decrease the tension on the strings and vary the pitch of the sounds produced. By bringing in an actual guitar, you (or a child) can demonstrate how the variation in pitch and loudness in music is produced.

Tuning Forks Feed Food for Thought

Tuning forks are excellent devices for demonstrating some of the basic principles of sound production and transmission. You will need a set of tuning forks and a rubber striker. First show the children that the fork is composed of two tines that have the ability to vibrate back and forth. Demonstrate this ability by striking one of the forks very gently with the striker and having a child touch the tines. The child will feel their vibrational movement. Now strike the various forks more harshly so that sounds are produced. Indicate that the vibration of a tuning fork causes particles of the air to receive energy. Show the children how they can amplify the sound produced by a tuning fork by striking it and then quickly pressing its base against a door or tabletop. The children will notice a significant increase in loudness, the result of the tuning fork causing the larger surface to vibrate and thereby a larger volume of air to receive energy.

chapter 16

The Natural Resource Crisis: Saving the Water, the Soil, and the Air We Breathe

DISCOVERY ACTIVITIES
AND DEMONSTRATIONS

DISCOVERY ACTIVITIES

Trash Masher: Can Nature Recycle All Our Garbage?*

OBJECTIVES

The children will observe the way in which nature is able to recycle some forms of litter.

The children will observe that nature is unable to recycle some materials.

Note: this is a long-term activity with observations carried out over a period of two or three months.

   *Asterisks refer to activities for young children.

Figure 16—1. Making and Using Air-Dirt Collectors (*Source:* J. Abruscato and J. Hassard, *The Whole Cosmos Catalog.* Santa Monica, Calif.: Goodyear Publishing Company, Inc. Used by permission of Goodyear Publishing Company.)

Observing
Hypothesizing
Classifying

MATERIALS

For each child or group

4 clear plastic tumblers or baby-food jars
Sufficient garden soil to fill each container
Access to a supply of the following materials:

Paper towels
Aluminum foil
Clear plastic food wrap
Plastic garbage bags (one is sufficient for the entire class)
Sheet of cardboard
Small collection of leaves and grass cuttings
Small cuttings from apples, carrots, and orange rinds
Plastic straws (six to ten for the entire class)

Source of water
Masking tape and marking pens

For the teacher

Collection of schoolyard litter (such as candy wrappers and bottles) in a paper bag

MOTIVATION

Display your collection of schoolyard litter so that everyone can see it. Ask the children what would have happened to each piece of litter if it had remained where you found it. Some children may suggest that someone else, such as a custodian or a member of a cleaning crew, might have picked it up and disposed of it. Ask the children what would happen to it after it was picked up for disposal. Children may be aware of land fills, incinerators, town or city dumps, and other ultimate destinations for garbage. At this point suggest that nature has its own way of breaking apart certain materials. Introduce the *idea* of biodegradable materials if you work with young children and/or the *term* biodegradable if you work with older children. Tell the children that in this activity they will have a chance to see how nature is able to break down some materials and not others.

DIRECTIONS

1. Distribute the tumblers or baby-food jars of soil to each group. Tell the children that they will be placing various materials in the soil to observe how nature acts on them.

2. Have the children use the masking tape and marking pen to label the containers 1, 2, 3, and 4. They should also place their name or some other identifying mark on the containers.

3. Tell the children that you would like them to place a very small quantity of each material you have provided below the surface of the soil in each container. Have them place as many of the materials as possible near the inside wall of the container. Children will be able to observe changes by directly viewing the materials through the side of the container.

4. The soil in each container should be kept moist for the duration of the activity, and each group's four containers should be placed in a warm area of the room.

5. Have the children begin making observations of their material by selecting container 1 for study at the end of one week. They should first observe as many of the materials through the container's side as possible. Then they should carefully remove the materials to observe and record changes.

6. Have the children observe container 2 after two weeks have gone by.

7. Repeat this process until the materials in all four containers have been observed.

KEY DISCUSSION QUESTIONS

1. Why do you think we kept the soil moist and warm? *It helps the tiny animals and plants in the soil to grow and "work on" the things we put in the container.*

2. Which things did you observe nature affecting and recycling? *Paper, cardboard, leaves, grass cuttings, vegetable pieces.*

3. Some people might say that we could simply get rid of those things that nature can't recycle by burning them. Do you think that would be a good idea? *No, those things would then pollute the air because they would be changed to gases.*

SCIENCE CONTENT FOR THE TEACHER

The accumulation of garbage is a serious ecologic problem. Each day human activity results in the production of large amounts of disposable material. Some of this material such as plant and animal parts and products, paper, and cardboard, can be broken down by nature. Such materials are called biodegradable. At the present time much of our garbage contains synthetic products that are not biodegradable. The incineration of these materials results in air pollution. Currently, very little can be done with these materials except to dump them in a sanitary land fill. It is hoped that scientific investigation will result in the development of more packaging products that are biodegradable.

EXTENSIONS

Science/Art. Some children may be encouraged to use coloring pencils to produce drawings that show the changes or lack thereof of various materials buried in the soil in this activity.

Science/Social Studies. You may wish to have some children investigate various community attempts to reduce the amount of nonbiodegradable materials that enter the environment. In particular they should contact local civic officials to find out if there are aluminum-can and bottle-recycling programs in the community.

Making an Air-Dirt Collector[1]

OBJECTIVES

The children will make air-dirt collectors.
The children will make observations of the extent to which air contains particles of matter.

SCIENCE PROCESSES EMPHASIZED

Observing
Making hypotheses

MATERIALS

Roll of Dennison Clear Seal contact paper (or a roll of waxed paper or clear plastic film and a small jar of Vaseline)
Box of thumbtacks (enough for 8 to 12 tacks per group)
Sheets of heavy cardboard that can be cut into enough squares about 10 centimeters (about 4 inches) on edge for each group to have 2 or 3 of them.
Roll of transparent tape
Hand lens for each group
Scissors

MOTIVATION

Ask the children if they think there is much pollution in the air they breathe. Remind them that air pollution may consist of invisible or visible gases as well as particles of matter (such as soot). Ask the children to suggest ways in which they could discover if there were many particles of soot or dirt in the air. Display the materials and ask the children for ideas about how they could be used to do an air-pollution activity. After some discussion describe the process for making an air-dirt collector as outlined below.

DIRECTIONS

1. Have each group prepare three or four air-dirt collectors by attaching a square of clean contact paper, sticky side out, or a square of waxed paper to each cardboard square with thumbtacks. If the children make the collectors with waxed paper, they will have to smear the surface with a thin coating of Vaseline in order to make it sticky. They should use equal-sized squares of collecting paper so that the results will all be based on surfaces of equal size.
2. Have the children write their names on the back of their collectors.

[1]The activity that begins on this page was adapted from "Making and Using Air-Dirt Collectors," in Joe Abruscato and Jack Hassard, *The Whole Cosmos Catalog* (Santa Monica, Calif.: Goodyear, 1977), p. 13.

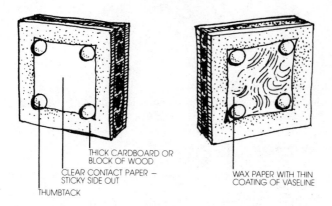

THICK CARDBOARD OR
BLOCK OF WOOD

CLEAR CONTACT PAPER —
STICKY SIDE OUT

THUMBTACK

WAX PAPER WITH THIN
COATING OF VASELINE

Figure 16—2. (*Source:* J. Abruscato and J. Hassard, *The Whole Cosmos Catalog.* Santa Monica, Calif.: Goodyear Publishing Company, Inc. Used by permission of Goodyear Publishing Company.)

3. The children should place their collectors at different locations within the school as well as outdoors. The outdoor collectors should be put near factories, near wooded areas such as parks or picnic areas, and in back of signs near streets. All collectors should be placed so that they are unseen by passersby. (This will increase the likelihood that they will remain undisturbed.) If possible, they should also be sheltered from precipitation.

4. After two or three days have the children gather their collectors and mark each to show where it came from.

5. The children should carefully remove the transparent sheets and count the number of particles on each square. The hand lens will make this easier. (In areas where the particle count is extremely high the children can simply make an estimate by counting the number on a small portion of the square and generalizing.)

6. When all groups have finished, call the class together for a discussion of their results.

KEY DISCUSSION QUESTIONS

1. Were you surprised by any of the results? If so, why? (*Answers will vary.*)

2. What do you think the tiny bits of matter that stuck to the collectors are? (*Answers will vary, but may include such things as dirt, soot from chimneys, and pollen.*)

3. What could be done to reduce the number of particles in the air? (*Answers will vary, but may include attaching particle collectors to chimneys and asking people to not burn leaves.*)

SCIENCE CONTENT FOR THE TEACHER

Many types of pollutants enter the air we breathe. Some emanate from natural sources—for example, soil particles picked up by the wind, gases, ash from volcanoes, and pollen. Human sources of air pollutants include the stirring up of surface soil in agriculture and construction and the burning of fuel oil, coal, and gasoline. Although much pollution is invisible to the naked eye, pollution caused by an abundance of air particles can be easily observed.

EXTENSIONS

Science. If you have access to a microscope you may wish to have some children make closer observations of the particles they have gathered. This will work best if they have used clear plastic film as the collector.

Science/Social Studies. You may wish to have some of the children draw a rough scale map of the school grounds or other outdoor areas where collectors were placed. This will give them some experience in geography. They should develop a legend for their map that identifies possible sources of the particles of pollution that reached the collectors.

Making a Litter Map

OBJECTIVES

The children will make a map displaying some areas near their school (such as parks and city streets) that have large amounts of litter.

The children will draw inferences about the sources of litter.

The children will make hypotheses about ways to control the littering of the environment.

SCIENCE PROCESSES EMPHASIZED

Observing
Classifying
Inferring
Making hypotheses

MATERIALS

Paper and pencil

MOTIVATION

Have a general discussion about types of environmental pollution. Ask the children whether they have polluted the environment. Some will probably indicate that littering is a type of pollution that many people do. Discuss the types of littering they have done or observed. Tell the children that this activity will help them see how big a pollution problem littering is.

DIRECTIONS

1. Provide each child or group with pencil and paper and have them draw maps of the area near their school that they will be studying.
2. Now take the children on a mini–field trip that will give them an opportunity to record

the locations of litter. They may wish to use various symbols to denote the types of litter they observe, such as paper wrappings, bottles, and cans.

3. When the children have completed their litter map have a class discussion focusing on the following questions.

KEY DISCUSSION QUESTIONS

1. Which areas had the most and the least litter? (*Answers will depend on local conditions.*)
2. What kinds of litter did you observe? (*Answers will include such things as food wrappers, glass or plastic containers, and metal cans.*)
3. What would be some things the schools (or community) could do to encourage people to stop littering? (*Answers will vary, but may include such things as providing more trash cans, fining people who litter, and passing laws that require a deposit on cans or bottles so that people will return them.*)

SCIENCE CONTENT FOR THE TEACHER

The surface pollution of land by litter is a common problem for communities. Much tax money is spent employing individuals and machines to pick up litter that people have simply thrown on the ground or the street. Litter is simply an eyesore. Moreover, health hazards may result from the attraction of insects to food wrappers and the sharp edges of cans and broken bottles. The control of littering rests on the ability of the school or community to encourage children and adults to refrain from doing it.

EXTENSIONS

Science/Math. You may wish to encourage some children to prepare a bar graph showing the number of pieces of litter of various types observed. For example, the graph might show that six bottles, three food wrappers, and two soda cans were observed.

Science/Art. Some children might be interested in using their artistic talents to create posters that encourage schoolmates to refrain from littering.

ADDITIONAL ACTIVITY IDEAS

"Drop Saving": Conserving Water in School*

You may wish to have a group of children carry out a survey to find out how much water is used each time a child drinks from a drinking fountain. This can easily be accomplished by having the children record the average time it takes for a child to get a drink of water—in other words, the amount of time in which the faucet is running. The children can then turn the fountain on and collect the water that is discharged in that time period. They can then make a pretty good estimate of the amount of water used during each trip to the drinking fountain in a school. The children can then find out how much of this water is usually drunk, by seeing how much water is in two or three mouthfuls. By comparing the amount of water drunk with the amount of water discharged by the fountain, the children will know how much water goes down the drain each time a child takes a drink. They can then estimate the number of children who get drinks of water during recess and calculate how much water is wasted. After this type of activity, the children in your class may wish to begin a poster campaign or some other school public-relations effort to conserve drinking water. Some children may wish to conduct a more detailed study of water use in schools, paying particular attention to the locations of dripping faucets, leaking pipes, and other water wasters.

Soil Survey

One activity you can do with children if you have access to land on or near your school grounds is to observe changes in the soil surface. Children can look for earthworm casts and piles of earth left on the soil surface by earthworms making their tunnels. The children can also look for signs of erosion of the soil surface. They may be able to find places where topsoil has been washed from higher ground to lower ground and where gulleys have formed, showing where soil-carrying water has moved down the slope and changed its surface. Some children may wish to dig a small hole to discover the depth of the topsoil in the area. If the area is rocky, children may be able to see the first stage of the soil-building process—lichens growing on rocks and breaking down their surface. The rock particles thereby released form the rough material that eventually becomes soil. These are a few of the ways in which children can observe that the soil surface is under constant change. They can document these changes by making a few drawings of the soil surface at various places near the school and revisiting these locations over a period of weeks and months.

How Can We Repair the Environment?

There are many activities that children can engage in on the school grounds that will give them an opportunity to make repairs to a deteriorating environment. Here are a few examples.

1. They can plant grass seed in lawn areas whose grass has worn away as a result of pedestrian traffic.
2. The children can plant some ground cover where soil seems to be eroding. See your local garden store for ideas on the appropriate ground cover for your area.
3. Even in urban settings children can do many things to beautify their natural environment. At the minimum, they can prepare flower boxes for classroom windows. An activity such as this can help children appreciate the effort involved in maintaining living things.
4. If the school grounds contain an area that can be gardened, the children can establish some mini-gardens. Children involved in planting and maintaining vegetables and flowers can acquire a better sense of the importance of water to living things.
5. Children may wish to become involved in cleaning up chalk marks and graffiti on exterior and interior building walls. Such a project can remind children of the ease with which the environment can be defaced and the efforts required to repair it.

What Do People Think about Pollution?

Children will be interested to find out how other children and adults in their community feel about pollution problems. A possible class project would be the design of a pollution survey that various groups in the class could use to ask people their views on such topics as litter laws, air pollution, water pollution, and noise pollution. Groups of children may be able to set up interview stations in the school where they can survey teachers and other children. With your supervision they may also be able to set up such stations in shopping centers and other places in the community where there is heavy pedestrian traffic. After various groups have gathered information for the survey, a class discussion would give the children a good indication of how others feel about the problems of environmental pollution.

DEMONSTRATION

Signs of the Times: Using Our Environment Properly*

OBJECTIVES

The children will guess at the meanings of a variety of outdoor signs intended to help people use the environment properly.

The children will create their own signs that could be posted at various places in the school environment.

SCIENCE PROCESSES EMPHASIZED

Observing
Making hypotheses
Communicating

MATERIALS

Prior to this demonstration you will need to redraw on large sheets of paper a selection of the signs depicted in Figure 16–3. You will also need enough sheets of poster paper and art supplies for each learning group to create one sign.

DIRECTIONS

1. Play a twenty-questions game that focuses on the meaning of the signs that you reproduced.
2. After the game have a discussion of the various ways in which the children use the natural resources available in the environment.
3. Have groups of children invent symbol signs that could be used around the school to help others use the school's resources appropriately.

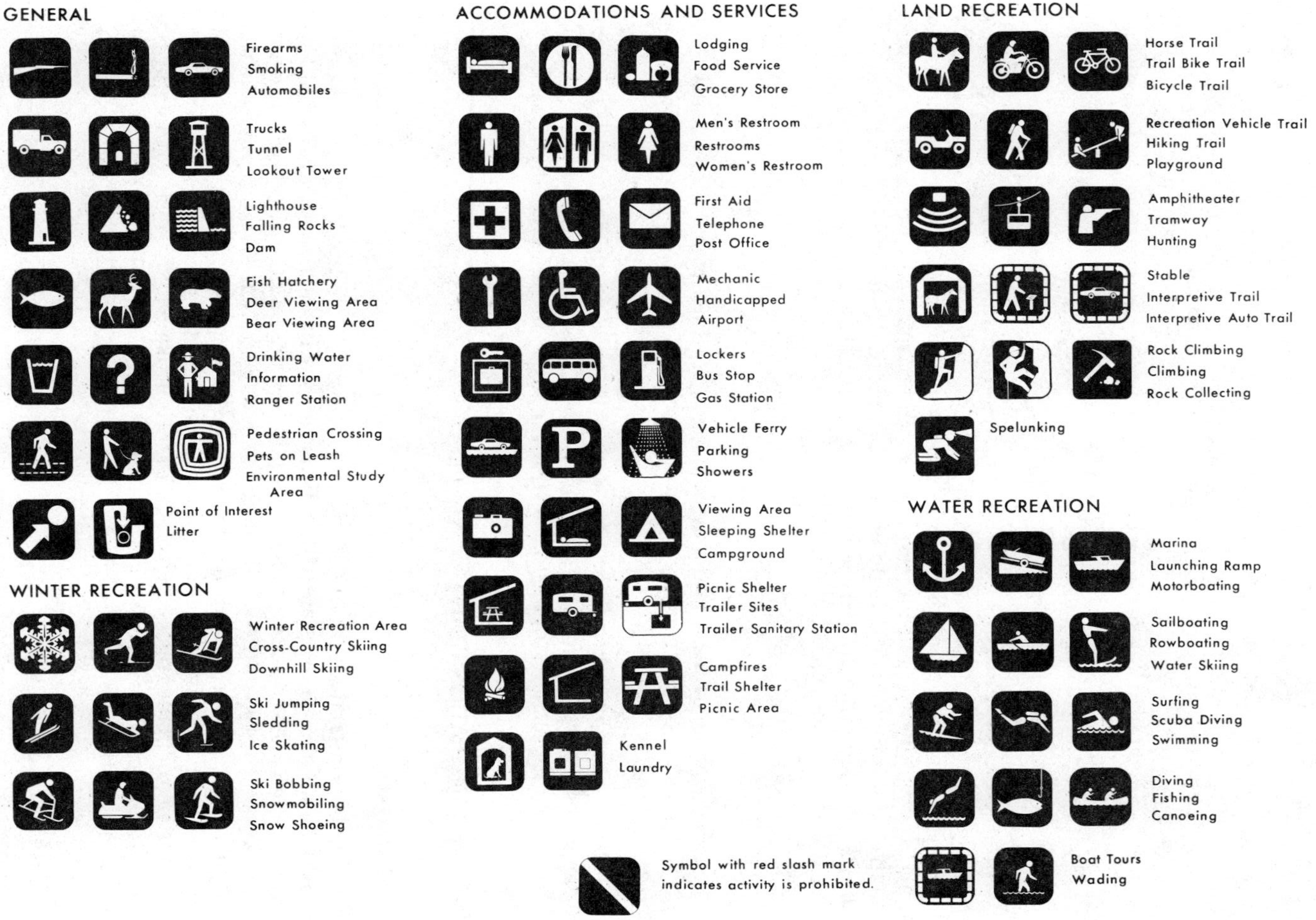
GENERAL
Firearms
Smoking
Automobiles
Trucks
Tunnel
Lookout Tower
Lighthouse
Falling Rocks
Dam
Fish Hatchery
Deer Viewing Area
Bear Viewing Area
Drinking Water
Information
Ranger Station
Pedestrian Crossing
Pets on Leash
Environmental Study Area
Point of Interest
Litter
WINTER RECREATION
Winter Recreation Area
Cross-Country Skiing
Downhill Skiing
Ski Jumping
Sledding
Ice Skating
Ski Bobbing
Snowmobiling
Snow Shoeing
ACCOMMODATIONS AND SERVICES
Lodging
Food Service
Grocery Store
Men's Restroom
Restrooms
Women's Restroom
First Aid
Telephone
Post Office
Mechanic
Handicapped
Airport
Lockers
Bus Stop
Gas Station
Vehicle Ferry
Parking
Showers
Viewing Area
Sleeping Shelter
Campground
Picnic Shelter
Trailer Sites
Trailer Sanitary Station
Campfires
Trail Shelter
Picnic Area
Kennel
Laundry
Symbol with red slash mark indicates activity is prohibited.
LAND RECREATION
Horse Trail
Trail Bike Trail
Bicycle Trail
Recreation Vehicle Trail
Hiking Trail
Playground
Amphitheater
Tramway
Hunting
Stable
Interpretive Trail
Interpretive Auto Trail
Rock Climbing
Climbing
Rock Collecting
Spelunking
WATER RECREATION
Marina
Launching Ramp
Motorboating
Sailboating
Rowboating
Water Skiing
Surfing
Scuba Diving
Swimming
Diving
Fishing
Canoeing
Boat Tours
Wading

Figure 16–3. Symbol Signs

1. Why do you think the signs don't have words? *So children and people who don't speak English can read them.*
2. Which of the signs help protect soil and water? *Rest room, house, trail-bike and bicycle trail, etc.*
3. Which signs help us keep safe when we are outdoors? *Swimming, falling rocks, sleeping shelters, etc.*

SCIENCE CONTENT FOR THE TEACHER

An interagency task force of the United States government has created a group of symbol signs describing the manner in which natural resources are intended to be used. Some of the symbols help people locate and identify services, accommodations, and other places of interest. These symbol signs lack words so that young children and individuals who do not understand English can interpret them. It is hoped that they will help people enjoy the natural resources of our environment and use them appropriately.

EXTENSIONS

Science/Social Studies. You may wish to engage the children in a discussion of the relationship of the country's natural resources to the quality of life that its citizens have.

Science/Language Arts. You may wish to have some children see if they can create a "sign story" using as many of the symbol signs and as few words as possible. They could then share these stories with the other members of the class.

ADDITIONAL DEMONSTRATION IDEAS

Showing Wind Erosion

For this demonstration you will need three or four aluminum pie plates and a small electric fan. Fill each pie plate with a different type of soil from your region. Hold the fan near each pie plate and have the children observe the effects of the wind it produces on the top of the soil. Extend the demonstration by dampening each soil sample and allowing the fan to blow air over it once again. Discuss the various factors that affect the rate at which the wind erodes the soil. For a long-term demonstration plant grass seed in some of the pie plates and repeat the demonstration after the grass has grown. The children will be able to observe how plant cover protects the soil from wind erosion.

How "Clean" Is Our Classroom Air?

You can demonstrate the extent of the dust and dirt in the classroom air by using a canister vacuum cleaner to filter the air. You will need two clean, well-worn handkerchiefs or pieces of cheese cloth and a strong rubber band in addition to the vacuum cleaner. One handkerchief will be used as a control. Stretch the other handkerchief over the end of the plastic tube to which the vacuum cleaner's attachments are normally fitted and fix it in place with the rubber band. The handkerchief should resemble a drumhead. Insert the free end of the tube into the vacuum cleaner and turn the machine on. Allow the vacuum cleaner to run for a half-hour and have the children observe the dust and dirt that accumulates on the cloth. You should probably schedule this demonstration before lunch or the end of school so that the noise from the vacuum cleaner does not disturb other classroom activities. If there is little dust or dirt in the air, children will observe that the cloth is clean.

How Much Paper Trash Do We Produce in Our Classroom?*

You will need to provide two labeled trash containers in the classroom over a five-day period prior to this demonstration. Label one container "paper and paper products" and label the other "other." You will also need five large plastic trash bags. At the end of each school day transfer the contents of the "paper and paper products" container to a trash bag. Label the bag with the day of the week and save the bag and its contents. Have the custodian dispose of the contents of the "other" container each day.

On the day you wish to do the demonstration, assemble all five bags of paper and paper products at the front of the room. Remove the contents of each and have the children observe the amount of paper thrown away each day. Also have them observe the amount of blank paper or paper with blank portions thrown away. Use this demonstration to raise questions and begin projects dealing with the reuse of paper as well as recycling in general.

It Hurts My Ears: Noise Pollution in the Classroom*

We are all so used to the amount of sound that reaches our ears that it is easy to forget what quiet really means. Children can be reminded of the presence of various sounds through this demonstration. Ask the children to be perfectly quiet for ten minutes (of course, if you have a particularly rambunctious group of children, you may need to reduce this allotment!) and write down each sound they hear. You should do the same. At the end of the ten minutes you may wish to have a discussion of all the sounds that reached their ears. Stress the sounds that they were unaware of prior to the demonstration. Ask the children to talk about the noises they experience each day—for example, noises from traffic, machinery, construction, and power lawn mowers.

Do You Mean We Breathe That Stuff?

This outdoor demonstration requires two adult assistants (perhaps two other teachers in the school), an automobile, and a sheet of cardboard to which a clean white paper towel is attached. Have the children stand a safe distance away from the car under the supervision of one adult. Have the second adult start the car, being sure that the emergency brake is engaged. Stand at the side of the car, not directly in back of it. Hold the cardboard to which the paper towel is attached about

15 centimeters (about 6 inches) from the exhaust so that the exhaust gases hit the towel. Turn your head so that you do not inhale the gases. After about four minutes remove the cardboard from the vicinity of the exhaust pipe and have the adult in the car shut the engine off. Take the children back to the classroom or to some other safe place outside the parking lot to observe the material that accumulated on the towel. *Note*: This demonstration must be carefully supervised since it occurs in a parking lot. You should not attempt it without the assistance of other adults.

chapter 17

The Ecology Crisis: Understanding and Preserving the Relationship between Ecosystems and the Environment

DISCOVERY ACTIVITIES AND DEMONSTRATIONS

A LOOK AHEAD

Discovery Activities

How Does a Natural Environment Change?

Are You Part of a Food Web?

What Is a Community Chart?

Grouping Consumers*

Additional Activity Ideas

Why Is This Man Crying?*

Touch-and-Feel Hike*

Cutting, Pasting, Thinking, and Talking*

Adopt an Endangered Animal

Demonstrations

What Are Some Things That Affect the Producers in a Community?

The Water Cycle*

Additional Demonstration Ideas

Whale Saver

Trash and Treasure*

Making Recycled Paper

Give a Hoot, Don't Pollute*

DISCOVERY ACTIVITIES

How Does a Natural Environment Change?

OBJECTIVES

Children will observe characteristics of a natural environment.
Children will infer the causes of changes in a natural environment.
Children will make predictions about ways in which a natural environment will change.

SCIENCE PROCESSES EMPHASIZED

Observing
Inferring
Predicting

MATERIALS

Access to a natural environment, such as a park, lawn, or woodlot
Paper and pencil

Figure 17—1. Why is this man crying? See the activity on page 402. (*Source:* Courtesy of Keep America Beautiful, Inc.)

MOTIVATION

Have the children discuss how the environment in their school changes over a twenty-four hour period. Temperature changes, lighting changes, and sound changes will probably surface during the discussion. Talk about how changes during the day (when the children are in school) affect them. Such actions as the ringing of bells, the opening and closing of windows, and the adjusting of shades all affect them in some way. Now turn the discussion to the more general topic of how changes in a natural environment affect the living things within it.

DIRECTIONS

1. Take the children outdoors to a natural environment and have them make observations of the types and amounts of living things they find there.
2. Have the children make observations of any signs of changes that have occurred, such as dead or broken branches and patios, sidewalks, paved parking lots, and other areas.
3. When you return to the classroom commence a discussion focusing on generations such as the ones listed below:

KEY DISCUSSION QUESTIONS

1. What signs of changes did you observe? (*Answers will vary.*)
2. Did you observe anything that might have caused some of the changes? (*Answers will vary, but may include "The wind might have blown the tree down" and "People left litter that covered some of the wildflowers."*)
3. How do you think the park (or whatever environment the class visited) will change in the future? What are some reasons for your answers? (*Answers will vary, but may include ideas such as "The lawn is going to get so covered with litter that grass isn't going to be able to grow in some places."*)

SCIENCE CONTENT FOR THE TEACHER

The natural environment is constantly subjected to forces that change it. Some of the causes of change are natural forces, such as wind, rain, and lightning. Other causes result from the presence of humans. The accumulation of litter on a lawn, the wearing down of plant life by footsteps, and accidental or purposely caused fires can all produce significant changes in an environment.

EXTENSIONS

Science. You may wish to take some children to visit more than one natural environment and then have them compare the changes that are occurring in the different areas. They can report the results of their visit to the class.

Social Studies. Some children may wish to create scale maps to depict some of the physical characteristics of a portion of a natural environment. Using symbols and a legend, they may be able to include information about observed changes and the variety of living things in the environment.

Are You Part of a Food Web?

OBJECTIVES

The children will trace the path taken by various foods they have eaten and discover their own place in a food web.

The children will discuss how various factors can affect the quantity and quality of the food that reaches them.

SCIENCE PROCESSES EMPHASIZED

Inferring

Hypothesizing

MATERIALS

For each child or group

Pencil and paper

For the teacher

Potato

Magazine picture of a hamburger

MOTIVATION

Have a discussion with the children about their favorite meals. Have them identify some of their favorite vegetables and meat. Ask them whether they ever think of how the food they eat was produced. At this point hold up the potato and ask the children to discuss what was needed for it to grow (soil, water, sunlight, etc.). Now hold up the picture of the hamburger and discuss how it was produced. You may wish to consider the production of both the meat and the roll.

DIRECTIONS

1. Have the children make a list of some of their favorite foods.
2. Have them make a chart showing how one such food was produced. They should try to think of all the stages of processing that change the food from its original form to the food they eat.
3. When they are done, have a class discussion of the various charts that were produced.
4. On the chalkboard reproduce the chart in Figure 17–2. Have the class focus on your chart as you raise questions such as those that follow.

KEY DISCUSSION QUESTIONS

1. Why do changes in soil, water, sunlight, or air affect the meat products you eat? *These changes may affect the grass and grain that cattle feed on. Changes in the grass and grain will*

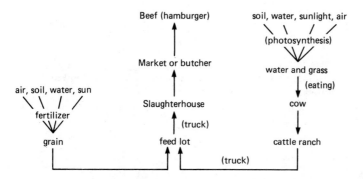

Figure 17—2. Sample Food Flow Chart (*Source:* U.S. Department of the Interior, Bureau of Land Management, *All Around You* [Washington, D.C.: Government Printing Office, 1977], p. 65. The pamphlet, stock number 024-011-0043-7, is available free from the Public Affairs Office, Department of the Interior, 18th and C Streets, N.W., Washington, D.C. 20240.

> *affect the amount of food cattle get. If the cattle don't eat good food, hamburgers will become scarce.*

2. How would a decrease in the amount of available gasoline affect the foods we eat? *If there was a shortage of gasoline, fewer food products would be moved from where they grow to the stores. Food would become more expensive because the higher price of gasoline would raise the cost of producing and transporting the food.*

SCIENCE CONTENT FOR THE TEACHER

The foods that reach us are the products of a complex series of interactions, which begin at the places where the foods are grown and end at the markets where we buy them. For example, meat production depends upon the availability of water, grass, and grain for cattle. The availability of grass and grain depends on the process of photosynthesis. Photosynthesis is dependent on the quantity and quality of soil, water, sunlight, and air.

EXTENSIONS

Science. If there is an organic-food store in your community, you may wish to have some children visit it to learn how the foods sold there differ (or are similar to) the foods sold in other stores. They should talk with the store owner about differences between the production of "organic" foods and the production of the foods available in other stores.

Social Studies. You may wish to have some children create ways to identify some of the places where their favorite foods originate. They may also wish to list the various modes of transportation of food products from the place they are produced to local stores and supermarkets.

What Is a Community Chart?

OBJECTIVES

The children will construct a chart that depicts the path of food and raw materials through a community of living things.

The children will explain how the living things in a community depend on one another for survival.

SCIENCES PROCESSES EMPHASIZED

Inferring
Communicating
Hypothesizing

MATERIALS FOR EACH CHILD OR GROUP

Large sheet of blank paper
Felt marker
Straightedge
3-by-5-inch index cards

MOTIVATION

Following a discussion of how animals and plants depend on one another, draw a community chart on the chalkboard on which the location of producers, first-level consumers, second-level consumers, decomposers, raw materials, and light are noted. See Figure 17–3.

Discuss how the types of organisms or materials labeled on the chart interact with one another. Indicate to the children that you will write on the board a list of organisms and materials in a make-believe community and that they will have an opportunity to see if they can place each at its proper location on a community chart.

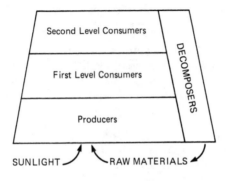

Figure 17–3. Community Chart

DIRECTIONS

1. Distribute the materials to each child or group.
2. Have the children make their own labeled community chart, using the chalkboard drawing for reference.
3. On the chalkboard list the following organisms and materials and have the children write them on the index cards, *one name per card.*

   Frogs
   Robins
   Worms
   Insects
   Bacteria
   Molds
   Yeasts
   Grass
   Green leaves

4. Ask the children to place each of the index cards in its appropriate location on their own chart.
5. Have a class discussion of the various arrangements that were created.
6. Ask the children to make hypotheses about the changes that would occur if various organisms or materials were removed from the community.

KEY DISCUSSION QUESTIONS

1. What do the plants in a community need in order to produce food? *Carbon dioxide in the air, water, minerals from the soil, sunlight.*
2. What do you think would happen to a community if all the decomposers were to die? *The materials in plants and animals could never be reused because after they died they would never rot.*
3. How would an oversupply of consumers affect a community's producers? *They might eat so many producers that none would be left. Then all the living things in the community would die.*

SCIENCE CONTENT FOR THE TEACHER

The feeding relationships in a community can be experienced through the preparation of a community chart that lists the materials and organisms that interact within the community. For the community studied in this activity, the organisms and materials would be grouped on the chart as follows.

Producers

Grass
Green leaves on trees

First-Level Consumers

Worms

Insects

Second-Level Consumers

Robins

Frogs

Decomposers

Bacteria

Mold

Yeast

EXTENSIONS

Science. You may wish to have some of the children create community charts for a city-park community. They should try to include such things as grass, acorns, grasshoppers, field mice, birds, cats, dogs, ants, spiders, flies, bacteria, and mold.

Science/Language Arts. A group of children might be interested in writing a story that describes a fictional island community that has an appropriate balance of producers, consumers, decomposers, raw materials, and adequate sunlight. In the story they could describe what might happen to the community if a group of people happened to be shipwrecked there.

Grouping Consumers*

OBJECTIVES

The children will identify first-, second- and third-level consumers.

The children will construct a food chain showing the relationships among first-, second-, and third-level consumers.

SCIENCE PROCESSES EMPHASIZED

Observing

Classifying

MATERIALS

For each group

List of consumers

Pencil and paper

*Asterisks refer to activities for young children.

For the teacher

Magazine pictures of an insect, a frog, a green plant, and a snake

MOTIVATION

Display the magazine pictures and ask the class to tell you the sequence of events that mark the movement of food energy among the consumers (insect to frog to snake). Indicate to the children that during this activity they will arrange the names of various consumers to show the path that food energy takes.

DIRECTIONS

1. Provide each child or group with a list of consumers.
2. Ask each child or group to study the list and then make their own groupings of consumers to show how food energy passes through them.
3. When they are done, ask various groups to explain the groupings they have made.
4. Have the children discuss the original source of food energy for the consumers.
5. Display the green plant and discuss its role as the original source of food for all the groupings made by the children.

KEY DISCUSSION QUESTIONS

1. What are consumers? *Living things that cannot make their own food.*
2. What are some examples of consumers that eat plants? (*Answers may include such animals as caterpillars, grasshoppers, and mice.*)
3. What are some examples of consumers that eat those consumers that feed on plants? (*Answers may include such animals as frogs and snakes.*)

SCIENCE CONTENT FOR THE TEACHER

Consumers are living things that cannot produce their own food. First-level consumers are animals that eat just plants. Second-level consumers eat first-level consumers. A given community can support a number of different levels of consumers. The following list of consumers can be the basis for the list of consumers required by the children.

Woodpecker	Cow	Mouse
Earthworm	Frog	Grasshopper
Robin	Moth	Raccoon
Bat	Fish	Deer
Wolf	Hawk	Owl
Bear	Human	Snail
Tiger	Snake	Duck

EXTENSIONS

Science. Have a group of children prepare a list of the consumers that exist in their own neighborhood. These children can construct groupings of these consumers to show the directions in which food energy moves through them.

Some children may be encouraged to construct chains and food webs that show the feeding relationships among all the living things in a particular community. They may be encouraged to first do library research to determine the types of living things in various communities.

Art. You may wish to have some children create a large drawing or painting that shows the variety of consumers that may exist in specific types of communities, such as forests, deserts, and the ocean.

ADDITIONAL ACTIVITY IDEAS

Why Is This Man Crying?*

You may wish to acquire a reproduction of the photograph at the beginning of this chapter. This native North American is looking at what has happened to his world and shedding a tear. The picture can be the source of an extended discussion of changes that are occurring in the environment. The children can be encouraged to think about and share the answers to such questions as, Why is this man crying? What do you think he is looking at? and If you could tell him one thing right now, what would it be? This activity could serve as the beginning of various direct-action activities within the school and on its grounds related to cleaning up the environment.

Touch-And-Feel Hike*

You may want to take the class for a walk, giving the following directions at intervals along the way.

1. Find the *hairiest* leaf around.
2. Find the *softest* leaf around.

Figure 17–4. (*Source:* © 1975 Ogilvy and Mather. Used with permission.)

3. Find the *smoothest* rock.
4. Find the *roughest* twig.
5. Find something *cool*.
6. Find something *warm*.
7. Find something *dry*.
8. Find something *bumpy*.

Add other "textures" when appropriate. The children should work in groups of three to four. They can make comparisons on the spot, without taking samples. It's important to leave things where they belong in the environment. You can ask the children questions such as these: What did you find that was dry, cool, etc.? Why was it dry, cool, etc.? How might these be different tonight? Next summer? Next winter? What have we discovered by touching and feeling things? The point of this activity is that our environment is made up of many textures. Being aware of the differences makes us ask why. By looking for the answers we can learn.

Cutting, Pasting, Thinking, and Talking*

An extended project for children that will keep their attention on current events that are affecting the environment is the maintenance of an ecology scrapbook. You may wish to take class time to have the children construct "empty" scrapbooks, using the unused sides of scrap paper for the interior pages and construction-paper remnants from art projects for the covers. When they have each constructed their own recycled-materials scrapbook they can begin cutting out newspaper and magazine pictures and articles concerning such ecologic matters as the world food supply, the use of pesticides, and noise pollution. At various times during the year you can have children discuss the various things they have included in their scrapbooks.

Adopt an Endangered Animal

You may wish to have each child "adopt" an endangered animal. The child adopting the animal should be encouraged to do library research to find out such things as where the animal lives, what its food supply is, and why it is endangered. The children can also draw pictures of their endangered animal and write poems or stories about it. You can have children make presentations to the class about their adopted animal.

DEMONSTRATIONS

What Are Some Things
That Affect the Producers in a Community?

OBJECTIVES

The children will predict the effects of the following factors upon the growth and health of producers (green plants): insufficient water, excess water, lack of light.

The children will observe the effects of these factors upon the growth and health of producers (green plants).

Children will explain why these factors affect the growth and health of producers.

SCIENCE PROCESSES EMPHASIZED

Observing
Predicting
Communicating

MATERIALS

5 healthy lima-bean or pea-plant seedlings, each in a separate container
Source of water
Masking tape
Marking pen
Sunny spot in the classroom

MOTIVATION

Display the seedlings so that all the children can observe them. Review the relationships among the producers, consumers, and decomposers in a community. Ask the children to tell you whether the seedlings are producers, consumers, or decomposers. Tell the children that you are going to do something to the seedlings that will help the children see how the environment can affect producers.

DIRECTIONS

1. After the children have had a chance to observe all four plants, use the masking tape to make a label for each container. The four seedlings should be labeled "Grown in sunlight—watered every 3 days," "Grown in sunlight—watered every day," "Grown in dark room—watered every 3 days," and "Grown in dark room—watered every day."
2. Have the children make predictions about how well each plant will survive.
3. Have children volunteer to carry out the plant watering.
4. Discuss various locations in the room that might be used for a dark environment and for a sunlit environment. (A closet can serve as the dark environment. If the classroom does not receive sunlight during the day, you can provide light for the plants with a fluorescent lamp. Such a lamp should be used only during the day so that the plant follows the same light/dark cycle that a plant growing outdoors experiences.)
5. Each day or every other day display all the plants and have children make observations. Return the plants to their respective environments after each discussion.
6. After two weeks have a general discussion of the demonstration. At this time have the children compare the results with their predictions.

KEY DISCUSSION QUESTIONS

1. In nature what might cause a plant to receive less sunlight than it needs? *Cloudy weather. Or a large plant growing over it might block the sunlight.*
2. In nature what might cause a plant to receive too little water? *Lack of rain.*
3. In nature what might cause a plant to receive too much water? *Floods.*

SCIENCE CONTENT FOR THE TEACHER

Various factors can affect the growth of producers. Since all other living things depend on the growth of green plants, anything that limits the growth of these plants limits the increase in other animal and plant populations. A period of sunlight and a period of darkness is required in order for a plant to produce and store food. Although water is essential for photosynthesis, too much water can cause the root systems of plants to rot.

EXTENSIONS

Science. A group of children may wish to find the effect of better soil on plant growth. They can accomplish this by adding plant fertilizer to the soil of some plants and not adding it to the soil of others. Both groups of plants should be maintained, and all other growing conditions should be the same.

Art. You may wish to have some children prepare before and after pictures of the producers used in this demonstration. Be sure to have them label their drawings so that the conditions in which each plant was grown can be observed.

The Water Cycle*

OBJECTIVES

The children will observe the recycling of water from a plant to its environment. The children will describe the path that water takes as it recycles.

SCIENCE PROCESSES EMPHASIZED

Observing
Communicating

MATERIALS

Large clear plastic bag
Potted geranium plant
Masking tape
Container of water

Discuss the concept of recycling with the children. Have them give examples of recycling they have observed. They may suggest the recycling of metal and of old newspapers. Some children may discuss the way in which water is recycled in nature. If no one does, introduce this topic and indicate that you will be doing a demonstration of one way in which water is recycled.

DIRECTIONS

1. Display the geranium plant, plastic bag, tape, and container of water.
2. Water the geranium plant.
3. Cover the plant with the plastic bag and tape the bottom of the bag to the pot. Be sure there is a good seal so that no water can escape.
4. Have groups of children come forward to observe and draw the setup.
5. For the next few days have the children make observations of the geranium plant and the plastic bag.
6. Eventually they will observe the accumulation of drops of water on the inside of the bag.
7. Have a class discussion about the source of this water.
8. Encourage the children to make a drawing of the path the water took during the demonstration.

KEY DISCUSSION QUESTIONS

1. Why do plants need water? *To make food and to carry dissolved food from place to place in the plant.*
2. What are the sources of water for a plant? *Water reaches the ground when it rains, and the roots take in the water. Also, some water from the air enters.*
3. What do you think happens to any extra water that a plant takes in? *It goes into the air from the leaves.*

SCIENCE CONTENT FOR THE TEACHER

Water is found in the cells of every living thing. Without water life as we know it cannot exist. Water can dissolve and transport materials needed for the life processes of both plants and animals. Water is constantly recycled in nature. It is absorbed by plants through their root system. Excess water leaves plants as water vapor, passing through openings in the leaf surfaces known as *stomata*.

In this demonstration excess water in the plant and soil was changed to a gas—water vapor. The water vapor condensed on the inside of the plastic bag. In nature some of the water vapor in the air becomes precipitation and returns to the ground.

EXTENSIONS

Science. Supply a group of children with life-science resource books that include cross-sectional diagrams of a leaf's cells. See if they can find the places where extra water leaves the plant as vapor. (They will see openings that show the stomata and surrounding specialized cells. Indicate that these openings allow a variety of gases to enter and leave the plant.)

Social Studies. You may wish to have some children consider ways in which people interfere with water cycles. They may wish to discuss their ideas with the remainder of the class. Encourage them to think about the effect of parking lots, paved streets, and buildings on the ability of the soil to receive water.

ADDITIONAL DEMONSTRATION IDEAS

Whale Saver

The possible extinction of the great whales is a matter that should be brought to the attention of children. There are a variety of things you can do within a demonstration format to focus attention on the plight of the whales. To lay the groundwork for the suggestions, you may wish to initiate a discussion of the characteristics of whales. In particular you should focus on the fact that whales are mammals, and as such bear the same essential characteristics that humans do. Following such a discussion you may wish to carry out the following demonstration for the benefit of the children.

Show the children how large various whales can become, using a measuring stick to mark off the size of some of them. When you run out of space take the children into the hallway or outdoors to mark off the lengths of the remaining whales. Use the following figures as a reference:

Type of Whale	Length in Meters	Length in Feet
White	5.5	18
Pacific Gray	14	45
Humpback	15.6	50
Sperm	19.2	63
Finback	25	80
Blue	31.3	100

You may also wish to discuss how whales communicate with one another and then play records that include the sounds they make.

Trash and Treasure*

For a week prior to this demonstration, save (without the children's knowledge) all the paper discarded in the classroom wastebasket. You can do this by transferring it to a cardboard box. On the day of the demonstration tell the children what you have been doing and display the cardboard box and accumulated papers. As you show the contents of the box have the children note the amount of paper that was wasted as a result of only one side being used. (The unused sides could at least have been used for scrapwork.) The children can then make estimates of the amount of paper that is discarded in the school's classrooms each week and each year.

Give a hoot!   Don't pollute!

Help Woodsy spread the word...

Figure 17-5. (*Source:* © 1975 Ogilvy and Mather. Used with permission.)

Making Recycled Paper

The essential steps in the paper-recycling process can be demonstrated in the classroom. The complete demonstration takes two class periods that are one day apart. On the first day you can produce raw paper pulp. By the second day the fibers in the pulp will have dried sufficiently for you to show the class the paper that was produced.

To show the children the basic steps, begin by tearing a sheet of newspaper into small pieces. Allow these pieces to soak in a bowl of water for one or two hours. Use an eggbeater to break up the soaked paper into the fibers of which it is made. The resulting mixture is paper pulp—the basis for papermaking. Now discard half the water in the bowl. Prepare a mixture of four tablespoons of cornstarch and one liter (about one quart) of water. Pour this into the pulp. The cornstarch will eventually cause the paper fibers to stick together. The pulp-and-cornstarch mixture should now be placed in a tray that is at least five centimeters (about two inches) deep. Use a flat square of window screening to begin the process of creating the paper. Lower the screen into the pulp-cornstarch mixture repeatedly until a layer about half a centimeter (about one fifth of an inch) thick forms on the screen. The screen should now be placed on some old newspapers. Place some waxed paper over the pulp on the screen and press *gently* on it with a book to squeeze out excess water. Let the pulp dry for about a day. Gently peel the fibers from the screen. What you have is raw paper.

Give a Hoot, Don't Pollute*

If you can play the piano or guitar or can locate a teacher or child who can, you may wish to use the "Help Woodsy Spread the Word" song plus some slides or photographs of pollution in your community to demonstrate the need to protect the environment and the responsibility that people have for the environment. You can use the song effectively by grouping the children around the musician and having the children first hum along with the music and then learn the words. You can then have some children write new words for the music so that the song includes references to school or community pollution problems. Have children or groups who create new lyrics come forward to sing them to the class.

chapter 18

The Energy Crisis:
Conserving the Energy We Have
and Searching for Alternative
Energy Sources

DISCOVERY ACTIVITIES
AND DEMONSTRATIONS

A LOOK AHEAD

Discovery Activities

How Do You Use Energy?*

Conserve, Conserve, Conserve*

Watt-Watcher

Additional Activity Ideas

Cube Saver*

My Dream Machine

Wind Machines

Demonstrations

I. M. Wright Holds a Press Conference

"Pardon Me, Sir, I'm with WKID News"

Additional Demonstration Ideas

Coal: What Is It and Where Does It Come from?*

Oil: What Is It and Where Does It Come from?*

It's in the Papers

DISCOVERY ACTIVITIES

How Do You Use Energy[1]*

OBJECTIVES

The children will name three ways in which they or others use energy.
The children will draw two pictures showing themselves or other people using energy.

SCIENCE PROCESSES EMPHASIZED

Observing
Communicating

MATERIALS FOR EACH CHILD

Energy-inventory sheet based on Figure 18–2
Battery-powered toy
String of colored lights that blink
Windup toy
Toy truck

MOTIVATION

Play "Simon Says" with the class, doing simple motions such as tapping your foot, clapping your hands, patting the top of your head, and rubbing your stomach. After about three minutes, ask the sudents to name some of the actions and record them or make stick drawings of them on the board. Tell the class that when they did these activities they were *using energy*.

Plug in several electric or battery-powered toys and ask the children what makes them move. Plug in the blinking colored lights and ask students what makes them light up and blink. (Possible answers: energy, battery, wires, electricity.) Wind up several toys and watch them move, or push a toy car or truck and ask what made them move. (Possible answers: We did. Our muscles. Our energy. I pushed it.) Lead students to observe that people, electricity, and anything else that make things *move* use energy.

---

[1]The first two activities in this chapter are based on activities found in the *Energy-Environment Mini-Unit Guide*. The illustrations are from this source also. This excellent book is available for purchase from the National Teachers Association, Washington, D.C. 20009.
*Asterisks refer to activities for young children.

Figure 18—1. Energy Inventory Sheet

DIRECTIONS

1. Give each student an energy-inventory sheet. Introduce it with lead questions such as "Let's look at the pictures on this page. What is happening in picture number one?" (A boy is pushing on a light switch.) "Have you turned the light switch on or off at home? What happens when you do?" (The lights go on or off.) "When we turn on our lights, we are using energy. Let's put an X in the box to show one way we use energy."

   "Let's look at the next picture. What is happening here?" (A girl is riding a bicycle.) "How many of you have ridden a tricycle or a bicycle? When we use our muscles to do things, we are also using energy. So if you ride a bicycle or tricycle, put an X in the box by this picture."

2. Ask the children to complete the rest of the energy-inventory sheet. Have the children make their own drawings of energy being used in boxes 14 and 15. Then they can show their drawings to the rest of the class and explain what is occurring in each.

KEY DISCUSSION QUESTIONS

The discussion questions are included in the two previous sections.

SCIENCE CONTENT FOR THE TEACHER

Since this activity simply helps children become aware of energy and its uses, there is little in the way of content that you will need to review. The essential concept stressed in the activity is that energy in its various forms is used by us every day.

EXTENSIONS

Science/Physical Education. You may wish to have groups of children invent dance movements to show various ways in which energy is used during a day. They can weave some of the events on the energy-inventory sheet into their dance.

Science/Health. You may wish to provide groups of children with magazine pictures showing people using energy in physical-fitness activities and pictures of people eating various foods. Each group could then use their pictures to make up a story about a person who used up more energy than he or she took in by eating food.

Conserve, Conserve, Conserve*

OBJECTIVES

The children will explain the meaning of the term *conserve.*
The children will separate sets of drawings into those that show energy being conserved and those showing energy being wasted.

SCIENCE PROCESSES EMPHASIZED

Observing
Classifying
Communicating

MATERIALS

Prepare twenty duplicating masters containing drawings of energy being used or wasted, such as those in Figure 18–1. Run off the masters, cut out the drawings, and paste them to index cards.

MOTIVATION

Tell the children that in this activity they will be learning to use a word that at present they may not be using very much. Also tell them that they will be taking a walk to various places in the school where it makes sense to use this word.

Figure 18–2. Sample Energy Cards

DIRECTIONS

1. Write the word *conserve* on the chalkboard, pronounce it, and ask the children to tell you what they think it means. After some discussion explain that it means "to save." Tell them that people usually use it when they talk about things that they do not want to use up.

2. Take the children for a walk to various places in the school where they can use *conserve* in sentences. For example, they can visit the cafeteria and make up sentences that deal

414

with saving water, saving heat energy used in cooking, and saving trees by using fewer paper products.

3. After this mini—field trip distribute a set of picture cards to each child or group and have the children separate them into two piles on the basis of whether or not something is being conserved.

4. After the groups have separated their cards, have them take turns holding up pairs of cards that display something being conserved and something being wasted.

KEY DISCUSSION QUESTIONS

Prior to the activity you may wish to prepare a list of questions to accompany the sets of index cards you develop. Prepare questions such as "How is the man in picture number two conserving energy." *He is mixing something without using the electric mixer.*

SCIENCE CONTENT FOR THE TEACHER

This activity is intended simply to teach children to use the term *conserve* and to raise their awareness of ways in which things can be conserved. There is no sophisticated content that you will need to review prior to the activity. However, you should prepare by taking your own field trip around the school to find suitable places to visit during the activity.

EXTENSIONS

Science/Art. Have each child prepare two large drawings of his or her own idea of something being conserved and the same thing being wasted. You can display these "picture pairs" on the bulletin board.

Science/Language Arts. Have the children pick up a pair of index cards to pantomime, and have the remainder of the class guess which cards are being acted out. After each pantomime have the children make up a two-line rhyme that explains the pair. For example, "Mr. Smith stopped using his mixer, to make his food quicker," or "Sally Jones put on her sweater, and then she felt better."

Watt-Watcher

OBJECTIVES

The children will gather information about the types of appliances used by various generations of people.

The children will calculate the average amount of electrical power used by various generations of people.

The children will discuss the possible consequences of increased electricity use.

SCIENCE PROCESSES EMPHASIZED

Observing
Using numbers
Communicating

MATERIALS

For each child or group

Watt-watcher survey form
Access to adults, including senior citizens

For the Teacher

2 small electrical appliances, the more exotic the better! (for example, an electric homemade-ice-cream machine and an electrically heated hot-air popcorn popper)

MOTIVATION

Display both of the appliances that you have brought to school. Ask the children if they know what the appliances are used for. Have them discuss whether they think the use of these appliances serves as a good use of electrical energy. Have the children discuss whether their parents or grandparents had such things. Indicate to the children that this activity will help them understand why we use so much energy.

DIRECTIONS

1. Tell the children that they will do three things outside of class. First they will determine which of the appliances on the watt-watcher survey form their parents had when they were children. Then they will find out how much energy is used by each appliance. Finally, they should locate a senior citizen (possibly a grandparent) and find out which of the appliances they had when they were children. Distribute the watt-watcher forms and have the children take them home to gather information with.

2. After a few days have the children bring their completed forms back to school. Have the children add up the number of kilowatt hours per month that are used now, the number used when their parents were children, and the number used when their grandparents were children.

3. Hold a general discussion of the results of the children's watt-watching. Be sure to avoid any specific discussion of particular appliances that some families in the class may or may not presently have. Focus instead on the big picture of increased electricity usage and its possible consequences.

KEY DISCUSSION QUESTIONS

1. Were there any surprises for you when you did your watt-watching? (*Answers will vary.*)
2. Can you find two or three appliances in the list that people could use less in order to conserve energy? Which ones? (*Answers will vary.*)

WATT-WATCHER SURVEY[a]

ITEM	AVG. KWH PER MO.*	YOUR FAMILY	PARENTS	GRAND-PARENTS
Dishwasher	35			
Microwave Oven	16			
Electric Range	98			
Blender	1			
Can Opener	1			
Electric Clock	1			
Automatic Coffeemaker	8			
Toaster	3			
Slow Cooker	12			
Refrigerator	152			
Vacuum Cleaner	4			
Clothes Washer	9			
Clothes Dryer	80			
Space Heater	75			
Water Heater	400			
Color TV	55			
B&W TV	30			
Radio-Record Player	9			
Power Saw	4			
Electric Blanket	12			
Hair Dryer	10			
Electric Toothbrush	1			
Room Air Conditioner	72			
Electric Fan	12			
Electric Furnace	1100			
Yard Light	30			
Garage Door Opener	1			

If you had lived in the year 1900, you would have used only one-fourth of the energy you use today. In the year 2000, you will use almost twice as much as you use today if demand continues at the present rate. What will happen if demand increases?

Figure 18–3.

[a]The Information on this survey chart is excerpted from *Your Energy World*, available from the Department of Energy, Technical Information Center, P.O. Box 62, Oak Ridge, Tennessee 37830
*Based on estimates made by Tennessee Valley Authority Power and Edison Electric Corporation.

3. If you wanted to save electrical energy, which two appliances could you use less so as to get large savings? *Water heater and electric furnace.*

4. What changes would you have to make in your daily habits if you were to use less hot water and less heat? (*Answers will vary.*)

SCIENCE CONTENT FOR THE TEACHER

The rate at which electrical energy is used is measured in kilowatt-hours. The number of kilowatt-hours used each month by an appliance can be found by multiplying the number of watts marked on an appliance by the number of hours the appliance is used each month and dividing by one thousand. The rate at which we use electricity is increasing significantly. In the year 1900 a person used only one fourth the electricity that a person uses today. It is estimated that by the year 2000 the amount of electrical power used by each person will be double today's use.

EXTENSIONS

Science/Social Studies. You may wish to have children do some research and prepare a drawing of a typical kitchen in the year 1900. They can base their drawing on follow-up interviews with senior citizens that focus just on kitchen appliances. The children can also prepare a drawing of a modern home kitchen. These drawings might stimulate an interesting class discussion of what has been gained and lost in over eighty years of "progress."

Science/Art. Some children may wish to make models or drawings of how some commonly used electrical appliances would look if they utilized an alternative energy source. Some examples that come to mind are wind-powered clothes washers and water-powered fans. The children should be able to invent many other surprising appliances.

ADDITIONAL ACTIVITY IDEAS

Cube Saver*

You can have children develop a better understanding of the function of insulation by having them assemble various containers to keep ice cubes solid. The children will need at least two class periods to do this activity. First they will have to time how long it takes for an ice cube to melt when it is placed on a saucer. While the ice cube is melting they can begin designing a container that will restrict the flow of heat from the room to the ice cube. You will need a large assortment of materials from which the children can choose construction materials. Try to secure such things as various thicknesses of cardboard, styrofoam coffee cups, aluminum foil, newspapers, sand, cloth, cotton, plastic food containers, tape, rubber bands, and glass, plastic, and metal tumblers. The children can design various containers and determine which combination of materials was able to preserve the ice cubes the longest. This activity can lead to a class discussion of the ways in which people insulate buildings in order to restrict heat exchange with the outdoors.

My Dream Machine

This activity will help children analyze the energy-conservation considerations that should accompany a decision about a car they would like to have when they are older. Prior to the activity visit as many automobile dealerships as you can in your community and obtain their most recent brochures describing subcompact, compact, standard, and luxury cars. Also write for some free copies of the most recent *Gas Mileage Guide For New Car Buyers*, available from the Fuel Economy Department, Federal Energy Administration, Washington, D.C., 20461. Also acquire a few copies of *Cost of Operating an Automobile* from the U.S. Department of Transportation, Federal Highway Administration, Office of Highway Planning, Highway Statistics Division, Washington, D.C. 20590. When you have all the brochures, have the children select their "dream machine" and conduct a study of such things as gasoline cost and mileage, base cost of the car, optional equipment that uses extra energy, and the cost of replacing a set of tires. Individual children or groups should prepare a presentation about their dream machine for the rest of the class.

Wind Machines

During a learning unit on alternative energy sources you may wish to have the children discuss the wind as a "free" and clean energy source. Such a discussion can be rounded out with an activity in which you provide some raw materials that they can use to build a variety of wind machines. They can use pictures from books that show various rotor designs, or they can develop their own idea for an efficient wind machine. After they have constructed a model wind machine you can bring an electric fan into the classroom and have the children assess how well their machine operates.

DEMONSTRATIONS

I. M. Wright Holds a Press Conference

OBJECTIVES

The children will role-play various participants in a press conference dealing with energy.

Children observing the press conference will write responses to questions dealing with the topics covered.

Children will explain the solution they have chosen for the energy problem dealt with in the press conference.

SCIENCE PROCESSES EMPHASIZED

Observing
Using information
Communicating

419

A copy of the script shown in Figure 18−4 for each person playing a participant in the press conference

A copy of the instant-analysis scorecard shown in Figure 18−5 for each child observing the role-playing

MOTIVATION

Lead into the demonstration by asking students questions about their concept of alternatives. For instance, you might ask them what they might do if they were at an ice-cream counter ordering a triple-dip of licorice-peppermint-banana ice cream and the clerk told them that he was all out of that flavor. Or, what would they do if the shirt they were planning to wear to school on Monday morning "bit the dust" during the touch football game on Saturday afternoon? They will probably tell you that they would simply order a triple dip of something else and get another shirt!

Now lead the children to a discussion of other energy sources. You can ask, What do you do in your homes when the lights go out during an electrical storm? How could you keep an appointment with your dentist whose office is on the tenth floor of a downtown high-rise if the elevators were out of order?

These questions can lead your students to the discovery of energy alternatives in their day-to-day living. Now they are ready, as a school board and as concerned citizens, to consider alternatives to petroleum and natural gas for the new school they are planning.

Tell the class that they will observe a short play to be read by several students. The simulated school board and concerned citizens attending the meeting are tuned into station NRG−TV, where a press conference is in session. Mr. or Ms. I. M. Wright, chairperson of the committee appointed by the school board to study energy systems, is fielding questions about these systems from the press corps. The reporters are raising the most frequently asked questions about each energy source. They are also voicing some of the most common objections to each source. Bring the role players to the front of the room and begin the demonstration discussion.

DIRECTIONS

1. Organize the seating at the front of the room so that it approximates a press conference. Have the children carry out the role playing.
2. After the role playing distribute copies of the instant-analysis scorecard to the remainder of the class and have them complete it.

KEY DISCUSSION QUESTION

See the instant-analysis scorecard.

SCIENCE CONTENT FOR THE TEACHER

You will need to review the characteristics of a variety of energy sources prior to the press conference.

LADIES AND GENTLEMEN OF THE PRESS . . .

Announcer:
We interrupt our program to bring you this NRG-TV news special. I. M. Wright, chairperson of the committee appointed to study possible energy sources for the new school building, is holding a press conference to announce the four sources that will be considered and is ready to field questions from the press corps about the choices.

Wright:
Our committee has considered many possibilities, but we've finally narrowed our choices down to four: Solar, Geothermal, Windpower and making oil and gas from coal.

Doogle of The Bugle:
What, exactly, is solar energy?

Wright:
Very simply, *solar energy is sunlight—sunlight collected on glass or metal plates or in special solar "cells."*

Bailey of The Daily:
How soon do we run out of solar energy and have to go through all this again?

Wright:
Never! *The sun will shine whether we collect its rays for energy or not. And it won't stop shining if we do use it.*

Parker of The Barker:
That's the good news! Now, let's have the bad. How much?

Wright:
Cost? Is that what you mean? *Well, it will be expensive in the beginning to install solar equipment because of the new technology involved, but once it's in, heating costs will be cheaper than using conventional systems.* Solar systems will need some kind of back-up heating system to help when the sun doesn't shine. However, using sun energy is *good for the environment.* It provides heat and light for animal and plant life all the time.

Hughes of The News:
Geothermal—what's that? Sounds like a new name for winter woolies!!

Wright:
If it were, you really would have a hot seat! *Geothermal energy is steam or hot water from under the earth's surface.* When this steam or hot water pushes through the earth's surface, it makes a hot spring or a geyser—like "Old Faithful."

Parr of The Star:
So, how do we use it for energy?

Wright:
We can pipe it directly into the school to fill the radiators, or we can pipe it to electric plants where it will turn turbines and generate electric power. Then we send it into the school building by wires.

Grimes of The Times:
Four quick questions. How much does it cost? How much do we have? Where is it located? How dangerous to the environment?

Wright:
It's expensive to find the reservoirs which are located mostly in the Western U.S., but once they're found, *steam is low in cost compared to fossil fuels.* Problem is, we don't have a lot of this energy source. And it will have *some bad side-effects as far as the environment goes. Wells, roads, ponds, large above-ground pipes and power plants are part of the package.*

Dunn of The Sun:
So why consider it? I heard *it can pollute streams and air, too.*

Wright:
That's true. Well, we considered it because it can be used directly and doesn't need to be mined, or processed, and it makes basically clean heat.

Doogle:
I thought I heard you say coal. Isn't that a step backwards?

Wright:
Not really. *Coal is our most abundant fossil fuel.* 90 percent of our fossil fuel reserve is coal, and we use only a very small amount of it.

Bailey:
If we start using it, won't coal begin to run out, too?

Wright:
Sure it will. But since there's so much of it there, we can use it to buy time for technology to catch up and find an effective alternative to fossil fuels.

Parker:
Isn't coal a terrible pollutant?

Wright:
Burning coal is polluting, but we're considering *gasified and liquefied coal. Gasification removes the sulfur and other pollutants and can give us a substitute for natural gas.* Coal liquefaction is the process of converting coal to a liquid. This liquefied coal can be refined like petroleum and can be transported through existing oil pipelines.

Hughes:
Is this an expensive alternative?

Wright:
It used to look expensive. Now, with the skyrocketing prices of petroleum, *it's starting to look like a bargain.*

Parr:
What's it going to do to the environment?

Wright:
Well, let's just say that the results aren't going to win a garden club award. *Coal first has to be mined; it could destroy thousands of acres of land unless the mines are reclaimed.*

Grimes:
Let's get to *windpower.* What could we do with the wind?

Wright:
Like solar, probably only hope to use it to supplement another energy source. But, like the sun, the wind is not something that nations can keep to themselves. *Every nation has a free supply. It requires no mining, and it is non-polluting as it has no dangerous by-products.*

Doogle:
(interrupting) Excuse me, but. . . what do we do if the wind doesn't blow? Get out our oars?

Wright:
That's the obvious problem. The wind would have to blow to create the energy needed to generate electricity.

Announcer:
Sorry, folks, that's all we have time for. Now stay tuned for an INSTANT ANALYSIS.

Figure 18—4.

421

INSTANT ANALYSIS SCORECARD

The press conference is over. U.R. Baffled, manager of the local movie theatre, stood up and said, "Whew! What'd he say? Did anyone write any of that down?" So, now you've got to play Cralter Wonkite and do an "instant analysis."

Think about what you heard in the press conference. Without looking back at the playlet, try to list as many of the important points mentioned about each energy source. Write your answers in the spaces under each energy source. Once you have finished, you can go back and check your answers with the press conference sheet.

WHAT DID THEY SAY ABOUT . . .

SOLAR ENERGY?
1. Where does it come from? *sunlight collected on glass or metal plates*
2. How much will it cost? *expensive in the beginning; cheaper than ordinary*
3. What is its effect on the environment? *good for the environment*
4. Is there a limited supply? *the sun won't stop shining*

GEOTHERMAL ENERGY?
1. Where does it come from? *steam or hot water from below earth's surface*
2. How much will it cost? *expensive to find; steam low-cost*
3. What is its effect on the environment? *wells, roads, ponds, pipes, power plants*
4. Is there a limited supply? *we don't have a lot of this energy source*

COAL GASIFICATION?
1. Where does it come from? *turning coal into gas after it's mined*
2. How much will it cost? *starting to look like a bargain*
3. What is its effect on the environment? *mining can destroy land; gasified coal is clean*
4. Is there a limited supply? *no we have a lot of it*

WINDPOWER?
1. Where does it come from? *moving air turns windmills*
2. How much will it cost? *a free supply to every nation*
3. What is its effect on the environment? *no dangerous by-products*
4. Is there a limited supply? *wind needs to blow*

NOW, put a check mark next to the source you like best and explain why you like it best. Maybe you have a better idea. Maybe you can think of an energy source that is not talked about here. If you can, put a check in the box that says "my suggestion," and use the space at the bottom to explain it. You might also like to see the new school use more than one of these sources. If this is your choice, mark the box that says "a combination of sources," and explain.

□ ONE OF THE FIVE   □ A COMBINATION   □ MY OWN SUGGESTION
   ENERGY SOURCES   OF SOURCES

EXPLAIN: _____

_____

_____

Figure 18—5.

Nuclear Fission. The uranium ores used in this process are found in the southwest United States, Canada, South Africa, and India. Heat created by the splitting of the nuclei of certain uranium atoms turns water to steam, which in turn drives turbines and produces electricity. Fission is a very efficient energy source: the heat value from 28 grams (about one ounce) of uranium 235 equals 388 barrels of petroleum. The United States now derives 9 percent of its electricity from nuclear fission. The two principal disadvantages of fission are that U 235 is scarce and radioactive waste from nuclear reactors must be safely stored for thousands of years in order to prevent leakage of radioactivity into the environment.

Oil Shale. Oil can be extracted from certain sedimentary rock found in the Rocky Mountain states. Although large amounts of oil exist in this form, its recovery requires enormous quantities of water, has adverse environmental effects, and yields only 30 gallons or less of oil per ton of shale.

Tidal Power. The rise and fall of the tides can be harnessed to rotate turbines and thereby generate electricity. Unfortunately, it is difficult to make the energy supply continuous.

Hydrogen. Hydrogen gas, the most abundant element in the universe, is burned for heat in the same way that natural gas is. It can also be used for the generation of electricity and can be converted to a liquid that operates motor vehicles and manufacturing equipment. It is a clean fuel: its only waste product is water. Its disadvantages are cost and its present low energy efficiency. It is sometimes dangerous to use because it can be explosive.

Nuclear Fusion. The fusion, or joining, of atoms of hydrogen (possibly from sea water) to create heat is an important potential energy source of the next century. It is an efficient energy reaction and releases only minute amounts of radioactivity into the environment. At the present time, it is very costly and technologically very difficult to produce.

Pyrolysis of Solid Waste. Waste material—such as manure, garbage, paper, logging residue, industrial waste, and sewage—can be heated to high temperatures in an oxygen-free atmosphere to produce oil and gaseous products. Pyrolysis helps clean solid wastes from our environment, thus reducing pollution. The problem is that of gathering these wastes together at a reasonable cost.

EXTENSIONS

Science. Have the children conduct an in-depth study of the energy sources, expenses, and problems associated with the school's energy use. They may wish to make direct observations of any energy-conservation measures that are being taken.

Science/Art. Some children may wish to design schools that would be extremely energy-efficient. They could draw the schools to rough scale on large sheets of poster paper. The drawings could then serve as the focus for a class discussion.

"Pardon Me, Sir, I'm with WKID News"

OBJECTIVES

The children will gather information among themselves and from adults about environmental damage, the world's supply of fossil fuels, and fuel costs.

The children will discuss the results of their information gathering.

The children will make hypotheses about people's knowledge and attitudes regarding the above topics.

SCIENCE PROCESSES EMPHASIZED

Observing
Communicating
Making hypotheses

MATERIALS

Interview form based on the one in Figure 18–6
Access to an adult for the demonstration
Access to other adults in the follow-up activity

MOTIVATION

Ask the children if they have ever seen people being interviewed on television. Have them talk about some of the interviews they have seen. Discuss the reasons reporters interview people. Indicate to the children that they will be observing a demonstration showing how to interview people and then doing a follow-up activity that will, in part, require them to interview an adult. An adult on the school staff, a member of their family, or any adult they choose can be the subject of the interview.

DIRECTIONS

1. Distribute copies of the "Problems, Problems, Problems" interview form. Tell the children that the first thing they are to do is write their own answer to the interview question.
2. Invite the adult who is going to help you with the demonstration to come to the front of the room. Demonstrate some techniques that the children might wish to use when interviewing adults. Don't leave out the importance of being polite, telling the adult what the interview is for, and explaining how the information gathered will be used.
3. After you have role-played the interview, have the children use the interview form to interview an adult. Allow a few days for this part of the activity.
4. When the children have completed their interviews, have a class discussion focusing on summarizing the results of the interviews. In particular, raise questions such as those listed below.
5. Ask the children to write a brief summary of what they learned during the activity.

	YOUR ANSWER	ADULT IN COMMUNITY
ENVIRONMENT 1. Have you ever had a cough or stinging eyes because of air pollution? How did it make you feel?		
2. Do you know if anything is being done in your town to make the air cleaner?		
3. (Your Question) _____		
LIMITED SUPPLY 4. Where in the world are the greatest deposits of fossil fuels found?		
5. What country in the world uses the most coal and petroleum?		
6. Is it possible to make more oil once it's gone?		
7. (Your question) _____		
COST 8. Name three fossil fuel products whose price has increased this year.		
9. (Your question) _____		
CONSERVATION 10. How can we make our fossil fuel energy supply last longer?		

Figure 18–6. Survey Form (*Source: Your Energy World,* available from the Department of Energy, Technical Information Center, P.O. Box 62, Oak Ridge, Tennessee 37830.

KEY DISCUSSION QUESTIONS

1. The answers to most of the questions on the interview form are either personal opinions or dependent on local conditions. The questions that tap specific knowledge are numbers 3, 4, 5, and 6. The answer to number 4 is debatable, but many experts believe that the coal reserves of North America represent the world's largest supply of fossil fuels. The answer to number 5 is the *United States.* The answer to number 6 is *no,* but we may be able to make synthetic fuel from coal.

425

2. Did any of the answers you got to the questions surprise you? (*Answers will vary.*)

3. Were there many differences between the children's answers and the adults' answers? (*Answers will vary.*)

4. What would be your guess about the best way to help children and adults become more aware of ways to protect the environment and make fossil fuels last longer? (*Answers will vary.*)

SCIENCE CONTENT FOR THE TEACHER

The fossil fuels—petroleum, natural gas, and coal—supply the United States with about 92 percent of the energy it uses. These fuels are nonrenewable resources. When they are gone they are gone! In recent years more attention has been paid to the production of synthetic fuels from fossil fuels. However, this is a case not of the production of new fuel but rather of the conversion of fossil fuels to some easier-to-use and more energy-laden forms.

The United States is considered the world's largest user of fossil fuels. With only one sixteenth of the world's population it uses about one third of the world's energy supply.

At the present time it is thought that the best way to extend our limited supply of fossil fuels is simply to conserve it. Each barrel of oil not used today will be available tomorrow.

EXTENSIONS

Science. You may wish to have some children do library research to find information about alternative energy sources that may be available to us in the future. These children may wish to create posters that depict some of the possibilities.

Science/Math. The information from this survey comes to the children in the form of words. Some children may wish to develop a way to change these words into percentages of respondents answering in a certain way. If they can accomplish this, they can then summarize their information with simple bar graphs and charts.

ADDITIONAL DEMONSTRATION IDEAS

Coal: What Is It and Where Does It Come from?*

The children you work with may not be familiar with coal as an energy source. Consequently, you may wish to include a lesson that conveys some information about this resource to the class. Before the lesson secure some samples of coal from a local coal dealer. You will also need magazine pictures of a mountain, the Midwest plains, a coal miner at work using a pick and shovel or mechanical equipment, and coal miners in an elevator or underground train cars on their way to work. Begin the demonstration by displaying the coal samples and having the children touch them. Use the pictures to begin discussions of where coal is found, how it is mined, and the dangers associated with removing it from the ground.

Oil: What Is It and Where Does It Come from?*

Many children have never seen petroleum. They also may not be familiar with the many uses to which it is put. To help them get a better understanding of the nature and uses of petroleum and the importance of conserving it you may want to do a demonstration-based lesson that includes an opportunity for children to observe petroleum and various petroleum products. Although it will be difficult for you to get a sample of raw petroleum, you can easily acquire some fuel oil to show the class. A fuel-oil dealer in the community would probably be happy to give you a small quantity. Place it in a clear plastic container so that the children can see, smell, and touch it.

Also have on hand various petroleum products, including petroleum jelly, plastics, and motor oil. (But don't bring gasoline into the classroom.) Display magazine pictures of oil wells, oil refineries, people working on oil wells, offshore-drilling platforms, and gasoline pumps. Use the pictures as starting points for a discussion of petroleum, its uses, and the importance of conserving it.

It's in the Papers

This demonstration can be used to help children increase their awareness of the existence of the energy crisis, the many problems associated with it, and the importance of energy conservation. You will need to save your daily newspapers for one week directly before the demonstration. Using a wide-tip, water-based marker, go through each newspaper and draw a line around each article dealing with the energy crisis, synthetic fuels, controversy over nuclear-power plants, the use of alternative energy sources, and so on. On the day of the demonstration attach each newspaper to the bulletin board (if you don't have enough space, you will have to use other surfaces as well) in a way that makes it possible to turn each page individually. Begin the demonstration with the first newspaper. Point out all the articles in it that deal with energy. Read each article's title to the class. Then cut out the articles and distribute them to the children. Do this for each of the other newspapers as well. When you have cut the articles from each issue, have the children suggest topics that could be used as a basis for grouping the articles. Make a small sign for each topic, and then have the children come forward to place the articles they received in the appropriate group. This demonstration can be used as a unit opener or a unit summary.

Appendixes

appendix A

Piagetian
Task Activities

SENSORIMOTOR KNOWLEDGE (0 TO 2 YEARS)

Diagnostic Activity 1

Hold a shiny object in front of an infant. Drop the object and observe the extent to which he or she follows its path. At the beginning of this stage of cognitive development the child believes that the object has disappeared the instant it drops from view. Later the child learns that it is simply moving from place to place.

Diagnostic Activity 2

Place a shiny object in the child's visual field. While the child is looking at the object, place a piece of paper in front of the object to shield it from the child's view. Early in this stage the child believes that the object has disappeared. Later in the stage the child learns that the object has permanency. The child will know it is simply behind the paper and will reach through or around the paper to get it.

PREOPERATIONAL (REPRESENTATIONAL) KNOWLEDGE (2 TO 7 YEARS)

Among other achievements, children at the end of this stage will have an understanding of the following concept:

Conservation of number: the number of elements in a group remains the same even if the elements are rearranged.

You can assess the existence of the ability to conserve number in many ways. Here are a few suggestions.

Diagnostic Activity 1

Spread eight to ten marbles out in a straight line. Then group the same marbles together in a cup. Ask the child if there were more marbles in the cup or in the straight line. Regardless of the child's response, ask "Why do you think so?"

Diagnostic Activity 2

Acquire twenty marbles, ten of one color and ten of another. Ask the child whether there are more of one color than the other. The child may count them or establish a one-to-one correspondence by lining them up: green/yellow, green/

432

yellow, etc. Now arrange the marbles in two rows, one row of green marbles equidistant from one another and one row of yellow marbles directly underneath. There should be a green marble directly above each yellow marble. Again ask the child if there are as many green marbles as yellow marbles. Now spread the row of green marbles out so that it is longer than the row of yellow marbles. Once again, ask whether there are more green marbles than yellow marbles. Ask the child why he or she thinks so. Continue this activity, rearranging the marbles into various groups.

CONCRETE OPERATIONS (7 TO 11 YEARS)

Among other achievements, children at the end of this stage will have acquired the following concepts:

> *Conservation of Substance*: the amount of a substance remains the same even if its shape is altered
> *Conservation of Length*: the length of an object (or line) does not change if it is displaced in space
> *Conservation of Area*: the surface covered by members of a set of objects remains the same even if the objects are rearranged
> *Conservation of Weight*: the total weight of the fragments of an object is equal to the weight of the original object.

You can assess a child's acquisition of these concepts in many ways. Here are a few strategies you may wish to try.

Diagnostic Activities[1]

CONSERVATION OF SUBSTANCE

Prepare a container of orange juice. "Empty it" into several glasses. Ask the child whether the total amount of orange juice has changed.

CONSERVATION OF LENGTH

Use two identical 25-centimeter (about 10-inch) lengths of string for this activity. Line them up on a table so that they are parallel to each other. Ask the child if they are of the same length and why he or she thinks so. Now move one piece of string so that it is partially to the right of the second piece of string. They should remain parallel. Ask the child if they are both the same length and why he or she thinks so. Now form a circle with one piece of string. Repeat the questions.

---

[1]The diagnostic activities assessing children's acquisition of the concepts of conservation of substance, length, area, and weight that I have presented in this appendix are based on strategies discussed in Jean Piaget, Barbel Inhelder, and Alina Szeminska, *The Child's Conception of Geometry* (New York: Basic Books, 1960), p. 26.

CONSERVATION OF AREA

Here is a rather ingenious approach to the analysis of a child's conception of area. It is based on a problem called "Cow in the Field" discussed by Piaget, Inhelder, and Szeminska in *The Child's Conception of Geometry*. You will need two toy cows (or two drawings of a cow), two sheets of green construction paper, and four or five play blocks of the same size. The paper will represent a field of grass and the blocks will represent buildings (see Figure A–1).

Place a cow at the same place in each field. Ask which has more grass to eat and why. Establish that both cows have the same amount of grass.

Now place a barn (block) in each field. Once again ask which cow has more grass to eat. Establish equivalence one more time.

Place a second barn in each field. In the first field, place the second barn away from the first one. In the second field, place the additional barn adjacent to the first barn. Ask which cow has more to eat now.

The child who cannot conserve will say that the cow in the second field (with the two adjacent barns) has more to eat. You can extend this activity by adding barns to the fields and placing them at a variety of locations.

Figure A–1. The placement of cows and barns (blocks) for the Piagetian "cow in the field" activity is to ascertain whether area is conserved.

CONSERVATION OF WEIGHT

Ascertain whether a child believes that a sandwich bag filled with cookies weighs more, less, or the same after the cookies are broken into very small bits.

FORMAL OPERATIONS (12 TO 15 YEARS)

By the end of this stage, children have gained an understanding of the following concept:

> *Conservation of Volume:* the volume of liquid displaced by a submerged object remains constant, regardless of any changes made in the shape of the object.

Diagnostic Activity

You can assess whether children "conserve volume" by asking them to predict changes in the level of water in a tall glass of constant diameter following the immersion in it of various clay shapes of equal volume. For example, you can take a ball of clay and ask a child to predict how much water will be displaced and then drop the ball in the water. You can note the volume of water displaced by observing the change in water level. The child can then change the shape of the ball, make another prediction, and reimmerse the clay. A child who "conserves volume" will understand that the volume of the clay is unchanged and that an equal volume of water will be displaced each time.

appendix B

The Metric System

EVERYDAY METRIC MEASUREMENTS[1]

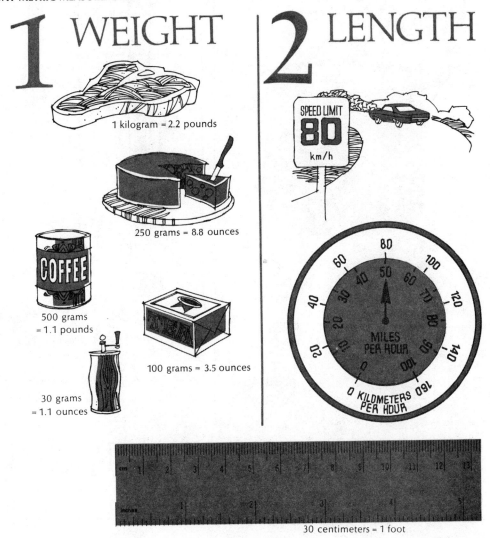

1 WEIGHT

1 kilogram = 2.2 pounds

250 grams = 8.8 ounces

500 grams = 1.1 pounds

100 grams = 3.5 ounces

30 grams = 1.1 ounces

2 LENGTH

SPEED LIMIT
80
km/h

30 centimeters = 1 foot

Figure B–1.

[1] The material in this appendix was reproduced from Louis E. Barbrow, *What about Metric?* (Washington, D.C.: Government Printing Office, 1974). This pamphlet (stock number G.P.O.-1974 O-560-335) is available for purchase from the Superintendent of Documents, Washington, D.C. 20402.

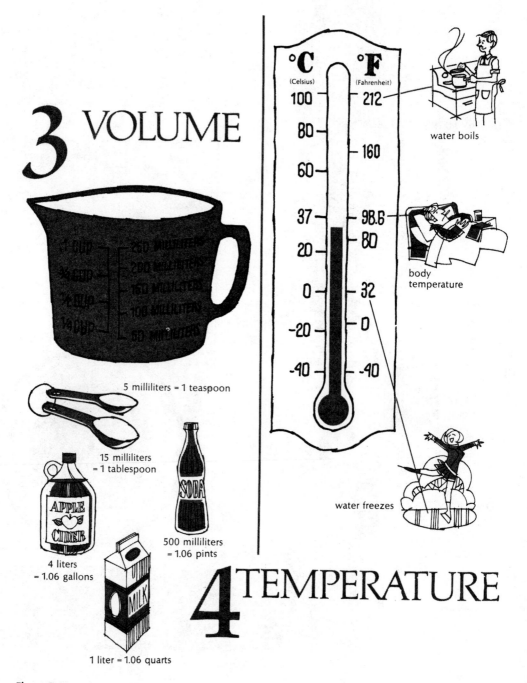

3 VOLUME

1 CUP — 250 MILLILITERS
3/4 CUP — 200 MILLILITERS
1/2 CUP — 150 MILLILITERS
1/4 CUP — 100 MILLILITERS
1/8 CUP — 50 MILLILITERS

5 milliliters = 1 teaspoon

15 milliliters = 1 tablespoon

500 milliliters = 1.06 pints

4 liters = 1.06 gallons

1 liter = 1.06 quarts

°C (Celsius)   °F (Fahrenheit)

water boils

body temperature

water freezes

4 TEMPERATURE

Figure B—1. (cont.)

APPROXIMATE SIZES OF COMMONLY USED METRIC UNITS

The few metric units of measurement that we will be using in our everyday lives and their approximate sizes are given on this page.

Measurement	Metric Unit	Approximate Size of Unit
Length	millimeter	diameter of a paper clip wire
	centimeter	a little more than the width of a paper clip (about 0.4 inch)
	meter	a little longer than a yard (about 1.1 yards)
	kilometer	somewhat further than ½ mile (about 0.6 mile)
Weight (mass)	gram	a little more than the weight of a paper clip
	kilogram	a little more than 2 pounds (about 2.2 pounds)
	metric ton	a little more than a short ton (about 2200 pounds)
Volume	milliliter	five of them make a teaspoon
	liter	a little larger than a quart (about 1.06 quarts)
Area	hectare	about 2.5 acres
Pressure	kilopascal	atmospheric pressure is about 100 kilopascals
Temperature	degree Celsius	see temperature scale below

TEMPERATURE	°C		−40	−20	0	20	37	60	80	100
	°F		−40	0	32		80 98.6		160	212

↑ water freezes　　↑ body temperature　　↑ water boils

Figure B−2.

439

WEIGHT, LENGTH, VOLUME, AND TEMPERATURE IN METRIC UNITS

1 WEIGHT

1 kilogram = 1000 grams
1 hectogram* = 100 grams
1 dekagram* = 10 grams
1 gram = 1 gram
1 decigram* = 0.1 gram
1 centigram* = 0.01 gram
1 milligram = 0.001 gram

2 LENGTH

1 kilometer = 1000 meters
1 hectometer* = 100 meters
1 dekameter* = 10 meters
1 meter = 1 meter
1 decimeter* = 0.1 meter
1 centimeter = 0.01 meter
1 millimeter = 0.001 meter

*units not commonly used

Figure B–3.

3 VOLUME

1 hecto**liter*** = **100 liters**
1 deka**liter*** = **10 liters**
1 **liter** = **1 liter**
1 deci**liter*** = **0.1 liter**
1 centi**liter*** = **0.01 liter**
1 milli**liter** = **0.001 liter**

*units not commonly used

4 TEMPERATURE

Prefixes are not commonly used with temperature measurements as they are with those for weight, length, and volume. Temperatures in degrees Celsius, as in the familiar Fahrenheit system, can only be learned through experience. The following may help to orient you with regard to temperatures you normally encounter.

0 °C	Freezing Point of Water (32 °F)
10 °C	A warm winter day (50 °F)
20 °C	A mild spring day (68 °F)
30 °C	Quite warm—almost hot (86 °F)
37 °C	Normal body temperature (98.6 °F)
40 °C	Heat wave conditions (104 °F)
100 °C	Boiling point of water (212 °F)

Figure B–3. (cont.)

441

appendix C

Suppliers of Science Materials and Equipment

American Science and Engineering, Inc.
955 Massachusetts Avenue
Cambridge, Mass. 02139

Cambosco Scientific Co.
37 Antwerp St.
Boston, Mass. 02135

Carolina Biological Supply Company
2700 York Road
Burlington, N.C. 27215

Cenco Scientific Company
2600 South Kostner Ave.
Chicago, Ill. 60623

Connecticut Valley Biological Supply Co., Inc.
Valley Road
Southampton, Mass. 01073

Damon Corporation
80 Wilson Way
Westwood, Mass. 02090

Delta Education Inc.
P.O. Box M
Factory Street
Nashua, N.H. 03061

Edmund Scientific Company
101 E. Gloucester Pike
Barrington, N.J. 08033

Educational Services, Inc.
108 Water St.
Watertown, Mass. 02172

General Biological Supply House
8200 South Hoyne Ave.
Chicago, Ill. 60620

Hubbard Scientific Company
Box 105
Northbrook, Ill. 60062

Lab-Aids, Inc.
130 Wilbur Place
Bohemia, N.Y. 11716

Nasco
901 Janesville Avenue
Fort Atkinson, Wis. 53538

Ward's Natural Science Establishment, Inc.
3000 Ridge Road East
Rochester, N.Y. 14622

Science-Education Books
for Elementary-School Teachers

ABRUSCATO, JOE, and JACK HASSARD *Loving and Beyond*. Santa Monica, Calif.: Good-year, 1976.

————, *The Whole Cosmos Catalog*. Santa Monica, Calif.: Goodyear, 1977.

BAEZ, ALBERT V., *Innovations in Science Education: World-Wide*. New York: UNESCO, 1976.

BLOUGH, GLENN O., and JULIUS SCHWARTZ, *Elementary School Science and How to Teach It*. New York: Holt, Rinehart & Winston, 1979.

BUTTS, DAVID P., and GENE E. HALL, *Children and Science: The Process of Teaching and Learning*. Englewood Cliffs, N.J.: Prentice-Hall, 1975.

CAIN, SANDRA E., and JACK M. EVANS, *Sciencing*. Columbus, Ohio: Charles E. Merrill, 1979.

CARIN. ARTHUR, and ROBERT SUND. *Teaching Science Through Discovery*. Columbus, Ohio: Charles E. Merrill, 1980.

DEVITO, ALFRED, and GERALD H. KROCKOVER, *Creative Sciencing: A Practical Approach*. Boston: Little, Brown, 1980.

ESLER, WILLIAM K., *Teaching Elementary Science*. Belmont, Calif.: Wadsworth, 1977.

FRIEDL, ALFRED E., *Teaching Science to Children: The Inquiry Approach Applied*. New York: Random House, 1972.

GEGA, PETER C., *Science in Elementary Education*. New York: John Wiley, 1977.

GEORGE, KENNETH D., MAUREEN A. DIETZ, and EUGENE C. ABRAHAM, *Science Investigations for Elementary School Teachers*. Lexington, Mass.: Heath, 1974.

GOLDBERG, LAZER, *Children and Science*. New York: Scribner's, 1970.

HANEY, RICHARD E., and JUANITA S. SORENSON, *Individually Guided Science*. Reading, Mass.: Addison-Wesley, 1977.

HILL, KATHERINE E., *Exploring the Natural World With Young Children*. New York: Harcourt Brace Jovanovich, 1976.

HOFMAN, HELENMARIE, and KENNETH S. RICKER, ed. *Sourcebook: Science Education for the Physically Handicapped*. Washington, D.C.: National Science Teachers Association, 1979.

HOLT, BESS-GENE, *Science With Young Children*. Washington, D.C.: National Association for the Education of Young Children, 1977.

HONE, ELIZABETH, ALEXANDER JOSEPH, and EDWARD VICTOR, *A Sourcebook for Elementary Science*. New York: Harcourt Brace Jovanovich, 1971.

HOUNSHELL, PAUL B., and IRA R. TROLLINGES, *Games for the Science Classroom*. Washington, D.C.: National Science Teachers Association, 1977.

HUBLER, CLARK, *Science for Children*. New York: Random House, 1974.

JACOBSON, WILLARD J., and ABBY BARRY BERGMAN, *Science for Children*. Englewood Cliffs, N.J.: Prentice-Hall, 1980.

KAUCHAK, DONALD, and PAUL EGGEN, *Exploring Science in the Elementary School*. Chicago: Rand McNally, 1980.

KUSLAN, LOUIS I., and A. HARRIS STONE, *Teaching Children Science: An Inquiry Approach.* Belmont, Calif.: Wadsworth, 1972.

LANSDOWN, BRENDA, PAUL E. BLACKWOOD, and PAUL F. BRANDWEIN, *Teaching Elementary Science: Through Investigation and Colloquium.* New York: Harcourt Brace Jovanovich, 1971.

LEWIS, JUNE E., and IRENE C. POTTER, *The Teaching of Science in the Elementary School.* Englewood Cliffs, N.J.: Prentice-Hall, 1970.

LOWERY, LAWRENCE F., *The Everyday Science Sourcebook.* Boston: Allyn and Bacon, 1978.

NAVARRA, JOHN G., and JOSEPH ZAFFORONI, *Science in the Elementary School: Content and Methods.* Columbus, Ohio: Charles E. Merrill, 1975.

New UNESCO Source Book for Science Teaching. New York: UNESCO, 1975.

PILTZ, ALBERT, and ROBERT SUND, *Creative Teaching of Science in the Elementary School.* Boston: Allyn and Bacon, 1974.

RENNER, JOHN W., and WILLIAM B. REGAN, *Teaching Science in the Elementary School.* New York: Harper & Row, 1973.

ROWE, MARY BUDD, *Teaching Science as Continuous Inquiry.* New York: McGraw-Hill, 1978.

SMITH, WALTER S., and KALA M. STROUP, *Science Career Exploration for Women.* Washington, D.C.: National Science Teachers Association, 1978.

STRONGIN, HERB, *Science on a Shoestring.* Menlo Park, Calif.: Addison-Wesley, 1976.

TALE, LARRY L., and ERNEST W. LEE, *Environmental Education in the Elementary School.* New York: Holt, Rinehart & Winson, 1972.

VICTOR, EDWARD, *Science for the Elementary School.* New York: Macmillan, 1980.

Index

LB1585 .A29 1982   010101 000
Abruscato, Joseph.
Teaching children science / Jo

0 2002 0018191 1
YORK COLLEGE OF PENNSYLVANIA 17403